Treatment of the Borderline Adolescent: A Developmental Approach
by James F. Masterson

Psychopathology: Contributions from the Biological, Behavioral, and Social Sciences
edited by Muriel Hammer, Kurt Salzinger, and Samuel Sutton

Abnormal Children and Youth: Therapy and Research
by Anthony Davids

Principles of Psychotherapy with Children
by John M. Reisman

Aversive Maternal Control: A Theory of Schizophrenic Development
by Alfred B. Hilbrun, Jr.

Individual Differences in Children
edited by Jack C. Westman

Ego Functions in Schizophrenics, Neurotics, and Normals: A Systematic Study of Conceptual, Diagnostic, and Therapeutic Aspects
by Leopold Bellak, Marvin Hurvich, and Helen A. Gediman

Innovative Treatment Methods in Psychopathology
edited by Karen S. Calhoun, Henry E. Adams, and Kevin M. Mitchell

The Changing School Scene: Challenge to Psychology
by Leah Gold Fein

Troubled Children: Their Families, Schools, and Treatments
by Leonore R. Love and Jaques W. Kaswan

Research Strategies in Psychotherapy
by Edward S. Bordin

The Volunteer Subject
by Robert Rosenthal and Ralph L. Rosnow

Innovations in Client-Centered Therapy
by David A. Wexler and Laura North Rice

The Rorschach: A Comprehensive System
by John E. Exner

Theory and Practice in Behavior Therapy
by Aubrey J. Yates

Principles of Psychotherapy
by Irving B. Weiner

Principles of Psychotherapy

Principles of Psychotherapy

IRVING B. WEINER
Case Western Reserve University

A WILEY-INTERSCIENCE PUBLICATION
JOHN WILEY & SONS New York • London • Sydney • Toronto

Library of Congress Cataloging in Publication Data

Weiner, Irving B.
  Principles of psychotherapy.

  (Wiley series on personality processes)
  "A Wiley-Interscience publication."
  Includes bibliographical references and indexes.
  1. Psychotherapy. I. Title. [DNLM: 1. Psychotherapy. WM420 W423p]

RC480.W373   616.8'914   74-26830
ISBN 0-471-92569-1

PRINTED IN THE UNITED STATES OF AMERICA

10 9 8 7 6 5 4 3 2

To Mollie Laevin Weiner
from a loving son

Series Preface

This series of books is addressed to behavioral scientists interested in the nature of human personality. Its scope should prove pertinent to personality theorists and researchers as well as to clinicians concerned with applying an understanding of personality processes to the amelioration of emotional difficulties in living. To this end, the series provides a scholarly integration of theoretical formulations, empirical data, and practical recommendations.

Six major aspects of studying and learning about human personality can be designated: personality theory, personality structure and dynamics, personality development, personality assessment, personality change, and personality adjustment. In exploring these aspects of personality, the books in the series discuss a number of distinct but related subject areas: the nature and implications of various theories of personality; personality characteristics that account for consistencies and variations in human behavior; the emergence of personality processes in children and adolescents; the use of interviewing and testing procedures to evaluate individual differences in personality; efforts to modify personality styles through psychotherapy, counseling, behavior therapy, and other methods of influence; and patterns of abnormal personality functioning that impair individual competence.

IRVING B. WEINER

Case Western Reserve University
Cleveland, Ohio

Preface

This book is addressed to the practitioner of psychotherapy and is primarily a manual of principles for conducting psychotherapy in clinical practice. To this end, guidelines are provided for the conduct of interviews from the initial evaluation sessions through the final termination phase of treatment. These guidelines are amplified throughout with illustrations of what the therapist should consider saying and doing in various circumstances.

In providing a guide for the conduct of psychotherapy, the text closely follows indications from available research. Without digressing from the clinical presentation to review relevant empirical findings, each chapter indicates the major data sources on which the discussion is based. Where adequate research studies bearing on proposed guidelines do not yet exist, clinical experience provides the basis of the recommendations made. Transcending both the supporting research and clinical evidence, there is an emphasis throughout the presentation on the importance of the psychotherapist to maintain at all times in the conduct of his work a conceptual framework—embracing the goals of the treatment and the possible strategies and tactics for achieving these goals—from which he can deduce the most appropriate and incisive ways of intervening in his patient's behalf.

It is hoped that this balanced approach to clinical and research guidelines for the practice of psychotherapy will contribute to narrowing an unfortunate gap that persists between them. Psychotherapy practitioners at times recommend their procedures as if personal conviction were equivalent to validity, while psychotherapy researchers sometimes present their data as if significant research results were an end in themselves, rather than only a means toward developing improved treatment procedures. The resulting dialogue has not always been friendly. Psychotherapy researchers have accused practitioners of ignoring or failing to comprehend the implications of empirical findings and of participating in a fraternity of "believers" who reinforce each other's dedication to their hallowed practices and disregard any data to the contrary. Practitioners in turn have accused researchers of failing to appreciate the complexity of real-life clinical interactions, and of designing experimental studies more with an eye to making them manageable than with adequate attention to making them reflect faithfully the transactions occurring within psychotherapy.

Both of these accusations have some basis. In every field of endeavor the applications of knowledge lag behind advances in theory and research, and so it is with psychotherapy; at the same time, sophisticated psychotherapy researchers readily admit to many unresolved difficulties in translating the intricacies of clinical interactions into meaningful operational definitions for investigative purposes. Yet the shortcomings of both practitioners and researchers should not obscure their substantial contributions to psychotherapy and the essential complementarity of their efforts. Hypotheses for research study emerge from the clinical practice of psychotherapy, and it is in the success and failure of the clinician's efforts that the conclusions from such studies must finally be examined for their utility. Clinical practice that is neither subjected to nor influenced by research studies can lead down many blind alleys and detract both from the pursuit of knowledge and from the delivery of responsible clinical service.

On the other hand, lack of unequivocal documentation should not dissuade a clinician from employing procedures he expects with reasonable certainty to benefit a troubled person who has sought his help. Cumulative clinical wisdom must be given its just due, lest uncertainty produce a paralysis of action. In the absence of empirically documented procedures for meeting every contingency, the psychotherapist must frequently turn for guidance to conceptual formulations and to the advice of experienced clinicians who have found certain techniques consistently helpful in their work.

To be systematically learned, taught, and practiced, psychotherapy must be grounded in a theoretical perspective on the nature of personality functioning and behavior change. A psychodynamic view of the psychotherapy process provides the primary theoretical context for the selection and discussion of topics in this book. Whatever theoretical perspective commands his primary allegiance, however, a psychotherapist requires some degree of eclecticism to function in full light of current knowledge. Useful contributions to understanding the ingredients of effective psychotherapy have emerged within numerous theoretical contexts, and research evidence supports hypotheses derived from many different theories of psychotherapy.

Accordingly, while the chapters that follow express primarily a psychodynamic point of view, they also stress a number of principles of psychotherapy central to transactional, client-centered, humanistic, and behavioral approaches as well: for example, that psychotherapy is an interpersonal process defined by the nature of the communication that takes place within it; that the capacity of the therapist to create a climate of warmth, respect, trust, and genuineness has considerable bearing on the outcome of psychotherapy; that psychotherapy is essentially a learning situation in which the amount of benefit a person derives depends on how extensively he can learn to understand and control his behavior; that the goals of psychotherapy include positive behavior change in addition to increments in self-understanding and self-control, and that positive behavior change is measured both in relief from emotional distress and in progress toward fuller realization of potentials for productive work and rewarding human relationships.

It is widely recognized that the agents of change in psychotherapy include both general and specific factors. General factors promoting change in psychotherapy reside in the treatment relationship and more specifically in (a) the opportunity it provides the patient to express himself and (b) the extent to which it fosters an atmosphere of candid self-observation, expectation of change, and amenability to the therapist's efforts to facilitate such change. Specific factors promoting change consist of the technical procedures employed by the therapist to facilitate change and promote progress toward the goals of the treatment. A good working relationship and sound therapist technique are thus complementary change agents in effective psychotherapy. Inept technical procedures limit or negate the benefits that might otherwise derive from an open and trusting patient-therapist relationship, while the most polished technical skills are of little avail in the absence of a treatment climate that nourishes receptivity to them. For this reason, concern with the general (relationship) and specific (technique) aspects of promoting personality and behavior change through psychotherapy are intertwined throughout the presentation.

The book is organized in four parts. Part One begins with an explanation of the nature and goals of psychotherapy. Chapters 2 and 3 are addressed to the characteristics of patients and therapists, respectively, with particular attention to how these characteristics affect treatment outcome. Chapter 4 presents an overview of the psychotherapy process, which is then elaborated in the remaining chapters of the book.

Part Two concerns the initial phase of psychotherapy and includes chapters on the evaluation and assessment of persons who seek psychotherapy (Chap. 5); on the role of the treatment contract in psychotherapy and procedures for establishing it (Chap. 6); and on principles for conducting psychotherapy interviews so as to maximize patient participation in the treatment process (Chap. 7).

Part Three, which treats the middle phase of psychotherapy, deals with methods for communicating understanding through interpretation (Chap. 8); for recognizing and minimizing interferences with communication that constitute resistance to the treatment process (Chap. 9); and for identifying and utilizing intercurrent influences exerted on the course of therapy by the treatment relationship, in both its transference (Chap. 10) and countertransference aspects (Chap. 11).

In Part Four of the text attention is given to determining when an appropriate termination point has been reached and bringing the therapy to an effective end (Chap. 12).

For their secretarial assistance in preparing the manuscript in its various stages, I would like to express my appreciation to Ms. Amy Garfinkel, Ms. Linda Honeycutt, and Ms. Carolyn Stigler.

IRVING B. WEINER

Cleveland, Ohio
August 1974

Contents

Principles of Psychotherapy

PART ONE

Introduction

CHAPTER 1

The Nature and Goals of Psychotherapy

Psychotherapy is an interpersonal process in which one person communicates to another that he understands him, respects him, and wants to be of help to him. Most of the procedures used by trained professionals to treat people with psychological problems involve understanding, respect, and helpfulness, but psychotherapy is unique in that the therapist strives to communicate his understanding of the patient's difficulties and to help him share in this understanding. Whereas other treatment methods such as drug therapy, shock therapy, mileu therapy, and behavior therapy may imply to the patient that his problems are being understood, this implicit communication is only a peripheral feature of the method, intended at most to facilitate the psychotherapeutic effects expected from the drugs, shock treatments, milieu setting, or behavioral techniques. In psychotherapy, on the other hand, the communication of person-related understanding is explicit and constitutes the central feature of the method.[1]

Yet psychotherapy and most other current methods for treating emotionally troubled people are not mutually exclusive. Sophisticated use of somatic, milieu, and behavioral therapies usually includes some explicit communication to the patient of where his difficulties appear to lie and in what ways the treatment procedures are expected to prove helpful. When the therapist is communicating this kind of understanding to his

[1]This approach to defining psychotherapy and distinguishing it from the broader category of what may be psychotherapeutic is elaborated by Reisman in *Toward the Integration of Psychotherapy* (1971). Reisman's careful synthesis of the relevant literature provides an excellent guide to the essential nature of psychotherapy. Overviews of the broader category of treatment methods most commonly used to alleviate psychological problems are available in Arieti (1959, Chaps. 64–78), Freedman and Kaplan (1967, Chaps. 28–30), Masserman (1973), Polatin (1966), and Wolman (1965, Chaps. 40–51).

patient, he is offering psychotherapy; when he shifts his focus from the communication of person-related understanding to doing something to or for his patient, then he is engaging in treatment procedures that are not psychotherapy, though they hopefully will be psychotherapeutic. In actual practice, the treatment of people with psychological problems frequently combines aspects of psychotherapy with aspects of other psychotherapeutic methods. The more the therapist concentrates his efforts on explicitly communicating understanding, the more appropriate it is to label what he is doing as psychotherapy; the less his focus is on communication, the more his work should be called something else.

Defining psychotherapy simply as the communication of person-related understanding, respect, and a wish to be of help raises the question of whether psychotherapy can be conducted by someone who has not been trained as a psychotherapist. For example, can the special kind of communication that constitutes psychotherapy take place between two friends discussing a problem together? There are compelling professional and ethical reasons for restricting the label *psychotherapy* to what trained psychotherapists do within the context of a formal patient-therapist relationship. Such a restriction serves to distinguish professional psychotherapy from random conversations between two people that happen to be psychotherapeutic for one of them, and it also helps protect the public from people who would portray themselves as psychotherapists without having had adequate training in psychotherapy.

However, psychotherapy does not have any independent identity as a profession, and there are no laws regulating who may or may not present himself to the public as a "psychotherapist."[2] Furthermore, any attempt to define psychotherapy in terms of who does it, rather than what it is, causes more problems than it solves. Psychotherapy consists of specific kinds of behavior. To posit that these behaviors constitute psychotherapy only when they are performed by a trained psychotherapist and not when they are performed by anyone else leads to to the untenable conclusion that the exact behavior engaged in by different people may somehow not be the same behavior.

[2]Influenced by Kubie's (1954, 1964) long-standing proposals to initiate training programs in "medical psychology," a number of arguments have emerged in recent years for establishing psychotherapy as an independent profession (see Abroms & Greenfield, 1973; Henry, Sims, & Spray, 1971; Holt, 1970; Mariner, 1967). Henry et al. bolster their argument with data to suggest that psychotherapists have many similarities in personality and outlook which cut across their membership in the four professional groups from which most practicing psychotherapists are drawn—psychoanalysis, psychiatry, clinical psychology, and psychiatric social work.

In order to teach and learn about psychotherapy as a set of behaviors intended to communicate a special kind of message, it is accordingly necessary to accept the possibility that these behaviors may emerge in any interpersonal situation. Yet to say that psychotherapy may take place inadvertently is not equivalent to saying that it is likely to do so. The likelihood of psychotherapy occurring between two people is considerably enhanced if one of them is a trained and knowledgeable therapist following a planned procedure of intervention intended to be of help. In fact, not only is psychotherapy more likely to take place when a trained professional and a troubled patient have agreed to work together on the patient's problems, it is very unlikely to occur under any other circumstances.

Several differences between the professional psychotherapy relationship and other interpersonal relationships account for the greater likelihood that psychotherapy will take place in the former. First, the therapist's training allows him to understand another person's psychological difficulties far more fully than any but the most unusually intuitive and sensitive nonprofessional, and it also provides him techniques for communicating this understanding in ways the other person can comprehend and accept.

Second, the professional psychotherapy relationship is not a mutual relationship, at least not in the sense that other kinds of ongoing interpersonal relationships tend to be mutual. In psychotherapy the interests, needs, and welfare of the patient always come first, while the therapist rarely asks for consideration of his interests, needs, and welfare in return. Unlike a friend or acquaintance, a therapist does not inject his own problems and preoccupations into the relationship, does not ordinarily respond to anger and criticism by defending himself or reciprocating in kind, and does not decide whether to continue the relationship on the basis of how pleasant he finds the other person's company.

It is not that the professional psychotherapist is free of problems and preoccupations, has no feelings toward his patient, or does not experience waxing and waning enthusiasm about the course of the treatment. It is rather that his training helps him prevent such human reactions from interfering with his dedication to his task. The trained therapist focuses throughout on understanding and interpreting his patient's behavior, and he brings his own feelings and experiences into the situation only when he decides that it would facilitate the treatment for him to do so.

Third, there are certain formal commitments and constraints in the professional psychotherapy relationship that seldom characterize other interpersonal relationships. The therapist and his patient agree to meet at specifically designated times on a regular basis and to continue meeting as long as it serves the patient's interests. These meeting times are kept as free from interruption as the therapist is able to make them, and, except for chance encounters, patient and therapist do not interact at other times or concerning matters other than the patient's emotional difficulties. These arrangements put a single-minded stamp on professional psychotherapy—helping the patient with his problems in living—that can rarely be maintained in other kinds of relationships between people.

To summarize this point, the professional psychotherapist's training, the nonmutuality of his relationships with his patients, and the formal arrangements he makes for ongoing psychotherapy maximize the prospects for his consistently communicating understanding, respect, and a wish to be of help. In interpersonal situations outside of professional psychotherapy, on the other hand, the lack of training in understanding and communicating the meaning of human behavior, the absence of formal arrangements for working on a defined problem, and the needs of each participant for his share of being understood, respected, and helped minimize the likelihood that one person will consistently provide psychotherapy for another.

APPROACHES TO PSYCHOTHERAPY

Although psychotherapy needs to be distinguished from the much broader category of treatment methods that may be psychotherapeutic, the task of doing psychotherapy can itself be approached in a variety of ways. First of all, the communication by one person to another that he understands, respects, and wants to help him is not limited to a two-person situation. It can be communicated by a therapist to several people together, as in group psychotherapy and family psychotherapy, and it can be communicated by more than one therapist at a time, as when co-therapists work together with groups, families, or sometimes even a single patient.

Second, there is no single or uniform approach to how human behavior can best be understood and how this understanding can most effectively be communicated. Instead, there are a number of systems or types of psychotherapy based on somewhat different ways of conceptualizing problems in living, including psychoanalytic psychotherapy (Greenson,

1967; Langs, 1973, 1974), client-centered psychotherapy (Hart & Tomlinson, 1970; Rogers, 1951), existential psychotherapy (Boss, 1963; May, Angel & Ellenberger, 1958), humanistic psychotherapy (Bugental, 1965; Maslow, 1962), gestalt psychotherapy (Fagan & Shepherd, 1970; Polster & Polster, 1973), and rational-emotive psychotherapy (Ellis, 1962).[3]

Although each of these approaches has its staunch adherents, their existence does not mean that the actual practice of psychotherapy is markedly different from one psychotherapist to the next. All of these systems of psychotherapy, in contrast to somatic, milieu, and behavioral therapies, stress understanding the patient and explicitly communicating this understanding to him. Furthermore, research studies indicate that the ways in which psychotherapists of various persuasions communicate person-related understanding are very much alike. Despite divergences in philosophy and strategy, experienced therapists with different theoretical orientations display more similarities than differences in their *tactics*, that is, in the kind of things they actually say to their patients (Fiedler, 1950; Raskin, 1965; Strupp, 1955a, 1955b, 1958a, 1958b; Wrenn, 1960).

There is parallel evidence from the patient's point of view that people who make similar changes in psychotherapy perceive similar factors in their psychotherapy as having been responsible for these changes, irrespective of the particular school of thought to which their therapist belonged (Heine, 1953). In reporting these latter data, Heine urged clinicians to work toward "developing a psychotherapy rather than a variety of psychotherapies" (p. 22), and considerable emphasis has indeed been placed by thoughtful clinicians on identifying the many factors common to all forms of psychotherapy (see Frank, 1971; Marmor, 1962; Strupp, 1973).

For these reasons aspiring therapists should be wary of parochial assertions that any one form of psychotherapy is inherently superior to the others or has a monopoly on the truth. Freud (1904a) appears to have had no less in mind: "There are many ways and means of practicing psychotherapy. All that lead to recovery are good" (p. 259). In this same vein, Luborsky and Spence (1971) conclude in a recent review of outcome research that "it is impossible to say that one type of psychotherapy is better than another or even that one type produces changes different from those produced by another type" (p. 416).

[3]Descriptions and comparative reviews of approaches to psychotherapy are provided by Corsini (1973), Ford and Urban (1963), Harper (1959), Heine (1971), and Stein (1961).

GOALS OF PSYCHOTHERAPY

The goal of psychotherapy is to relieve a patient's emotional distress and help him modify personality characteristics that are preventing him from realizing his human potential or enjoying rewarding interpersonal relationships. There are many possible routes to such a goal, including treatment procedures other than psychotherapy and fortuitous life experiences that improve a person's emotional state and expand his opportunities to find self-fulfillment. As already noted, the defining characteristic of psychotherapy as a route to symptom relief and positive personality change is that the vehicle for pursuing these goals consists of helping a person to understand himself better.

At times the methods of psychotherapy are confused with its goals, prompting some harsh but unfounded criticisms of the psychotherapy approach. For example, behavior therapists have been wont to accuse psychotherapists of being satisfied with achieving empathy and insight, thereby

> . . . mistaking private intellectual pleasures for accomplishments of actual goals. These pleasures may cause the clinician to regard *insight*, or understanding of the causes of his behavior by the patient, as a *sine qua non* of treatment, instead of seeking removal of symptoms. . . . Behavior change, not understanding, is the clinician's main goal (Kanfer & Phillips, 1970, p. 29).

This criticism reflects a failure to distinguish between patient understanding as a means to an end and patient understanding as an end in itself. No adequately trained psychotherapist regards insight in the absence of behavior change or symptom relief as a satisfactory treatment outcome. Such a circumstance indicates either (a) that the insight achieved has not been relevant to the patient's needs and problems or (b) that certain resistances to behavior change remain to be identified and understood. Persistent absence of behavior change or symptom relief, whatever the patient's level of self-understanding, conveys to the knowledgeable psychotherapist that his patient needs either a different therapist or a different form of therapy.[4]

The goals of psychotherapy are discussed in more detail in Chapter 12, which deals in part with identifying when an appropriate termination

[4]For a balanced perspective on the relationships between psychotherapy and behavior therapy, including their complementarity in the treatment of many patients, the reader is referred to contributions by Feather and Rhoads (1972), Hersen (1970a, 1970b), Marmor (1971), Murray and Jacobson (1971), Sloane (1969), Weitzman (1967), and Woody (1971).

point has been reached. The following three chapters in this introductory section take a closer look at the three central elements of psychotherapy: the patient who comes for help, the therapist who attempts to provide this help, and the treatment process to which they commit themselves.

CHAPTER 2

The Patient

Probably the first mistake a therapist can make is to assume that someone who consults him knows what psychotherapy consists of, is prepared to undertake it, and should receive it. Far from being assumed, these are matters that need to be carefully explored before psychotherapy is begun. For each prospective patient it is important to determine how, why, and with what preconceived notions he has come; the hopes and fears he brings into a treatment situation; and whether his personal characteristics indicate great or little likelihood of his benefiting from psychotherapy.

HOW PEOPLE COME TO PSYCHOTHERAPY

The two major routes by which people come to psychotherapy are referral from a physician and self-referral. In instances of physician referral the patient has sometimes asked directly for help with a personal problem; in other instances he has been examined in connection with some somatic complaints that the physician has concluded are of psychological origin. Self-referrals occassionally include people who have decided entirely on their own that they should seek psychological help from a qualified professional. More commonly, however, the self-referred patient has come for help after discussing his concerns with someone close to him, such as his spouse, his clergyman, or a good friend.[1]

After physician referral and self-referral, the most frequent path by which people enter psychotherapy is at the suggestion of various

[1]For a detailed description of the steps by which people seeking help come into contact with a psychotherapist, the reader should consult Kadushin, *Why People Go to Psychiatrists*, 1969. As the title indicates, Kadushin elaborates on the reasons why people seek professional psychological assistance as well as the process by which they obtain it.

community agencies, including family service centers, welfare agencies, schools, and courts. Agency referrals highlight a very important aspect of how a person comes to psychotherapy, namely, the degree to which his coming is on other than a voluntary basis. The growing public recognition and acceptance of psychotherapy has made consulting a psychotherapist a common condition of being placed on probation for a criminal act, being allowed to return to school following expulsion, or even being allowed to continue receiving welfare aid.

Such involuntary entry into psychotherapy is less immediately apparent in physician-referred and self-referred patients than in those referred by agencies, but it nevertheless occurs. For example, a husband or wife may insist that his spouse seek psychological help as a condition of continuing their marriage, or a physician may prescribe psychological treatment as a requirement of his continuing to serve as a patient's doctor. These types of involuntary entry into psychotherapy do not preclude successful treatment, but whether a person is coming voluntarily or under duress can influence his response to psychotherapy. Determining the conditions under which a patient comes to psychotherapy therefore needs to be included in the initial evaluation for treatment (see Chap. 5).

WHY PEOPLE COME TO PSYCHOTHERAPY

However people come to psychotherapy, they come for many different reasons. Most often a person who seeks psychotherapy is experiencing painful problems in his life situation that he wants help to eliminate or at least minimize. Yet prospective patients vary considerably in the extent of their psychological distress, and some consult a psychotherapist for reasons other than being particularly troubled—some because they are curious about what psychotherapy is like, some because they regard entering psychotherapy as "an in thing to do," and some because they think psychotherapy can make their already productive and rewarding life style an even better one.

Furthermore, people may come to a psychotherapist not because they want to become engaged with him in some way, but because they do *not* want psychotherapy. These are people who, rather than hoping the therapist will be able to help them with their psychological problems, hope to hear from him either that they have no significant psychological problems or that the problems they have cannot be resolved by psychotherapy (implying that the problems are being caused by other people or by environmental circumstances, and that they are in no way personally culpable).

Prospective patients who want to be told they do not need help are very often people for whom psychotherapy has been mandated. Armed with a therapist's clean bill of health, they could then report to their referring probation officer, school official, or spouse that "I'm all better now" or "See, it's not my problem, it must be yours." Sometimes a psychotherapist's most appropriate response to an involuntary patient will be to indicate no need for treatment, while at other times an initially unmotivated patient can and should be helped to undertake therapy addressed to psychological problems he has. To proceed effectively in either of these directions, a therapist must first ascertain why a particular person has come to see him, which along with the how of his coming is a topic for the initial evaluation process.

PRECONCEIVED NOTIONS BROUGHT TO PSYCHOTHERAPY

Except for psychotherapists themselves and patients who have previously been in psychotherapy, most people arrive at a therapist's office with limited information and many preconceived notions about what to expect. Self-referred patients are particularly likely to be uninformed, unless they have been "prepared" by a friend or spouse who has been in psychotherapy. Yet not even an "unprepared" patient comes without preconceptions, although he may deny having any prior knowledge about psychotherapy. With the visibility of psychotherapy in the movies, on television, and in magazines and books, very few people remain innocent of at least literary or theatrical versions of what transpires in it.

Among people referred for psychotherapy by a physician or agency, many are likely to have been "prepared" by some discussion of their need for psychological treatment. However, a physician- or agency-referred patient does not necessarily come better informed about psychotherapy than someone who is self-referred. A referring person may have reservations about psychotherapy or know very little about it himself, so that his preparation conveys negligible useful information to the patient. Or, in his efforts to encourage the patient to accept a referral for psychotherapy, he may foster misconceptions about how rapid, painless, and curative the process is.

The kind of preconceived notions people bring to psychotherapy usually center around expectations of what the treatment will consist of and what it will accomplish. Some patients come expecting to talk about themselves and be listened to, whereas others expect to be medicated, hypnotized, advised on how to lead a better life, or presented with a detailed analysis of their psychological makeup. Some patients anticipate that psychotherapy will be an ongoing process involving regular sessions for some indefinite period of time, whereas others anticipate that a few visits will be adequate to meet their needs. Some patients come to psychotherapy expecting it to relieve them of distressing symptoms, whereas others expect it to help them understand themselves better.

As a further difference, some people approach a first visit with the expectation that they are entering psychotherapy and will continue to work with that therapist; others expect that the initial sessions will constitute an evaluation period to determine whether they should enter psychotherapy and, if so, with whom; and still others begin with no expectations regarding psychotherapy or the particular therapist, but rather see the first meeting solely as a diagnostic consultation for the benefit of a referring physician or agency. Like the how and why of a patient's coming to psychotherapy, all such notions about it need to be explored before treatment is begun, particularly since success in psychotherapy depends in part on congruity between a patient's expectations and the therapist's plan for treating him (see Chap. 5).

HOPES AND FEARS ON BEGINNING PSYCHOTHERAPY

Everyone who enters psychotherapy does so with mixed feelings. The most highly motivated patient will have some reservations about undergoing psychological treatment, as will the involuntary patient have some interest in the possibility of being helped. Such ambivalent attitudes are seldom expressed in the early stages of psychotherapy, at least not spontaneously. The highly motivated patient hesitates to air his reservations for fear of diminishing the therapist's interest in working with him, and the involuntary patient resists giving others the satisfaction of knowing that he sees any possibility of receiving help from psychotherapy.

What most patients hope for when they begin talking to a psychotherapist is to feel better as soon as possible. For some people "feeling better" means relief from specific symptoms, for some it means increased self-understanding, and for others it may mean achieving a greater sense of self-satisfaction and purpose in life. Whatever "feeling better" means, it is a hope also shared by those who come to psychotherapy under duress and are reluctant to admit having any personal problems. The fact that the involuntary patient is regarded by other people as needing psychological help can be taken as presumptive evidence that his life circumstances are causing him difficulty. Psychotherapy may not be a means of improving his circumstances, but he can certainly hope it might be.

As for feeling better quickly, almost all patients who enter psychotherapy hope for rapid or magical improvement. Even those who understand that a satisfactory outcome may require months or even years of work may still feel disappointed when the first few sessions do not produce noticeable change. Furthermore, many people begin psychotherapy with the hope that it will solve all of their emotional problems completely and permanently. When a therapist appreciates that his patient is likely to have such hopes, whether they are expressed, he is better prepared to discuss meaningfully with him the goals of the treatment and the outcomes that are possible from it.

A patient's fears may be less apparent than his hopes when he consults a psychotherapist, but apprehension in some form or other is almost certain to be present. Some patients are afraid of being considered crazy or dangerous and put in a hospital. Some are afraid they will learn terrible things about themselves or their past that they were better off not knowing. Some are concerned that entering psychotherapy will undermine their independence as a person, interfere with their creativity, or disrupt their life in various ways. And many people, in contrast to those who see psychotherapy as a status symbol, fret about the social stigma of being a "mental" patient.

The voluntary patient's concerns about being crazy, bad, or too dependent put him in a particularly difficult bind when he comes for his first meeting with the therapist. On the one hand, he is motivated to put his best foot forward and to demonstrate that he is a sane, competent, worthwhile person capable of managing his own affairs. On the other hand, he is motivated to reveal enough of his emotional problems to ensure that the therapist will recognize and respond to his need for help. An accurate assessment of a potential patient's current status and need for help accordingly depends on the therapist's sensitivity to the influence such conflicting motivations may have on how the patient presents himself in a first visit.

PATIENT CHARACTERISTICS AFFECTING OUTCOME

In past years much attention was paid to selecting patients for psychotherapy and identifying the characteristics of the "good" psychotherapy patient. More recently this focus of attention has been altered in two important respects. First, because many demonstrably effective methods for treating people with psychological difficulties are now available, the therapist's task should no longer be seen as selecting patients for psychotherapy, but rather as selecting a treatment approach or combination of approaches suited to the patient's needs (see Abroms, 1969). If the indicated treatment approach for a particular patient is not within the therapist's competence, he should refer the patient to a colleague better prepared to provide the necessary help. The pool of therapists and therapeutic methods is many and varied, whereas the patient is only himself. A troubled person should never be obliged to fit the mold of one particular form of treatment or else be rejected as a patient; rather, he should have potentially available to him a wide range of treatment methods and therapists qualified to apply them in his behalf.

Second, accumulating research evidence indicates that patient characteristics probably have less bearing on the outcome of psychotherapy than the personal qualities and technical competence of the therapist who conducts the treatment. The therapist must be able to create a helping relationship through which he can influence the patient's ways of thinking, feeling, and acting. More specifically, improvement in psychotherapy appears to be largely a function of the therapist's capacity to communicate understanding and respect to the patient and his skill in facilitating the patient's self-awareness and self-determination (see Chap. 3).

Nevertheless, certain patient characteristics generally seem to increase the likelihood of a favorable outcome in psychotherapy, whereas other characteristics occasionally have this effect and still others are sometimes presumed to influence outcome but do not. Therefore, separate comments are in order concerning patient characteristics generally related, occasionally related, and unrelated to improvement in psychotherapy.[2]

Characteristics Generally Related to Outcome

On the basis of available data, the following three characteristics can each be expected to increase a patient's prospects of benefiting from psychotherapy:

[2]In addition to the specific studies cited in the text, this discussion of patient characteristics related to outcome in psychotherapy is based on reviews of research by Garfield (1971), Luborsky, Auerbach, Chandler, and Cohen (1971), Meltzoff and Kornreich (1970, Chap. 9–10), and Truax and Carkhuff (1967, Chap. 5).

1. *The patient comes to psychotherapy with minimal generalized personality disturbance but with a high level of felt distress.* Regarding personality disturbance, it has been observed clinically and confirmed by research studies that the patients who are most likely to improve in psychotherapy are those whose personality functioning is the most adequate to begin with. Indeed, the clearest result to emerge from the Menninger Psychotherapy Research Project (Kernberg et al., 1972; Wallerstein, 1968; Wallerstein & Robbins, 1958), which is the most extensive naturalistic study of psychotherapy reported in the literature, was that good initial ego strength predicts improvement in psychotherapy. Limited personality resources did not necessarily prevent a favorable outcome in the Menninger sample; however, consistently with the emphasis placed above on therapist rather than patient characteristics in determining psychotherapy outcome, it was found that the lower the initial ego strength of the patient, the more crucial was the skill of the therapist in determinining whether the treatment was beneficial.

Unfortunately, the direct relationship between adequate personality functioning and positive outcome in psychotherapy is sometimes interpreted to mean that psychotherapy works best with patients who need it least, or that the ideal candidate for psychotherapy is a person who has no psychological problems at all. The absurdity of such an inference can be resolved by distinguishing carefully between generalized personality disturbances and specific psychological problems. Among surgical patients, those who are in the best general physical condition enjoy the best prospects for an uncomplicated recovery, assuming they need the surgical treatment, and the prognosis for someone who does not need surgery is an irrelevant consideration. Similarly, the person who will do best in psychotherapy is one who needs and wants it because he is experiencing emotional distress, but whose general personality integration has remained reasonably intact. Luborsky and Spence (1971) note in this regard that marked anxiety has proved an especially positive predictor of favorable outcome among psychotherapy patients with initially good general personality functioning.

2. *The patient is motivated to receive psychotherapy, hopes to change how he is feeling or behaving, and expects that the treatment will help him accomplish this change.* Considerable evidence has accumulated to demonstrate that the more positive the attitudes and expectations with which a patient enters and pursues psychotherapy, the more likely he is to benefit from it. Most experienced clinicians accordingly regard it as an important task of the therapist to nourish a patient's expectations of

receiving help and to provide him success experiences that sustain these hopes (see Frank, 1971).[3]

Yet, while initially strong motivation, high hopes, and positive expectations enhance the likelihood of a patient's benefiting from psychotherapy, none of these is essential for a good response to follow. The committed or involuntary patient, the pessimistic patient, and the skeptical patient can all benefit from psychotherapy if the therapist is skillful enough to get them involved in the treatment process (see Gendlin, 1961a; Vriend & Dyer, 1973). However, since the therapist's task will be less difficult if he does not have to surmount major obstacles to change, the patient who comes to therapy already motivated, hopeful, and optimistic has better prospects for improvement on the average than one who does not.

3. *In therapy the patient is a likeable person with good capacity for expressing and reflecting on his experience.* The psychotherapist's work has sometimes been regarded as an impersonal procedure in which any feelings he forms toward a patient constitute countertransference and should not be allowed to influence his conduct of the treatment (see Chap. 11). Yet a therapist cannot entirely avoid having feelings about whether his patient is a worthwhile person; moreover, not surprisingly, therapists may encounter difficulty working with patients they dislike (Strupp, 1960; Strupp & Williams, 1960). It is toward patients regarded as worthwhile human beings that a therapist is best able to display the respect that contributes to a helpful treatment relationship. Likeability is a general predictor of outcome, then, because it increases the patient's prospects for having his therapist hold him in positive regard. Furthermore, numerous studies indicate that the more a therapist is attracted to a patient, the more fully and openly the patient will talk and the less resistance he will display to the treatment process (see Goldstein, 1969).

The capacity of a patient to express and reflect on his experience is perhaps the most obvious of the patient characteristics associated with improvement in psychotherapy. A therapist's understanding of a patient derives from what the patient is able to communicate to him, whether verbally or nonverbally. Additionally, a patient's ability to profit from his

[3]Wilkins (1973), reviewing the literature on expectancy of therapeutic gain, criticizes the adequacy of research in this area and concludes that empirical data have yet to confirm that expectancy of improvement contributes to actual improvement in psychotherapy. Nevertheless, given the generally acknowledged impact of expectancies on human behavior, it seems justified to assign them an influential role in psychotherapy, even though research to date may fail to satisfy all behavioral scientists as to its conclusiveness.

therapist's efforts to communicate understanding depends on his capacity to ponder the therapist's comments in light of his own self-observations. Accordingly, the more a patient can express and reflect on his experiences, the more information will become available to work with in the treatment and the more fully this information will be utilized in pursuing the goals of the therapy.

Characteristics Occasionally Related to Outcome

Two additional patient characteristics sometimes prove useful in predicting improvement in psychotherapy, although neither is as uniformly applicable as the three characteristics discussed above. First, people who have previously demonstrated competence in life situations tend to have relatively good prospects for benefiting from psychotherapy. Competence overlaps in many respects with minimal generalized personality disturbance but it refers more specifically to what a person has been able to accomplish in his life. Individuals who have been relatively successful in utilizing their talents and opportunities to achieve academically, vocationally, and socially are similarly likely to achieve in psychotherapy:

> The more an individual has had a general pattern of persistent effort in a goal-directed fashion, and of success in the various ventures he has undertaken, the more likely will he be to sustain his effort during the course of the treatment, and ultimately to achieve some measure of success (Dewald, 1971, p. 116).

Second, people with higher intelligence and greater intellectual skills tend to derive more benefit from psychotherapy than those who are less well-endowed. However, this patient characteristic should be applied very cautiously in estimating prognosis in the individual case. Although there is a generally positive relationship between intelligence and progress in psychotherapy, a high level of intelligence has not been found necessary for effective psychotherapy to take place. To the contrary, there is ample evidence that psychotherapy can help alleviate the emotional problems of mentally retarded as well as intellectually advantaged patients (see Lott, 1970; Szurek & Philips, 1966).

Characteristics Unrelated to Outcome

Several other patient characteristics, including age, sex, race, marital status, and social class, have little or no necessary bearing on whether a person will benefit from psychotherapy. Of these, age, race, and social class require special comment, since each is at times proposed as a predictor of psychotherapy outcome.

With regard to *age*, there is some slight tendency for younger patients to profit more from psychotherapy than older patients, presumably because they have fewer fixed commitments in life, fewer entrenched characterological problems, and thus more freedom for pointing themselves in new directions. On balance, however, research findings provide little support for estimating a patient's response to psychotherapy on the basis of his age, and effective psychotherapy even with elderly and dying patients is extensively described in the literature.[4]

With respect to *race*, increasing concern in recent years with the psychological problems of minority groups has fostered impressions that black and Spanish-speaking patients come to psychotherapy with different needs and attitudes from those of English-speaking Caucasians; that new theories and methods are necessary to achieve therapeutic success with these patients; and that favorable outcome requires the patient's therapist to come from the same minority group as he does. In contrast to these impressions, however, the bulk of research data indicates that the attitudes minority group members hold toward psychotherapy and the needs with which they seek it vary on an individual rather than a culturally-determined basis and are indiscriminable from the needs and attitudes of the majority population; that current theories and methods, if appropriately tailored to meet the needs of the individual patient, are as applicable to minority as to majority group members; and that the race of the therapist is relevant only to the extent that it influences his capacity to empathize with a particular patient and to sustain positive regard for him. As long as racial differences do not impair the therapist's capacity to understand his patient or to consider him a worthwhile person, the patient's race will not predict his likelihood of benefiting from psychotherapy.[5]

As for *social class*, it has frequently been suggested that psychotherapy is a treatment of choice only for members of the middle and upper socioeconomic classes, whereas working-class people lack the necessary sophistication, introspectiveness, psychological-mindness, and verbal capacity to participate effectively in psychotherapy. Concerns about the presumed inadequacy of traditional psychotherapy for meeting the

[4]For representative discussions of psychotherapy with older people, see Baltes (1973), Butler (1960), Grotjahn (1955), Hammer (1972), Hiatt (1971), Norton (1963), Peck (1966), and Wolff (1963).

[5]Relevant research on the import of racial characteristics in psychotherapy is reported by Banks (1972), Fitzgibbons, Cutler, and Cohen (1971), Jackson (1973), Khaton and Carriera (1972), Waite (1968), Winston, Pardes, and Papernik (1972), and Wolkon, Moriwaki, and Williams (1973).

psychological needs of low-income patients have stimulated the development of various innovative treatment methods for working with them (see Goldstein, 1973; Guerney, 1969; Minuchin et al., 1967). As noted in a review by Lorion (1973), however, socioeconomic status has *not* been demonstrated to relate to treatment outcome, and the emergence of differential treatment methods carries a risk of creating separate and unequal services for various social groups. Hence, as with race, it is necessary to look closely at the characteristics of different social classes as they are presumed to bear on response to psychotherapy, with particular attention to whether there are generalized class differences that cut across individual variation.

On closer examination, the common presumptions about the attitudes and orientations of working-class people being antagonistic to psychotherapy appear unfounded. The help-seeking attitudes of working-class people are no more uniform than those of middle-class people, and the impression that working-class patients come to treatment primarily for symptom relief is refuted by evidence that, as much as middle-class patients, they come expecting to talk about their problems and to have the therapist focus on the meaning of their thoughts and feelings.[6]

Two investigations employing traditional verbal psychotherapy with low-income patients merit special attention. First, Lerner (1972) and Lerner and Fiske (1973) report that at least two-thirds of a sample of inner-city patients showed positive changes with psychotherapy, and they conclude from their data that favorable outcome was related not to any measured individual differences among these patients but to differences among the patients' therapists in their democratic values, their preference for working with lower-class patients, and their self-ratings of skill in working with such patients.

Second, Gould (1967) reports a similar 67% improvement rate among members of an auto workers' union to whom psychoanalytic psychotherapy was made available. This outcome figure, like Lerner's, compares favorably with findings for patients in general, which indicate a 65% average improvement rate with psychotherapy and only a 30% likelihood of improvement among untreated neurotic adults (Bergin, 1971). Gould additionally observed that the union members, whether they sought treatment, generally had a favorable, accepting, nonantagonistic response to its being made available; that those who came for help were less embarrassed and secretive than many middle-class patients about

[6]Findings to this effect are reported by Aronson and Overall (1966), Fisher and Cohen (1972), Gliedman, Stone, Frank, Nash, and Imber (1957) and Goin, Yamamoto, and Silverman (1965).

receiving psychotherapy; and that these patients were able to speak easily and expressively about themselves once their therapist was able to reduce the role distance between them.

The observations by Lerner on therapist attitudes and skill and by Gould on the therapist's reduction of role distance between himself and his working-class patient explain why psychotherapy has so often been considered inapplicable to lower-class people. Psychotherapists, as highly educated people usually drawn from the middle-class, tend to react less positively to lower-class patients, to feel less comfortable talking with them, and to see them as less treatable by psychotherapy (Brill & Storrow, 1960; Lee & Temerlin, 1970; Stein, Green, & Stone, 1972). Hence a working-class patient may in fact have a guarded prognosis in psychotherapy, but only because his middle-class therapist is likely to have difficulty understanding and communicating with him, sustaining positive regard for him, and fostering his trust and expressiveness.

What is needed, then, is for the therapist to know *how to conduct psychotherapy* with working-class patients and other groups of people who may differ from him, and *not* to conclude that it is inapplicable. As Truax and Carkhuff (1967, p. 175) note, the ideal therapist is one who can overcome his personal and professional prejudices so as to provide relatively high levels of therapeutic conditions to virtually all patients and can therefore be helpful *even* to those who might be regarded as poor therapy candidates. The role of such therapist behavior in promoting good treatment outcome is the subject of the next chapter.

CHAPTER 3

The Therapist

Psychotherapists come from a number of disciplines and represent a variety of training backgrounds. The great majority of professional psychotherapists are drawn from the fields of clinical and counseling psychology, psychiatry, and social work, although increasing numbers of nurses, clergymen, educators, and mental health aides are being trained to provide psychotherapy. How people from different professions become psychotherapists and the nature of the training they receive are reviewed by Henry, Sims, and Spray (1971, Chap. 7) and Wolberg (1967, Chap. 14) and will not be elaborated here. However, two comments are in order concerning the general question of who should do psychotherapy.

First and foremost, psychotherapy should be conducted only by people who are trained to conduct it. This prescription is not as gratuitous as it may sound. Self-appointed experts in human behavior are plentiful, and there are very few people who do not consider themselves prepared by their own experiences in living to understand the problems of others. Furthermore, psychotherapy can seem deceptively simple after hearing or reading a few things about it—the therapist just listens and reports his impressions of what is being said, and the patient gets better. Hence it is not uncommon for well-intended individuals who are interested in helping others to fancy themselves as being able to do so, and such fancy poses a risk for anyone who seeks psychological help without discriminating among it would-be providers.

For psychotherapy is not a benign procedure. Ample evidence indicates that it can be harmful as well as helpful to patients and that the major factors influencing good and bad outcomes reside in the therapist and how he conducts the treatment.[1] An untrained person may

[1]Research concerning the potential of psychotherapy for ill as well as good is reviewed by Bergin (1966, 1967, 1971), Truax and Carkhuff (1967, Chaps. 1–3), and Truax and Wargo (1966). For clinical discussions of success and failure in psychotherapy, books by Chessick (1971) and Wolman (1972) are recommended.

inadvertently conduct psychotherapy in a way that fulfills the necessary conditions for a good outcome, and a patient may benefit just from talking with someone who listens, whether the listener has any knowledge of how best to respond. As noted in Chapter 1, however, it is unlikely that an untrained person will perform the salutary functions of psychotherapy as well or as consistently as a professional who has been trained to perform them, and it is reasonable to expect that someone who benefits from talking with an untrained person would have derived greater and more lasting benefit from working with a knowledgeable psychotherapist.

These comments are not intended to depreciate the preparation of nonprofessional people as mental health counselors. Yet it should be noted that in the best-known and most successful effort of this kind—namely, the housewife training program conducted by Rioch and Elkes for the National Institute of Mental Health—the nonprofessional counselors were very carefully selected and received over 2500 hours of traditional didactic instruction and practicum supervision (see Rioch et al., 1963; Magoon, Golann, & Freeman, 1969). While such extensive skill training can prepare nonprofessional people to conduct psychotherapy, the lack of a broader professional background in the mental health field confines the clinical effectiveness of these people to a limited domain of settings and roles (see Durlak, 1973).

The second point about who should conduct psychotherapy concerns whether psychotherapy is a medical treatment to be performed solely by or under the supervision of a physician or whether it is a psychological procedure to be conducted by whomever can become competent to do so. This issue has generated pleas, polemics, pronouncements, and even legal suits emanating from both sides of the argument. The substance of the controversy is thoughtfully reviewed by Wolberg (1967, Vol. 1, pp. 331–347), who encourages an "ecumentical spirit in the mental health field." After noting that medical supervision is necessary for patients who require somatic therapy and that all psychotherapy patients should be under the coordinate care of a general medical practitioner who tends to their physical health, Wolberg draws the following conclusions:

1. Competence as a psychotherapist has little to do with the particular degree the therapist has.
2. The sense of ethical responsibility necessary for assuming patient care can be appreciated by any professional person.
3. Professionals who have been trained to do psychotherapy, including sufficient supervised clinical experience, are capable of doing psychotherapy under whatever continuing supervision their level of training demands.

BEING A GOOD THERAPIST

Just as considerable effort has been expended to identify the "good patient" for psychotherapy, so there have been numerous attempts to define the "good therapist." Most texts on psychotherapy list at least a few essential requirements for being a good therapist, and the 1947 report of the American Psychological Association's Committee on Training in Clinical Psychology offers no less than 15 characteristics a psychotherapist should possess (Shakow, 1947). The problem with most such lists is that they attempt to define the good therapist in the abstract, rather than in the terms of therapist characteristics that contribute to positive outcomes in specific treatment situations. In the same way as the "good patient" concept is relative to finding the appropriate treatment to meet a particular patient's needs, a good therapist is one who proves helpful to the patients with whom he works.

The essence of being a good therapist is possessing interpersonal skills that promote positive outcome in psychotherapy and the ability to display these skills in encounters with patients. It needs to be emphasized that having these interpersonal skills is not tantamount to the capability of displaying them in clinical situations. An individual with a gift for understanding personality processes may not be able to draw effectively on this sensitivity in the situation of a treatment relationship, confronted with a disturbed person for whom he must shoulder clinical responsibility. This chapter summarizes the qualities of an effective psychotherapist, first with regard to the interpersonal skills he needs to have and second in terms of the major factors that influence his capacity to utilize these skills clinically.

INTERPERSONAL SKILLS

Research data identify the successful therapist as one who genuinely cares about and is committed to his patients. These studies confirm that the most crucial element in the therapist's contribution to successful outcome, and the personality characteristic that most consistently differentiates successful from unsuccessful therapists, is interest in people and commitment to the patient (Swenson, 1971). The interpersonal skills of the effective psychotherapist have frequently been translated for research purposes into the three attributes of therapist *warmth*, therapist *genuineness*, and therapist *empathy*. A brief discussion of what these concepts mean describes in general how a psychotherapist needs to conduct himself so as to create a climate conducive to progress in the treatment.

Warmth

The psychotherapist must provide an atmosphere in which his patient can feel safe, secure, and respected as a person. Therapist warmth is the means of creating such an atmosphere. The warm therapist values his patient as a person, independently of any evaluation he makes of his patient's thoughts or behaviors; he unconditionally accepts whatever his patient says or does as something that is part of him and hence worthy of being understood; he refrains from passing judgment on his patient's actions or assuming responsibility for his decisions; and he maintains at all times a friendly, receptive, and nondominating attitude. It is by valuing and accepting his patients, without judging or dominating them, that a therapist displays the warmth that is necessary for his patients to feel safe in the psychotherapy situation and to become profitably engaged in it.

In illustrating expressions of therapist warmth, it is helpful to clarify what warmth is *not*. Although it is through warmth that a therapist communicates his interest in his patient's welfare, warmth does *not* mean sympathy. A therapist's response to a saddening experience in his patient's life usually should not be "Oh, that's terrible!" or "I'm so sorry to hear that." Such expressions of sympathy imply some caring, but their warmth is limited in that they convey the *therapist's* evaluation ("that's terrible") and the *therapist's* reaction ("I'm sorry") to the situation, as opposed to giving primary attention to the *patient's* thoughts and feelings. To display respect as well as caring, a warmer response to misfortune would be "That must have been very upsetting for you" (for an obviously devastating experience) or "It sounds like that was upsetting for you" (for a less obviously disturbing experience). These latter responses convey the caring that warmth demands, while at the same time they emphasize that it is the patient's feelings and attitudes, not the therapist's, that take precedence in the treatment relationship.

Warmth also does *not* mean that the therapist is a passive, entirely benign figure who keeps the treatment situation as free from anxiety as possible. The therapist's job is to help his patient understand himself better, and the quest for expanded self-awareness is not a painless pursuit. A warm therapist avoids threatening the integrity and dignity of his patient as a person, but he does not shrink from challenging the rationality of the patient's thoughts, feelings, and behavior when it is appropriate to do so. It is a caring person who makes an effort to understand and confront another person with actions and underlying attitudes that are causing him psychological difficulty. A therapist who rarely makes the effort to be challenging comes across not as warm and accepting, but as aloof and uncaring.

The point to keep in mind, then, is that the warm therapist does evaluate and challenge his patient's statements and actions, but he does not judge or denigrate him as a person. There is a world of difference between saying to a patient "That was a dumb thing to do" (which, if properly expressed at an appropriate time, can be a warm and constructive observation) and "You certainly are dumb" (which is a personal attack conveying no warmth, and which could be an effective comment only under very unusual circumstances). In other words, the concept of "unconditional positive regard," first explicated by Carl Rogers (1951, 1957) as essential for effective psychotherapy, means that the therapist unconditionally respects the patient's dignity and integrity, but not necessarily everything the patient thinks, says, and does.

Finally, although warmth should not be possessive, as it is if the therapist assumes responsibility for deciding what is best for his patient, it cannot be impersonal either. For a therapist to say, "Here's what I'd like you to do" is caring but possessive, in that it strips the patient of responsibility for making his own decisions. Although such a comment may serve the purposes of some forms of psychological treatment, it seldom constitutes effective psychotherapy. Yet to convey warmth a therapist does need to inject himself as a person into the treatment situation and to use personal pronouns. Thus to say "It seems to me that you didn't handle that situation as well as you might have" or "I think there may be something more on your mind than you feel like talking about" expresses that the therapist, without intruding on the patient's prerogatives, is using his own observational skills and personal impressions in the effort to be of help. A therapist who confines himself to impersonal language communicates an objectivity that patients perceive as detachment and indifference.[2]

Genuineness

For a patient to derive maximum benefit from psychotherapy, he must be able to present his thoughts and feelings in an open, truthful, and

[2]For an elaboration of the nature of warmth as a therapist quality and as a personality characteristic the reader is referred to Raush and Bordin (1957).

nondefensive manner. To some extent patient candor is facilitated by therapist warmth, which promotes a sense of trust and security in the treatment situation. However, patients find it difficult to be open and truthful unless they perceive their therapist as relating to them in an open and truthful fashion.[3] The essence of therapist genuineness is engagement with the patient in a direct personal encounter, rooted in honesty and unmarred by artificiality.

For the therapist, being genuine means simply being himself, that is, being an authentic person who says only what he means and does only what is comfortable and natural for him to do. Freud (1915, p. 164) felt that "psycho-analytic treatment is founded on truthfulness," and he warned that a therapist who is caught in a lie by a patient can never again generate the level of trust necessary for the patient to confide in him fully. As part of being truthful, a therapist must avoid trying to sound definitive when he lacks conviction. Unless he is a consummate actor, his patient will recognize any such discrepancies between what he is saying and what he thinks and will stamp him as ungenuine without further ado.

Patients are also quick to identify when a therapist is behaving in ways that are not natural for him. A customarily somber therapist who decides his patient needs an additional show of warmth and forces himself to smile is being ungenuine. A forced smile, which most patients will recognize immediately, bears eloquent testimony to therapist insincerity, not genuine warmth. Warmth is meaningful only when it is expressed by a person who is being real. Similarly, a therapist who attempts to improve communication with his patient by talking in the patient's vernacular, when he cannot do so comfortably, will appear ungenuine. Anyone not trained in the performing arts who makes a conscious effort to use profanity, slang, dialect, pedantic words, or technical terms that are not ordinarily a part of his speech will stumble and strain in ways that communicate phoniness and pretense.

On the other hand, being genuine does *not* mean that a therapist must express every feeling he has and disclose all of his personal concerns. It simply means that whatever feelings a therapist does express are sincere and congruent with his inner experiences, and that what he chooses to disclose represents a real aspect of himself.

Furthermore, although there are times when openness and self-disclo-

[3]Extended discussions of the beneficial aspects of self-disclosure and of the relationship between therapist openness and patient disclosure in the treatment situation are provided by Cozby (1973), Jourard (1964, 1971), and Jourard and Jaffee (1970).

sure by a therapist facilitate psychotherapy, instant intimacy can be as ungenuine as exaggerated distance from a patient. Just as a patient will have difficulty identifying the real person in a therapist who hides behind a professional facade and never deviates from an impersonal stance, so too he will see as unreal a therapist who ushers him into the office for a first visit saying, "Hi, my name is Fred, and I'm feeling a little anxious because you remind me of a fellow I knew in college who always made me feel I wasn't good enough to compete with him." Even a patient who is prepared to be very open, and one who will benefit from an opportunity to work with a particularly open therapist, knows that people have to get to know each other a bit before they share deeply personal experiences, and premature self-disclosure by the therapist will strike him as unnatural and insincere.

Empathy

Empathy is the ability to put oneself in another person's shoes and comprehend his needs and feelings. In the psychotherapy situation empathic understanding consists of the therapist's special sensitivity to the meaning of what his patient says and does. The empathic therapist is able to perceive his patient's thoughts and feelings accurately and to recognize their significance, not only for what the patient is experiencing at the moment but also for what may lie outside of his conscious awareness. Theodore Reik (1948) captured the essense of empathy very well when he titled his classic book on therapist sensitivity *Listening with the Third Ear.*

It is therapist empathy that serves the work of the psychotherapy relationship, for it is by communicating accurate understanding that the therapist helps his patient broaden his self-awareness and understand himself better. Empathy can run aground on many shores—on misinterpretation of the patient's thoughts and feelings, on failure to listen attentively, on preoccupation with making judgments and giving advice, or on excessive attention to the content rather than the meaning of the patient's verbalizations. Each of these errors represents missed opportunities for the therapist to empathize with his patient and help him amplify his self-awareness.

To be effectively empathic, a therapist must not only be able to understand his patient, but he must also be able to communicate this understanding in ways the patient can understand and accept. As with therapist warmth and therapist genuineness, then, there may be a gap between what the therapist experiences and what he is capable of expressing well. The most psychologically sensitive individual cannot become a good therapist until he learns techniques for establishing a good working relationship with his patients and for helping them share in the understanding he gains about them.

To summarize this discussion of interpersonal skills, research findings indicate that the effective therapist is one who is friendly, interested, and understanding, whereas the ineffective therapist is one who appears to be less friendly, not so understanding, and reserved (Reisman, 1971, Chap. 4). Therapist expressions of nonpossessive warmth, genuineness, and accurate empathy contribute to positive outcomes in psychotherapy, whereas therapist expressions of aloofness, detachment, and insensitivity detract from positive outcomes. Moreover, these relationships hold for therapists with many different theoretical orientations, for many different kinds of patients, and for both individual and group psychotherapy (Truax & Mitchell, 1971, p. 310). This chapter concludes by examining some of the factors that are likely to influence a therapist's capacity to display these interpersonal skills to the benefit of his patients.

CAPACITY TO DISPLAY INTERPERSONAL SKILLS

The therapist's capacity to display the interpersonal skills that contribute to good outcome in psychotherapy is a function primarily of the following three factors: (a) the extent to which his training and experience have taught him how to communicate warmth, genuineness, and empathy to his patients; (b) the extent to which he is free from neurotic difficulties that interfere with his ability to respond to his patients' needs; and (c) the extent to which his interaction with a particular patient promotes his potential for being helpful to that patient.

Training and Experience

It has already been pointed out in this chapter that psychotherapy should be conducted only by people who are trained to conduct it. Being a warm, friendly, and empathic person is only the beginning of being an effective therapist—a necessary beginning, but *only* the beginning. To be maximally effective, a therapist needs a thorough education in the nature of personality processes and extensive training in the techniques of psychotherapy. Only with a solid grasp of personality processes and a repertoire of polished technical skills on which to draw can a therapist make meaningful decisions about what he should actually do: when should he express empathic understanding and when should he express warmth, how much of either should he express at a particular time for a particular patient, and with what words of gestures should he express it?

Considerable research indicates that therapists cannot be uniformly effective simply by being indiscriminately warm and empathic. For example, the more direct and probing an empathic statement is, the more anxious and defensive a patient becomes (Frank, 1964; Garduk & Haggard, 1972; Speisman, 1959). In addition, although therapist warmth and genuineness are equally important for patients who differ in motivation for change, accurate empathy is probably more critical in helping the low prognosis patient who is not eagerly seeking change than the high prognosis patient who is very much ready to change (Truax & Carkhuff, 1967, p. 188). Also, trained therapists vary the amount of empathic understanding they express to their patients from one session to the next and in relation to the particular content of what is being discussed (Gurman, 1973; Moos & MacIntosh, 1970). Finally, identical therapist behavior may facilitate responsiveness in some patients and inhibit responsiveness in other patients (Murray & Jacobson, 1971).

These and other related studies confirm that such personal qualities as warmth and sensitivity can facilitate psychotherapy only to the extent that the therapist is adequately trained in how, when, and to whom to express them. It has sometimes been suggested that anyone who can listen sympathetically, foster a good interpersonal relationship, and give sound advice can be as effective as a trained professional theapist. However, there is no sound evidence to support this view. To the contrary, the amount of genuineness, warmth, and empathy therapists are capable of expressing to their patients appears related to the amount of training and experience they have had (Beery, 1970; Perlman, 1973). Furthermore, numerous studies have demonstrated (a) that there is a significant positive relationship between therapist level of experience and patient improvement and (b) that experienced therapists have lower drop-out rates and more successful terminations than inexperienced therapists.[4]

Freedom from Neurotic Difficulties

To conduct psychotherapy effectively, a therapist must be free from neurotic difficulties that interfere with his responding openly and flexibly

[4]These studies are reviewed by Bergin (1971), Luborsky et al. (1971), Meltzoff and Kornreich (1970, Chap. 11), and Strupp and Bergin (1969).

to the needs of his patients. Freedom from interfering neurotic difficulties means first of all that the therapist must be keenly aware of his own personality dynamics—in particular, what tends to make him angry or anxious, how he feels about the important figures in his life, and why he behaves as he does in various situations. Only with a high level of self-awareness can a therapist differentiate clearly between patient behavior and his reaction to that behavior. Although he can often draw on his own reactions to understand better what is going on in the treatment, he can do so only if he recognizes that his reactions to some behavior are not necessarily the same reactions his patient is having.

Therapists who lack self-awareness tend to interpret what they observe within their own frame of reference, and they are consequently handicapped in their efforts to help their patients understand themselves better. For example, a male therapist who is unaware of underlying concerns about his masculinity may become angry at a male patient who tells him he looks effeminate and proceed to interpret the patient's behavior as an expression of hostility. In doing so he may miss a much more important element of homosexual seductiveness in the patient's comment, which was a reflection of positive rather than negative feelings toward him. The therapist in this example would have been better prepared to recognize the meaning of his patient's behavior if he had been able to avoid or at least understand his own anger in response to it.

In addition to preventing his personality dynamics from clouding his objectivity, a therapist must also be able to avoid using the psychotherapy relationship to gratify inappropriate personal needs. It is appropriate for a psychotherapist to seek and expect certain gratifications in his work, such as the opportunity to be of help, to learn more about human behavior, and to make a living. However, if a therapist is compelled to bolster his own self-esteem by dominating or depreciating his patients, if he has sadistic needs that lead him to be cruel or dependent needs that lead him to curry favor, or if he has fears of failure that cause him prematurely to discharge patients who are progressing slowly, then his behavior is being governed by inappropriate personal needs that prevent his giving the necessary priority to his patient's needs.[5]

This does not mean that an effective psychotherapist must be a paragon of psychological adjustment, free from any neurotic symptoms or

[5]An excellent discussion of the various rational and irrational needs that may influence the psychotherapist's work is provided by Singer (1965, pp. 117–124), Bugental (1964) elaborates on gratifications that are appropriate and inappropriate for the therapist to seek from his patients.

personality quirks. Rather, it means that whatever neurotic elements a therapist may have in his personality they must not be either (a) of a kind that will interfere with his objectivity and commitment to his patient's needs in the psychotherapy situation or (b) sufficiently within his self-awareness and self-control for him to counteract any such interference with his ability to understand his patients and address their needs.

It is sometimes maintained that a therapist must himself undergo therapy in order to attain sufficient objectivity, commitment, self-awareness, and self-control to function effectively in his work. Such an assertion, if unqualified, confuses the goal of being an effective therapist with the means of becoming one. The goal is for the therapist to be free from neurotic interferences with his work, and therapists whose effectiveness is hampered by neurotic difficulties may find personal psychotherapy a useful and necessary means of increasing their skill. However, for therapists whose personal capacities and previous experiences have already prepared them to understand and meet the needs of their patients, personal psychotherapy may be irrelevant except as an educational venture. The notion that personal psychotherapy is a prerequisite for becoming a good therapist is now generally regarded as a myth, and there is no research evidence to suggest that therapists who have had personal psychotherapy are more effective than those who have not.[6]

Therapist-Patient Interaction

Whatever their level of training, experience, and freedom from neurotic needs, therapists do not work equally well with all patients. Every therapist is more sensitive to the difficulties of some patients than others, and every therapist is more interested in helping some type of patients than others. Most therapists learn in the course of their experience not only what type of treatment techniques they are most comfortable and adept with, but also what type of patients and patient problems they treat most effectively. Although it is difficult for the beginning therapist to make such judgments about his clinical functioning, he nevertheless needs to keep in mind that one of the critical factors promoting optimal psychotherapy outcome is the matching of a patient with a therapist who can best communicate interest, understanding, and respect to him. In this

[6]Arguments and evidence relating to this point are presented by Fierman (1965), Leader (1971), and Meltzoff and Kornreich (1970, Chap. 4).

sense, then, the interpersonal skills of the therapist are dyadic variables, influenced by the nature of his interaction with a particular patient as well as by his intrinsic qualities and the training he has received (see Beutler et al., 1973; Gurman, 1973; Truax & Mitchel, 1971).

It is less clear what contributes to the best possible match of therapist with patient. Considerable attention has been given in this respect to the notion of "A-type" and "B-type" therapists introduced a number of years ago by Whitehorn and Betz (1954). Therapists who are oriented primarily toward establishing a meaningful patient-therapist relationship are classified as A's, while B's are therapists who focus more on helping their patients achieve insight into their difficulties. In terms of their personality style, A-type therapists appear to be relatively intuitive individuals with ready access to their inner feelings and a readiness to relax their reality orientation in response to those feelings, whereas B-type therapies are more rational, realistic, and intellectually oriented in their dealings with people and events. Although there is some evidence to suggest that A-type therapists communicate more effectively with schizophrenic patients and B-type therapists with neurotic patients, more work needs to be done to confirm and account for this and other possible treatment implications of the A-B variable.[7]

There are also indications that similarity between patient and therapist in age, sex, race, religion, social class, and cognitive style promotes a good treatment outcome. Here again, however, the research findings are not uniform, and it is always possible to identify exceptions in the individual case. For example, a male patient who is extremely fearful of being criticized or humiliated by men may feel more secure and work more productively with a female rather than with a male therapist, and a younger person may do better with an older therapist because he has higher expectations in working with someone he presumes, because of his age, to be relatively experienced and skilled. Interestingly, some studies suggest that the relationship between patient-therapist similarity and success in psychotherapy is curvilinear, that is, communication proceeds most helpfully between two people who are neither too much alike nor too different from each other (e.g., Carson & Heine, 1962).

Until more is known on this subject, all that can be said is that the match between therapist and patient is important to the extent that it

[7]A representative sample of the numerous reports and reviews of research concerning the A-B variable in psychotherapy includes articles by Berzins et al. (1972), Beutler et al. (1972), Bowden et al. (1972), Carson (1967), Chartier (1971), Fancher et al. (1972), Razin (1971), and Silverman (1967).

influences the degree to which a particular therapist can communicate effectively with a particular patient. Each therapist needs to devote his treatment time to those people he feels respect and empathy for and to refer elsewhere those toward whom he feels disinterested, disapproving, or insensitive.[8]

SUMMARY

As defined in Chapter 1, psychotherapy consists of the communication of understanding, respect, and a wish to be of help. Chapter 2 notes that the patients most likely to benefit from this particular form of treatment are those who are motivated to receive it, have minimal generalized personality disturbance but a high level of felt distress, and are likeable people with good capacity for reflection and self-expression. The present chapter identifies the effective psychotherapist as one who can display high levels of warmth, genuineness, and empathy.

Yet it needs to be recognized that psychotherapy may not be *effective* psychotherapy. Psychotherapy is defined by the communication of understanding, respect, and a wish to be of help, irrespective of whether a patient benefits from receiving this communication. Whether psychotherapy will be effective psychotherapy in a given instance depends on (a) the extent to which the patient's needs are best suited for psychotherapy as opposed to some other form of treatment; (b) the extent to which the match between the patient and therapist maximizes the therapist's capacity to display warmth and understanding, and (c) the extent of the therapist's ability to judge how, when, and to what degree he should express understanding and warmth.

The therapist's ability to judge what he should try to communicate to a particular patient, when he should communicate it, and what words he should use constitute his technical skill. Following a brief overview of theory and process in psychotherapy in Chapter 4, the remaining chapters of this book concern the technique of psychotherapy, that is, the principles of conducting psychotherapy interviews during the initial, middle, and final phases of a treatment relationship. Some approaches to psychotherapy have focused largely on technical skill with little attention to the personal qualities of the therapist. Others have stressed the personal interest and warmth of the therapist as the major agent of change

[8]Further discussion and reviews of research about therapist–patient interaction are to be found in Carr (1970), Gassner (1970), Goldstein (1971), Luborsky et al. (1971), Meltzoff and Kornreich (1970, Chap. 12), Strupp and Bergin (1969), and Swenson (1971).

in psychotherapy and have minimized the importance of technique. Yet most psychotherapy practitioners and researchers concur that effective psychotherapy requires a balanced combination of personality and technical skills, which Strupp (1970, 1972) aptly refers to as the general and specific factors promoting change in psychotherapy.

Technical mastery is useful in the hands of a therapist who can foster a good personal relationship with his patients, a relationship that allows them to listen to, understand, and trust in what he is trying to communicate, no matter how painful the message may be. Without such a relationship the most brilliant insights and deftly turned phrases will fall on deaf ears. Likewise, a therapist's interpersonal skills can be turned to his patient's fullest advantage only if he has sufficient knowledge of personality dynamics and treatment techniques to build self-understanding on the foundation of a good working relationship. A good therapist is neither a good friend nor a good technician; he is a little of both, in a combination distilled from his personality skills and his professional training.

CHAPTER 4

Theory and Process in Psychotherapy

To be an effective psychotherapist, one must work within the context of a cohesive theory of personality and an overall conception of the psychotherapeutic process. Planned intervention is always more likely to be productive than accidental behavior, and a therapist can do his job best if he operates with a set of principles that help him formulate what is happening in the treatment and what his next move should be. The principles for doing psychotherapy as presented in this book are derived from dynamic personality theory, from the distinction between uncovering and supportive psychotherapy, and from the complementary roles of strategy and tactics in conducting psychotherapy.

DYNAMIC PERSONALITY THEORY

Dynamic personality theory is most clearly represented by, but not limited to, the various psychoanalytic approaches to understanding human behavior.[1] Three major premises of dynamic personality theory are especially relevant to understanding and implementing psychotherapy: the notion of the unconscious, the notion of conflict and defense, and the notion of an experiencing self and an observing self.

[1]For a sound introduction to dynamic personality theory the reader is referred to Blum (1966), Brenner (1973), Cameron (1963), Hall and Lindzey (1970, Chap. 2), Holzman (1970), Mahl (1971), and Munroe (1955).

The Unconscious

The notion of the unconscious refers to the fact that people may have thoughts and feelings of which they are not fully aware. Although existing outside of a person's conscious awareness, unconscious thoughts and feelings can nevertheless exert powerful influences on his behavior. This means that some of the reasons why a person behaves in a certain way may be entirely unknown to him. For example, a man may find to his puzzlement and consternation that he is slacking off in his work just when he is coming up for promotion, and he may have no idea that his declining performance is being influenced by underlying concerns he has about becoming a more successful person than his father was.

Behavior determined by largely unconscious influences is not necessarily self-defeating, however. A woman who chooses a husband without realizing that he bears many resemblances to her father, whom she loves dearly, may make an excellent choice that she will never regret. On the other hand, the more a person's behavior is determined by influences he does not or cannot recognize, the more prone he is to encounter problems in living.

Unconscious determinants of behavior are potential sources of emotional difficulty precisely because they are not available for conscious consideration. Sorting out their feelings, weighing pros and cons, and wrestling with alternatives are the means by which people decide on courses of action that are consistent with their needs. When important feelings and attitudes are not sufficiently conscious to participate in such decision-making, then the possibilities are increased for a person to behave in ways that are not fully satisfying to him. Thus a woman motivated by unconscious fears of sexual intercourse may avoid having relations with her husband even though she is consciously frustrated by the lack of physical intimacy in her marriage and concerned about her husband's losing interest in her.

Another way of conceptualizing the meaning of the unconscious is to distinguish between the *manifest* and *latent* content of behavior. The manifest content of behavior is what is readily observable, while the latent content of behavior consists of its underlying meanings. Distinctions between the manifest and latent content of behavior are often apparent in psychotherapy and play an important role in the treatment.

For example, suppose that following a session for which the therapist was delayed, a patient arrives late for the next session and explains that he was held up by heavy traffic. Perhaps he was involved in a traffic jam and is not aware of any other reason for his being late. Yet the latent content of his tardiness could well involve anger at the therapist and an unconscious wish to replay him in kind for having kept him waiting previously. If such be the case, careful exploration will usually turn up some corroborating evidence, for example, the traffic was no worse than usual but the patient "somehow" managed not to leave for the appointment until 10 minutes later than he customarily does.

As this example illustrates, one of the ways in which psychotherapy proceeds is by making the unconscious conscious. The more the therapist can identify the unconscious determinants or latent contents of his patient's behavior and help the patient become aware of them, the more he expands the patient's self-awareness. With expanded self-awareness, a person's underlying needs and attitudes, rational and irrational, become increasingly subject to his conscious control, so that he can evaluate and deal with them more constructively than he could when he had no idea of what they were or how they were influencing him.

Conflict and Defense

Conflict and defense in dynamic personality theory refer to aspects of behavior that may be motivated more by needs to avoid anxiety than by the pursuit of self-fulfillment. In this model of ineffective behavior it is presumed that a person may have unconscious wishes that run counter to his sense of right and wrong, and that such conflicts may generate anxiety. Thus a man who is sexually attracted to other men but views homosexuality as perverse may become highly anxious in situations that put him in close proximity with other men, such as a lockerroom or an Army barracks. For another example, a woman who unconsciously hates her mother but consciously considers it the moral duty of a woman to love her mother may feel very uncomfortable when she is in her mother's presence.

Since anxiety is a painful affect, people tend to defend against it by behaving in ways that keep it under wraps. To continue with the above examples, a latently homosexual man with strong conscious aversion to homosexuality may defend against anxiety about his own masculinity by becoming a Don Juan, preoccupied with demonstrating his sexual prowess as often and with as many women as possible, or by becoming a hypermasculine individual constantly intent on displaying his strength, bravery, and capacity to be a "man among men." A woman with underlying hostility toward her mother may minimize the discomfort these feelings cause her by keeping away from her mother as much as possible (leaving the field) or by bending over backwards to be kind and loving toward her mother (reaction formation).

Sometimes these defensive maneuvers work well in that they ease the anxiety stemming from a conflict without creating serious new conflicts. At other times, however, a defensive maneuver may take the form of symptoms or maladaptive behaviors that are in turn anxiety provoking. The Don Juan may be extremely unhappy that he cannot settle down with and be satisfied with one woman, and a woman who is repressing hostility toward her mother and relying on reaction formation to present a loving facade may find herself getting a headache whenever she and her mother are together for an extended period of time.

Because the origins of their conflicts are unconscious, neither of these two people will understand why they are behaving as they are or experiencing the symptoms they have, but both are likely to want to improve their situation. The role of the psychotherapist lies in helping such people to recognize the defensive quality of their behavior and to explore the underlying needs or wishes they are defending against. Psychotherapy helps a person better his life by helping him identify and resolve buried conflicts and thereby increase his potential for conscious control of his behavior.

The Experiencing Self and the Observing Self

In dynamic personality theory people are viewed as having the capacity to experience themselves and to observe themselves. Although all people are capable of both types of activity, individuals differ in the degree to which their personality style favors one or the other. Some people are primarily experiencers, who do what they do and feel what they feel without much pause for looking critically at themselves. Other people are primarily observers, who self-consciously weigh the implications of their behavior without having much tolerance for spontaneous expression in thought or deed. Self-experiencing and self-observing exist on a continuum, neither end of which is conducive to good adjustment: the total experiencer is prone to impulsive, inconsiderate, poorly planned behavior, and the total observer is subject to a paralysis of action or reaction.

In psychotherapy the therapist needs to have both of these aspects of his patient's personality in operation, and he needs to be able to help the patient shift back and forth between them as the occasion demands. The patient who only observes himself produces abundant reflections on his experience but does not report the kinds of spontaneous ideas and feelings that could offer clues to new or different ways he might experience himself. The patient who only experiences himself is unable to participate with the therapist in an effort to reflect on and understand the meaning of his experiences.

Progress in psychotherapy requires a flexible split between a patient's experiencing self and his observing self, originally described by Sterba (1934) as an "ego split." He must be able to relate what he is thinking and feeling spontaneously and with minimal self-consciousness. Yet he must also be able with the therapist's help to take distance from himself, that is, to sit back and look at his behavior as something that needs to be understood. Psychotherapy is in many ways a learning process in that the patient's progress is closely tied to his learning about himself. Experiencing oneself facilitates such learning, but for learning to take place self-experience must be balanced by self-observation.

UNCOVERING AND SUPPORTIVE PSYCHOTHERAPY

Uncovering and *supportive* describe two approaches to psychotherapy that differ in the degree to which attention is focused on unconscious determinants of the patient's behavior. In uncovering psychotherapy, which is also referred to as "insight," "intensive," or "depth" psychotherapy, the goal is to help the patient achieve some reorganization or restructuring of his personality by helping him recognize and express his unconscious conflicts and concerns. In supportive psychotherapy the goal is helping the patient deal more effectively with his real-world problems without delving into his unconscious conflicts and concerns; some uncovering with accompanying personality change may take place secondarily in the course of successful supportive psychotherapy, but such developments are independent of the primary intent of the supportive approach.

Despite this difference in goals, uncovering and supportive psychotherapy share many features in common. In both the overriding aim is to expand the patient's self-awareness so that he may enjoy a richer, more satisfying life. Uncovering psychotherapy seeks to bring many previously unconscious thoughts and feelings into the patient's awareness, whereas supportive psychotherapy focuses on increased understanding and control of thoughts and feelings of which the patient is already at least dimly aware.

Furthermore, the course of both uncovering and supportive psychotherapy proceeds largely through interpretive comments made by the therapist of what the patient says and does. These interpretations may point out connections between past experiences and current behavior (genetic interpretation), or they may identify relationships among various current events in the patient's life (here-and-now interpretations). What is different in the two approaches to psychotherapy is that in uncovering psychotherapy interpretations may be addressed to the patient's personality style as well as to the content of what he says, whereas in supportive psychotherapy the therapist focuses on content and does not challenge the patient's personality style.

To appreciate the meaning of this distinction, it is necessary to recognize that any interpretive comment by the therapist constitutes a challenge. As elaborated in Chapter 9, an interpretation suggests to the patient some new or different way of looking at his experiences and hence always implies that his current views are incorrect or incomplete. In uncovering psychotherapy this type of challenge is offered not only in relation to the thoughts and feelings a patient expresses, but also in relation to various means of coping with new or problem situations and the defense mechanisms that define his personality style. In supportive psychotherapy the patient's personality style is accepted as it is, and the therapist concentrates on thoughts and feelings as they are expressed within this style.

As an example of the distinction between interpreting or accepting a patient's personality style, an obsessive-compulsive man may describe the pros and cons of a decision he is unable to make in excruciating detail. In uncovering psychotherapy the therapist may encourage this patient to step back from the decision for the moment and look at his style of decision-making, which consists of becoming so preoccupied with details that he cannot arrive at an objective, satisfying solution. This may lead to exploring why he needs to be so pedantically careful in dealing with his experience and from there to some resolution of the conflicts that have given rise to his obsessive personality style. Subsequently, then, his characteristic ruminativeness should decrease, allowing him to make this and other decisions with considerably less vacillation than before.

In supportive psychotherapy with such a patient the therapist would work instead within the context of his obsessive-compulsive style to help him make the decision in question. He might, for example, set up a very orderly procedure for reviewing the various pros and cons and assigning them some relative weight, so that by increasing his capacity to differentiate among the more and less crucial considerations the patient will be able to reevaluate the choices open to him and arrive at a reasonable decision.[2]

The distinction between uncovering and supportive psychotherapy needs to be qualified in three important respects. First, uncovering and supportive psychotherapy describe a continuum and not a dichotomy. Psychotherapy exists in a spectrum from a very intensive, uncovering relationship, as in classical psychoanalysis, to an exclusively supportive relationship, and in between there is a considerable range of limited or moderate insight approaches. How uncovering or how supportive a particular approach is depends on the extent to which the patient's unconscious is probed and his defensive style is interpreted. To put it the other way around, a therapist should decide how extensively to interpret his patient's behavior and personality style on the basis of how uncovering or how supportive he feels the psychotherapy ought to be. Without such a judgment to guide him, a therapist may err in flitting randomly between various depths of approach and thereby conduct a chaotic psychotherapy that poorly serves his patient's needs.

Second, uncovering and supportive approaches are not mutually exclusive. Because psychotherapy exists in a spectrum of intensity, effective psychotherapy usually combines efforts to help the patient gain insight and efforts to support him. As Schlesinger (1969) has pointed out, psychotherapy for the individual patient requires a "prescription" indicating for that particular person which aspects of his personality need to be uncovered and which need to be supported for him to derive maximum benefit from psychotherapy.

Furthermore, prescriptions of this type have to be altered from time to time in the course of psychotherapy. During primarily uncovering psychotherapy, for example, various circumstances may arise that call for the use of supportive techniques. A patient faced with a crisis or situational difficulty in his life may temporarily become too anxious or depressed to be able to step back from his experiences and look objectively at himself; in other words, his experiencing self becomes so occupied that he has no time or energy available for his observing self. In such a case the therapist may have to suspend the uncovering emphasis in

[2]For a thorough discussion of the distinction between uncovering and supportive psychotherapy the reader is referred to Dewald (1971), who delineates the technical implications of these differing approaches in various phases of the treatment process.

the treatment and focus for a time on supporting the patient through his intercurrent difficulty.

It is also not uncommon for patients to experience mini-crises during a psychotherapy interview and to need some support and reassurance from the therapist. A patient exploring painful memories or disturbing unconscious impulses may become so upset that further uncovering at that point will do more harm than good. In such situations it may be advisable for the therapist to change the subject to something that is "safer," which supports the patient by allowing him to reestablish his defenses; or the therapist may say, "I can see this is a difficult thing for you to talk about," which reassures the patient that the therapist recognizes and cares about how distressed he is.

In other instances a patient who is being treated with a primarily uncovering approach may give indications that he cannot tolerate the anxiety it produces, or that he cannot strike an optimal balance between experiencing himself and observing himself in the psychotherapy situation. Such developments usually mean that the patient's capacity to participate in and benefit from uncovering psychotherapy has been misjudged, and the therapist may then have to shift from a primarily uncovering to a primarily supportive approach for the duration of the treatment.

On the other hand, a patient whose initial capacities were underrated or who has been helped to resolve a crisis situation that brought him for help may want and need his prescription for psychotherapy changed from primarily supportive to primarily uncovering. However, the therapist should be forewarned that a shift from supportive to uncovering psychotherapy is more difficult to accomplish than the reverse. Uncovering psychotherapy is primarily an *investigative* approach, whereas supportive psychotherapy is primarily a *giving* approach. For a therapist to become less investigative and more giving is easy for a patient to accept, but a therapist who becomes less giving than before is often experienced by the patient as depriving and rejecting.

For this reason, a therapist who has initially treated a patient supportively and subsequently decides than an uncovering approach should be started will usually do well to refer the patient to another therapist. This will not entirely solve the problem, since patients who go through such a referral frequently complain to the new (uncovering) therapist that he is not doing as much for them and does not seem as interested in them as the old (supportive) therapist. Yet this change is still easier to accomplish when the uncovering therapist is a different person from the supportive therapist.

The third qualification that needs to be made in distinguishing between uncovering and supportive approaches to psychotherapy concerns the value assigned to each. It is easy to fall into the error of regarding uncovering psychotherapy as a thorough and effective approach for patients who have many personality strengths, and supportive psychotherapy as a second, less desirable choice for those people who fail to qualify for uncovering psychotherapy. This all-too-common view overlooks the fact that effective psychotherapy is defined not by its brand name, but by how well it meets the needs of the patient. In the abstract, no approach to psychotherapy is better or more desirable than any other approach. For each individual patient there is an approach which promises to be best and most desirable for *him*, and this best and most desirable approach may be uncovering or supportive psychotherapy, or it may be group or family psychotherapy, or it may be some form of psychological treatment other than psychotherapy.

STRATEGY AND TACTICS

To conduct psychotherapy effectively a therapist needs to operate with a sense of both strategy and tactics. *Strategy* refers to the objectives the therapist is trying to achieve at a particular time, and *tactics* have to do with the specific methods he employs to gain these objectives. Strategy may involve such general objectives as helping the patient talk more freely, helping him recognize the nature and origins of his maladaptive behaviors, or helping him identify alternative ways of thinking or feeling. Within the context of a single interview or portion of an interview, strategy may consist of more specific objectives, such as helping the patient uncover some feelings of inferiority or helping him realize that he is experiencing anger toward the therapist. Tactics include whatever the therapist may say or do, including questions, assertions, interpretive comments, facial expressions, or gestures, as a means of implementing his strategy.

Having a sense of strategy and tactics means that at every point in the course of psychotherapy the therapist knows exactly what he is trying to accomplish and how he is trying to accomplish it. Strategy without tactics is an abstract conception of what psychotherapy should be like without the necessary therapist operations to make it that way; tactics without strategy is a technical exercise that meanders in the patient's psyche without fostering any systematic progress toward increased self-understanding. For a therapist to want his patient to achieve certain objectives but not be able to help him do so (strategy without tactics) is ineffective psychotherapy, because the objectives, no matter how correctly conceived, will not be attained. For a therapist to say the right thing for the wrong reason (tactics with poor strategy) or for no reason at all ("It just felt like the thing to say"—tactics with no strategy) is unpromising therapy, because it offers no likelihood of the therapist's being able to say the right thing at other times or in other situations.

THE PROCESS OF PSYCHOTHERAPY

Although the actual course of psychotherapy varies greatly from one patient to another, there is a general sequential process in all psychotherapy relationships. The elements of this process may not always appear in the same order or with the same degree of importance, but some awareness of how psychotherapy may generally be expected to proceed aids the therapist in knowing where he is in his work with a particular patient and mapping this strategy accordingly.

Psychotherapy begins with a patient who comes for help and participates with the therapist in deciding whether psychotherapy is the kind of help he should receive. This initial phase of the treatment relationship consists of (a) evaluating the nature of the patient's problems and what there is about himself he would like to change; (b) assessing the patient's needs, motivations, and capacities for psychotherapy or for some other form of treatment; and (c) if psychotherapy is indicated, making a "contract" to proceed with it. The psychotherapy contract is an explicit agreement between patient and therapist about how their meetings will be arranged, what their respective roles will be in the treatment relationship, and the specific nature of the goals toward which they will be working.

Following the period of evaluation and assessment and the agreement on a treatment contract, psychotherapy enters its middle phase. The middle phase is usually the longest phase in psychotherapy, and it is the time when a therapist does the major portion of his work in communicating psychological understanding to a patient. During this middle phase the therapist's major tasks are to help his patient talk, to understand what the patient is able to reveal about himself, and to make interpretive comments that help the patient share in this understanding.

In the middle phase of psychotherapy the therapist can expect to encounter certain interferences with the process of listening, understanding, and communicating understanding. These interferences or *resist-*

ances constitute a paradoxical reluctance on the part of the patient to participate in the therapy. When resistance occurs, a patient who is apparently eager to learn more about himself and change his behavior becomes unable or unwilling to talk freely.

Resistances arise from a number of sources—sometimes from a patient's underlying reservations about being a patient or changing himself (resistance to treatment), sometimes from an entrenched personality style that resists being challenged (character resistance), sometimes from anxiety about a particular subject that is being discussed (resistance to content), and sometimes from feelings about the therapist that he is reluctant to express (transference resistance). In one sense all of these forms of resistance disrupt patient-therapist communication, and the therapist needs to find ways of proceeding through or around them in order to make continued progress in the middle phase of psychotherapy. At the same time, however, these resistances can themselves provide useful information about a patient's personality style, underlying attitudes, and sources of anxiety.

Transference, which consists of feelings and attitudes that patients experience toward their therapist, is a potential form of interference with patient-therapist communication that merits special comment. Psychotherapy seldom gets off the ground unless a patient has some positive feelings toward his therapist, since such positive regard is a key factor in the patient's willingness to talk freely and accept interpretations of his behavior. Yet positive feelings toward the therapist, if they become strong enough, can motivate a patient to want the therapist's approval and affection more than his help and understanding. Communication then becomes disrupted, because the patient reports primarily what he thinks will find favor in the therapist's eyes and keeps to himself anything he expects the therapist might disapprove.

As therapy continues, patients also develop negative feelings toward their therapist, primarily for two reasons: first because the therapist frustrates them by not expressing the affection and approval they would like to receive from him, and second because negative feelings toward important people in the patient's life tend to be stirred up in the course of the treatment and directed, or *transferred*, onto the therapist. Negative transference can disrupt the communication process by making the patient feel angry or dissatisfied with the therapist, and hence unwilling to cooperate with him or with the treatment procedures.

One additional interference with the communication of psychological understanding that may complicate the middle phase of psychotherapy stems from the therapist's attitudes. Every therapist experiences fluctuating positive and negative feelings toward his patients, sometimes in response to something they have said or done and sometimes as a result of intercurrent events in his own life that are affecting his frame of mind. The therapist needs to recognize and control such *countertransference* reactions in order to prevent them from distorting his perception of his patient or adopting incorrect treatment strategies. At the same time, countertransference reactions can be utilized productively if the therapist has sufficient knowledge of himself to find in them clues to latent features of the patient's behavior that may have prompted his reactions.

Interpretation, resistance, transference, and countertransference are the main themes of the middle phase of psychotherapy. When the work of communicating psychological understanding has been achieved as much as is possible or was planned for, that is, when the goals of the treatment have been realized, psychotherapy enters a final phase of termination. Termination consists of reviewing the course of the treatment, tying up various loose ends, and contemplating what the future may hold for the patient with regard to his personality functioning.

This brief overview of the process of psychotherapy indicates the ground to be covered in this form of treatment. The chapters that follow consider in more detail these aspects of the initial, middle, and final phases of psychotherapy, with specific attention to the strategy and tactics they embrace.

fluctuating positive and negative feelings toward his patients, sometimes in response to something they have said or done and at other times as a result of other, usual events in his own life that are influencing his frame of mind. The therapist needs to recognize and [illegible] such [illegible] reactions in order to prevent them from distorting his perception of his patient or leading to incorrect treatment strategies. At the same time, countertransference reactions can [illegible] the therapist has sufficient knowledge of himself to [illegible] at the patient's behavior that may have prompted his reactions.

Interpretation, resistance, transference, and countertransference are the main themes of the middle phase of psychotherapy. [illegible] understanding has been [illegible] as much [illegible] termination. Termination consists of reviewing the course of the treatment, tying up various loose ends, and contemplating what the future may hold for the patient with respect to his personality functioning.

This brief overview of the process of psychotherapy [illegible] ground to be covered in this [illegible]. The chapters that follow [illegible] in [illegible] detail these [illegible] initial, middle, and final phases of [illegible] the [illegible] to [illegible] and [illegible]

PART TWO

The Initial Phase of Psychotherapy

CHAPTER 5

Evaluation and Assessment

The initial phase of psychotherapy begins with a period of *evaluation* and *assessment*, in which the therapist learns something about his patient and decides whether continuing psychotherapy is indicated. Evaluation and assessment are followed by the making of a *treatment contract*, in which the patient agrees to continue in psychotherapy and works out with the therapist the arrangements for doing so. A third key aspect of initiating psychotherapy is the proper *conduct of the interview*, which deals with how the therapist helps his patient talk freely and become involved in the work of the therapy. The treatment contract and the conduct of the interview are considered in Chapters 6 and 7, and the present chapter treats the evaluation and assessment of prospective psychotherapy patients.

EVALUATING THE PATIENT

The process of evaluating a prospective psychotherapy patient takes place in four sequential steps: (a) identifying the presenting problems; (b) exploring the background of these problems; (c) beginning to understand the patient as a person; and (d) arriving at an adequate working formulation.

Identifying the Presenting Problem

The first step in evaluating a patient is identifying the nature of the problems that have brought him to seek help. Many patients facilitate this task by self-initating an explanation of why it is they have asked to be seen. Some open the initial interview with complaints of diffuse symptoms or interpersonal difficulties ("I don't know if you can help me or not, but I've been feeling awfully anxious lately, and I can't sleep well, and I've been irritable and yelling at my husband and children"); some present one or more specific symptoms that have prompted their seeking help ("I suppose you want to know why I wanted to talk to someone, so I'll just come out with it—I'm impotent and it's messing up my life"); and some do not mention symptoms at all but instead express general dissatisfaction with their life style ("The reason I'm here is that I've realized I'm just not happy in what I'm doing, I feel I've been wasting myself, and I want to get at the bottom of what's best for me before it's too late for me to change").

These types of patient opening give the therapist a good start in knowing what subjects should be pursued in the first interview. On the other hand, it is not uncommon for patients to begin with statements that contain little or no information about their problems and concerns. In such cases the therapist needs to provide some direction toward an explication of the presenting complaints:

Pt. Dr. Smith told me I should come to see you.

Th. What was that about?

. . .

Pt. I don't know where to begin.

Th. You can begin anywhere you like.

Pt. You mean you want to hear all about my childhood?

Th. Well, perhaps you could begin by telling me what led to your coming to see me.

Still other patients do not begin at all, but instead sit quietly and wait for the therapist to open the interview. In this situation it behooves the therapist to inquire directly about the patient's chief concerns. In contrast to this recommendation, it is sometimes suggested that the initially silent patient should be responded to with silence. The rationales offered for such therapist silence include that it avoids taking a directive stance in relation to the patient, that it helps assess the patient's willingness and capacity to talk about himself, and that it constitutes a useful measure of how well the patient can tolerate anxiety in an interpersonal situation.

However, extended therapist silence at the beginning of a first interview is an example of erroneous tactics based on incorrect strategy. Therapist silence can be an effective treatment tactic if it is employed at the right time. But the correct strategy for the beginning of an initial interview is not to test the patient's anxiety tolerance, or to assess his capacity to talk, or to demonstrate the nonpossessivenes of the therapist. These are all important strategies, but the time for them comes later. At the beginning of an initial interview the overriding strategy must be to find out what the patient's problem is, and this strategy dictates the appropriate tactic—if he does not tell you, ask him.

Another frequent suggestion that needs to be looked at critically is that the therapist should begin with whatever dynamic implications are contained in the patient's opening remarks. For example, with this approach the therapist's response to the opening comment "I don't know where to begin" might be "It's hard for you to get started with things." Such an interpretive tactic at the beginning of a first interview is inopportune both because it defers the strategy of identifying the patient's current difficulties and because it may interfere with the subsequent course of the therapy.

To elaborate this latter point, the pitfalls of an immediate interpretive focus on personality dynamics are threefold. First, since the therapist has only very limited knowledge of his patient at this point, he runs a high risk of making an incorrect interpretation, which, at the beginning of psychotherapy, conveys the impression that the therapist is not very understanding and is inclined to jump to conclusions.

Second, because every interpretation is a challenge, the patient who encounters immediate interpretive comments is likely to view the therapist as someone who shoots from the hip and is likely to shoot him down with regularity. And third, interpretations at the beginning of an initial interview mean that the therapist has undertaken the work of the treatment before the patient has agreed to a treatment contract, which is authoritarian and patronizing on the therapist's part. In sum, then, premature interpretive focus can cause the patient to doubt the therapist's sensitivity, can preclude the patient's developing a sense of security in the treatment relationship, and can undermine the therapist's efforts to communicate warmth and respect—all of which are obviously to be avoided.

One other cautionary note should be made about beginning an initial interview. Often the therapist will know something about a patient's current problems before he sees him, usually because the patient has been referred by a colleague who has discussed the referral with him. In such cases the therapist should not play dumb ("Perhaps you could tell me what brings you here"), but should instead state exactly what the situation is: "I know from Dr. Brown that you have been having a number of troublesome thoughts on your mind." After such an opening remark the therapist can wait for the patient to elaborate on the problem, without necessarily spelling out everything he has learned from the referral source. If the patient does not take up this cue to begin talking about himself, the therapist can then add, "Perhaps you could tell me something about it" or "What has it been like for you?"

The therapist's prompt acknowledgment of a referral helps get the treatment relationship off to a good start. A referred patient knows he has been referred, and if his therapist fails to mention this fact, he is likely to draw one of two conclusions: either the therapist has some prior information about him that he is not acknowledging, which means he is asking questions he already knows the answer to and hence is being ungenuine; or he has no prior information, which means he was not sufficiently interested to take the trouble of making some inquiries of the referral source. The therapist can easily avoid or repair such inadvertent communication of ungenuineness or disinterest if he is alert to the importance of doing so:

Th. Why don't you begin by telling me what brings you here.

Pt. (with some irritation) Dr. Jones said he had talked to you about seeing me. Didn't he tell you anything about the problem?

Th. (correcting his error) Yes, he did, and I know it has to do with your relationship with your husband. But I'd like to hear your view of things.

. . .

Pt. (midway in the first interview) I think that's all there is to say about what's bothering me right now. I guess you know about my past since I was a patient here before.

Th. I know you were seen in the clinic a couple of years ago, and I've had a chance to look through your records. But I think it would be helpful if you could tell me about yourself in your own words.

Exploring the Background of the Presenting Problems

After the therapist has identified the major problems and concerns that have brought a patient for help, his next step is to learn something about the background of these presenting difficulties. If the patient has come with a very specific complaint, such as anxiety attacks, the therapist's inquiry likewise needs to be fairly specific: when did the anxiety attacks first begin, how are they manifest, what seems to bring them on, and so forth. With a more general patient concern, the inquiry may take a correspondingly general tack:

Pt. I don't know how to deal with people, and that's the big thing I'm worried about.

Th. Tell me something about your relationships with people.

Whether it is specific or general, the purpose of this initial inquiry into the patient's presenting problems is to get some elaboration of their nature, history, and connection with possible precipitating circumstances. Should the patient present multiple problems and concerns, the therapist may have to be selective in which ones he pursues and how extensively he attempts to elaborate them in a first interview. In some instances, faced with a litany of complaints that all seem central to the patient's difficulties, the therapist may be unsure which ones to select for further exploration. When this is the case, it is usually helpful to call on the patient's judgment: "You've mentioned a number of things you're concerned about; which are the ones that are bothering you the most or that you'd like to talk about first?"

It should be recognized that the patient may not necessarily respond to such a question by selecting his core or most serious problems. He may feel it would be too painful or embarrassing to begin with what is bothering him the most, and he may prefer to start with matters that are relatively easy to talk about; or perhaps he himself does not have an accurate sense of which of his concerns are the more basic or serious ones. Yet for the therapist to request such a choice serves to elicit some topics to be pursued in the initial interview and also to communicate warmth and respect. The patient is being told that he will share responsibility for deciding what goes on in the treatment, and furthermore that he will be accepted as he is and not called on to do more than he is psychologically prepared to do.

As for how extensively to explore aspects of a patient's presenting complaints during an initial interview, there are two guidelines to keep in mind. On the one hand, the more it appears that ongoing psychotherapy will follow the initial phase of evaluation and assessment, the less actively the therapist should pursue any particular topic in the first interview. Detailed information about the patient's problems is not necessary for making a treatment contract and can be expected to emerge gradually during the psychotherapy. Furthermore, vigorous questioning in the initial phase of psychotherapy may hamper the patient's spontaneity and give him the impression that psychotherapy consists of a question-and-answer interaction in which the therapist takes the initiative.

On the other hand, the more a patient's presenting complaints suggest an emergency or crisis situation, the more actively and thoroughly the therapist needs to explore them during a first interview. This is particularly the case for patients who are depressed to the point of contemplating suicide, or who have problems with impulse control that may lead to assaultive or homicidal behavior, or whose difficulties in thinking and reality testing suggest an impending schizophrenic breakdown. With such patients careful assessment of risk, followed as necessary by immediate supportive and preventive intervention (e.g., medication, hospitalization, contacting the family) take precedence over planning for ongoing psychotherapy.

The therapist also needs to recognize when patients with physical complaints and certain psychological disturbances may need medical evaluation prior to or instead of psychotherapy. Additionally, people embroiled in difficult social situations may be served better by prompt referral to an appropriate social agency or counseling service than by further assessment for psychotherapy. Whenever such possibilities arise, they should be explored thoroughly until the therapist is satisified that they do not contraindicate psychotherapy as a treatment of choice.

Understanding the Patient as a Person

Thus far the discussion of evaluation has focused on the patient's *problems*. It is also essential in the initial evaluation to get some understanding of the patient *as a person*. Most patients provide considerable information about themselves as they describe their current concerns. Just by listening to this description, the therapist will usually hear many things about his patient's family situation, his occupation or avocation, his attitudes toward the significant people in his life, and even his views on how earlier life experiences may have contributed to his present difficulties.

However this may be, the therapist will reach a point in the evaluation where he has as much initial information as he needs about the patient's presenting problems, and it is then time for him to concentrate on filling in his picture of the patient as a person. This shift in focus may occur imperceptibly, with the therapist merely following the patient's lead into talking about himself. Should the patient continue to talk only about his symptoms, the therapist may have to be more directive in implementing a change of subject: "I think you've given me a pretty good idea of what's troubling you; perhaps you could tell me something about your background."

When the therapist begins to inquire about his patient's background, he must again decide what topics to pursue and how much detail to obtain about them. To know what background topics to pursue in a diagnostic interview, the therapist needs to be broadly knowledgeable about normal and abnormal personality development and about the dynamics of interpersonal relationships. To determine how much detail to obtain, he must find a middle ground between too much and not enough. If the therapist does not get enough information about his patient as a person, he is not in a good position to assess whether psychotherapy is indicated. On the other hand, if he seeks too much information, he risks promoting the type of question-and-answer atmosphere than can impede subsequent spontaneity and progress in psychotherapy.[1]

The guiding principle of information gathering in the initial evaluation phase of psychotherapy is to learn enough to arrive at an adequate working formulation of the patient and the patient's problems. The particular amounts and kinds of information required for an adequate working formulation vary among therapists and from one patient to the next. Therapists differ in how definitive they prefer their initial formulations to be before they propose a treatment contract, and they also differ in their degree of clinical sensitivity and their knowledge of personality processes. The more a therapist can tolerate uncertainty (within the limits of good clinical judgment), and the more sensitive and knowledgeable he is, the less information he will require to complete his initial evaluation of prospective psychotherapy patients.

Whatever the amount and kind of information a therapist would like to have initially, the patients he sees will vary in how readily they can provide it. Some patients talk more freely and rapidly than others, some keep to the point while other ramble, and some have fewer and more focused concerns than others. Hence it takes longer to complete an initial evaluation in some cases than in others, and no exact number of interviews can be specified for this process. However, it is possible to elaborate further on what needs to be accomplished in arriving at a working formulation.

Arriving at a Working Formulation

An adequate working formulation in the initial phase of psychotherapy has two facets, a *clinical* formulation and a *dynamic* formulation. A

[1]Guidelines for the evaluation interview, together with various perspectives on the technique of diagnostic interviewing, are elaborated in numerous books and papers. The reader is referred especially to contributions by Bordin (1968, Chaps. 9–10), Deutsch and Murphy (1955), Dollard, Auld, and White (1953), Garrett (1972), Gill, Newman, and Redlich (1954), Kelly (1955, Chaps. 18–19), MacKinnon and Michels (1971), Ripley (1967), Sands (1967), Stevenson (1974), Stevenson and Sheppe (1974), Sullivan (1954), Whitehorn (1944), and Wolberg (1967, Chaps. 20–34).

working clinical formulation consists of more or less traditional diagnostic judgments about the nature and severity of a patient's psychological condition. Although a highly specific, thoroughly documented diagnosis is not necessary for a working formulation, an initial evaluation is not complete until the therapist has reached three general diagnostic conclusions: (a) whether his patient is suffering primarily a psychotic, characterological, or psychoneurotic disorder; (b) whether the presenting symptoms are primarily psychogenic in origin or instead related to organic brain dysfunction or some toxic condition that requires medical evaluation; and (c) whether the patient's psychological difficulties are so slight as not to require ongoing psychotherapy or so severe as to call for immediate supportive intervention.

In addition to telling the therapist whether he should continue to explore his patient's interest in and capacity to benefit from psychotherapy, the working clinical formulation provides some guidelines as to whether a primarily uncovering or primarily supportive approach is likely to be indicated. Uncovering psychotherapy is most likely to be the treatment of choice for people with psychoneurotic disorders, whereas the more a patient gives evidence of an impending or overt psychotic disturbance or of entrenched characterological problems, the more likely he is to require supportive psychotherapy. Likewise, people whose psychological difficulties represent efforts to adapt to brain disorders or other physical disabilities will usually be served best by a primarily supportive approach.

A working dynamic formulation consists of a general impression of what the patient is like as a person and how he got to be that way. Included in this formulation are some fairly clear ideas of the nature of the conflicts the patient is experiencing; the defenses he uses against the anxiety these conflicts produce; his style of coping with social, sexual, and achievement-related situations; his attitudes toward significant people in his life and what he perceives their attitudes to be toward him; and how his past and present life experiences have contributed to his becoming distressed and seeking help.

An extensive dynamic formulation is a tall order, and even at the conclusion of psychotherapy there may be aspects of a patient's personality that have not fully come to light. Yet the initial dynamic formulation must be sufficiently complete for the therapist to have some sense of the kind of person with whom he will be working and of what the focal points of the treatment are likely to be. Only then can psychotherapy proceed as planned intervention and not as fortuitous tampering.

In contrast to the emphasis being placed here on arriving at a working formulation in the initial phase of psychotherapy, some therapists object to beginning in this fashion. The usual grounds for these objections are that traditional diagnostic categories have questionable reliability and hence limited value; or that diagnostic labels, whether reliable or not, are morally and socially undesirable because they place people in negatively valued pigeonholes and presume the right of one person to pass judgment on another; or that, even if diagnostic evaluation is a reliable and ethical procedure, it interferes with subsequent psychotherapy by depriving the patient of his initiative in talking and his responsibility for trying to understand himself.[2]

Two distinctions are usually lost sight of when these objections are raised. First, a working diagnostic formulation does not have to be made in terms of any particular set of traditional diagnostic categories. All that is needed is for the therapist to have in mind some set of rational distinctions that can guide him in meeting his patients' needs. Menninger (1963), in *The Vital Balance*, rejects traditional psychiatric classifications as pejorative and theoretically unsound, and his views are frequently echoed by those who oppose diagnosis in therapy. Yet Menninger in fact presents his own scheme for classifying the nature and severity of psychological dysfunction and insists on adequate initial assessment within this scheme:

> Treatment depends upon diagnosis, and even the matter of timing is often misunderstood. One does not complete a diagnosis and then begin treatment; the diagnostic process is also the start of treatment. Diagnostic assessment is treatment; it also enables further and more specific treatment (p. 333).

Menninger's comments point to the second distinction that is frequently overlooked by critics of diagnosis in therapy, namely, the difference between an initial working diagnostic formulation and a diagnostic case study. A diagnostic case study is a detailed and thorough assessment of personality functioning, and its explicit aim is to obtain information with or without the communication of understanding to the patient. As such, a case study is usually not psychotherapy and may

[2]For the reader who is interested in pursuing this subject, the most influential antidiagnosis positions have been presented within the framework of client-centered therapy (Rogers, 1951, 1961) and humanistic psychology (Bugental, 1965; Buhler & Allen, 1971; Maslow, 1962). Criticisms of the reliability and utility of diagnostic judgments, and some ringing rebuttals these criticisms have evoked, are reviewed by Beck (1962), Brill (1965), Eron (1966), Frank (1969), Gough (1971), Phillips and Draguns (1971), Shakow (1966), Weiner (1972), and Zubin (1967).

indeed interfere with subsequent efforts to help the patient talk spontaneously and work toward understanding himself.

A working diagnostic formulation, on the other hand, consists of just enough information for the therapist to decide whether psychotherapy might be an appropriate treatment approach to pursue. As Menninger implies, diagnostic evaluation in an initial interview is an integral part of psychotherapy for those patients who continue in treatment, not just a prelude to it. Rather than interfere with subsequent psychotherapy, the initial evaluation gives the patient a sample of what talking with a therapist is like, and it furthermore conveys the message that the therapist takes him seriously enough to inquire into the problem he is presenting. In fact, if the therapist concentrates too much on encouraging the patient's initiative, at the expense of asking any diagnostic questions about the concerns he is having, he may inadvertently communicate disinterest ("I don't care about your problems") or disrespect ("Your problems are not important").

Furthermore, it is widely acknowledged that ongoing evaluation of the patient during psychotherapy is essential in guiding the selection of appropriate strategies and tactics (see Schlesinger, 1969; Sturm, 1972). Without continuous diagnostic appraisal, there is no roadmap for the therapist to follow in attempting to lead his patient toward a more symptom-free and self-fulfilling life. Significantly, even within the client-centered approach from which numerous criticisms of evaluation in psychotherapy have emerged, the thinking of many therapists has been influenced by the compelling importance of an adequate working formulation. Truax and Carkhuff (1967), for example, espouse a client-centered approach but nevertheless stress the usefulness of diagnosis and its particular importance for empathic understanding:

> The more we know about the client we seek to help, the more able we will be able to correctly understand his moment-to-moment communications. Beyond this consideration, lack of adequate diagnosis may allow a counselor or therapist to do the patient irreparable harm (p. 175).

ASSESSING THE APPROPRIATENESS OF PSYCHOTHERAPY

When a therapist has learned enough about a patient and his problems to arrive at a working clinical and dynamic formulation, his next task is to assess the appropriateness of psychotherapy for meeting the patient's needs. Although a great many guidelines have been proposed for assessing a person's capacity to participate in and benefit from psychotherapy, the research discussed in Chapter 2 points to three major criteria: (a) whether the patient is motivated for psychotherapy, (b) whether he is able to reflect and talk about himself, and (c) whether despite his difficulties he has retained a generally well-integrated level of personality functioning.

As noted in Chapter 2, none of these criteria is essential for effective psychotherapy to take place, and it is possible for unmotivated, unreflective, untalkative, and poorly integrated people to be helped in psychotherapy. Other things being equal, however, the three variables of motivation, reflectiveness, and personality integration will indicate the likely extent to which a patient who needs psychotherapy will be able to engage in and profit from it. Hence an adequate assessment of these variables guides the therapist in deciding whether to recommend psychotherapy to someone who has come to him for help or, instead, to recommend some other form of treatment or no treatment at all.

Assessing Motivation

The key to assessing a patient's motivation for psychotherapy is determining how much acute distress he is experiencing. In general, the more acutely distressed a person is, the more he would like things to be different from how they are and the more willing he will be to bear the burden of being in psychotherapy. Specifically, the more a person wants to change and the more unhappy he is with his current psychological state, the more inclined he will be to attend sessions regularly, to talk about himself even when talking becomes painful or embarrassing, to consider interpretations that challenge his previous views, and to persevere in the treatment process until an advantageous termination point is reached.

People with strong masochistic needs may appear to require an exception to using level of distress as an index of wish to change, since they often complain bitterly about their difficulties while nevertheless finding solace in them. However, careful diagnostic evaluation of the masochistic patient usually reveals that most of his complaints relate to long-term problem situations that he has cultivated and endured when other options were open to him, and these complaints do not constitute *acute* distress. When a masochistic individual does give evidence of acute concerns in addition to his chronic characterological complaints, then his current distress is likely to represent suffering beyond what his masochism requires and to have the same implications for psychotherapy motivation as the acute distress of any other patient.

A patient's level of acute distress can be judged partly from the amount of anxiety he displays about his presenting complaints and partly from how he responds to the following two kinds of indirect question: "How have these problems (symptoms, difficulties, concerns) been affecting your life in general?" and "In what way would things be different for you if you weren't having these difficulties?" The answers to these questions clearly illuminate the extent of a patient's underlying wish to change and hence of his motivation for psychotherapy. The more extensive and disturbing he reports the effects of the presenting complaints to have been, and the more significant the changes he feels would result from their disappearance, the more highly motivated for psychotherapy he can be assumed to be.

This indirect approach to assessing motivation for psychotherapy is illustrated by the following two responses to the question, "How has this problem been affecting your life in general?":

Pt 1. It's just that I worry about it from time to time, and then I get a little irritable or have trouble sleeping.

Pt 2. I'm becoming a nervous wreck. I think I may be losing my mind, and everything is going sour for me. I've been told at work that if I keep on this way I'll have to be transferred to a less responsible job, and, as if that isn't bad enough, my wife is getting fed up with my temper outbursts and some of my best friends are starting to avoid me.

The contrast in these two responses is evident between one that indicates passing concern over a mildly disruptive problem and one that indicates considerable anxiety over a problem that is interfering with the patient's work, marriage, and social relationships. Because the implications of the presenting problem for the patient's life in general provide such important clues to his level of motivation for psychotherapy, it is usually helpful for the therapist to broach this subject if the patient does not bring it up himself. The initial assessment in psychotherapy cannot be considered complete unless it includes some information about the patient's subjective attitude toward his presenting problems and about how these problems are affecting his friendship patterns, his heterosexual relationships, and his performance in school or at work.

A similarly informative contrast can be illustrated for responses to the question, "In what way would things be different for you if you weren't having these difficulties?":

Pt 1. I'd be able to relax a little more.

Pt 2. It would be a different world for me. I know I could get a promotion in my job if this thing weren't holding me back, and I could stop worrying about my marriage going on the rocks.

Again the difference is striking between an attitude that indicates only a slight wish to have things be different and one that suggests considerable motivation for change. It is the latter attitude that sustains a patient through the arduous and challenging task of learning about himself in psychotherapy, whereas the former attitude tends to predict minimal investment in treatment, spotty attendance, and dropping out when the treatment sessions become difficult or uncomfortable.

These indirect questions often yield more reliable information about a person's motivation for psychotherapy than direct inquiries. A patient asked directly about his attitudes toward entering psychotherapy may say, "I really want very much to have some psychotherapy and I hope you'll be able to take me on as a patient"; or he may say, "Well, I don't really see much need for it, and I think the problems I'm having will probably work out by themselves." Although the first of these comments may in fact reflect strong motivation for psychotherapy and the second comment weak motivation, it is also possible that neither gives an accurate indication of the patient's underlying wish to change.

There are both psychodynamic and situational reasons why a patient's true level of motivation for psychotherapy may be quite different from what he says or thinks it is. An apparent lack of motivation in patients who would prosper in psychotherapy is described particularly well by Holt (1967), who points out that a patient's conscious attitudes toward psychotherapy are inextricably tied up with the unconscious conflicts that are causing his psychological difficulties. For example, people who feel they do not deserve to be happy or successful may express reservations about psychotherapy because the idea of receiving help makes them uncomfortable. Other people who are eager to receive help may still express only lukewarm interest in doing so because they anticipate not being able to make a success of the treatment venture. These are people whose psychological difficulties include powerful fears of failure and who dread the disappointment of failing as a psychotherapy patient.

Also to be expected are a certain number of people who feel the need for psychotherapy but have reservations about becoming a patient. Although they would like very much to undertake psychotherapy, they are inclined to reject it because they regard patienthood as an admission of weakness or as an embarrassment to their families. Whenever the therapist perceives such concerns about entering psychotherapy, discussing them directly with the patient becomes an important part of arranging the treatment contract (see Chap. 6).

Whereas psychodynamic factors may contribute in these ways to lack of expressed motivation in patients who need and can benefit from psychotherapy, situational factors can produce expressions of very positive attitudes toward psychotherapy in patients who do not particularly need it and are not especially likely to work hard at it. People who come under duress, for example, with psychotherapy held over their head as a condition for staying in school, on the job, in the home, or out of jail, may wax eloquent about their interest in psychotherapy to promote their being accepted as a patient. For the same reason, people who have some intellectual curiosity about psychotherapy or regard it as a social badge of merit may attempt to impress the therapist with their terribly urgent need to be treated by him.

What the therapist needs to keep in mind is that the more a patient appears to have come on his own volition to get psychological help, the more highly motivated for psychotherapy he is likely to be. Conversely, the more he has come at someone else's urging or for reasons other than to receive help for psychological difficulties, the more doubtful his motivation will be. Like motivation itself, however, this index of motivation is not an infallible predictor. A self-referred, psychologically oriented patient may come with little appreciation for the effort and commitment psychotherapy will require of him and quickly demur once he becomes accurately informed. In the opposite case, an involuntary, nonpsychologically oriented patient who needs psychotheapy badly may become highly invested in the treatment once he senses its potential for helping him.

Hence, although knowing how and why a patient has come for psychotherapy may provide some important clues to his level of motivation, attention must be paid to possible differences between what a patient says in response to direct inquiries about his motivation and what his true motivation will turn out to be once psychotherapy gets under way. In trying to assess whether a person will work and remain in psychotherapy, a therapist should rely primarily on his impressions of how distressed the person is and how much he would like to change. As already noted, these impressions will come primarily from observations of the patient during the interview and from information about the impact his psychological difficulties are having on his current and prospective life situation.

Assessing Reflectiveness

A patient's capacity to reflect and talk about himself can usually be assessed from his behavior during the evaluation phase of psychotherapy. Does he describe his presenting complaints in relation to himself as a person, or does he enumerate his symptoms as if he were talking about someone else or about no one in particular? Does he volunteer information spontaneously, or, like someone on the witness stand, does he confine himself to answering the questions asked of him? When answering a question, does he provide abundant detail, or does he make only the minimum response consistent with being courteous? As he gives details, does he remind himself of related topics which he then elaborates, or does he merely follow the leads provided by the therapist? The more the patient's interview style resembles the former of these pairs of alternatives, the more likely it is that he will be sufficiently talkative and reflective in subsequent psychotherapy to benefit from it.

For the therapist to make an accurate estimate of his patient's ability and willingness to talk, he needs to be careful that his own interview style does not become too directive. A rapid-fire flow of questions, intended to accumulate as much information as possible, will prevent the therapist from learning much about the patient's capacity to talk and reflect about himself. Unless the presenting difficulties appear to call for a primary focus on making a clinical diagnosis to meet some emergency, the therapist should conduct his evaluation interviews in a manner that allows ample opportunity for the patient to pause and reflect, to bring up ideas spontaneously, and to pursue directions his thoughts may take him in. The patient who cannot or will not take advantage of such opportunities to talk about himself is the one who has a low probability of being able to participate in and benefit from psychotherapy.

Some additionally useful information about a patient's capacity for reflectiveness can be obtained by the use of a few trial interpretations during the assessment phase of psychotherapy. A trial interpretation is a superficial, relatively nonthreatening reflection or recasting of what the patient is saying, and its purposes are to give the patient a sample of how psychotherapy proceeds and to observe how he reacts to having his behavior interpreted. For example, a patient in an initial interview may talk at one point about feeling anxious at home whenever he and his wife are having company and at a later point about feeling anxious whenever he has to attend an office meeting. Unless there is clear evidence to the contrary, the therapist might venture, "So it appears that one thing that makes you anxious is having a lot of people around, whether at home or at work."

The patient may respond to a trial interpretation by ignoring it completely, by acknowledging it grudgingly and with irritation that his story has been interrupted ("Could be . . . who knows?) or by becoming overtly angry and resistive ("Why would you say a thing like that? What could one thing have to do with the other?"). Patients who respond in these ways to trial interpretations—assuming the therapist has been careful in selecting an interpretation that is minimally threatening and almost certainly correct—are not particularly likely to do well in subsequent psychotherapy. They will find it difficult to shift from experiencing to observing themselves, and they will not be receptive to considering connections between various aspects of their behavior.

On the other hand, a patient's response to a trial interpretation may express interest and curiousity ("Well, you may have a point there; I wonder what one thing has to do with the other?"); or warm endorsement ("That's right, I do have a thing about having a lot of people around, wherever it is"); or even the excitement of discovery ("Hey, you know, I never thought of that before, but that could really explain a lot of things"). The patient who treats a trial interpretation as something to stop and think about is displaying a readiness to observe himself. If he in addition accepts the interpretation, he is revealing openness to the psychotherapeutic process. And if he furthermore appears enthused about having his behavior interpreted, he is responding to the interest and empathy expressed by an interpretation rather than its threatening aspects. Such indications of self-observation, openness, and a positive attitude toward the therapist's efforts predict a high level of reflectiveness and willingness to talk in subsequent psychotherapy.

Assessing Personality Integration

The therapist's assessment of his patient's personality integration is based primarily on what the patient can tell him about his past and current life experiences. The relationship of personality integration to potential for benefiting from psychotherapy is discussed in Chapter 2 and earlier in this chapter in relation to the working clinical formulation. Rather than further considering the technique of diagnostic interviewing (see p. 57), this section instead calls attention to two useful adjuncts to the diagnostic interview in assessing a patient's personality integration—psychological testing and contacts with people other than the patient.

Psychological Testing. Some clinicians regard psychological test data as important predictors of whether a patient will improve in psychotherapy, particularly with respect to test indices of verbal fluency, anxiety tolerance, and capacity for social relatedness (e.g., Pope & Scott, 1967, pp. 254–260). Others rely on test data not so much to predict outcome as to predict behavior in psychotherapy. In this approach supplementary information gleaned from the tests about a patient's attitudes, conflicts, and personality style is used to plan the therapy, to decide which areas to focus on, and to anticipate how the patient will react at different points in the treatment process (e.g., Blank, 1965).

Some therapists prefer to have initial test data available on all patients with whom they are going to work, both as a treatment guide and as a baseline against which retesting during or at the conclusion of psychotherapy can be compared (see Harrower, 1958). On the other hand, therapists who question the importance of an initial working formulation in psychotherapy have little interest in psychological test assessment, and there are some who feel that testing may interfere with subsequent psychotherapy. The main objections raised against psychological testing for psychotherapy patients are (a) that it has the same disadvantages as beginning with highly structured diagnostic interviews (see p. 55) and (b) that the information obtained will prematurely crystallize the therapist's view of his patient, thereby restricting the flexibility and open-mindedness with which he conducts the psychotherapy.

These possibilities need to be recognized when psychological testing is considered for a prospective psychotherapy patient. In the end the therapist's decision about testing should depend on whether his initial interviews have given him sufficient information to arrive at an adequate working formulation, that is, one that provides a comfortable basis on which to proceed. If they have, there is no call for psychological testing, unless it is to be done for research purposes. But if they have not, then the data from a psychological examination may significantly add to his understanding of his patient's needs and his preparations for meeting these needs.

How often and with what kind of patients a therapist will require psychological testing to help him formulate his initial clinical and dynamic impressions will depend on how skillful and sensitive an interviewer he is and how puzzling and complex the interview data are. Some therapists will turn to psychological test data rarely and others frequently, but in any case, concern about the impact of being tested on the patient's subsequent relationship with the therapist should seldom decide the issue.

This potential source of difficulty in the treatment can usually be avoided by having someone other than the therapist conduct the testing. In this way the therapist can maintain his role with the patient as someone intent on understanding rather than merely obtaining information, without having to forego test data that might help him decide on and plan for subsequent psychotherapy.

Of the three variables involved in assessing the appropriateness of psychotherapy—motivation, reflectiveness, and personality integration—it is the last one that is most likely to require the kind of supplementary information provided by psychological testing. If a therapist misjudges a patient's motivation or reflectiveness, subsequent psychotherapy may be bogged down and time will have been wasted, but more dire consequences are unlikely. Likewise, if a therapist proceeds with an incomplete or incorrect conception of his patient's personality dynamics, he can adjust his impressions as new information emerges in the treatment, usually without adverse effects.

However, if a therapist initially overestimates his patient's level of personality integration, the results may be very unfortunate. When people with minimal capacity to tolerate anxiety and frustration are taken into uncovering psychotherapy and confronted with the ambiguity, lack of structure, and focus on painful experiences that characterize this treatment approach, they may become acutely anxious or depressed, even to the point of psychotic breakdown or suicidal behavior. The adequately trained psychotherapist should be able to recognize such personality decompensation as soon as it begins to appear and to appreciate its relationship to his having instituted an inappropriate treatment approach. He can then take steps to correct his error and avert further breakdown, primarily by becoming more supportive. It is far better, of course, for the therapist to avoid making this type of mistake in the first place.

To the extent that any questions about a patient's level of personality integration remain in the therapist's mind when he is satisfied in other respects about the appropriateness of pursuing psychotherapy, he should utilize psychological testing. Although many issues have been raised about the validity and utility of psychological test interpretations, the ability of psychological tests to identify weaknesses in personality integration is well-documented and has been spelled out in numerous texts.[3] Whatever its value as a source of information, however,

[3]For further information about the application of psychological tests to the assessment of personality integration the reader should consult Allison, Blatt, and Zimet (1968), Kaplan et al. (1970), Rapaport, Gill, and Schafer (1968), and Weiner (1966).

psychological testing should not be used as a replacement for adequate diagnostic interviewing. It is too costly and specialized a procedure for routine employment, and the therapist who regularly turns to test data for information that could be obtained from interviews is not fulfilling his responsibility to his patients.

Contacts with Others. By contacting other people in the patient's life, the therapist can usually obtain information about his social, heterosexual, and work adjustment that the patient has overlooked or been reluctant to mention. Yet, however helpful this information may be in constructing a complete case history, considerable caution is advisable in seeking and relying on it.

First, although a patient's family, friends, and employer may be more objective observers of his behavior than he is, the information they provide will not necessarily be more reliable that what the patient himself has to say. Anyone coming for psychotherapy will be having some interpersonal difficulties, whether as a primary manifestation of his psychological problems or as a secondary consequence of his being emotionally troubled, and the important people in his life will accordingly be involved in his problems: some contributing to the problems, some suffering as a result of them, and all regarding the patient with varying degrees of concern, impatience, sympathy, or annoyance. The impressions these people have of the patient's behavior will be influenced by the role they are playing in his problems and by their relationship to him as spouse, parent, son or daughter, friend, or employer. Hence the therapist will have to regard the information they provide with qualifications, particularly since he is unlikely to know them well enough to appreciate their motivations and judge the reliability of what they tell him.

Second, even if reliable and useful information should come from talking with people other than the patient, it may come at the expense of the subsequent psychotherapy relationship. As with extensive diagnostic procedures in general, talking with other people can suggest that the therapist's emphasis is on obtaining rather than understanding information. Furthermore, the fact that the therapist has talked to other people about him can create concern in the patient's mind about the confidentiality of psychotherapy and about how much he can safely reveal. The therapist's wish to talk with others may also imply that he regards the patient as incapable of providing adequate information. Thus the use of informants can limit the degree to which a therapist helps his patient feel secure and respected in the treatment relationship.

Third, the therapist has little control over what the other people to whom he talks may subsequently say or suggest to the patient. Without malice, and sometimes with, informants may give a distorted report of what transpired between them and the therapist, and these slanted reports can foster patient antipathies toward further treatment that the therapist cannot easily counteract. Consider the following comment from a patient being evaluated for psychotherapy: "My wife says you told her she'd have to be more tolerant of me because I'm just a mean person by nature and unlikely to change; if that's what you think of me, why should I even bother to become your patient?" The therapist who has permitted such a situation to come to pass, no matter how good his intentions were, will have slim chances for rekindling his patient's enthusiasm for entering treatment with him.

These potential disadvantages of seeking evaluative information from other people in the patient's life can be minimized if the therapist anticipates or circumvents them. For example, talking with informants only in the patient's presence allows the patient to know exactly what has been said by and to each informant and gives him no cause for concern about the confidentiality of his relationship with the therapist. Unfortunately, however, some informants cannot or will not provide the crucial information known to them while the patient is there to hear, and the therapist has little leverage for resolving this kind of problem unless he intends to structure the treatment as family or group psychotherapy. Furthermore, even if the patient is present to hear all that is said about him, he can still be left wondering why the information he was able to give in private was not sufficient. To add one more complication, the patient who observes his therapist's interest in what someone else has to say may be upset at having to share the therapist's attention instead of remaining the sole focus of it. And once a patient has reacted adversely to the therapist's conversations with other people about him, his concerns may not be completely resolvable, since the act itself cannot be undone. There are difficult situations that are best avoided in the first place, and talking with a prospective psychotherapy patient's friends and relatives can at times be one of these.[4]

In view of this caution, the therapist needs to consider carefully whether he needs to talk with other people about a patient for whom he is considering individual psychotherapy. Like psychological testing, other informants should not be used as a replacement for careful interviewing of the patient himself, now should other people be consulted to fill in details about the patient that do not bear significantly on the initial working formulation. Instead, contacts with others should usually be reserved for patients whose level of personality integration is initially in

[4]These and other issues in the therapist's contacting relatives and referral sources are discussed by Mariner (1971).

doubt. In common with psychological test data, then, the most important purpose served by additional informants in the assessment phase of psychotherapy is the identification of patients for whom psychotherapy, at least of an uncovering nature, may be contraindicated by virtue of their personality limitations or crisis condition.

COMPLETING THE INITIAL EVALUATION AND ASSESSMENT

At this point in the course of his work with a prospective psychotherapy patient, the therapist will be completing his initial evaluation and assessment. He will have identified the nature of the presenting problems, learned something about the background of the patient's concerns, filled in his picture of the patient as a person, and arrived at a working clinical and dynamic formulation. He will also have assessed the patient's motivation for psychotherapy, his capacity for reflectiveness, and his level of personality integration. With this information, which may take from one to several interviews to piece together, the therapist is in a position to decide whether psychotherapy appears to be a treatment procedure the patient can participate in and benefit from. To complete his initial evaluation and assessment, the therapist has only to determine whether a patient for whom psychotherapy is indicated is able to continue with it.

The ability of a patient to continue in psychotherapy is determined by a number of reality factors in his life. As reviewed in an excellent paper by Dewald (1967), particular attention has to be paid to whether the patient has sufficient time, money, and freedom from distraction to engage in the work of psychotherapy. With regard to time, will the patient be able to attend sessions regularly when the therapist can make them available, or will responsibilities at home or work prevent him or her from doing so? Can the treatment contact continue for some length of time, or will it be limited by an imminent move or interrupted frequently by prolonged vacations or business trips? As for money and freedom from distraction, can the patient afford the cost of ongoing psychotherapy, and is his life situation sufficiently stable for him to be able to concentrate on the work of the treatment?

Patients who have adequate time, money, and concentration to devote to psychotherapy are the ones who should be encouraged to continue with it. In his work with people who could benefit from psychotherapy but are less fortunate with respect to these reality considerations, the therapist should be prepared to explore various alternatives. In some cases people whose time for treatment is limited will do best to defer further psychotherapy until they can arrange to be in one place for an extended period and fit regular sessions into their schedule. People embroiled in a chaotic life situation that is not directly related to their wish to have psychotherapy might also be advised to wait for psychotherapy until matters around them have stabilized and they can concentrate on their particular goals in psychotherapy. Patients with financial limitations may need help to pursue their eligibility for various kinds of insurance or to become familiar with available low-cost clinics.

The exploration of these practical reality-oriented matters with patients for whom psychotherapy is indicated provides a bridge between evaluation and assessment in the initial phase of psychotherapy and the making of an agreement between patient and therapist about continuing treatment. This agreement constitutes the psychotherapy *contract*, which is the subject of the next chapter.

CHAPTER 6

The Treatment Contract

The treatment contract in psychotherapy is an explicit agreement between patient and therapist to work together toward alleviating the patient's psychological difficulties. To arrive at this contract patient and therapist need first to agree that treatment is indicated and will be undertaken. Next they need to agree on the objectives of the treatment and on the procedures they will follow in working toward these objectives. And finally they need to agree on such specific treatment arrangements as the time, place, frequency, and fee for sessions. This chapter is concerned with the therapist's task in explicating these three aspects of the treatment contract.

AGREEING ON PSYCHOTHERAPY

For psychotherapy to start well, there must be an explicit agreement between patient and therapist that the treatment is indicated and will be undertaken. As obvious as it may seem, this first step in arriving at a treatment contract is easy to overlook, especially with patients who have been eager and responsive during the initial evaluation interviews. With such patients it may seem appropriate to assume that they want psychotherapy and are ready to discuss arrangements for it. The disadvantage of making this assumption is that it denies the patient an explicit opportunity to share in the decision about further treatment. Assumptions and unilateral decisions should generally be avoided in psychotherapy, because they communicate disrespect for a patient's integrity and competence. To show respect, the therapist needs to offer his patient the choice of accepting or declining ongoing psychotherapy *before* he proposes any specific treatment arrangements.

The therapist furthermore needs to help his patient make an *informed* decision about continuing in treatment. Just as the parties to any contract should have the right of informed consent, a patient has rights to certain information before he decides about psychotherapy.[1] He has a right to know how the therapist views his psychological problems and what means he recommends for dealing with them; he has a right to know something about the psychotherapeutic process and the nature of the commitment it requires; and he has a right to inquire about the qualifications of the therapist to provide the treatment that is being offered.

Recommending Psychotherapy

Following his initial assessment, the therapist's next task is to summarize the impressions he has formed and make some recommendation to the person who has sought his help. This summary should usually be limited to a brief recasting of what has been discussed in prior interviews and should not attempt to reconstruct the patient's personality development or the origin of his difficulties. The therapist is still working with minimal information at this point, and he is likely to make errors if he attempts a full reconstruction of the patient's personality development and symptom formation. Furthermore, the more hypotheses he elaborates in his summary statement, the more he limits the patient's opportunities for arriving at hypotheses on his own in subsequent psychotherapy. The following summary, presented to a 33-year-old professional man with a classical success neurosis, illustrates the form such a statement might take:

I think this would be a good point for me to share with you the impressions I have. You came to see me mainly because you were feeling depressed and irritable and generally dissatisfied with the way your life is going. As we've talked, it has become clear that the most likely source of these feelings is your work situation. Everything was going pretty well until you were told you were in line for a promotion. Then your job performance deteriorated, you didn't get the promotion, and your depression, discouragement, and irritability set in. We've also learned that a similar kind of thing has apparently happened to you before, at

[1]Menninger and Holzman (1973, pp. 15–38) provide an excellent discussion of how the psychotherapy relationship operates as a two-party contract. Also recommended is a classic paper by Freud (1913), "On Beginning the Treatment," which is concerned with many of the topics covered in this chapter.

times when you were on the verge of some success, and you have vivid memories of the very high standards of accomplishment you saw being set around you in your family while you were growing up. Putting all this together, it seems to me that your problem lies in some mixed feelings you have about being successful and some underlying attitudes you have towards people in your life who have been successful. Mostly these are feelings and attitudes that you haven't been fully aware of, but that have nevertheless been preventing you from doing as much with your life as you could or as you would find satisfying. How does all that sound to you?

As this example indicates, there is nothing dramatic or startling about the summary presented at this point. The patient will have realized most of it before he came for help, and the rest will have been brought out during the initial assessment interviews. Yet it is very important for the therapist to construct this kind of summary and present it with some emphasis. There is considerable difference between having a point brought out during an initial interview and having it restated as part of a summary of impressions. Whereas the former can sometimes be lost sight of, especially if the patient's defenses are geared to repressing it or denying its implications, the latter stands out as a definite statement made by the therapist after he has completed his full evaluation.

There are several advantages in having the therapist's initial impressions stand out as a definite statement. First, an accurate and clearly presented summary is a convincing demonstration that the therapist has taken the trouble to listen carefully and think about what he has heard, that he is capable of understanding the patient's difficulties, and that he regards the patient as entitled to a straightforward disclosure of his impressions. Second, a good summary statement usually identifies what the specific goals of treatment should be and thereby paves the way for subsequent agreement on these goals. Third, a vivid and unequivocal summary helps spare the therapist from the previously mentioned pitfall of implicit understandings.

In this regard, implicit understandings about the treatment contract should be avoided not only because they undermine the therapist's capacity to be effective when communication in psychotherapy becomes complicated by the difficulty of the material being discussed or the attitudes of the patient and therapist toward one another (see Chaps. 9–11). At these times patients may experience a temporary disenchantment with the treatment and raise such complaints as, "You never even asked me if I wanted to get into psychotherapy," or "You never told me what you thought my problem was," or "You never gave me any idea about what this would be like."

Faced with such complaints, the therapist should be able to remind his patient that all these matters were discussed directly, and he can then focus on what may be happening at the present time that is troubling the patient and distorting his recollection of the treatment contract. If the therapist has proceeded on the basis of implicit understandings, however, and failed to make all aspects of the treatment contract explicit, he is ill-prepared to deal with these kinds of patient reactions when they arise.

The final sentence of the summary statement quoted above illustrates one further technical recommendation: the therapist should end his summary statement by asking the patient to comment on it. The respect and mutual participation communicated by asking for the patient's reactions are obvious, and in addition, the response he gives will provide some useful information. If he concurs with the therapist's formulation, the eagerness and whole-heartedness with which he agrees give some indication of how open and expressive or defensive and reserved he is likely to be in subsequent psychotherapy. If on the other hand he rejects the therapist's formulation, he indicates that some reassessment is called for. It may be that he is not as prepared to look at himself as the therapist thought, or it may be that the therapist has not been particularly sensitive to his problems and needs. In the former case some treatment approach other than uncovering psychotherapy may be in order, and in the latter case a different therapist may be what is needed.

When a summary statement has been made and acknowledged as correct, a firm and unambiguous treatment recommendation is the next order of business. Like the summary, this recommendation does not require any lengthy exposition, and it certainly does not call for the therapist to indicate why each of a number of possible treatment approaches is or is not suited to the patient's needs. Rather, he should recommend the treatment of choice as he sees it and then answer any questions that may be raised about other possibilities.

When psychotherapy appears to be the treatment of choice, the therapist should simply say so: "I think it would be worthwhile for you to have psychotherapy, and I'd like to talk further with you about what that might consist of." Stated in this way, the therapist's recommendation leaves little room for doubt about his opinion or about his readiness to be of help, and it furthermore lets the patient know that he is going to have an opportunity to talk about psychotherapy before being asked to decide about pursuing it.

Under these circumstances a patient will usually reserve any questions he has about psychotherapy until he has heard more of what the therapist has to say. If procedural questions begin to emerge as soon as a treatment recommendation has been made (e.g., "What exactly is psychotherapy?" "How long will it last?" "How often would I have to come for sessions?"), the therapist can indicate that these are among the matters he is about to discuss: "Let me tell you something about psychotherapy, and I think as we talk about it the questions you have will be answered." Similarly, questions that reflect ambivalent feelings about entering psychotherapy ("Do I really need it?") can usually be deferred until the psychotherapeutic process has been discussed in general.

However, when a question such as "Do I really need it?" appears to reflect patient anxiety about the severity of his condition or denial of the problems he is having, further clarification of the therapist's summary and recommendations may be necessary. With the anxious patient this will involve eliciting and correcting any misconceptions he has of how disturbed he is and how extensively he will have to be treated. With the patient who minimizes his need for help, it will involve restating what the apparent problems are and what kinds of difficulties they may continue to cause if some ameliorative steps are nt taken.

In no case, however, should the therapist threaten or frighten the defensive patient into accepting a psychotherapy recommendation, any more than he should minimize the problems of the anxious patient or falsely reassure him. Rather, the therapist needs always to be guided by respect for the patient and a code of genuineness, which means presenting and reaffirming his summary and recommendation as clearly and directly as he can and leaving the decision about how to respond in the patient's hands.

A second question by the patient that requires a direct response when it is asked has to do with other possible treatment modalities. Acting on various kinds of prior information, patients may respond to a recommendation for psychotherapy by asking about the equal or greater appropriateness of group therapy, sensitivity training, hypnotherapy, shock treatment, conditioning therapy, or psychotropic drugs.

When such questions arise, the psychotherapist needs to steer a middle course. He must avoid representing psychotherapy as the only treatment that is likely to be of help, because that is seldom the case; yet he also needs to avoid getting into a discussion of the possible appropriateness of a wide range of treatment approaches, because doing so can easily become a didactic exercise that sidetracks the therapist from describing what he is prepared to offer. Simplicity and directness remain the guidelines to answering such questions: "There are a variety of treatment approaches that have proved helpful to people with problems similar to yours, just as there is usually more than one way to solve any kind of problem. The approach that I use is individual psychotherapy, and this is what I am recommending you consider."

On the other hand, there are many individual psychotherapists who practice or at least maintain familiarity with other approaches as well. A therapist who conducts group as well as individual psychotherapy and also sees patients for hypnotherapy and behavior modification may feel that one of these approaches is clearly more suitable for a particular patient than another and may recommend it. Or, if he sees no such clear adavantage of one approach over another, he may elect to describe two or three alternative approaches he is prepared to employ and help the patient decide among them. In other situations a psychotherapist may be sufficiently familiar with a treatment approach he himself does not use to decide that it is probably more clearly indicated than his own approaches, and his task is then to convey this impression to the patient and help arrange a referral to a colleague who does provide the indicated treatment. It should also be kept in mind that some patients will not require any further psychological help following the assessment interviews, and for them a no-treatment recommendation is what is called for.

For the therapist to choose wisely among these possibilities, he has to know more than just how to conduct psychotherapy. He must also know how to judge whether a patient needs treatment and, if so, whether psychotherapy or some other treatment approach is more likely to benefit him. It is for this reason that psychotherapists, especially if they are to practice independently or assume responsibility for the initial evaluation of patients, need to have broad clinical training as well as schooling in psychotherapeutic skills.

Explaining the Process of Psychotherapy

To allow a patient to make an informed decision about continuing in psychotherapy, the therapist should follow his treatment recommendation with some explanation of the psychotherapy process. A good way to begin this explanation is to ask the patient what information or ideas he may already have. Most people come for help with a mixture of accurate and inaccurate notions of psychotherapy, and knowing what these notions are can guide the therapist in formulating his description of the treatment process, especially with regard to where he needs to confirm or correct prior impressions.

As in recommending psychotherapy, the key to explaining the psychotherapeutic process effectively is being explicit and avoiding assumptions. To this end the therapist should never accept at face value a patient's statement that he knows all about what psychotherapy entails. No matter how informed he professes to be, he should be asked to spell out his notions so that the therapist can assess their accuracy. Furthermore, even patients who can give a thorough and accurate description of how psychotherapy proceeds should have an opportunity to hear the therapist do so. When a patient is moved to complain during the middle phase of treatment that he was never adequately informed about what psychotherapy would be like, the therapist as already noted cannot respond effectively if the most he can say is "I thought you knew" or "You seemed to have a good idea about it at the beginning."

The explanation of psychotherapy itself can be accomplished in a relatively brief discussion with the patient that covers the following points. In psychotherapy the patient talks about himself while the therapist listens, facilitates the talking, and helps the patient understand the significance of what he says and does. In the course of this talking thoughts, feelings, and experiences in the patient's past and present life come to light in ways that clarify the nature of his personality and the origin of the difficulties he has been having.

This simplified explanation of how psychotherapy works can usually be elaborated in reference to what has already transpired in the evaluation interviews. Thus the therapist, if he has made adequate use of trial interpretations, should be able to paint an accurate and easily understandable picture of psychotherapy with such statements as the following:

> Psychotherapy consists of talking together pretty much as we have been so far, with you doing most of the talking, telling me about your experiences and the things on your mind, and me listening and trying to help you understand yourself better. For example, you mentioned at the very beginning that one of the things you were concerned about was never having met a man that you could feel attracted to, and then later, when I asked you something about your experiences growing up, you recalled how much you idolized your father. From this we came up with the idea that perhaps one reason you have had difficulty feeling attracted to men is that you could never find one who could live up to your father, and this was a possibility that made sense to you but had never occurred to you before. And that's how psychotherapy operates.

Once he has given the patient this basic outline of the psychotherapy process, the therapist has to consider carefully how much detail to add. A particularly important question in this regard is whether he should anticipate interferences with the communication process, as by telling the patient that there will be times when he finds talking difficult, or that he is likely to develop strong positive and negative feelings toward the therapist. The usual guideline to follow is that the therapist should explain enough to get the patient off to a good start in psychotherapy, but not so much as to leave no room for surprises in the treatment.

More specifically, it is important for reasons already noted that the patient receive some information about the basic process of psychotherapy before he contracts to undertake it; however, this information should consist of telling the patient what psychotherapy is like, *not* how he will react to it. Reactions to the psychotherapeutic process can be used to facilitate patient self-understanding, especially if they can be treated as unique individual experiences. If the therapist spells out in the beginning how people generally react to psychotherapy, then the patient will not attach any particular significance to reactions he has.

To illustrate this point further, it is advantageous when interferences with communication arise to be able to focus on why the patient, having come for help and having been able to talk freely about himself, has suddenly begun to find talking difficult. If he has been told that all patients experience such difficulty, or that he can expect to form strong feelings toward the therapist, the impact of such resistance and transference reactions is diluted and the possibility for making constructive use of them minimized. To facilitate uncovering psychotherapy, the patient who experiences problems in talking or feelings toward the therapist should be puzzled and surprised by them, or at least be susceptible to being helped to feel puzzled and surprised. The patient who asks "Isn't it natural to feel this way in psychotherapy?" or "Don't all patients go through this kind of thing?" should be told "The important thing is that *you* are having these feelings and reactions right now, and we have to wonder where they came from and what they mean with respect to you as an individual."

While avoiding details about probable reactions to psychotherapy, the therapist should add to his initial explanation some indication of the commitment of time that will be required of the patient. First in this regard he needs to clarify that sessions will be held regularly according to a fixed and prearranged schedule. Although the exact frequency and time for appointments will not be worked out until the discussion moves to a consideration of specific arrangements, the therapist in providing his general description of psychotherapy should indicate that this form of treatment does not proceed on the basis of the patient's calling for appointments when he has a problem or feels like coming in to talk. Such an informal arrangement may be suitable for some kinds of counseling and supportive psychotherapy, but it does not lend itself to ongoing personality exploration in uncovering psychotherapy.

Second, the therapist must say something about how long the treatment will last, even though the duration of psychotherapy is difficult to estimate. Not only is it hard to know in advance just how rapidly a patient will progress in psychotherapy, but patients do not always work toward precisely the goals originally agreed on. Some after achieving their original objectives decide to continue working on other problems or toward deeper self-understanding, and some decide to settle for lesser treatment accomplishments than they originally had in mind.

Hence, unless there is some specific reason or basis for fixing the duration of the treatment (e.g., a clinic policy, participation in a research study of time-limited therapy, or the expected departure of patient or therapist), it is best to structure the length of psychotherapy as indefinite and open-ended. At the same time, it should be clearly indicated that the time necessary for substantial progress in psychotherapy is measured in months or years and not in days or weeks.[2] For a patient who has difficulty comprehending that the treatment process will take longer than just a few sessions, it is usually sufficient to point out that it has taken a long time for him to become the person he is and that it will accordingly take some time to understand how he got to be that way and to bring about any changes.

Before concluding his explanation of the treatment process, the therapist may also have to respond to questions from the patient about his prospects for benefiting from psychotherapy. Some markedly different opinions have been expressed on how this question should be answered. On one hand, there is a traditional concern about holding out any promises of "cure" or marked behavior change, since there can be no guaranteed outcome in psychotherapy and it is insincere for a therapist to provide assurances on which he may not be able to deliver (see Menninger & Holzman, 1973, p. 30). On the other hand, the nonspecific factors that contribute to successful outcome in psychotherapy are often considered to include an element of suggestion (see Frank, 1971, 1973; Shapiro, 1971; Strupp, 1972, 1973). From this point of view, the more the therapist assures the patient that psychotherapy will help him, the more help he is likely to derive from it.

The research findings in this regard, although somewhat ambiguous, appear to indicate (a) that patients who are initially given some

[2]Some readers may be surprised that "months" of treatment should be considered potentially adequate for uncovering psychotherapy to take place. It is interesting to note in this regard that Freud, discussing this same aspect of informing the patient about psychotherapy, states that "psycho-analysis is always a matter of long periods of time, of half a year or whole years" (Freud, 1913, p. 129).

explanation of the process of psychotherapy are more likely to continue in treatment and benefit from it than patients who are not given any initial explanation, but (b) that patients who are given both an explanation *and* assurances that psychotherapy will help them do not improve any more than patients who receive just an explanation. Furthermore, patients who are given assurances of benefits from psychotherapy but no explanation of the psychotherapeutic process do not display any more improvement than patients who are told nothing at all (see Heilbrun, 1972; Hohen-Saric et al., 1964; Sloane et al., 1970).

In other words, the therapist who has adequately explained the process of psychotherapy will probably not facilitate subsequent improvement by adding any promise of improved functioning, and he might just as well avoid promising something he cannot guarantee. What he can safely do, however, is indicate the *possibility* of the patient's being helped. This kind of statement, for example, can promote a positive attitude toward the treatment without stretching the boundaries of genuineness:

> It's difficult to know in advance whether psychotherapy will relieve the problems you've been having. However, it is a process that will aid you in understanding yourself better, and it has proved beneficial to other people with problems similar to yours.

Presenting the Therapist's Qualifications

When the therapist has completed his explanation of the treatment process and answered the patient's questions about psychotherapy, he is next obligated to satisfy the patient regarding his professional qualifications. This does not mean providing a complete resumé of his training and experience. What it means is that the patient has a right to know whether the therapist is qualified to provide the treatment that is being offered, and a right to raise any questions he may have in this regard.

In deciding how to respond to such questions, the therapist needs to differentiate between those that concern him as a *therapist* and those that concern him as a *person.* Within limits, questions about the therapist as therapist should always be answered directly and honestly, such as whether he is a psychologist, psychiatrist, or psychiatric social worker and where he received his education and training. At the same time, the therapist needs to recognize questions that call for equally direct but less denotative answers.

For example, the patient who asks "How many years have you been in practice?" or "How many patients have you treated with problems like mine?" is really not after a numerical answer. He has no basis for judging how many years of experience with what kind of patients the therapist shoud have had, and what he really wants to know is whether the therapist will be able to understand and help him. An appropriate response to such questions is , "You're wondering whether I will be able to understand your problems and help you with them, and the best way I can answer your question is to tell you that I have had the experience necessary to be able to work with you; if I did not feel prepared to be of help, I would be referring you to another therapist."

Most patients will be satisfied with such an answer, which tells them what they want to know. When patients persist with demands for more specific information about the therapist's credentials, it then becomes appropriate to comment on the unusual nature of their behavior; namely, that since as laymen they have no basis for judging how much training and experience are necessary to guarantee competence, their demand for such information must have some underlying meaning. Perhaps a generalized need to have more information than should be necessary for making decisions is one of their neurotic difficulties, or perhaps they characteristically antagonize people by refusing to take what is said to them at face value, or perhaps they are having second thoughts about continuing in psychotherapy or about their ability to be helped—in which case no number of years of experience or patients successfully treated will satisfy them concerning the therapist's competence.

In contrast to questions about the therapist as a therapist, questions raised by a patient about the therapist as a person should usually not be answered. Even though a good psychotherapy relationship requires the therapist to be warm and genuine, to invest himself as a person, and to foster an atmosphere of shared participation in problem-solving, psychotherapy is not a friendship. The problems to be solved are the patient's, and the only personal information relevant to working effectively on these problems is personal information about the patient. A patient who needs psychotherapy needs a trained therapist whose contribution to the patient's welfare will be through his interest, understanding, and willingness to help, not through promoting a mutual friendship.[3]

[3]Schofield (1964, 1970) elaborates on two prime reasons why psychotherapy should not ordinarily be structured as a friendship: first, because of the short supply of trained psychotherapists relative to the numbers of psychologically disturbed people who need their specific therapeutic skills, a therapist should not devote his energies to working with people whose needs can be met solely by having a personal relationship; and second, the therapist who functions as a substitute friend may inadvertently interfere with his patient's search for and handling of truly spontaneous relationships in which mutuality and interdependence exist outside of the protective therapeutic umbrella.

Hence personal questions about the therapist ("Are you married?" "How many children do you have?" "Are you interested in sports?") need to be construed as statements to be understood, not answered. Often such personal questions can be responded to with "How would you like it to be?" or "How would you feel about it either way?" The patient who has asked whether the therapist is married, for example, may then be able to explore feelings he has that only a married or only an unmarried therapist could really understand and help him. It is these feelings that are important to discuss, not the specific answer to the patient's question. Except perhaps for some mild curiosity, a patient who needs and wants psychotherapy is not really concerned about the therapist as a person. He is concerned only with whether the therapist is someone he will be able to confide in and be helped by, and any personal questions he raises are almost certain to reflect such concerns.

For the patient who dwells on personal questions or asks directly why the therapist is not talking about his own life, it is usually sufficient to point out that the focus of the treatment relationship will be on the patient and his problems. Patients who are truly interested in psychotherapy will usually accept this explanation, because it is exactly the focus they wish the treatment to have. Those who are not satisfied with the therapist's statement that the focus will be on them, and instead insist that the therapist will have to talk about his personal life, may be looking for some excuse not to pursue psychotherapy, or they may be seeking some kind of encounter experience different from what the therapist is prepared to provide. In such cases further exploration of the patient's motivations may be necessary to reevaluate both his wish for help and his expectations of the kind of treatment he will be receiving.

There are two other points that need to be kept in mind with respect to this issue. First, as is true of virtually every aspect of conducting psychotherapy, there can be no fixed, immutable rules. At some times with some patients a therapist will feel there is good reason to mention some aspect of his personal life, and he should then do so. Flexibility based on sound clinical judgment, not hard and fast rules, is the key to conducting good psychotherapy. The empathic therapist who has a good grasp of personality dynamics and psychopathology will be able to recognize when it is in a patient's best interests to answer a personal question or volunteer some information about himself.[4]

[4]In some forms of supportive psychotherapy, particularly in the treatment of adolescents, expressions of the therapist's personal attitudes and interests may figure prominently in the therapy relationship. This aspect of adolescent psychotherapy is discussed by Holmes (1964, pp. 102–108), Meeks (1971, pp. 120–126), and Weiner (1970, pp. 362–369).

Second, it is mistaken for the therapist to think that by treating his personal life as classified information he can preserve his anonymity. The main reason for the therapist's not answering personal questions is to keep the emphasis on the patient and his problems, not to shroud himself in mystery. Although it may be advantageous for the patient to have limited knowledge of the therapist's personal life, especially to allow maximum latitude for him to form impressions of the therapist on a transference basis (see Chap. 10), the fact is that patients seek out and absorb considerable information on their own.

Patients notice styles of dress and grooming, office decor, a wedding band, family pictures, and a variety of other clues to the reality of the therapist's personal life and tastes. To attempt to limit these sources of information by conducting the treatment in a bare, impersonal cell detracts from the therapist's image as an authentic person and is much more damaging for psychotherapy than, for example, evidence from a pipe rack that the therapist is a pipe-smoker. In addition, patients often prove very resourceful in checking out their therapist in the telephone book to see where he lives, determining his exact rank and position if he works in a public facility, and picking up other bits of information from one source or another. The smaller the community or the professional circle in which the therapist works, the more the patient learns about him, and even in the largest metropolis a therapist deceives himself if he believes that through careful control of what he says he is guaranteeing anonymity for himself as a person.

The Patient Responds

When the therapist has finished recommending psychotherapy, explaining the psychotherapeutic process, and answering questions about his qualifications, it is time for the patient to respond. The patient's response will take one of three forms: he will either accept the recommendation for psychotherapy and indicate his readiness to continue, reject the offer of treatment, or express some mixed feelings about what he wants to do. The first type of response needs no further comment, since it completes the initial agreement phase of making a treatment contract and leads directly to the discussion of goals, procedures, and arrangements. The second and third types of response require the therapist to give some additional attention to the patient's attitudes toward receiving psychological help.

The patient who flatly declines further psychotherapy at this point should always be asked the reason for his decision. Sometimes the reasons given open avenues for further exploration (e.g., "I just don't have any clear picture of how this kind of treatment works or how just talking can really be of any help to me"), and the therapist can then review whatever areas of information may not have been covered sufficiently.

At other times a patient may reject psychotherapy in a manner that leaves little room for discussion ("I don't think I need it"; "I appreciate your interest in helping me, but getting into psychotherapy is not something I want to do right now"). When presented with such clear and definite rejections of psychotherapy, the therapist should have sufficient respect for the patient's integrity to accept his wishes. The patient is, after all, a free agent—free to accept or decline an offer of psychological help no matter how much someone else thinks he needs it, just as he is free to decline financial aid or medical care. The therapist needs to resist any temptation to cajole, seduce, or frighten him into reconsidering his decision about psychotherapy. Glowing portents if psychotherapy is undertaken and dire predictions if it is not are forms of hucksterism that demean both patient and therapist, and they also exaggerate the transcendence of psychotherapy—it is not the only solution to everybody's problems.

Emergency situations such as suicidal risk and imminent personality breakdown do of course call for a firm and persistent treatment recommendation. As noted in Chapter 4, however, such emergencies should be identified and responded to early in the evaluation process, long before work with a patient has reached the point now being discussed. Hopefully by the time the therapist has begun to discuss ongoing psychotherapy with a patient, any emergencies have been ruled out. Hence the patient's unequivocal rejection of a psychotherapy recommendation deserves to be taken at face value.

Yet there are two additional steps the therapist should take with a patient who appears to have potential for benefiting from psychotherapy but who declines to undertake it. First, the therapist should inquire whether there is any other way he might be of help. Some patients may be convinced that, contrary to the therapist's opinions, they would benefit more from marriage counseling, hypnotic treatment, or an encounter experience than from psychotherapy, and they may appreciate being recommended to someone else for this purpose. Even though the therapist may sincerely believe that these other approaches are potentially less beneficial for the patient than psychotherapy, he should avoid pouting at the expense of executing his professional responsibility. If the patient is going to explore some form of treatment that the therapist does not provide, the least he can do is refer him to a practitioner of this other treatment whom he knows to be qualified.

Second, the therapist should help the patient who rejects a psychotherapy recommendation look to the future. Without being overly dramatic, he can point out that the patient's problems may persist, that he may at some future time wish to reconsider psychotherapy, and that the therapist will remain available and interested in working with him. In this way the therapist can subtly encourage the patient to reconsider while leaving the door open for him to return without prejudice. It is not uncommon for initially disinterested patients who are treated in this manner to return for psychotherapy following some subsequent events that convince them of their need for help.

On the other hand, when a patient initially expresses some mixed feelings in response to a psychotherapy recommendation, the therapist should attempt to explore these feelings and resolve them in favor of a decision to continue. Some people are embarrassed or anxious about being a psychotherapy patient, others may resent being told they need help (even though they have come seeking it), and others may be uncertain whether they can meet the time and financial commitments of psychotherapy. Usually these and other such hesitancies about accepting an otherwise appealing psychotherapy recommendation can be worked through if the therapist is sufficiently sensitive to recognize them and help the patient talk about them.

One final point needs to be clarified in concluding this discussion of agreeing on psychotherapy. As stated previously (p. 73), for psychotherapy to have a good beginning, there must be an explicit agreement between patient and therapist that treatment is indicated and will be undertaken. This statement may seem inconsistent with the point made in Chapter 2 that patients who come to the therapist under duress or without much intrinsic motivation are not necessarily incapable of being helped. Yet what happens is that the involuntary patient or the patient who doubts that treatment is indicated does *not* get off to a good start. He may eventually benefit from psychotherapy, but his prospects for doing so hinge on how effectively the therapist can surmount his lack of motivation and generate some intrinsic commitment to the treatment. In this way an inauspicious beginning can be turned into a reasonably successful outcome.

AGREEING ON OBJECTIVES AND PROCEDURES

The psychotherapeutic process is facilitated if the treatment contract includes an explicit agreement between patient and therapist on the objectives of their work together and on the procedures they will follow in attempting to reach these objectives. By the time an initial evaluation has been completed and an agreement has been made to undertake psychotherapy, it may seem that the treatment objectives are obvious and already known to both parties: the general purpose of the treatment will be to help the patient understand himself better, and the more specific objectives will be some alleviation or resolution of the problems that they have been discussing. As previously explained, however, nothing in the treatment contract should be presumed or taken as implicitly understood. Explicit statements of each facet of the contract, no matter how apparently redundant, help resolve any uncertainties or misconceptions held by either party and solidify the foundation for subsequent psychotherapeutic work.

To clarify the objectives of the treatment following a patient's agreement to undertake psychotherapy, the therapist can begin by saying, "Now that we've decided to work together, let's review for a moment exactly what you see as the main objectives we'll be working toward." The patient may respond by summarizing his problems and concerns just as he has previously presented them, in which case the therapist can simply (a) acknowledge and repeat this summary in order to give it additional emphasis and (b) move on to talk about procedures and arrangements.

On the other hand, the patient may now present a somewhat different list of objectives or a somewhat different set of treatment priorities than he presented initially. It is not unusual for people to gain new perspectives on themselves and their problems in the process of just one or two evaluative interviews. Concerns that seemed particularly pressing may take on a paler cast after having been discussed briefly, and previously suppressed or denied difficulties may emerge as primary sources of concern. By asking for a summary at this point, the therapist can avoid proceeding on the basis of an outdated view of what the patient most wants to accomplish in treatment.

Not only does psychotherapy progress more rapidly, follow fewer blind alleys, and promote a more congenial working relationship if patient and therapist have reached an explicit agreement on their objectives,[5] but

[5]Research supporting this relationship between congruent patient-therapist expectancies and positive treatment outcomes is reviewed by Meltzoff and Kornreich (1970, pp. 257–264; see also Goldstein (1962) and Pope et al., 1972). Although the influence of patient expectations on the treatment course has not yet been studied adequately in all its ramifications, available evidence indicates that patients who do not share a common view with their therapist concerning objectives and procedures of the treatment tend to experience more anxiety and dissatisfaction during interviews and are more likely to drop out of treatment than patients who enjoy mutuality of patient-therapist expectations.

such an explicit statement of objectives also provides an excellent guideline for judging when the treatment should stop. As discussed in Chapter 12, the therapist's task in terminating psychotherapy is as much a matter of knowing *when* as *how*. One of the main ways of avoiding a situation in which psychotherapy drifts aimlessly or endlessly is to include in the treatment contract an explicit and mutually agreeable list of specific objectives. Even though the objectives may change during the course of the psychotherapy, as long as they remain explicit and mutual the patient and therapist will be able at any time to review together where they stand in relation to reaching their treatment goals.

Little more need be said here about treatment procedures, since the therapist will have covered in his explanation of the psychotherapeutic process most of what the patient needs to know at this point. However, there may be some specific questions the patient wants to raise now that the therapist is talking about psychotherapy for *him* rather than just about psychotherapy in general. For example, he may want to know whether any drugs will be used as part of the treatment, whether he will lie on a couch, whether he will be talking with the therapist on the telephone as well as in the office, whether other members of his family will be brought into the treatment, and so on.

Although it is impossible to anticipate all such procedural questions and suggest responses to them, two guidelines can be offered to help the therapist answer them. First, the more a therapist intends the psychotherapy to be uncovering in nature, the more he will be confining his role to interpretive behavior within the treatment sessions and the less likely he will be to have contacts with the patient outside of these sessions, to meet with family members, or to provide counseling and advice. Conversely, the more a therapist plans on a supportive approach, the more likely he is to become a "real" person in the patient's life (someone who reacts to the patient's behavior) rather than solely an "as if" person (someone who concentrates on interpreting the patient's behavior), and the more he will be injecting himself into the patient's life beyond providing interpretations within the treatment session.[6]

Second, with respect to many procedural details the therapist should conduct psychotherapy in ways that he is accustomed to and has confidence in. Thus, for example, a therapist who occasionally uses drugs in collaboration with psychotherapy might tell his patient that medication during the treatment is a possibility if it appears indicated, whereas a

[6]For a further elaboration of this very useful distinction between the therapist as a "real" object and as an "as if" object in the patient's life, the reader is referred to Tarachow (1963, Chaps. 2–3).

therapist who neither prescribes drugs nor wishes his patients to use drugs prescribed by others will say so if asked. Similarly, a therapist who prefers to use a couch will recommend its use, and one who does not will not.

This approach to procedural details may appear cavalier or naive, especially since very strong opinions have been expressed on such points. However, psychotherapy is no stranger to shibboleths, and it is not unusual to find firmly held beliefs masquerading as confirmed facts (see Fierman, 1965). For example, many clinicians regard the use of drugs as incompatible with dynamically oriented psychotherapy, yet there are both an excellent rationale and empirical data to support combined psychotherapy and pharmacotherapy in selected cases (May, 1971; Ostow, 1962).

Regarding use of the couch, there is a wide range of opinion concerning the circumstances in which it will facilitate or impede psychotherapy. However, there are in fact no empirical data to demonstrate the superiority of either couch or face-to-face interviewing in any form of psychotherapy, and experienced therapists listening to tape-recorded treatment sessions have not been able to identify when the patient was being seen on the couch and when he was being interviewed face-to-face (Hall & Closson, 1964). Until some evidence is forthcoming, then, the therapist should decide on the use of a couch through a combination of what his clinical judgment, the nature of his training and experience, and his expectations tell him would be most beneficial in the treatment of a particular patient, and this same conclusion applies to numerous other specific procedural details.

AGREEING ON ARRANGEMENTS

When patient and therapist have agreed to work together in psychotherapy and have clarified the objectives and procedures of the treatment, the final step in cementing the treatment contract is agreeing on specific arrangement for the time, frequency, place, and fee for sessions. The remainder of this chapter is concerned with the major points the therapist should keep in mind in making these arrangements.

Time

Specific appointment times for psychotherapy interviews should be arranged to suit the mutual convenience of patient and therapist and should usually involve sessions of 45 or 50 minutes in length.[7] The most important aspect of making these arrangements is communicating that session length will be uniform throughout the treatment. If the time period for sessions is left free to vary with the nature of the material being discussed, a number of disadvantages may accrue. For example, a patient struggling with upsetting thoughts that are difficult or embarrassing for him to express may sit quietly or talk about the weather for 15–20 minutes and then indicate that he is ending the session because "There's nothing much on my mind today." In the absence of a previously fixed and specified time period for sessions that he can refer to, the therapist is in a poor position to help this patient realize there is something unusual about his behavior that constitutes an interference with communication and is not a customary and appropriate feature of the treatment arrangements.

A fixed time period also helps the therapist work effectively with patients who are inclined to measure his interest and helpfulness according to how much time he gives them. Dependent and narcissistic patients in particular are likely to save material they consider important or captivating for the last few minutes of a session, in the hopes of getting the therapist to extend their time. Unless a fixed session length has been set and adhered to, the therapist is hamstrung in such situations: if he allows the patient to go on, he gratifies his dependency or narcissism without helping him understand it; if he cuts the patient off, he risks appearing disinterested and unsympathetic.

By operating within a fixed time limit, the therapist can end sessions without communicating dislike for the patient or disinterest in what he is saying. When a patient interprets "Our time is up for today" as a rejection, the therapist can remind him that the end of the session is based solely on the agreed time period for their meetings, not on the therapist's feelings or attitudes. Additionally, a fixed session length helps the therapist resist being influenced by any feelings or attitudes he does have. Every therapist experiences temptations to abbreviate dull or difficult sessions and extend productive ones, and the fixed time period protects him against introducing such surplus meanings into session length.

Thus a clear initial staement of a fixed duration for sessions serves two related purposes. First, it promotes a relationship in which the therapist's saying "Our time is up for today" is interpreted to mean simply that the

[7]The psychotherapy "hour" has traditionally involved something less than a 60-minute session in order to allow the therapist a few moments to reflect, make notes, answer telephone calls, and tend to other personal needs between appointments. Lindner (1955) among others has popularized the concept of the "50-minute hour."

time is up, not as "I don't like you," or "I don't want to spend any more time with you," or "You and your problems aren't very important," or "You're boring me." Second, it provides a definite basis for regarding any such patient impressions as misconceptions that need to be understood. Yet the advantages of fixed-length sessions do not mandate inflexibility in this regard. A therapist should always be prepared for unusual situations that seem to call for abbreviated or extended interviews, particularly in the context of relatively supportive psychotherapy.

It should also be noted that there is nothing sacrosanct about any particular length of time for therapy sessions. Although the advantages of a fixed duration for interviews and of some breathing space between appointments have compelling face validity, there are no data to indicate that a 45–50-minute hour is either the best or only effective time period. To the contrary, some promising results have been reported using a "20-minute hour" (Tedesco, 1967, 1970), and developments in the area of group psychotherapy have tended to favor a 90-minute hour or even much longer "marathon" sessions (see Yalom, 1970, pp. 210–215). No careful research has examined the differential effectiveness of various length "hours" in psychotherapy. Hence even though the 45–50-minute hour is the most widely recommended and commonly used time period, there is no basis for considering it inviolate.

Frequency

For the same reasons that psychotherapy should consist of sessions of specified and uniform length, the sessions themselves should be scheduled at regular and fixed intervals. Systematic progress toward self-understanding is difficult to sustain if appointments are made or canceled according to the patient's felt needs for a session. The patient who feels disinclined to talk may be struggling with some difficult material that should be talked about, and a patient who feels no need for a session because things are currently going well in his life may be in an excellent state of mind, free from intercurrent pressures, for recalling and thinking productively about past events.

The therapist likewise needs some protection from his underlying needs, so that he does not find himself scheduling additional sessions when the patient is presenting interesting material and progressing well, and cutting back on the frequency of the interviews when progress becomes slow or difficult. There may be times when it appears appropriate to alter the frequency of sessions, particularly in relatively supportive psychotherapy, but such alterations should be based on the patient's needs and not on how fascinating, easy, or rewarding the therapist's work is.

It is usually helpful to begin discussing the frequency of sessions by asking the patient about his expectations in this regard. Some people come for therapy with little idea that regular sessions on at least a weekly basis are likely to be required, while others may have the notion that psychotherapy always has to involve daily sessions. By eliciting any misconceptions the patient may have before he proposes a particular session frequency, the therapist can be prepared to close any gaps in this regard between the patient's expectations and what the treatment will consist of.

As for deciding on the most desirable session frequency, there are no hard and fast rules to be followed. In general, the more intensive the treatment is to be, as defined by how ambitious the treatment goals are and how deep a level of self-understanding is to be sought, the more frequently interviews should be scheduled. Yet there is no uniform relationship between depth of psychotherapy and frequency of sessions. Some patients work faster and are less rigidly defended than others, so that a relatively open and spontaneous patient may work as intensively in once-a-week psychotherapy as a relatively restrained and guarded patient can in two or three sessions per week.

Furthermore, it is necessary to recognize that there is no direct relationship between how frequently sessions are scheduled and how quickly therapy will be completed. Some patients may expect that if they are seen twice weekly they will finish treatment sooner than if they have appointments just once a week. In fact, however, just the opposite is likely to occur. Patients who have relatively frequent sessions tend to bring up more kinds of issues than patients seen less frequently, to get more deeply involved in these issues, and to require more time to resolve them. Hence when the therapist makes his recommendation for how frequent the sessions should be, he should clarify that the frequency has no necessary bearing on how long the treatment will last.

The actual decision the therapist makes concerning session frequency will be determined by his assessment of what is suitable for helping the particular patient work on the problems that have been outlined and toward the goals that have been agreed on. Although relevant research evidence is limited, what data there are suggest that at least once-a-week sessions are necessary for significant personality change to occur in psychotherapy.

Accordingly, the therapist should have a once-a-week minimum in mind if he intends to conduct uncovering psychotherapy, and the more guarded, rigid, or resistive a patient appears, the more a frequency greater than once weekly may be indicated to attain a given set of goals.[8]

Place

In making the treatment arrangements, the therapist should not overlook stating clearly where the sessions are to be held and where the patient is to check in when he arrives for appointments. This advice may seem gratuitous, especially when viewed from the vantage point of an established practitioner conducting psychotherapy in an office that bears his name on the door and is adjacent to an obvious reception area. However, it becomes less gratuitous as one considers (a) the extensive amount of psychotherapy being provided by professionals in training, who may or may not have the luxury of their own office, and (b) the amount of psychotherapy being conducted in hospital, clinic, and agency settings in which a series of interviewing rooms rather than individual offices are used for treatment, and in which a large and complex physical plant may challenge even the brightest and most adventurous patients to find out where they are supposed to be. A few words of direction from the therapist will be appreciated by the patient and may make the difference in his arriving on time for his first several sessions.

With further respect to settings in which an individual private office may not be available, the therapist should try to see his patients in the same place each time they come in. People talk about themselves more easily when they feel "at home," and the trappings of a therapist's office take on a familiarity that helps make a patient comfortable. Even a relatively barren interview room containing few of the therapist's personal effects has features to which a patient becomes accustomed and which give him a sense of being in a familiar place—the type and placement of the furniture, the color of the walls, the view from the window, and so forth. Constant haphazard shuffling from place to place for each interview leaves the patient feeling a stranger in the treatment room and may inhibit his spontaneity.

[8]Research on session frequency is summarized by Meltzoff and Kornreich (1970, pp. 354–356) and Reisman (1971, pp. 32–37). Although available evidence has not yet confirmed that session frequencies of more than once weekly arc generally conducive to better outcomes than weekly interviews, clinical experience with individual patients leaves little question that some people whose defensiveness prevents them from becoming meaningfully engaged in once-a-week psychotherapy can make considerable progress if interviews are scheduled more frequently.

There is a second, more subtle disadvantage in repeated shifting of interviewing rooms that has to do with the therapist's image. Patients tend to invest themselves more eagerly in the treatment process if they feel that their therapist, whatever his age or years of experience, is a competent professional who has the respect of his colleagues. Accordingly, it may hinder the course of psychotherapy if the therapist comes across as such a low-status person and therapist-errant that he cannot command a regularly scheduled interviewing room for an ongoing therapy patient. Even without having his own office, a therapist can avoid this possible interference with the treatment by putting himself in the position of being able to say, "We will be meeting each Wednesday at one o'clock, then, and we will have the use of this room for our sessions."

Fees

Opinion is divided concerning whether the payment of a fee is necessary for progress to occur in psychotherapy. Whereas some therapists are convinced on the basis of their clinical experience that a financial sacrifice by the patient is essential for benefits to accrue, others view the fee as incidental to outcome. The meager research evidence in this area appears to indicate that fees are not *necessary* for a successful outcome, but the data do not negate the possibility that in some situations fees may benefit the treatment.[8]

This uncertainty notwithstanding, the fact is that most psychotherapy patients are charged fees, and the matter of fees must therefore be included in the treatment contract. Because money is not an easy topic for most people to talk about, the therapist may find himself tempted to talk around rather than about it. Rationalizations for avoiding money talk are readily available ("I want the patient to feel I am interested in him as a person, regardless of how much money he has or how much he is paying to see me"), and there is usually a clinic fee clerk, billing secretary, or someone else around other than the therapist to whom money matters can be referred.

But it is the therapist's responsibility, whether he is setting his own fees or having them set by institutional policies, to make sure that his patient knows what the fee will be, considers it fair and acceptable, and has an opportunity to raise questions about it. Although the setting of a fee

[8]See Meltzoff and Kornreich (1970, pp. 254–255) for a brief summary of this research. An interesting discussion of psychodynamic implications of fee-setting is provided by Dewald (1971, pp. 146–150).

should not be a bartering affair, the therapist must be prepared to discuss fee variations with individual patients, based on realistic considerations, just as he is prepared to schedule sessions on a Wednesday rather than a Tuesday for a patient who would have difficulty keeping Tuesday appointments.

An explicit discussion of fees, in addition to providing information to which the patient is entitled, also helps communicate that all aspects of the patient's life are appropriate subjects for discussion in psychotherapy. Money matters play some role in everybody's life, and the therapist who omits discussing such an obvious money matter as the fee for his services may inadvertently imply that financial concerns, and perhaps other unspecified subjects as well, should not be brought up in the treatment.

Finally, it is helpful for the therapist to keep in mind what the patient has a right to expect in return for his money. The psychotherapy patient is purchasing the therapist's professional services. He is not purchasing a piece of merchandise with a money-back guarantee if he is not satisfied with it, nor is he accepting a free trial offer. In other words, the patient is expected to pay his bills regularly from the beginning of the treatment, assuming of course that the therapist is keeping his part of the treatment contract. Whether a patient is getting his money's worth is solely a function of whether a qualified therapist is exercising a conscientious effort in his behalf.

CHAPTER 7

Conduct of the Interview

As a patient becomes increasingly comfortable with talking and his therapist becomes increasingly familiar with him and his difficulties, psychotherapy gradually progresses from its initial, preparatory phase to its middle, interpretive phase. To promote such progress, the therapist needs to conduct the interviews following agreement on the treatment contract in ways that acclimate the patient to the methods and procedures of psychotherapy, help him talk productively, and elicit further information about his life experiences and personality functioning.

ACCLIMATING THE PATIENT

No matter how informed a patient has been about psychotherapy before coming for help and no matter how perceptively he has endorsed his role as a patient in discussing the treatment contract, he is unlikely to be fully prepared to participate in the treatment. To make the transition from talking about the patient's role to actually filling it, most patients require some continuing education aimed at helping them become acclimated to the psychotherapy situation. A useful beginning in this direction is a capsule review of patient and therapist roles:

> Now that we've made our arrangements to continue working together, let me say something about what our roles will be. Your role will be to talk as freely as you can about yourself and whatever may be on your mind, and my role will be primarily to listen and to help you talk.

A brief statement of this kind is sufficient to clarify for the patient what his task is and how the therapist intends to respond. Having made such a clear and definitive statement, the therapist can refer back to it in helping the patient recognize role distortions that he may express from time to time (e.g., "I've been talking a lot lately, it's your turn now"). Likewise, patients who have understood the therapist's explanation of how psychotherapy proceeds may still have specific questions about how they should actually begin, what they should focus on in talking, how they can tell what is important to bring up and what is not, and so forth. The therapist can respond adequately to most such questions by briefly amplifying the patient's task:

The main thing is that you should talk about whatever is on your mind. It's difficult to know in advance whether something will be important or not in understanding more about you, and we can't tell for sure until we've had a chance to discuss it. For this reason, you should try not to censor any thoughts or feelings you may have, but just express them as they come to you.

The need for continuing patient education is likely to arise at a number of points in the interviews immediately following agreement on the treatment contract. It is not unusual for a patient to begin one or more of these early sessions by sitting silently or otherwise indicating his preference for the therapist to open the interview (e.g., "I don't know where to begin"; "What should I talk about today?"; "I wish you would ask me some questions"). In response to such beginnings early in psychotherapy the therapist should focus on communicating that the responsibility for starting sessions rests on the patient's shoulders:

We have been learning something about you and have seen how this emerged from what you were able to say about yourself. It will work best if we continue to begin each time with what may be on your mind, and then take it from there.

It should be noted that this type of response to initial silence purposely ignores any elements of resistance that may be involved. In the initial phase of treatment the therapist needs to guard against jumping on every possible hint of resistance in the patient's behavior. Unless resistances are threatening to interrupt the treatment, they are better left alone until the middle phase of therapy, when they arise following a period of comfortable participation in the treatment process (see Chap. 9). The initial phase is the time for educating the patient in his role, not offering challenging interpretations of his behavior. Hence the instructional approach illustrated above is the preferable way of responding to a patient who has difficulty starting interviews early in the treatment.

Once a patient has begun an interview and raised some topics for discussion, he may become uncertain about how to continue and ask for guidance: "Should I tell you more about that?"; "There are a number of things I could talk about next, but I'm not sure what you're interested in finding out or what's proper for me to bring up." Like silence, such questions usually reflect some resistance operations (e.g., a wish to change the topic because the subject being discussed is leading toward material that is painful or embarrassing), and they are also likely to have rich implications for the patient's personality dynamics and attitudes toward the therapist (e.g., why does he feel a need to ask permission to continue talking, or why does he allude to what the therapist wants to find out rather than to what he wants to learn more about, or why is he concerned about being "proper?").

Again, however, the therapist's task in the initial phase of psychotherapy is not to demonstrate his brilliance at picking up subtle clues to the patient's underlying thoughts and feelings, but rather to cement the patient's involvement in the treatment process and prepare him for subsequent interpretive work.[1] Hence the focus at this point belongs on instructing the patient who expresses uncertainty about how to proceed, and not on trying to probe the origins of his uncertainty.

The most effective instructional technique with the uncertain patient is repeating as necessary the basic elements of the "free association" method that define his role: he should talk as freely as he can about whatever comes to his mind; he should try not to censor or withhold any of his thoughts or feelings; and, since it is difficult to know in advance what is more or less important to discuss, he should avoid any prejudgments about whether something should or should not be said.[2]

Whenever a patient is talking freely in these early interviews, the

[1]Hasty and undisciplined interpretation of a patient's unconscious mental life is known as "wild analysis" (Freud, 1910a). Practiced usually by inexperienced or inadequately trained therapists who regard psychotherapy as a flashy and sensational lunge for the psychic jugular, rather than as the painstaking pursuit of understanding it needs to be, wild analysis seldom serves a patient's best interests.

[2]The free association method of was devised by Freud, who considered it the "fundamental rule" of psychoanalysis (Freud, 1913, pp. 134–135). Although various types of psychotherapy can be differentiated in terms of how the therapist responds to the patient's productions, they share the basic concept that the patient should talk about himself as freely as he can. Fuller discussions of free association are provided by Bellak (1961), Kanzer (1961), Loewenstein (1963), Rosner (1973), and Singer (1965, Chap. 8).

therapist can acclimate him to the treatment process simply by adopting the role he has told the patient he will fill and by displaying the therapist behaviors that contribute to good outcome (see Chap. 3): he listens attentively, he provides an accepting climate in which nothing that is said elicits censure, scorn, or ridicule, and he demonstrates his ability and willingness to help the patient understand the meaning of his experiences. As just noted, however, this is not yet the time for the therapist to attempt to demonstrate his empathy and helpfulness by offering penetrating insights or sweeping interpretations. Instead, he needs to accustom the patient gradually to the interpretive aspect of the treatment process through occasional clarifications and relatively superficial observations.

These clarifications and observations will consist for the most part of repeating or asking the patient to repeat some bits of information that seem potentially important ("As I understand it, then, it was the combination of your being criticised about your work and having the criticism come from someone you admire that led to your feeling particularly bad"; "Could you go over that again so I can be sure I have a clear picture of what it was your husband did that made you angry?"). With such occasional interjections the therapist helps familiarize the patient with how psychotherapy works, while at the same time he demonstrates his interest, attentiveness, and capacity to understand.

One additional aspect of continuing education in psychotherapy involves questions the patient may raise about the content of his thoughts and feelings. As a patient begins to associate freely and to come up with novel ideas and recollections, he is likely to ask the therapist's opinion of them: "Why did I think about that now?"; "What does it mean that I'm feeling angry as I talk about my brother?"; "How have I become such a rigid person as I seem to be?" In some instances, when the answer to such a question would constitute the type of clarification or superficial interpretation that helps accustom the patient to the psychotherapy process, the therapist may offer a direct answer. More often, however, it is preferable not to answer such questions, but instead to use them to help the patient work toward discovering his own answers.

Two approaches in particular allow the therapist to respond to content-oriented questions so as to foster further self-exploration by the patient. One approach is to elicit the patient's own associations ("I wonder what ideas might occur to *you* about that question"), and the other is to call attention to the question itself ("Perhaps it would be helpful to look at why that particular question occurred to you at this point"). In addition to encouraging the patient to plumb his own mental contents further, these types of response also help educate the patient to the fact that in psychotherapy questions are to be treated as statements to be understood and not necessarily answered.

HELPING THE PATIENT TALK PRODUCTIVELY

Whereas the general process of acclimating the patient to psychotherapy helps to induce him to talk freely, there are a number of more specific technical procedures by which the therapist can further promote productive talking. Productive talking consists of a readiness on the patient's part to elaborate what he is saying, sufficient spontaneity for him to report new feelings and ideas as they arise, and a willingness to continue talking even when it becomes difficult or uncomfortable to do so. The patient can be helped to achieve and sustain these elements of productivity by a number of techniques for phrasing statements, responding to silences, handling discomfort, and arranging the physical setting for interviews.

Phrasing Therapist Statements

Perhaps the most effective way in which a therapist can foster spontaneous production of material is by interviewing without asking questions. Although there are times when a direct question is the most suitable means of getting at some necessary information, a predominantly inquisitive interview style has a number of disadvantages for ongoing psychotherapy. First, it sets a question-and-answer model for the interview, thereby giving the patient the impression that his task is simply to answer each of the therapist's questions as it is asked. Second, it implies that the therapist will be taking responsibility for determining what subjects are to be discussed and in how much detail. Third, it tends to suggest that, once the patient has finished answering all of the therapist's questions, he will receive an answer that solves his problems, in the same way as a physician asks about symptoms, conducts a physical examination and necessary laboratory tests, and then tells the patient what is wrong with him and how it can be remedied.

For these reasons, a question-oriented interview style tends to discourage a patient from elaborating his remarks or spontaneously volunteering information on subjects of his own choosing, while at the same time it obscures the patient's responsibility for producing material and working toward self-understanding. With practice and careful attention to how he phrases his statements, a therapist can learn to avoid taking a questioning or directive stance even when he is trying to elicit a specific bit of information or lead the patient into a particular subject area.[3]

For example, "How did you feel about that?" can be phrased "I wonder what feelings you may have had about that"; "Tell me more about your mother" can be phrased "You've been mentioning your mother but you really haven't told me much about her"; "How old is your mother?" can be phrased "You've been talking about your mother but you haven't said how old she is"; and so on. Despite the seeming insignificance of these changes in wording, they do alter the therapist's overt role. Instead of being a questioner, he becomes someone who listens and clarifies, and instead of overtly leading the discussion, he subtly influences its direction without imposing any direction. Questions ("How old is your mother?") call for an answer, whereas statements ("You haven't mentioned your mother's age"), no matter how compelling, do not demand any specific answer. To borrow an apt phrase from Sullivan (1954, pp. 19–25), it is as a "participant observer" who can translate his questions and directives into observations and clarifications that the therapist best facilitates productive talking by his patient.

In addition to avoiding questions and directives, the therapist can also foster patient productivity by being concise. As few words as possible should be used to phrase whatever observations or clarifications appear indicated to help the patient keep working productively. Lengthy commentaries and elaborate reconstructions of the therapist's impressions impede rather than facilitate progress: they impose a role shift, with the therapist becoming the talker and the patient the listener, and they interrupt the patient's flow of ideas and efforts at self-understanding.

Psychotherapy is not an occasion for speech-making. The therapist who finds himself engaging in long-winded interventions should ask himself two questions. First, is he gratifying needs of his own (e.g., to be in control, to exhibit perspicacity, or to win admiration) at the expense of meeting the patient's needs? If so, a change in style is clearly called for. Second, is he insufficiently aware of what he is observing to formulate it concisely? If so, the attempt at formulation should be deferred until he

[3]Although research studies of this aspect of the interview process are neither as extensive nor conclusive as one might wish, Reisman (1971, p. 56) reviews data confirming that a directive, inquisitorial therapist approach stifles patient spontaneity and leads to fewer patient statements of self-understanding than a therapist approach based on clarifications and interpretations. There is also evidence that relatively experienced therapists are less likely to ask questions than relatively inexperienced therapists, and that increased experience is accompanied by increasing use of nonquestioning responses to patient verbalizations (see Ornston et al., 1968; Ornston et al., 1970; Strupp, 1960).

knows enough to do a better job of it.

Responding to Silences

To help a patient talk productively, the therapist must be prepared to deal with periods of silence that inevitably occur during psychotherapy interviews. Patient silences, whatever their origin, represent an obstacle to communication that must be removed or circumvented before progress can be resumed. This is the case particularly when a silent patient does not appear to be actively thinking about or trying to find the words for what he will say next, but instead is looking around blankly or squirming uncomfortably at an apparent loss for ideas. Faced with such silences, the therapist has four primary options open to him:

1. He can sit silently himself and wait for the patient to resume talking. Prolonged silences make most patients progressively more uncomfortable and motivate them to talk as a way of relieving discomfort. In this sense the interview situation can be likened to a vacuum, which compels being filled, and sooner or later the patient will say something if the therapist does not.

However, extended therapist silence should be recognized as a potentially self-defeating tactic. Although it is consistent with the therapist's role as listener, it may make the patient so anxious that he cannot express himself clearly or perhaps cannot even tolerate remaining in treatment. Furthermore, prolonged therapist silences often give a patient cause to wonder whether the therapist has been paying attention to what he has been saying and is really interested in helping him.

For these reasons, the therapist should be cautious about greeting silence with silence, especially in the early phases of treatment. Occasional brief silences educate the patient about the treatment process and foster his spontaneity and sense of responsibility for talking; extended painful silences, on the other hand, occurring before the patient is accustomed to his role as talker and prepared to deal interpretively with his reactions to silence, are more likely to be damaging than productive. The therapist who sits in stony silence during early interviews, believing that he is appropriately requiring the patient to demonstrate his motivation or assume his responsibility for the treatment, is abdicating his own responsibility for helping the patient talk, and he is in for more than his share of inordinately anxious and prematurely terminating patients.

2. He can assume responsibility for sustaining the conversation. Whereas the above option of therapist silence is the most radical and anxiety-provoking of the four responses to patient silence being discussed

here, this second option is the most conservative and anxiety-reducing response. In sustaining conversation, the therapist responds to a patient who has fallen silent by commenting on what he had been talking about or by suggesting a new topic for him to take up: "You were talking a few moments ago about what it was like when your parents got divorced, and I wonder if there is more you could say about that"; "So far today you haven't mentioned anything about how things are going at work."

Although this means of responding to patient silences avoids the potential disadvantages of the therapist's also remaining silent, it too has serious drawbacks. When comments or suggestions are offered to sustain conversation following a patient silence of a few minutes or more, they implicitly contradict what the therapist is trying to convey about his role in the treatment. That is, they imply that the therapist stands ready to indicate what the patient should talk about, whether he should elaborate on a topic, and when he should change the subject.

Hence the therapist should use this direct method of ending a patient's silence only sparingly, usually in just two circumstances. First, there may be occasions when it appears so important to elaborate certain aspects of content or background information that getting this further information takes precedence over instructing the patient in his role or exploring his difficulty in talking. In this circumstance the therapist might respond to a patient who has fallen silent by encouraging him to continue with the topic he was discussing. Second, there may be times when a silent patient appears to have become so upset about what he had been saying that reducing his anxiety takes precedence over trying to understand its origin. In this circumstance the therapist might choose to change the subject, helping the patient talk about something he is relatively comfortable with and deferring the upsetting subject for some later time.

3. He can ask the patient for his associations. Asking for associations ("What's going through your mind right now?"; "I wonder what thoughts or feelings you may be having") helps to break through a patient's silence without having most of the drawbacks of the therapist's remaining silent or becoming directive. A request or suggestion that the patient associate is sufficiently active to let him know the therapist is paying attention and trying to be helpful, while at the same time it is sufficiently inactive to leave in the patient's hands the responsibility for deciding how much to say about what.

Because the free association method can help a silent patient talk productively without compromising the therapist's role as an interested but nondirective listener, it is generally preferable to remaining silent or attempting to sustain the conversation. Yet all three of these ways of handling silence have in common the fact that they are efforts to circumvent a silence and cause a patient to talk again, rather than to understand the origin and meaning of the silence. Circumventing silences, especially by the free association method, is an important therapist activity while the patient is learning about the nature of psychotherapy. As the patient becomes accustomed to the treatment process, however, exploring silences takes priority over merely breaking through them, and the therapist should begin to replace asking the silent patient for associations with a fourth way of responding to patient silence.

4. He can offer observations and interpretations of the patient's silence. When a patient who has had ample opportunity to become acclimated to psychotherapy is extensively silent without displaying a degree of anxiety that appears to call for support, the most productive response to his silence is to focus on it as behavior that needs to be understood. A variety of approaches can be used to introduce such a focus, depending on how fully the therapist understands the silence and how much pressure he feels should be placed on the patient.

To illustrate, in a situation where the therapist has little idea why a patient has fallen silent, he might simply comment, "You haven't said anything for the last several minutes." An observation of this kind puts no pressure on the patient to respond in any particular way, but it does constitute both a suggestion that the silence is worth paying attention to and an invitation for the patient to give some thought to what it might mean. An alternative statement in this situation, one that puts a little more pressure on the patient to reflect on his silence rather than just begin talking again, would be, "I wonder why it is you've stopped talking."

Should the therapist sense some relationship between a patient's silence and what he was saying prior to falling silent, he might then observe, "You've been sitting silently for a while now, and just before you stopped talking you were describing some feelings you have about your mother." Whereas such a response to silence is more directive than merely commenting on the silence without any reference to content, it still leaves it up to the patient to consider whether his silence is in fact saying something about his feelings toward his mother.

In still other situations the therapist may be fairly certain that a patient's silence is the result of upsetting thoughts or feelings generated by the subject under discussion. He can then choose to offer a direct interpretation on the order of, "There's something about talking about your mother that is upsetting to you." In this manner of responding to silence the therapist puts direct pressure on the patient to explore further an apparently difficult subject, and the silence is used as partial evidence for a content interpretation rather than as the focus for an observation.[4]

Handling Patient Discomfort

If psychotherapy is proceeding in productive directions, a patient will inevitably experience moments of psychological discomfort. In fact, if someone presumably engaged in uncovering psychotherapy rolls along session after session in unmitigated good spirits and with no transient indications of being angry, anxious, or depressed, it behooves the therapist to look closely at whether anything constructive is taking place. The consistently comfortable patient is either not being helped to explore anything about himself that he is not already familiar with, or he is rigidly defending against any affective involvement in the treatment process. In such cases the therapist must take steps to help the patient confront new material and relax his defenses, or else the treatment will bounce around ineffectually on the surface and produce little benefit.

When a patient is affectively involved in expanding his self-awareness, on the other hand, he will become upset from time to time, perhaps to his dismay. Having entered psychotherapy in hopes of feeling better, a patient needs time to adjust to the fact that learning about himself may at points make him feel worse. Until he has made this adjustment, there is some risk that his becoming upset may discourage him from talking or even suggest to him that he has little to gain from continuing in the treatment. It is at these points that the therapist must be prepared to recognize and handle patient discomfort.

The most useful way of handling such discomfort in the early stages of psychotherapy is to explain it. For example, the therapist can point out that when a person begins to look at aspects of himself he has not previously been aware of, some uneasiness is to be expected. He can furthermore indicate that it is usually the things that are going well in a person's life that are most pleasant to talk about, whereas if someone wants to explore aspects of his life that trouble him, he can anticipate some discomfort with the subjects that come up.

Such comments serve only to relieve or circumvent patient discomfort, and they should be gradually replaced with interpretation of patient discomfort as therapy progresses. Early in the treatment, however, when the therapist's attention should be focused more on helping the patient talk than on interpreting what he is saying, education in psychotherapy

[4]Research reported by Auld and White (1959) confirms that interpretations of silence do appear effective in enabling silent patients to resume talking.

takes precedence. Not until the patient has come to accept psychological discomfort as an inevitable by-product of his quest for greater self-understanding is he ready to profit from the therapist's shifting from an instructive to an interpretive stance.

It should also be noted that an explanation of patient discomfort offered in the early stages of psychotherapy is not inconsistent with the recommendation in Chapter 6 that the therapist avoid telling the patient in advance that there will be times when he finds talking difficult. Anticipating difficulty before it occurs is different from responding to it after it has appeared, and telling an uncomfortable patient that he is apparently dealing with a subject that is troubling to him does not strip his discomfort of any uniquely personal meaning.

Arranging the Physical Setting

The previous chapter refers to the advantage of seeing a patient in the same room for each session, in order to foster a sense of familiarity with the surroundings and make talking easier. There are additional ways the therapist can arrange the physical setting so as to make his patient comfortable and enhance the likelihood of his talking productively, especially with regard to the style and placing of furniture in the interviewing room.

For one thing, it is important for interviews to take place without any large physical barrier interposed between patient and therapist. A therapist ensconced behind a desk is less likely to be seen as a warm, open, genuine person than one who allows himself to be seen and could even be reached out to and touched. Whether a patient actually experiences or acts on a wish to touch his therapist, there is something much more engaging in talking with someone who *could* be touched than with someone so far removed or so sheltered behind his furniture that he is untouchable. Hence the therapist who uses a desk will do well to have his patients sit at its side, rather than directly across from him, and he might do even better to consider changing to a seating arrangement that puts no furniture between himself and his patients.

As for the style of furniture used, both patient and therapist should obviously be comfortable, and the therapist may justifiably feel that his long hours of sitting call for a particularly comfortable chair. What needs to be avoided, however, is any use of furniture that might convey disadvantageous surplus meaning. Consider, for example, the possible implications of the therapist's settling into a comfortable easy chair while the patient perches on a hard, straight-backed model; or having the patient buried deep in the folds of an over-stuffed chair with the therapist in his regular desk chair towering several inches above him. Although there are no uniform ways in which such features of the seating arrangment can be expected to affect all patients, they are likely to generate feelings that can inhibit productive talking, such as feelings of being in a dependent, babied position, feelings of being judged, feelings of being accorded second-class status, and so forth. Approximate equality of seating, on the other hand, contributes to demonstrating therapist respect for the patient.[5]

ELICITING FURTHER INFORMATION ABOUT THE PATIENT

When a patient has become reasonably acclimated to psychotherapy and able to talk productively in his sessions, the treatment is ready to progress from its initial, preparatory phase to its middle, interpretive phase. What remains initially is for the therapist to fill in the picture he has of the patient's personality structure and dynamics, since he cannot begin to interpret effectively until he has sharpened his earlier working formulations.

Hence this last part of the initial stage of psychotherapy is a time when a therapist should concentrate on eliciting and absorbing further information about his patient. As he becomes increasingly confident that he has a full and accurate grasp of various aspects of the patient's life style, past experiences, and current difficulties, he can gradually shift his focus from gathering information to interpreting it. In the process, the treatment itself will gradually shift from the initial to the middle phase. As discussed earlier, no specific length of time or number of sessions can be specified as necessary or sufficient for this shift to be accomplished; how easily the patient talks about himself and how sensitively the therapist can listen are among the many factors that determine the duration of the initial phase of treatment. However, three helpful tactics the therapist can employ to facilitate sharpening his formulations include probing the patient's personal dimensions, calling attention to what is not stated, and

[5]Although there is some evidence that seating distance can affect the interviewer-interviewee relationship (Boucher, 1972; Lassen, 1973), the effects of placement and style of furniture in the interviewing room on communication in psychotherapy have not been examined in controlled research studies. In the absence of such confirmatory data, however, the face validity of some relationship between the seating arrangement a patient is provided and the feelings he forms about the treatment relationship justify attention to this aspect of the physical setting.

encouraging a balanced expression of thoughts and feelings.

Probing the Patient's Personal Dimensions

One person can learn a great deal about another person simply by finding out how he defines the dimensions of his experience, or, to put it more simply, what things mean to him. Consider, for example, someone who says, "I feel happy today." What does feeling happy mean to this person? In what ways does he experience the feeling of happiness? What kind of things generally tend to make him feel more or less happy? And how does he feel about feeling happy? Is he surprised at feeling happy or is it something he takes for granted? Is happiness a totally pleasant experience for him or one that is bittersweet because he feels underserving or anticipates a rude letdown? The answers to such questions provide a great deal of information about a person, and similar amplification of what other feeling states mean to him can yield a very full picture of his personality style.

In the psychotherapy situation, then, the therapist should listen closely for words that have individual meaning and should encourage the patient to elaborate on them. Adjectives like "happy" and "sad" illustrate only one part of speech that provides a basis for the therapist to probe his patient's personal dimensions in this way. Colorful nouns and verbs offer similar opportunities. When a patient says his wife is "a real shrew," the therapist may have a fairly good idea what he means; however, he should not miss the opportunity to question the meaning of "shrew" (e.g., "What do you mean by a shrew?" or "Your wife is a *shrew?*") and thereby invite the patient to elaborate on his marital relationship and on what there is about his wife that bothers him.

Suppose in responding this patient describes an incident in which he "chewed out" his wife. What does "chewing out" consist of for him, how does he feel about doing it, and is it a common or uncommon thing for him to do? Suppose he contrasts his wife with someone else whom he regards as a more "sympathetic" person. What does being sympathetic consist of in his mind, in what circumstances and from what people in his life is he likely to feel sympathy being extended to him, and how does he usually react to being sympathized with?

The therapist also should not take for granted the meaning of slang expressions or metaphors the patient uses, especially if he is unsure what is meant by them. While taking care not to make a production of every instance in which the patient uses colorful language, so as not to discourage his spontaneity, the therapist should pose enough questions of the "How do you mean?" variety to make sure he understands what is being said, to elicit elaborations of the patient's feelings and attitudes, and to help communicate that the focus in psychotherapy will not be on what things mean in general, but on what they mean specifically to the patient.

Calling Attention to What Is Not Stated

Calling attention to what the patient has not said is generally an effective way to lead an interview without appearing to. It is also a technique that can be adapted successfully to the therapist's aims at various points during the treatment. In the initial assessment phase of psychotherapy a comment like "You haven't said anything about your work" can help to open up a broad and diagnostically important area of discussion. In the middle phase of psychotherapy a similar statement ("You're not saying anything about your work") can be intended not to elicit general information about the patient's work situation but rather to focus on whatever reasons there might be for his omitting to talk about this subject.

At the treatment point being discussed now, when the therapist is bridging the initial and middle phases of psychotherapy, an observation of what is not being said serves an intermediate purpose: its objective is specific information rather than the introduction of a general subject area, but it is still focused on *what* is being said or not said (content) and not yet on *why* (process). For example, the therapist may have learned from earlier interviews a fair amount about the nature of the patient's work and how it relates to his difficulties, and now observe at an appropriate point, "You've been talking about your job but you haven't said anything about how you got into your line of work."

Encouraging a Balanced Expression of Thoughts and Feelings

For psychotherapy to be maximally beneficial, it must be comprised of more than either an emotionally detached discussion of ideas and events or an unbridled outpouring of affect. A person can understand himself and realize his full human potential only if he can both think and feel, and overemphasis on one at the expense of the other will always constitute a characterological handicap. Accordingly, an important way for a therapist to promote the progress of his patients is to help those who are primarily thinkers to feel more and those who are primarily feelers to think more.

The transition period between the initial and middle phase of psychotherapy is a good time to begin helping a patient strike an optimal balance between thinking and feeling. A useful start in this direction is simply for the therapist to comment at appropriate points on which aspect of his experience the patient is omitting to mention: "You've given me a detailed description of what went on in that situation, but you haven't said anything about how you felt"; "You've told me a lot about the feelings you experienced in the situation, but you haven't given much of a description of what actually took place." Comments of this kind elicit additional information the therapist can use to supplement his picture of the patient's personality, and at the same time they subtly convey that both thoughts and feelings need to be recognized and explored. Later in treatment the therapist's observations that thoughts or feelings are not being expressed can serve the same purpose as is generally served by observations of what is not stated—namely, to focus on the process aspects (why) rather than merely the content aspects (what) of the material.

One final point to make in concluding this discussion of tactics for conducting psychotherapy interviews is that the therapist should avoid relying too heavily on any one of them. Whenever the therapist gets in a rut, the treatment loses its spontaneity and becomes a stilted and formal exercise in the patient's eyes. To prevent this from happening the therapist should have in mind a variety of methods for helping a patient talk and for eliciting items of information, and he should vary his use of these methods so as to make them as natural and as unobtrusive as possible.

PART THREE

The Middle Phase of Psychotherapy

CHAPTER 8

Communicating Understanding: Interpretation

The middle phase of psychotherapy is the period during which the therapist concentrates on communicating understanding to his patient. As noted earlier, there is no fixed number of sessions necessary to reach this middle phase of treatment. The therapist may require anywhere from a few sessions to a few months to complete his evaluation and assessment, establish a treatment contract, accustom the patient to therapy, and arrive at a solid grasp of the patient's personality style. Sooner or later, however, the therapist will find himself prepared to shift his efforts from learning about the patient to helping the patient learn about himself.

The main tool for communicating understanding in psychotherapy is interpretation. To use this tool effectively, the therapist needs to be familiar with the nature of the interpretive process and with specific aspects of offering interpretations, including (a) what to interpret, (b) when to interpret, (c) how to interpret, (d) judging the effectiveness of interpretations, and (e) working through. The present chapter examines these aspects of interpretations, and the following three chapters consider ways in which resistances and the treatment relationship influence communication in psychotherapy.

THE NATURE OF INTERPRETATION

An interpretation is a statement that refers to something the patient has said or done in such a way as to identify features of his behavior that he has not been fully aware of. Interpretations are intended to expand the patient's awareness of his thoughts and feelings and thereby enhance his understanding of himself. Accordingly, the desired effect of an interpretation can be seen as helping the patient achieve restructuring of his cognitive and affective experience and reorganization of his behavior patterns.

It is possible to conceive of any therapist intervention as an interpretation, since even the most noncommittal remark can influence what the patient is attending to and result in restructuring. A simple observation ("I notice you've been smoking more than usual today") may direct the patient to an aspect of his behavior—his chain-smoking—that he had not been aware of, and a grunting "Mm-hmm" or even a nod of the head may communicate that what the patient is saying is interesting, important, or commendable. However, such a broad concept of interpretation eliminates any systematic differentiation among kinds of therapist intervention, which muddles matters both for the clinician who aspires to conduct psychotherapy and for the researcher who seeks to study the psychotherapy process.

For both clinical and research purposes it is advantageous to adopt a relatively narrow definition of interpretation, namely, that interpretation is an attempt to expand a patient's conscious awareness of himself by pointing out unconscious determinants of his behavior. This definition of interpretation excludes observations on readily apparent aspects of a patient's behavior ("You're smoking more than usual today"), although such observations may be a prelude to pointing out some unconscious significance of the behavior ("You seem to smoke more when you're feeling angry about something"). Similarly, incidental comments that are not intended to expand a patient's self-awareness should not be considered interpretations, even though they may have some interpretive effect, in the same way that psychotherapy is defined by what the therapist is attempting to do, not by whatever happens to have a psychotherapeutic effect (see Chap. 1).

To distinguish further between interpretations and other kinds of therapist interventions, it is useful to employ the following scheme for classifying five therapist behaviors in increasing order of their potential impact on the patient:

1. *Questions.* The simplest and most superficial way for the therapist to intervene is by asking questions about the patient and his experiences. Although direct questioning may elicit useful information and also help the therapist vary his interview style, it is not a particularly productive technique in the psychotherapy situation, as is noted in the preceding chapter.

2. *Clarifications.* Clarifications are statements intended to emphasize

some aspect of the patient's manifest productions. Often such an emphasis is achieved simply by inviting further attention to what the patient has been saying, thereby implying its possible importance ("I wonder if you could tell me something more about that"; "Could you go over that incident again so I can be sure I have a clear picture of what it was like for you?"). At other times clarification consists of recapitulating the patient's remarks, perhaps in somewhat different language but without any elaboration or attempt to draw inferences ("As I hear it, then, you were feeling fine all the time you were watching the movie up to the point when someone sat down in the seat next to you, and then you began to feel so nervous and edgy that you had to leave the theater"). Either way, a clarification does not present the patient with any ideas or possibilities that are not already in his conscious awareness, although it may initiate a sequence of interventions that leads to such new material.

3. *Exclamations.* Exclamations are brief therapist utterances that let the patient know he is being listened to and encourage him to continue talking. Like clarifications, exclamations lend emphasis to what the patient is saying, even when they consist of no more than "Mm-hmm" or "I see."[1] Moreso than clarifications, however, exclamations convey endorsement of the patient's comments as well as interest in them. Remarks like "Mm-hmm" and "I see" imply not only "I'm listening" and "I understand," but also "I agree" and "I approve." Exclamations can of course be disapproving as well as approving, as in "Uh-uh" or "No way." However, should the therapist intend to challenge or disagree with what the patient is saying, his remarks, no matter now brief, will have more in common with confrontations than with exclamations, which are meant to be at least relatively noncommittal.

4. *Confrontations.* In contrast to clarifications and exclamations, both of which address a patient's manifest productions, confrontations call attention to something the patient could be talking about but is not. By observing that the patient has described an incident without mentioning any of his feelings about it, for example, or that the incident is notably similar to some previous episodes in his life, or that he has been drumming his fingers incessantly while relating the incident, the therapist focuses on some potentially significant data that might otherwise have gone unnoticed.

[1]Beginning with work by Greenspoon (1955), numerous studies have demonstrated that minimal therapist exclamations can influence a patient's verbal behavior and reinforce his selective attention to some subjects rather than others. Research in this area is reviewed by Kanfer (1968), Krasner (1965), Matarazzo et al. (1965), Matarazzo et al. (1968), Matarazzo and Wiens (1972), Salzinger (1959), Williams (1964), and Williams and Blanton (1968).

Although confrontations bring new material to the patient's attention, they refer to observable events that should be obvious to the patient once they are pointed out. The therapist may sometimes fail to keep his facts straight, if, for example, he misjudges the similarity of a current incident in the patient's life to experiences in his past. With allowances for therapist error, however, confrontations are meant to be factual statements of how things are or how they were, not hypotheses about how they could be or might have been. Because confrontations refer to observable facts of which the patient can readily become aware, they address the level of *preconscious* awareness. They go beyond what the patient is immediately attending to but not so far as to introduce possibilities from his unconscious.

5. *Interpretations.* An interpretation calls attention to some aspect of the patient or his behavior of which he is not fully aware or cannot immediately become aware. In contrast to other therapist interventions, interpretations (a) deal with unconscious material rather than manifest productions, (b) seek to explain rather than merely describe the patient's behavior, and (c) consist of inferences, probabilities, and alternative hypotheses rather than observations, facts, and certainties.

Research studies lend support to the utility of defining interpretations in this relatively narrow way so as to distinguish them from such other therapist interventions as questions, clarifications, exclamations, and confrontations. Of particular note in this regard is an investigation reported by Garduk and Haggard (1972), who operationally defined interpretation as consisting of (a) one or more specific connections suggested by the therapist between the patient's thoughts, feelings, behaviors, dreams, other phenomena, and (b) the inclusion in these connections of reference to nonmanifest material, not just simple similarities or juxtapositions (p.17). In a detailed analysis of patient-therapist interactions in ongoing psychotherapy, Garduk and Haggard identified the following differential effects between interpretation and any other kind of therapist intervention:

1. Patient reaction times are longer following interpretations than following noninterpretive interventions.
2. Patients display less verbal activity and more silence in response to interpretations than in response to noninterpretive interventions.
3. Patients manifest more affect following interpretations than following noninterpretive interventions.
4. Patients manifest more oppositional and defensive associations in

response to interpretations than in response to noninterpretive interventions.

5. Patients give more indications of understanding (e.g., "Yes, I can understand that") and insight (e.g., "I wouldn't have thought of that but I recognize it now") following interpretations than following noninterpretations.

6. Patients deal with more transference-related material following interpretations than following noninterpretations.

Garduk and Haggard account for some of their findings by pointing out that interpretations are by nature more complicated to deal with than noninterpretations: "It seems logical that it would take longer to 'process'—to receive, to think about, to understand, to integrate, and to react to—interventions that, by definition, present something new and may be quite intricate" (p. 42). Hence, they continue, patients would be expected to respond more slowly and with more silence to interpretations than to other therapist interventions. In addition to providing construct validity for the distincfion between interpretations and noninterpretive interventions, the Garduk and Haggard research has implications for when interpretations should be offered and will be referred to later in this context.

In concluding this section, it is important to identify two additional characteristics of interpretation that make them difficult for patients to respond to. First, because interpretations convey something new to a person about himself or his behavior, they take something away from his previous frame of reference. To entertain new ways of thinking, feeling, or acting, a person must contemplate giving up old ways; the cognitive, affective, or behavioral restructuring toward which interpretation aims can be achieved only through the modification of existing structures. Asking a person to give up aspects of his psychic functioning that he is familiar with and accustomed to, even if they constitute demonstrably maladaptive or self-defeating patterns of behavior, is asking him to endure a sense of loss. With this point in mind, Tarachow (1963, p. 20) posits that the principal consequence of interpretation is object loss and that correct interpretations are therefore likely to be followed by momentary mild depression.

Second, because interpretations imply that the patient's current mode of doing or looking at things is not as effective or as realistic as it might be, they always constitute an attack. Suggesting to a person that there are alternative ways for him to think, feel, or act, and furthermore that these alternatives are likely to direct him toward a richer and more rewarding life, tacitly conveys that there is something bad, wrong, or misguided in how he has been living. Hence even a mild interpretation challenges the patient's integrity and deflates his self-esteem, and it thereby constitutes an attack against which he may feel a need to defend himself.

WHAT TO INTERPRET

In a typical psychotherapy session the therapist will form many more hypotheses about the meaning of his patient's thoughts, feelings, and actions than he can or should express. Time is never sufficient to interpret every pertinent feature of an interview, and some priorities are therefore necessary to guide the therapist in deciding what kinds of patient behavior should be interpreted when they occur.

Because interpretations are intended to communicate understanding, a first step in establishing priorities for what to interpret is to recognize that increased self-understanding is not uniformly beneficial across all areas of a person's life. Consider, for example, an attorney who is successful and happy in his work, even though he is not fully aware of why he chose a career in law, and who has come for help because he is depressed about a perceived or actual decline in sexual potency. Although expanded self-awareness concerning his career choice might be of some interest to him, it would have minimal impact on his life style and feeling of well-being, whereas learning more about his sexual attitudes may make considerable difference in how he feels and acts. On the other hand, if this attorney has sought help not because he is concerned about sexuality but because he feels frustrated and unfulfilled in the practice of law, the benefit he derives from increased self-understanding is likely to be much greater in the area of occupational choice than in the area of sexual behavior.

These hypothetical instances identify a general principle that should govern decisions about what to interpret: interpretations should focus on those aspects of a patient's behavior that are causing him difficulty. To this end, the therapist should constantly ask himself the following three interrelated questions as he listens to his patient and thinks about offering interpretations:

1. What is making the patient anxious? Anxiety is always present in people in the form of *trait* or characterological anxiety, which constitutes a person's general anxiety level and his disposition to experience anxiety in various kinds of situations. In addition, all people experience *state* or

situational anxiety from time to time when life events threaten them psychologically. Trait anxiety results from unresolved psychological conflicts and state anxiety reflects an irrational anticipation of dire consequences; both are obviously important subjects for interpretations intended to focus on sources of difficulty in a person's life.[2]

2. What is the patient handling ineffectively? As a result of anxiety or faulty learning people sometimes handle aspects of their life in ways that are neither as satisfying nor as self-fulfilling as they could be. Such ineffectiveness usually generates additional anxiety that in turn leads to even further ineffectiveness. Interpretations addressed to ineffective coping strategies can help the patient replace them with more rewarding ways of handling his experiences and at the same time reduce the likelihood of his becoming anxious.

3. What is the patient perceiving in a distorted fashion? Although clinicians tend at times to regard distorted perceptual functioning as associated only with severe disturbance, various needs and attitudes cause all people to misperceive themselves and their environment from time to time.[3] When a person is misperceiving the nature and significance of his experiences, he is particularly likely to encounter psychological difficulties and to handle them ineffectively. Hence what a patient is perceiving in a distorted fashion provides a third major subject area for interpretation.

To summarize this general principle, then, interpretations should focus on sources of difficulty in the patient's life as they become apparent in what is unusual, ineffective, inappropriate, contradictory, irrational, self-defeating, or anxiety-arousing in his actions, thoughts, and feelings. In addition to this general principle, the therapist's selection of what apparent sources of difficulty to interpret and what to let pass can be guided by two priorities, which if followed contribute to a systematic interpretive effort and maximum patient self-understanding: (a) interpretation of *defense* should take precedence over interpretation of *conflict,* and (b) interpretation of *process* should take precedence over interpretation of *content.*

[2]For a detailed analysis of the important distinction between state and trait anxiety the reader should consult the work of Spielberger (1966, 1971).

[3]The observations that a person's needs can influence what he perceives, even to the extent of grossly distorted perceptions that serve as a defense against anxiety, have rested on solid empirical grounds since the research work of Bruner and Goodman (1947), Eriksen (1951), and McGinnies (1949). Contributions by Blake and Ramsey (1951), Solley and Murphy (1960), and Wolitsky and Wachtel (1972) provide a good introduction to study of this phenomenon.

Conflict and Defense

As described in Chapter 4, unresolved conflicts tend to generate anxiety that in turn evokes various defenses against anxiety. Whenever a person is motivated more by needs to avoid anxiety than by pursuit of self-fulfillment, he becomes likely to engage in ineffective and unrewarding behavior. Hence both the nature of underlying conflicts and the defenses they evoke are potential sources of difficulty in a person's life that bear interpreting in psychotherapy.

In terms of priority, however, it is usually advantageous to interpret a patient's defenses against anxiety before attempting to interpret the conflicts that are giving rise to his anxiety. If interpretations of underlying conflicts and sources of anxiety are offered before a person has been helped to recognize and modify his defensive style, they tend to be integrated within his existing defensive framework and to add little to his self-understanding. On the other hand,the more a person has previously been helped to identify and alter how he uses defenses, the more likely he is to learn something from conflict interpretations rather than ward them off with habitual defenses against anxiety.

For example, a patient whose preference runs to ideational defenses may thoughtfully mull over an interpretation but intellectualize it into an abstract personality description devoid of personal significance. The following response was made by a college student whose therapist had just told him that his failing grades were probably related to fears of surpassing his high school-educated father:

> Yes, Doctor, I think that's a very good point. I can easily see how somebody who is worried or guilty about being more successful than his father might end up not working to capacity in school. It makes good sense, and I can think of a number of fellows I know who it probably applies to.

The conflict interpretation made in this instance had not been preceded by adequate attention to the patient's intellectual defensive style, and the result was the above sterile intellectualization. The patient praises the therapist's acuity, comments on how "somebody" might feel, and claims increased understanding of the behavior of other people. Absent from the response are any emotional reactions or relevant associations to indicate that the interpretation has had some uniquely personal impact on him. Instead, the anxiety that might accompany such emotions or associations is warded off by an intellectualization of the interpretation, and no increment in self-understanding takes place.

To illustrate further what can happen when conflict is interpreted before defense, consider how this same college student might have responded to the same interpretation if his preference were for repressive defenses:

I don't see how that could be. I know my father wants only the best for me, so I don't have to worry about his feelings, and I know I've never been afraid of doing well. You must be on the wrong track.

Assuming that the therapist is not on the wrong track, the above response demonstrates characteristic uses of repression and denial to avoid the anxiety an interpretation might stir up. Nothing is wrong with my father or me (denial), the response indicates, and furthermore the whole thing is not worth looking into (repression). Interestingly, when a patient is responding to a conflict interpretation defensively, it may make little difference whether the interpretation is correct. Just the fact that the therapist is attempting to probe beneath the surface is sufficiently anxiety-provoking to lead an ideational patient to endorse intellectualized versions of interpretations and a repressing patient to discount interpretations completely, regardless of whether they are correct.

Whatever a person's preferred defenses may be, he continues to use them to ward off possible sources of anxiety until he has learned to do otherwise. Such learning is fostered by helping the patient recognize behavior patterns by which he typically seeks to protect himself against anxiety. Defenses do not promptly disappear on being interpreted, never again to characterize the person's behavior or hamper his adjustment. Identified and understood, however, defenses become more subject than before to voluntary control and hence more flexible and adaptive in how they are employed. As a patient in psychotherapy gains control over his defenses, he becomes more capable of relaxing or suspending them in the face of conflict interpretations, and it is for this reason that interpretations of underlying concerns are more likely to enhance self-understanding if they follow, rather than precede, relevant interpretations of defense.[4]

Situational and Characterological Defensive Operations. To recognize

[4]The modification of defenses subsequent to their being interpreted, with particular respect to their coming increasingly under voluntary control, is elaborated by Gill (1963), Kris (1954), Lichtenberg and Slap (1972), Loewenstein (1954), and Weiss (1967). A recent paper by Sampson et al. (1972) provides a good illustration of the striking correspondence often found between relaxation of a patient's defenses and the emergence of related concerns that he had previously been unable to verbalize.

defensive behavior in order to assign it priority for interpretations, it is helpful to listen carefully for and differentiate between manifestations of *situational* and *characterological* defensive operations. Situational defensive operations consist of specific steps a person takes to reduce his felt anxiety in threatening circumstances (secondary prevention), whereas characterological defensive operations comprise the ways a person generally conducts his life so as to minimize the likelihood of his becoming anxious (primary prevention).

Situational defensive operations typically become apparent in psychotherapy when patients are describing their response to anxiety-provoking events outside of the treatment or are reacting to anxiety-provoking aspects of the ongoing interview. For example, a patient may report developing a headache and having to leave work after being criticized by his boss, or he may tell the therapist he is pressed for time and wants to end his session early. Both statements suggest situational defense by leaving the field, and an appropriate interpretation in either case might be, "Your way of handling that (this) situation was (is) apparently to run away from it."

Characterological defensive operations become evident in the attitudes, values, and preferred behavior patterns that make the patient the kind of person he is. In selecting subjects for interpretations, however, it is important to distinguish characterological defenses from the broader category of characterological style. Some of the attitudes, values, and preferred behaviors that make someone the kind of person he is are defensive operations, generated by or serving to ward off anxiety. Other values, attitudes, and preferred behaviors are positively motivated and self-fulfilling, neither resulting from nor directed against anxiety. Interpretation involving characterological style should be focused for the most part on those aspects of the patient's style with which he is defending against anxiety, at the expense of self-fulfillment, rather than those with which he is effectively promoting his best interests. The following therapist statements, each of which refers to a fairly common pattern of self-defeating behavior observed in people seeking psychological help, illustrate the form that interpretations of characterological defensive operations are likely to take:

You apparently try to organize everything in your life down to the last detail.

You seem to have a tendency to do or say whatever comes into your mind, without taking much time to think over the consequences.

Whenever you start to get into a close relationship with someone, you find some reason for breaking it off.

When something goes wrong, your first tendency is to blame yourself and feel that the fault lies with your not being as good a person as you should be.

Your usual way of deciding what to do in a situation seems to be based on what you think other people would like you to do, rather than on what you yourself would really like to do.

The Particular Importance of Interpreting Characterological Defensive Operations. Dynamic psychotherapy as originally formulated by Freud concentrated on tracing maladaptive aspects of current behavior to specific sources of anxiety lying deep in the unconscious and related to events occurring early in life. Subsequent to the influence of Wilhelm Reich's (1933) work on character analysis and Anna Freud's (1936) contributions on ego mechanisms, however, the emphasis on origins of conflict became balanced by an equal or even greater emphasis on the handling of conflict. Reich explained the necessity of characterological interpretations ("the loosening of the character armor") as a prelude to interpretations of underlying conflicts, while Anna Freud described how specific defense mechanisms, if unchallenged by the therapist, can prevent the patient from coming directly to grips with his underlying concerns. As one result of their work, it is now generally recognized that effective interpretation of characterological defensive operations can by itself bring psychotherapy to a satisfactory conclusion in many cases.[5]

To elaborate this point, it may not always be possible or necessary to help a patient understand the early origins as well as the nature of his personality style. In the first place, because the conflicts that lead to the emergence of characterological defenses have usually occurred in the developmental years, an adult may have difficulty recapturing them in vivid detail. The more intensive psychotherapy is and the longer it lasts, the more likely the patient is to reexperience early life events that placed him in conflict, made him anxious, and influenced his choice of defensive operations. But psychotherapy should be conducted with an eye to the point of diminishing returns, when further uncovering does not appear to promise sufficient increments in self-understanding and self-satisfaction to justify the effort it would require. At such a point patient and therapist

[5]It is interesting to note that, in a recent survey in which 90 analysts were asked "What do you consider the three most important technical advances in psychoanalysis during the past 30 years?", the item most frequently mentioned was "ego analysis," which consists of interpretations focused on defensive operations both as symptoms and as character traits (Hofling & Meyers, 1972). The history of the change from an id-emphasis to an ego-emphasis in psychoanalysis is recounted by Lorand (1972–1973).

may concur that termination rather than further probing will best serve the patient's interests.

Second, conflicts originating in early experiences may be so remote from a patient's current concerns and life style as to have little impact in the present, even if he is able to become aware of them. Once a characterological pattern of defensive operations has become established and persisted over a number of years, it tends to become autonomous and provides its own rewards, so that reexperiencing and reworking the events that evoked it exerts little influence on current behavior, defensive or otherwise.[6]

On the other hand, being able to grasp how he is using defensive operations to cope with his experience has considerable potential for helping a person modify his defensiveness and increase the effectiveness of his coping style. Hence the interpretation of defense can constitute a significant end as well as a means to an end in psychotherapy.

Content and Process

The content of a psychotherapy interview consists of *what* the patient is saying; the process refers to *how* and *why* he is saying what he is and why he is *not* saying something else. Accordingly, content interpretations typically focus on connections between current concerns and events outside of the psychotherapy session, whereas process interpretations focus on connections between current concerns and ongoing behavior in the interview. Content interpretations establish continuity between what a person is at the moment and what he has been and might be, whereas process interpretations help a patient see his personality style currently in action. Although both kinds of interpretation serve important functions in psychotherapy, there are two reasons for favoring process over content interpretations when both are equally compelling.

First, process interpretations are generally more vivid and incisive than content interpretations, since they are addressed to currently observable behavior rather than to recollected or reported events. Second, whereas an interpretable item of content will probably be mentioned again by the patient or can be reintroduced by the therapist,

[6] The possibility that cumulative life experiences can minimize or transcend the importance of connections between characterological defenses and the conflicts that engendered them relates closely to Gordon Allport's (1937) concept ot the "functional autonomy of motives." Allport's point, subsequently subscribed to by most behavioral scientists, was simply that a person's behavior can become an end or a goal in itself, independently of the reasons for which it was originally engaged in.

interpretable aspects of process are one-shot affairs that rarely recur in exactly the same fashion. This means that missed opportunities to interpret sources of difficulty apparent in content can usually be recouped, but a lost occasion to make constructive use of ongoing process is lost for good.

To distinguish process from content in psychotherapy interviews, the therapist needs to observe his patient's behavior closely. With respect to how the patient is talking, for example, is he stammering, squirming, perspiring, or in some other way manifesting more anxiety than he is admitting to, or is he instead being more casual or flippant than seems consistent with the seriousness of what he is saying? With respect to why the patient is saying what he is, does he appear more concerned with making some kind of impression on the therapist than with expressing things that trouble him, or is there perhaps something about the sequence of the subjects he is talking about that seems to say more about his underlying concerns than the subjects themselves? Whenever the answer to such questions is in the affirmative, an interpretation addressed to process rather than content may be indicated.

Finally, with respect to the process underlying why the patient is *not* saying something, it is helpful to identify four content alternatives in psychotherapy interviews: (a) the patient can talk about relatively current events ("Yesterday I . . .") or relatively remote events ("When I was much younger I . . ."); (b) he can talk about himself in the abstract ("I have a bad temper") or in reference to actual behavior ("This morning I lost my temper"); (c) he can talk about his life independently of the treatment or in specific reference to the role of the therapy and the therapist in his life; and (d) he can report thoughts or he can express feelings. Repeated focus on any one of these pairs of content alternatives to the exclusion of the other is an aspect of the psychotherapy process that should be interpreted when it occurs.

Obviously, many of these process aspects of a patient's behavior in psychotherapy involve elements of resistance and transference. As noted in Chapter 4, resistance is a paradoxical reluctance on the part of the patient to participate in the treatment, and transference refers to feelings and attitudes that patients develop toward their therapist. Resistance and transference frequently account for a patient's difficulty in talking, his attempts to impress the therapist, and his emphasis on some subjects to the exclusion of others. Hence interpretations of resistance and transference can be very productive in opening up lines of communication and, like process interpretations in general, they usually take precedence over interpretations of content.

Despite their key role in the treatment process, however, resistance and transference still should be interpreted selectively, when they constitute a source of difficulty for the patient. This means that indications of resistance and transference do not always call for an interpretation, but only when they become so marked or repetitive as to interfere with communication. More is said on this point in Chapters 9 and 10. For the present, it is relevant to introduce one additional concept that can help the therapist decide whether to call attention to an aspect of the psychotherapy process, namely, the distinction between *near derivatives* and *remote derivatives*.

A near derivative is an instance of behavior that is relatively clearly and closely tied to some underlying concern it reflects, whereas a remote derivative consists of behavior that is relatively distant in time and in psychological relatedness from conflicts that have engendered it.[7] For the same reasons that interpretations of defense and process take precedence over interpretations of conflict and content, interpretations of near derivatives are more likely to be productive than interpretations of remote derivatives—they are more vividly and easily grasped by the patient, they bear more directly on his current concerns, and they initiate a potential sequence of interpretations (from near derivatives to remote derivatives) that cannot readily be initiated in the opposite direction (from remote to near derivatives).

To illustrate the distinction between near and remote derivatives, suppose that a female patient is telling a male therapist about being envious of her more attractive sister and is sitting with her legs spread apart. Her posture could conceivably be a sexual overture reflecting transference feelings of wanting to love or be loved by the therapist. In the absence of strong supporting evidence for such transference feelings, however, her way of sitting is a remote derivative: there is neither a previous basis for connecting her open legs with love for the therapist, nor does the content of what she is saying (envy of her sister) provide much current basis for a transference interpretation of her posture. Some tortuous reasoning could construct such a basis (e.g., if it were speculated that her concern about being less attractive than her sister means she

[7]Classical psychoanalytic theory suggests that repressed material tends to seek outlets in the form of events that permit some discharge of energy, and that the displacement of energy in this way produces a wide variety of *derivatives*, including dreams, daydreams, screen memories, and neurotic symptoms (see Fenichel, 1945a, pp. 148–150, 193–194). Whether one embraces the psychoanalytic model of energy flow, the concept of some behavior being derived from and indirectly expressing conflict is very useful in deciding what to interpret in psychotherapy, especially if distinctions are made between near and remote derivatives.

wants to prove she can attract men which means that she wants the therapist to be attracted to her), but complex chains of logic dangling from remote derivatives seldom end in useful interpretations. They are subject to multiple errors of inference, because of the multiple suppositions they involve, and even if correct they may be too complex for the patient to wade through without losing his sense of personal engagement.

In contrast, suppose this same woman sitting with her legs apart is saying, "I enjoy talking with you so much I wish I could see you every day." Although a wish for more therapist time can mean many things, such as a felt need for additional help or a general belief that the more therapy the better, an explicit statement like "I enjoy talking with you so much I wish I could see you every day" is almost certain to reflect strong positive transference feelings. In addition, the manifest content of the statement, with its "I-you" emphasis, refers directly to the patient-therapist relationship. Hence, because of its clear connection to underlying feelings toward the therapist and its manifest relevance to the nature of these feelings, this expressed wish for additional sessions would constitute a near derivative and lend itself well to being interpreted. In the course of using this near derivative (the patient's expressed wish to see the therapist every day) as a basis for exploring possible feelings of wanting to love and be loved by the therapist, there might be opportunities to allude to the remote derivative (her inviting posture) as related or supportive evidence. Beginning with the remote derivative, however, would be to lead from weakness (a less certain connection) rather than from available strength (the more certain connection).

Lest this example suggests that what a patient *does* will always be a remote derivative in relation to what he *says*, consider the following situation: a male patient stalks into the office for his session, slams the door, drops heavily into his chair banging it against the wall behind him, crosses his legs with a kick to the therapist's desk, drops an ashtray on the floor, and then scowls and says, "I've been having dreams about beating people up." Such behavior leaves little room for doubt that the patient is angry at his therapist, and in this case what has been said, not the accompanying behavior, constitutes the relatively remote derivative. The patient's comment reflects an aggressive theme, but it concerns dreaming rather than waking fantasy and refers to "people" in general. On the other hand, what he is actually doing—breaking up the therapist's office—approaches being an assault on the therapist himself and constitutes a relatively near derivative of probable negative transference feelings. In light of his behavior, an appropriate interpretive response to the patient's statement "I've been having dreams about beating people up" might well be "It looks like you're beating me up right now."[8]

Distinguishing between near and remote derivatives can help the therapist avoid becoming sidetracked by process details, which at times are given more attention than they merit. Such process details in this regard often involve the kinds of behavior described by Freud (1901) in *The Psychopathology of Everyday Life*, including forgetting, slips of the tongue, mistakes in reading and writing, and various types of accidental behavior and "erroneously carried-out actions." Because of its dramatic flair and apparent simplicity, interpreting slips and errors has enjoyed great vogue among some therapists and many self-styled amateur analysts, including use as a parlor game or form of one-upmanship. In fact, however, even slips and errors whose meaning is transparently clear tend to be remote derivatives that rarely provide prime subjects for interpretation in psychotherapy.

For example, consider a female patient who "accidentally" refers to her husband as her father ("I said to my father just the other night—er, I mean my *husband* of course—that we should take a vacation") or who repetitively "forgets" her purse or umbrella in the therapist's office. The therapist may have little doubt that the first behavior reflects some unresolved paternal attachment and the second some longing for a closer patient-therapist relationship. Despite the certainty of such connections to the therapist, however, for the patient they involve remote derivatives: the chain of evidence linking the overt behavior to the underlying wish it indirectly expresses is long, complex, and only loosely anchored in the content of what the patient is saying.

In contrast, suppose that in the first of the above examples the patient, instead of talking about taking a vacation, is describing some problem in her marriage. Suppose further that these problems appear to derive from

[8]As derivatives, dreams themselves can vary in how closely they are related to the thoughts and feelings that elicit them. Whether a dream as experienced or reported by a patient in psychotherapy is a relatively near or relatively remote derivative will depend on the extent to which the "dream work," consisting of condensation, displacement, symbolization, and secondary revision (see Freud, 1900, Chap. VI), has intervened between the latent and manifest content of the dream. The less disguised the meaning of a dream, the more suitable it is for interpretation in psychotherapy. Yet Freud (1911) cautioned that the therapist should not become so preoccupied with dreams that he loses sight of the patient's current thoughts and emotions Once undertaken, dream interpretation proceeds according to the same general principles of interpretation being outlined in the present chapter. The technique of utilizing dream material in psychotherapy is elaborated by Bonime (1962), Freud (1923), Fromm-Reichmann (1950, pp. 161–175), Gutheil (1951), and Wolberg (1967, pp. 633–654).

her acting more like a child than a wife, and suppose that her slip occurs in this context ("I keep telling my father—I mean my husband—that he expects too much of me"). She then would be describing a near and readily interpretable derivative of an unresolved attachment to her father (a wish to have her husband baby her or, at a deeper level, perhaps a wish to receive paternal love through the person of her husband), and the remote derivative included in her statement (the husband-father slip) could be adduced secondarily as evidence to support such an interpretation.

To summarize this point, a patient's slips and errors, together with his gestures, mannerisms, posture, and other peripheral interview behaviors, are usually too distant from the underlying concerns they reflect and too discontinuous with the content of the interview to be interpreted fruitfully. Furthermore, repetitive focusing on such process details can make a patient so self-conscious and preoccupied with observing himself that he loses the capacity to report his thoughts and feelings spontaneously. Should a detail of the psychotherapy process seem to provide the only available leverage for opening up an area of concern that is being strongly resisted, an interpretation may be called for. By and large, however, process details are useful mainly as supporting evidence for other interpretations and should be assigned low priority for interpretation in their own right.[9]

WHEN TO INTERPRET

Deciding when to offer interpretations is primarily a matter of attention to their *timing* and *dosage*. As introduced earlier in this chapter, timing pertains to the specific moment when interpretation is made and dosage to the number of interpretations being made. Because interpretations challenge a patient's existing ways of doing or looking at things, and because they often dredge up unwelcome thoughts and feelings, they always evoke some defensiveness. With proper timing and dosage, however, it is possible to minimize a patient's aversion to interpretations and promote his openness to learning from them.

[9]Fromm-Reichmann (1950, pp. 154–157) elaborates further on the reasons why process details in psychotherapy should be interpreted conservatively, if at all. However, for the reader to expand his understanding of process behavior and its potential role in treatment, he should consult contributions by Deutsch (1947, 1966), Ekman and Friesen (1968), Ekman et al. (1972), Feldman (1959), and Mahl (1968).

Timing of Interpretations

The best time to make an interpretation is when the patient is prepared to receive it and the therapist is prepared to offer it. For the patient to be prepared to receive an interpretation, he should have a level of awareness bordering closely on the content of what is to be interpreted, and he should be in a reasonably positive frame of mind regarding the therapist and the treatment process. For the therapist to be prepared to offer an interpretation, he should be reasonably certain that the interpretation is accurate and that there are adequate data to document it.

Patient Level Of Awareness. Interpretations are most useful in communicating understanding when the patient is verging on becoming aware of them and is just one step away from full awareness. This does not mean that the therapist sits passively waiting for the patient to work himself into psychological proximity to an underlying concern, which can then be safely interpreted. Rather, the therapist's task is to use questions, clarifications, and confrontations as part of an interpretive sequence that leads up to an interpretation by gradually bringing the patient into near-awareness of some previously unrecognized aspect of himself or his behavior.

Interpretations made before a patient has been helped to approach awareness of them have negligible prospects for enhancing his self-understanding. Learning new things about oneself requires experiencing them as personally meaningful, not just having them pointed out, and it is difficult for a person to experience as personally meaningful anything that is remote from his conscious awareness. Freud (1910a, p. 225) pointed out in this regard that if knowledge about the unconscious were important in its own right, it would be sufficient for a patient to read books or go to lectures, and he further observed that descriptions of the unconscious have as much influence on neurotic symptoms as "a distribution of menu-cards in a time of famine has upon hunger." It is not psychological knowledge in the abstract, but learning about uniquely personal aspects of underlying concerns and experiencing them as relevant to one's past and current behavior, that enhances self-understanding. For interpretations to facilitate such learning and experiencing, they must be deferred until the matters they involve have been brought to a point close to the patient's awareness.

In addition to being of limited usefulness, interpretations offered before the patient is prepared to receive them may also mobilize resistance to the treatment process. Like a plunge into cold water, inter-interpretations are potentially bracing but also nerve-jangling, and careful preparation of the patient for an interpretation readies him for the icy waters with a sequence of progressively cooler immersions. Without having been thus prepared, the patient is likely to clamber straight out of the water and resent the therapist's having dumped him in without warning. Hence premature interpretations not only fail to promote self-understanding but also foster negative feelings toward the treatment process and toward the therapist.

Such negative consequences of a premature interpretation are almost inevitable if the therapist compounds his error by insisting that the patient come to grips with it. Therapists sometimes become overly impressed with their omniscience and with the staggering significance of their insights, and they then may fall prone to the erroneous convictions that (a) it is essential for the patient to accept and integrate every interpretation they make and that (b) any disinterest or disagreement on the patient's part reflects resistance rather than their having offered an incorrect or poorly timed interpretation. As important as it is for the therapist to recognize and respond to resistance when it occurs, it is equally important for him to guard against holding his patient responsible for every interpretive sequence that goes awry. The infallible therapist does not exist, and a therapist with presumptions to such status will frequently fail to sustain a positive working relationship with his patients.

Premature interpretations have the further disadvantage of diluting the impact the interpretation might have had later on, when the patient was prepared to receive it. Interpretations are more likely to be effective when they state fresh ideas than when they repeat possibilities that have previously been considered and found wanting. Such reduced effectiveness of an accurate interpretation becomes particularly likely when a premature presentation has mobilized strong defenses against it. In this sense premature interpretations are analogous to opening fire at too great a distance to hit anything; by the time the range has been closed the quarry has had sufficient notice to take evasive action. For an accurate interpretation to have its full impact on a patient who is prepared to receive it, it should not come compromised by prior fittings in which it has been tried on for size and found wanting.

Patient Frame of Mind. With regard to the patient's frame of mind, interpretations communicate best when a patient is in a state of relatively low resistance to the treatment process and has a relatively positive regard for the therapist. Resistance is a means of defending against the anxiety stirred up by psychotherapy, and a resistant patient has little tolerance for the additional anxiety interpretations generate. Resistance and receptivity are mutually exclusive, since a patient who is wrestling with concerns about participating in the treatment does not have an open mind for learning more about himself as a person. Hence interpretations during periods of marked resistance should be limited to interpretations of the resistance itself and aimed at helping the patient understand and resolve his aversive reaction to the treatment process.

Positive regard for the therapist, like low resistance to therapy, creates a climate of receptivity to interpretations. It is when a patient feels that his therapist respects him and is interested in helping him that he is most likely to consider an interpretation carefully, even if it causes him anxiety or embarrassment. Should the patient have reservations about how much his therapist respects him or is devoted to helping him, he will be inclined to take interpretations as criticisms and to respond to them defensively rather than open-mindedly.

It should be stressed, however, that receptivity to the therapist's interpretations consists only of trusting him and appreciating his efforts, not of liking or loving him. Feelings of liking or loving the therapist are aspects of positive transference that develop during the middle phase of treatment, and it is neither necessary nor advisable to delay offering interpretations until this point. The patient does not need to like his therapist in order to tolerate having him interpret his behavior; he needs only to feel that the therapist genuinely respects his integrity and is sincerely trying to be of help to him. Furthermore, because interpretations provide concrete evidence of the therapist's work on his patient's behalf, they can aid in building and sustaining positive patient regard. Hence, not only should interpretations be timed to coincide with periods of positive attitudes toward the therapist, but they should also be begun in the therapy as soon as such a positive feeling tone has begun to emerge, as a means of fostering an effective treatment relationship and facilitating receptivity to subsequent interpretations.

Therapist Certainty. Turning next to the preparation of the therapist, an interpretation will be well-timed when the therapist is reasonably certain of its accuracy and has adequate evidence to document it. The value of an accurate interpretation is self-evident: it helps the patient learn something new about himself, and it demonstrates that the therapist is capable of understanding him. Incorrect interpretations, on the other hand, because they lack congruence with the nature of the patient's past and current experiences, add little to his self-knowledge and give him cause to question the therapist's capacity to understand and help him.

The potential disadvantage of inaccurate interpretations does not mean that the therapist must refrain from making any interpretive statements until he is absolutely certain of their validity. What it does mean is that more certain interpretations should be favored over less certain ones and that interpretations should be couched in language commensurate with the certainty they command. An interpretation that the therapist has every reason to believe is correct might be introduced with "It seems clear now that you. . . ."; given some expectation but less certainty that an interpretation is accurate, he could begin with "It may be that . . .", or "It seems to me that . . .", or "Could it be that . . . ?"; should he wish to explore a hunch, based only on suggestive evidence, the therapist might start with "Is there any possibility that . . . ?" or "I just had a thought I want to check out with you."

It should be noted that some clinicians take exception to the importance of accurate interpretation. Hobbs (1962), for example, argues that the therapeutic relationship itself, in which the patient learns to be close to another person without getting hurt, is a much more significant source of gain in psychotherapy than increased self-understanding. Hence, concludes Hobbs, "The therapist does not have to be right; he mainly has to be convincing" (p. 742). As summarized by Roback (1972, 1974), other contributions in this vein have led to the proposition that inexact interpretations and general personal descriptions offered by the therapist in the context of a positive patient-therapist relationship can be as effective in producing cognitive restructuring and behavior change as accurate interpretations.

Unfortunately, there are no conclusive empirical data to resolve the question of whether behavior change requires increased self-understanding or can occur without it. It can be said, however, that there has been little continuing support for the view that an individual can learn to give up old ways of feeling, thinking, and acting and replace them with new ways without having some awareness of the difference between the old and new ways. Introduced in the framework of behavior modification approaches to therapy, this view held that enduring behavior change could be accomplished by reinforcement alone without the mediation of cognitive and affective experiences, that is, without increased self-awareness. However, the current writings of most behavior therapists stress that the goal of their treatment method is not to establish the therapist as absolute controller of the patient's behavior, to shape it as he sees fit, but rather to help the patient become capable of managing his own life and working effectively toward whatever goals he deems desirable. Such self-direction and self-control are seen in contemporary behavior modification as being achieved through a patient's conscious deliberation about and selection of the ways he would like to act (see Goldfried & Merbaum, 1973; Kanfer, 1970; Locke, 1971; Marston & Feldman, 1972).[10]

Furthermore, serious question can be raised whether an emphasis on being convincing rather than accurate can sustain a positive treatment relationship, while inaccurate interpretations suggest lack of understanding and erode the patient's confidence in the therapist's ability to be helpful. It may be that "convincing" presentation of inexact interpretations and general personality descriptions can carry sufficient authority to convey an aura of therapist understanding. But how consummate an actor is a psychotherapist expected to be? To what extent must he be naturally gifted or well-trained in feigning complete assurance while making statements that he has little reason to believe are correct or specifically applicable?

From the perspective of the treatment relationship, there is no satisfactory answer to this question. If therapists need to excel in conveying more certainty than they know to exist, then they will have to be drawn from the ranks of actors and confidence men—which is obviously neither a feasible nor attractive possibility. Most people, being neither skilled in acting nor comfortable with dissimulation, have difficulty being convincing when they lack conviction; instead, they telegraph insincerity when they do not believe in what they are saying. Hence most therapists who strain to be convincing without regard for accuracy will end by appearing ungenuine, and their patients will profit less fully from psychotherapy than patients who perceive their therapist as being genuine with them (see Chap. 3).[11]

To summarize this important point, any effort to be more convincing in offering an interpretation than the data justify jeopardizes the quality of the treatment relationship by stripping it of its genuineness. For this reason, accurate interpretation cannot be adequately replaced with inexact interpretations and general personality descriptions. Accurate interpretations convey understanding because they are congruent with the patient's past and current experiencing of himself, and they

[10]Fuller explication of these current directions in behavior modification approaches to therapy are available in textbooks by Bandura (1969), Kanfer and Phillips (1970, Chap. 9), and Yates (1970, Chap. 20).

[11]Wexler (1974) argues cogently in this regard that therapist genuineness derives from empathic responding, and that the *only* way a therapist can demonstrate genuineness is by devoting his full attention to understanding his patient and communicating such accurate understanding to him.

strengthen the treatment relationship because they demonstrate the therapist's sensitivity and potential helpfulness. Inexact interpretations and general personality descriptions, on the other hand, convey understanding only if the therapist draws on the patient's positive regard for him to make them seem convincing, and the insincerity of proceeding in this way sooner or later undermines the relationship on which it is based.

Therapist Documentation. The final guideline for deciding whether an interpretation that seems accurate should be offered at a particular time consists of whether there are sufficient data available to document it. Documentation is almost always required to make an interpretive sequence effective, since patients seldom greet even correct and well-timed interpretations with an enthusiastic surge of insight. The therapist who waits for his patient to respond to an interpretation with "Aha, I see it all now, it's perfectly clear to me, and it explains exactly what's been going on" will have a very long wait indeed.

In fact, prompt and ecstatic endorsement of an interpretation should be regarded with suspicion, because it usually is a way of warding off rather than exploring whatever possibilities are being suggested. With such unequivocal acceptance the patient is in effect saying that the interpretation has been so clear, precise, and comprehensive that there is no need to consider it further. When patients are prepared to work on rather than ward off an interpretation, they typically respond to it not with unqualified agreement, but with increased attention ("I never thought of that before"; "I had a real pang of anxiety when you said that, so it must have some important meaning for me"), with self-reflection ("I wonder if that could be why I'm so afraid to meet new people"; "That makes me think of having had the same feelings toward one of my teachers when I was in school"), or with questions about it ("I'm not sure how you came to that conclusion"; "How would that account for the feelings I have toward my husband?").

It is in relation to the questions a patient raises about an interpretation that the therapist should be able to provide documentation based on the previous content of the therapy. Such questions may of course be turned back to the patient ("What ideas do you have?"), and they may also be regarded as manifestations of resistance rather than as a genuine request for information. However, resistance should not be presumed to lurk behind every minor hesitation in a patient's progress toward understanding himself better, and a patient who appears about to come to grips with an interpretation should be given information to help him with his task when he raises relevant questions about it. Consider the following example of a female patient to whom it has just been suggested that she seems to place herself in subservient roles to men, whom she then resents:

Pt. I'm not sure how you came to that conclusion.

Th. The same pattern has been apparent in your relationship with three different men we've discussed, first your father, then your husband, and now me.

Pt. I'm beginning to see what you mean . . . yes, I'm like that. But how can this account for my getting more irritable with my husband when he is doing so well?

Th. He's a man, and you tend to downgrade yourself in relationship to men and then resent them for being in a superior position.

Pt. So I resent him . . . and that explains why the more successful he is, the more I resent him. And it's my own doing, because I feel I have to be subservient to a man in order to please him, like with my father. That's it, isn't it?

Note that the therapist's answers to these questions about an interpretation do not spell out every detail of his reasoning. Rather they call to the patient's attention bits of additional information intended to demonstrate some basis for the interpretation and stimulate her exploration of its implications. Further questions would be answered with further, more detailed documentation, up to the point where the questions became so numerous or tangential as to suggest that the patient is trying to avoid rather than wrestle with what the interpretation might mean to her.

If the therapist cannot document an interpretation with information he and the patient have previously shared, he will have created the same treatment disadvantages as result from a premature interpretation. That is, especially if he has been uncompromisingly certain in presenting an interpretation that he subsequently cannot justify, the therapist will impress his patient as being careless and inconsiderate, and both the quality of the treatment relationship and the potential effectiveness of the interpretation if better-timed will suffer in the process. The undisciplined offering of interpretations that cannot be adequately documented constitutes another aspect of the previously mentioned "wild analysis" approach that the therapist should carefully avoid.

It should also be noted in this regard that the misapplication of interpretive techniques, particularly in the various forms that wild analysis takes, can lead to poor treatment results for which some presumed inefficacy of the interpretive method is mistakenly held responsible. Hence it is of utmost importance for therapists, both in their clinical practice and in their reading of the literature, to base their impressions of the effects of interpretive psychotherapy on instances in which it is appropriately conducted, and to regard inappropriately conducted psychotherapy as testimony to the inexperience of the therapist and not as a basis for drawing evaluative inferences about the method.

Dosage of Interpretations

Effective interpretation requires that dosage—the number of interpretations offered per unit of time—be kept at a level the patient can tolerate. As already noted, every interpretation generates some anxiety and evokes some defensiveness. If interpretations are offered in rapid-fire succession, patients tend to become increasingly anxious, which interferes with their attention to the interpretations, and increasingly defensive, which interferes with their participation in the treatment process. An interpretation should be made only when the patient appears able to tolerate the anxiety it will arouse, and one interpretation should not follow another until the patient has adequately worked through any defensiveness evoked by the first one. In this regard, the findings of Garduk and Haggard (1972, p. 31) confirm that experienced psychotherapists tend to use interpretations cautiously rather than persistently, and that, once having made a point through an interpretation, they tend to proceed next with other types of interventions rather than further interpretations.

The Garduk and Haggard data on the effects of interpretation also indicate that the dosage of interpretations should be regulated according to the type of patient response that it seems desirable to elicit. Thus if the therapist feels it would be useful for his patient to talk less or respond less fully, he should offer interpretations; if on the other hand he would like his patient to become more discursive and spontaneous, he should limit his interventions to observations and clarifications and avoid interpretations. Similarly, if the therapist feels it would be helpful for his patient to express understanding, to manifest anxiety or defensiveness, or to talk about the treatment relationship, interpretation should be his intervention of choice; but if he prefers to have the patient talk freely with minimal anxiety or defensiveness, then he should use interventions other than interpretation.

An advantageous dosage of interpretations is therefore relative to the needs of each individual patient at specific points in his treatment. Yet, as one general guideline for dosage, the therapist should avoid offering interpretations whenever there will be limited opportunity for the patient to respond to them. Interpretations made during the early and middle portions of an interview allow the patient time to explore their implications and work through the discomfort they may cause him, whereas an interpretation delivered in the waning moments of an interview leaves the patient hanging, unable to discuss it with the therapist and uncomfortable about it until the next session.

Certainly a case may be made for the importance of a patient's having to explore the implications of interpretations on his own and having to endure the discomfort that inevitably accompanies exposure to the interpretive process. But the patient's own reflection on interpretations should occur in addition to, not instead of, adequate opportunity to reflect on them jointly with the therapist, and his discomfort should be a natural consequence of his decision to look closely at himself, not painful affect artificially and unnecessarily stimulated by poor timing of interpretations.

Hence the therapist should avoid interpretations that crowd the latter part of a treatment session, and he should be similarly circumspect about major interpretive efforts just prior to some interruption of the treatment. When vacations or other anticipated breaks in the treatment routine occur. the last session prior to the interruption should be used more for review and consolidation than for breaking ground in new areas. Frequently patients themselves sense that the session preceding an interruption is a poor time to stir up new problems and concerns, and they accordingly limit their conversation to mundane and uncomplicated matters. The therapist will do well to follow such a lead from his patient just before a break in the treatment, and he should particularly avoid interpreting his patient's superficiality as resistance. The major exception to this guideline involves instances in which the patient gives evidence of some unexpressed feelings toward the therapist related to his interrupting the treatment. To prevent such feelings from building into a negative transference reaction that interferes with the resumption of the treatment, they should be identified and aired promptly, even if there is insufficient time to explore them fully. A further explanation of recognizing and responding to transference in this circumstance is given in Chapter 10.

HOW TO INTERPRET

To sustain an effective interpretive style, the therapist must prepare his patient for any interpretations he plans to offer, encourage the patient's participation in developing and evaluating interpretations, and phrase his interpretations as concisely and incisively as he can. Adhering to these guidelines, as elaborated below, enhances the likelihood of offering interpretations in a manner that capitalizes on accurate prior judgments about what and when to interpret.

Preparing the Patient

The previous discussion of timing emphasized the importance of offering interpretations when the patient is on the verge of becoming aware of them. To be most effective, the therapist should direct his interpretations at material that is just below the surface, or just outside of the patient's conscious awareness. Research by Speisman (1959) confirms in this regard that both superficial interpretations dealing with matters already obvious to the patient and deep interpretations dealing with matters quite remote from his conscious awareness evoke more resistance than interpretations of moderate depth—those that fall between the obvious and the remote. Since resistance, although interpretable in its own right, interferes with the patient's efforts to participate in the interpretive process, the most productive interpretations will be those that evoke least resistance, namely, those of moderate depth.[12]

Accordingly, effective interpretive technique requires the therapist to take steps to bring aspects of the patient's thoughts, feelings, or actions that he believes *should* be interpreted into close awareness where they *can* be interpreted usefully. Simply listening and waiting for the patient to bring himself to the brink of expanded self-awareness provides relatively few opportunities for well-timed interpretations. Instead, the therapist must work systematically to guide his patient toward interpretations that appear indicated.

[12]Meltzoff and Kornreich (1970, p.427) correctly point out that "depth of interpretation" is a difficult concept to objectify for research purposes, since whether a particular interpretation is deep or shallow varies from one patient to the next and for individual patients from one moment to the next. Furthermore, a therapist may not be able to judge whether an interpretation he has made is too shallow or too deep until he observes the patient's reaction to it, a fact that complicates research by suggesting an after-the-fact definition of depth of interpretation. The task of the clinician, operating as he often must with imperfect knowledge, is to judge as best he can what would constitute a moderately deep interpretation for a particular patient at a particular time, and then to modify his judgment if the patient's response suggests he was mistaken.

Guiding the patient toward an interpretation is usually accomplished with a sequence of increasingly penetrating interventions, beginning with questions and clarifications, proceeding with confrontations, and ending with the interpretation to be made. The following exchange illustrates how such a sequence often unfolds:

Pt. We had a salesman's meeting, and a large group of us were cramped together in a small room, and they turned out the lights to show some slides, and I got so jumpy and anxious I couldn't stand it.

Th. So what happened? [Question]

Pt. I just couldn't stand it, I was sweating and shaking, so I got up and left, and I know I'll be called on the carpet for walking out.

Th. You became so anxious and upset that you couldn't stand being in the room, even though you knew that walking out would get you into trouble. [Clarification]

Pt. Yeah . . . What could have bothered me so much to make me do a dumb thing like that?

Th. You know, we've talked about other times in your life when you've become upset in close quarters with other men, once when you were in the army and again in your dormitory at college. [Confrontation]

Pt. That's right, and it was the same kind of thing again.

Th. And if I'm correct, this has never happened to you in a group of men and women together, no matter how closely you've been cramped together. [Further confrontation]

Pt. Uh . . . Yes, that's right.

Th. So it appears that something especially about being physically close to other men, and especially in the dark, makes you anxious, as if you're afraid something bad might happen in that kind of situation. [Interpretation]

Pt. (Pause) I think you're right about that . . . and I know I'm not physically afraid of other men. Do you think it might be sexual, that I might get worried about something homosexual taking place?

This sequence illustrates several typical features of the interpretive process. First, note that it does not end with a dramatic conclusive statement delivered by the therapist, to the accompaniment of the patient's adulation and gratitude. The clinician seeking such drama will rarely find it in the practice of psychotherapy. Instead, the sequence proceeds gradually from a reported experience (the patient's anxiety in the dark, crowded, all-male environment), through clarification of the experience and confrontation with its similarity to other experiences in the patient's life, to an interpretation that takes the patient one small step ahead in understanding himself more fully than before (the apparent fact that he fears something bad might happen in situations of close proximity to other men).

Second, note that the interpretation serves not only to summarize what has previously been said but also to stimulate new lines of inquiry ("Do you think it might be sexual?"). Once an interpretation of connections or relationships heretofore outside the patient's conscious awareness has been made and accepted, it can function in turn as a confrontation that helps pave the way for further interpretations. In the above example, the therapist goes only so far as to point out the patient's apparent fear of being too close to other men. Then the patient, having agreed with this interpretation, uses it as a basis for suggesting a new topic, possible homosexual concerns, that can provide the subject for an additional sequence of questions, clarifications, confrontations, and interpretation.

Third, note the extent of the patient's activity in pulling the interpretation together and beginning to explore its implications. In light of the suggestive information available, the therapist might have extended his interpretation to include "Could it be that you have some concerns about homosexual activity that cause you to become anxious in such situations?" To have done so, however, would have been to take more of an interpretive leap than would have been necessary or productive. An effectively managed interpretive sequence prompts the patient to take the next step on his own, as happened in this instance. But if an interpretive sequence is too far off the mark or is generating too much anxiety for the patient to pursue it spontaneously, then efforts by the therapist to push him further are more likely to increase resistance than to promote progress. Furthermore, should the therapist "succeed" in pushing the implications of an interpretation beyond where the patient was prepared to go, he will have abrogated rather than fostered the patient's participation as a respected partner in the interpretive process.

Fostering the Patient's Participation

Active participation by the patient in the interpretive process is necessary to keep both the nature of interpretations and the nature of the treatment relationship in proper prespective. Interpretations are, after all, alternative hypotheses.[13] They suggest different ways in which the patient might look at himself and his experiences, and, if apt, they will prove more congruent with the patient's basic personality, present emotional state, and past history than his current views. However, it is not the therapist's expressing it that makes an interpretation accurate, or even useful; accuracy lies in the patient's acknowledging that the interpretation has some personal meaning to him and has helped him to know himself better. As Schonbar (1965) notes, interpretations cannot be imposed on a patient, but can only emerge in concert with the unfolding of his intrinsic nature. It can be safely said that no effective interpretations occur in psychotherapy without the patient's participation in developing and evaluating them.

In the same way as interpretations comprise alternative hypotheses, not oracular pronouncements, the psychotherapy patient is not a student to be lectured but a partner in an exploratory venture. Not only is he entitled to judge the accuracy and usefulness of interpretations, but he also should share responsibility for arriving at interpretations. Contributing actively to an interpretive sequence enhances the patient's sense of being able to generate his own self-understanding and to become the master rather than the victim of his fate. Hence interpretations that the patient can formulate for himself, no matter how much help he receives from the therapist along the way, tend to have more impact and a more lasting effect than interpretations set before him in finished form. To excuse a patient from responsibility for arriving at interpretations is to demean and patronize him while at the same time depriving him of valuable opportunities to formulate his own new ideas about himself.

The patient's role in the interpretive process can be understood and illustrated further in terms of the distinction introduced in Chapter 4 between a person's experiencing self and his observing self. To recapitulate this distinction, people differ from each other and from one moment to the next in whether they are oriented primarily toward experiencing or observing themselves, and a rewarding life style usually requires a flexible balance between the two. Too much self-observation produces paralyzing self-consciousness and eliminates spontaneity, so that a person cannot enjoy thinking, feeling, or doing anything simply for its own sake. Too much self-experiencing fosters mindless, uncritical immersion in thoughts, feelings, and actions for their own sake, without

[13]Note should be made of an important book by Levy (1962), *Psychological Interpretation*, which elaborates the manner in which interpretations serve as alternate hypotheses.

concern for their consequences or implications. For interpretation in psychotherapy to achieve personal meaning to the patient and to generate understanding that takes firm root in his consciousness, the patient must have both the experiencing and the observing parts of his personality available and the therapist must be able to call on them alternately as the situation demands.

When the situation involves preparation for an interpretive sequence, the therapist needs to emphasize the patient's experiencing self, to help him feel and report the life events that will be the subject of clarifications, confrontations, and interpretations to come. But when the situation becomes ripe for interpretation, the therapist needs to focus on and establish an alliance with the patient's observing self, in order to assure his participation in the interpretive process.

To establish such an alliance the therapist needs to communicate first that he has formed certain impressions of the experiences reported to him, and second that, if the patient will put part of himself where the therapist is sitting and join him as an observer, he will be able to share in evaluating his impressions. By thus encouraging the patient to function as both an observing and an experiencing person in the psychotherapy session, the therapist actively promotes his participation in the interpretive process. The following example illustrates such an effort to activate the patient's observing self:

Pt. I wish I could understand why people are always taking advantage of me, so that I end up doing things their way instead of how I would like to.

Th. From what you've been telling me, it sounds to me not so much that you're taken advantage of, but that you always go along with what other people say, without saying what you would like to do or how you would like to see things done. I wonder if you can see it that way? [An invitation to the patient to separate his observing self from his experience of being taken advantage of, so that he can join the therapist in looking at it]

Pt. Well, I haven't thought of it that way before, but I suppose I am that way. I sort of ask for people to make decisions for me by not making them for myself.

Th. So you're not a passive victim. [An invitation to the patient to consider further that he may be actively bringing about some of the interpersonal difficulties he previously thought he was undergoing passively]

Pt. No, I guess if you look at it that way I get myself into these situations that aggravate me by avoiding expressing any strong opinions or trying to influence what is decided on. But why would I want to avoid telling people, especially my friends, what I really feel or want?

Th. What thoughts do you have about that? [The patient's observing self has been activated in this sequence to help him participate in learning something new about himself, namely, that his subordination to others is at least in part his own doing; he is now on the verge of recognizing that his interpersonal passivity may serve some defensive purposes, in that he avoids asserting himself in order to avoid anxiety associated with being assertive, and the stage is set to begin exploring a conflict-defense sequence in this area][14]

One additional technique useful in promoting a patient's participation in the interpretive process is *partial interpretation.* Partial interpretation consists of offering an abbreviated version of an interpretation and thereby encouraging the patient to provide the rest of it. In the above example the therapist's statement, "So you're not a passive victim," constitutes such a partial interpretation. A full interpretation at this point might have been, "In other words, you're not a passive victim of what other people do to you; you avoid expressing strong opinions or trying to influence decisions that are made, and it is because you avoid being decisive that other people end up making decisions for you." What actually happened, however, was that the therapist went only so far as to make the somewhat elliptical statement, "So you're not a passive victim," and the patient, his participation having been engaged, formulated the rest of the interpretation in his own words.[15]

Partial interpretation is not always as successful as it was in this case, even when the full interpretation toward which it points is accurate and

[14]This illustration is based in part on guidelines for the interpretation of defenses provided by Fenichel (1941, p. 77), who was among the first writers to stress the importance in uncovering psychotherapy of isolating the patient's observing self from what he is experiencing.

[15]Consistently with these comments about the potential utility of partial interpretations, research findings confirm that relatively ambiguous, nondirective therapist remarks are followed by relatively long and productive patient responses exploring the meaning of what is being discussed, whereas relatively specific and directive therapist communications lead to relatively brief and nonproductive patient responses focused on descriptions of symptoms and problems (see Frank, 1964; Lennard & Bernstein, 1960).

timely. Sometimes a patient's reluctance to confront the full interpretation causes him to dig in his heels a bit, and sometimes dependent or manipulative needs lead him to shirk his responsibility and prefer the therapist to do more of the work. In these circumstances a partial interpretation would have to be buttressed with additional statements intended to prod the patient toward the full interpretation. The above interaction might then have taken the following course:

Th. So you're not a passive victim.

Pt. What do you mean? (Therapist remains silent) Oh, you mean I may be bringing some of this aggravation on myself. But how do you see me doing that?

Th. Someone has to make decisions.

Pt. You mean it's my own doing, that because I don't express strong opinions other people end up making the decisions. But why don't I express strong opinions?

Th. Why indeed?

Pt. Oh, now I see what you're getting at; it's like for some reason I'm avoiding telling people what I really feel or want.

Th. What thoughts do you have about that?

This second, hypothetical version of the example provides some instructive contrasts with the first. The patient appears equally sensitive to his behavior and equally prepared to explore its defensive aspects. However, whether due to elements of resistance or aspects of the transference, he seems just not ready to move as fast; he needs or wants the therapist to help him through the interpretation. The therapist provides such help, but notice that he does not do so at the cost of sacrificing the patient's active participation. He follows his partial interpretation first with silence and then with two other elliptical statements ("Someone has to make decisions"; "Why indeed?"), and thus gradually elicits the same response that emerged more quickly in the example as it actually happened.

The partial interpretation technique offers much to gain and virtually nothing to lose. If it provokes an immediate and full response, as in the first case above, some time is saved and the patient has the beneficial experience of formulating his own self-understanding. If it does not promptly strike a responsive cord, as in the second case, it is merely necessary to supplement it with further comments or explanations. The latter process of gradually eliciting an interpretation through a series of elliptical statements requires the therapist to be patient, but no more so than is generally necessary to minimize his patient's resistance and promote his active participation in the treatment. Furthermore, if an interpretation should be incorrect or poorly timed, approaching it with partial statements can provide the therapist some opportunities to recognize and correct his error before he has already put the hook in his mouth with a comprehensive, elaborate statement of the interpretation.

Phrasing of Interpretations

Interpretations constitute reasonable but not incontrovertible inferences about the patient, and their effectiveness usually depends on how actively the patient participates in arriving at them. Accordingly, interpretation should be *tentative,* couched in the language of possibilities and probabilities rather than certainties, and they should be *concise,* consisting of no more words than are necessary to communicate the intended message and elicit the patient's reaction to it.

Phrasing Interpretations Tentatively. The overriding consideration in phrasing interpretations effectively is to make them tentative statements and not pronouncements. A pronouncement leaves no room for error and casts the therapist as an infallible authority; at the same time, it allows no opportunity for the patient to participate in its formulation, which casts him as a passive recipient. To avoid having interpretations foster either of these unprofitable roles, the therapist needs regularly to precede them with some qualifying remark indicating possibility or probability: "It's as if . . ."; "Perhaps . . ."; "I get the feeling that . . ."; "I wonder if . . ."; "Could it be that . . ."; "Apparently, then, . . ."; "Maybe it's because . . ."

Interpretations introduced in this way leave the door open to alternatives and invite the patient to weigh any such alternatives against what is being suggested as possible or probable. At times the patient may not hear that an interpretation is being made tentatively, or he may not recognize that he is being invited to evaluate it. If so, his response may imply the message, "If that's the way it seems to you, I guess that's the way it is." Any such response to an interpretation, whether direct or implicit, calls for immediate intervention to prevent the patient from drifting into an inactive role. Depending on the circumstances, this intervention may be directed either at process features of the patient's behavior (perhaps his acquiescence reflects submissiveness to the therapist or sullen resistance to the treatment) or at the content of his response. At the content level, for example, a therapist whose patient responds passively to a tentative interpretation ("If that's the way it seems to you, I guess that's the way it is") may usefully reemphasize the active role expected of a psychotherapy patient: "My thinking it doesn't make it so." This elliptical comment implies (a) that the therapist is not omniscient, (b) that conclusions can be drawn about the patient only in light of his estimate of these conclusions, and (c) that the next step in exploring the accuracy of the interpretation that has been offered is up to him. Should such an elliptical comment not immediately elicit all the points it is intended to make, the therapist can lead the patient through them one at a time at whatever pace he can follow.

It is important to distinguish such elliptical statements and partial interpretations, which are usually made bluntly and without hedging ("My thinking it doesn't make it so," or, from the previous example, "So you're not a passive victim"), from interpretations, which need to be offered tentatively. Elliptical statements and partial interpretations consist of information about which the therapist is almost totally certain, and they are intended to stimulate the patient's observation of his experience. Interpretations are inferences intended to suggest some meaning of experiences that the patient and therapist have shared in observing. The therapist may be very emphatic and uncompromising in guiding the patient toward increased self-understanding by encouraging him to observe himself more fully. When he arrives at the point of attempting to communicate such understanding, however, it behooves him to exercise restrained suggestion rather than unequivocal pronouncement.

In striving to phrase his interpretations tentatively, the therapist should also take care to vary his style. If he precedes every interpretation with "Could it be that . . ?" or "It's as if . . .", his work will take on an automatic, stereotyped quality. Stereotyped therapist behavior can make a patient more conscious of his therapist's technique than of his remarks. Furthermore, the more a therapist is perceived by his patient as playing out a formalized role, the less he is seen as being interested in and sensitive to his individual needs. The therapist too can suffer from falling into repetitive speech patterns, since the more he begins to sound to himself like a broken record, the more he risks becoming bored and inattentive. Hence it is important for the therapist to alternate among a variety of suitable ways of expressing himself, whether in offering interpretations or conducting any other aspect of the treatment.

Phrasing Interpretations Concisely. Turning next to the number of words used in phrasing an interpretation, considerable attention has already been given in principle and through example to advantages of the therapist's saying no more than is necessary to help his patient talk meaningfully about himself. The therapist's words have no importance in their own right; they are important only to the extent that they aid the patient to achieve the goals of the treatment. Erudite exposition belongs in the lecture hall, not in the treatment session. The less a therapist says about a subject being discussed, the more his patient will say about it, because (a) there will be more time for him to talk and (b) there will be more left for him to say. And it is what the patient says that gives him his sense of participating in the treatment and learning to understand himself better.

In this regard, available evidence indicates that there is little to be gained by efforts to offer comprehensive rather than parsimonious intervention. Garduk and Haggard (1972) include in their study some comparisons between lengthy, detailed interpretations and interpretations that were limited to sparse statements of the main point the therapist wished to convey. As measured by various dimensions of patient response, they found no advantage of comprehensive over more limited interpretations. Indeed, the one significant difference they did find in this area was that patients say less and are less active following comprehensive interpretations than in response to briefer interpretations. Given the potential disadvantage of the therapist's being comprehensive—namely, in limiting the patient's potential participation in treatment process—therapist wordiness emerges as antithetical to progress in psychotherapy.

JUDGING THE EFFECTIVENESS OF INTERPRETATIONS

The specific indications that an interpretation has been effective are threefold: the patient will accept it, he will understand it, and he will use it as a stimulus to additional self-exploration. Of these, the first is the most crucial. Only if the content of an interpretation is experienced by the patient as a part of himself can he derive any lasting benefit either from reconstructing the evidence for it or from projecting its implications into his present and future life. Unless such acceptance occurs, any professed understanding or apparent use of an interpretation amounts to little more than an abstract exercise in personality dynamics, without an accompanying increment in personal self-understanding.

Is the Interpretation Accepted?

The extent to which a patient has accepted an interpretation is indicated by, but not always obvious from, how he responds to it. For example, consider a patient who responds to an interpretation with "Yes, I think you're right," or "As you say that, it feels right to me." Such comments usually indicate agreement with the interpretation, and the second type of comment in particular suggests that the patient is experiencing the interpretation as congruent with himself. Yet such agreeable responses have at least two other meanings not infrequently encountered in psychotherapy.

First, patients who are characterologically submissive or momentarily concerned with courting the therapist's favor may be motivated to acquiesce to whatever he says. A "yes" in these circumstances does not necessarily mean that the patient agrees with the interpretation, but only that he does not want to disagree with the therapist.

Second, patients who find an interpretation particularly threatening may agree with it in order to close the issue, just as one may seek to end an unpleasant argument simply by agreeing with whatever the other person says. Thus, particularly before he has sufficient experience in the treatment to appreciate the therapist's patience and tenacity, a patient may agree with an interpretation not because he has accepted it, but because he hopes to end discussion of the subject it concerns.

The indications that a patient who says "Yes" really means something else are usually to be found in process aspects of his behavior. Sometimes an endorsement of an interpretation will just not ring true, as when agreement comes too readily without reflection, or too grudgingly without enthusiasm. In other instances the therapist may recognize feelings and attitudes in his patient, such as a wish to court favor, that are probably influencing him to agree without being in agreement.

More than these intercurrent clues, however, what the patient says next will indicate the genuineness of his expressed agreement with an interpretation. An interpretation that is experienced and acknowledged as congruent stimulates new associations and leads the patient into previously unexplored or imperfectly understood aspects of his behavior. When a patient agrees to an interpretation but then drops it, without spontaneously reporting some ideas or events related to and suggested by it, it can safely be inferred that the interpretation has not really been accepted, whether because it was inaccurate, poorly timed, ill-conceived, or whatever.

As a further demand on the therapist's alertness, there are also times when a patient disagrees with an interpretation that he recognizes as being accurate. A patient who is characterologically obstinate or counter-dependent, for example, or who feels negatively toward the therapist, or who is upset by the implications of what is being said to him may reject an interpretation because he dislikes having to agree with others, or because he resents giving the therapist the satisfaction of having been perceptive, or because he wants to avoid any further discussion of the subject involved. The more such motives are in evidence, the more likely it is that a rejected interpretation has in fact struck home, especially when a patient who has rejected an interpretation proceeds to reflect on it in ways that leave little doubt about its meaningfulness to him.

Is the Interpretation Understood?

Turning to the second criterion for judging the effectiveness of interpretations, a patient needs to understand an interpretation if he is to learn anything from it. Understanding an interpretation means being able to recognize how the evidence for it fits together and how it could account for some thoughts, feelings, or actions that have previously been puzzling or unaccountable. A patient who has understood an interpretation will usually demonstrate his understanding by being able to recapitulate it in his own words:

> Let me think about that for a minute . . . yes, I see it now. I turned him off by being nasty to him and yet I wasn't angry at him, just worried he might put me down if I gave him a chance; and this must be the fourth or fifth time the same thing has come up in our sessions. So you must be right—I've got some fear of having people not like me or reject me, and I protect myself by rejecting them first, and that would explain a lot about why I do such a poor job of trying to make and keep friends.

The therapist should listen for such glimmers of understanding as the patient responds to an interpretation, and he should try to elicit them if they do not emerge spontaneously ("I wonder what thoughts you have about that possibility"; "You haven't said anything about what meaning such a connection might have to you"). It has already been noted that professed understanding in the absence of basic acceptance of an interpretation is a hollow accomplishment. Likewise, inability to demonstrate understanding of an interpretation, no matter how enthusiastically it has been accepted, indicates that more work needs to be done to make it effective.

Limited understanding of an interpretation that has been accepted may mean that factors other than a true experience of its being accurate have motivated the patient to agree with it, as illustrated above. If so, then the therapist needs to defer further consideration of the interpretation until he has been able to explore and resolve with the patient his reason for saying "Yes" to it when he meant "No." However, inability to understand an accepted interpretation may also indicate that the patient's experiencing self has temporarily outstripped his observing self—that is, he has had a sudden flash of experiencing the interpretation as truly characteristic of himself, as "feeling just right," even though he cannot yet put his finger on why it feels so right.

Although the experiencing of an interpretation as "feeling just right" provides strong evidence of its accuracy, no interpretation can be fully effective until the patient's powers of reasoning and observation are also brought to bear on it. An emotional experience, no matter how powerful, is a thing of the moment. For a person to learn from his experience, he must be capable not only of experiencing but also of understanding why he experiences as he does, what his experiences mean, and what implications the experiences of one moment have for experiences of the next. Hence it may at times be necessary for the therapist to use further questions, clarifications, and confrontations to promote understanding of an interpretation that appears to have been accurate. The therapist should not consider the interpretation effective until the patient has been able to supplement his acceptance of it with indications that he understands it.[16]

Is the Interpretation Used?

The third clue to the effectiveness of an interpretation is the extent to

[16]This emphasis on the patient's understanding interpretations as well as experiencing them runs counter to the emphasis in some treatment approaches on experiencing for its own sake and on the attainment of personal growth solely through becoming open to experience. It cannot be denied that poignant emotional experiences can institute a sequence of events leading to personality or behavior change, as noted by Alexander and French's (1946) "corrective emotional experience" and by Gendlin's (1961) "the process of feeling." To be enduring, however, such change must be accompanied by cognitive frames of reference that help a person appreciate the present and future significance of what he has experienced. It is noteworthy in this regard that even in the framework of client-centered therapy (Rogers, 1951, 1957, 1961), which stresses personal growth through openness to experience, recent developments emphasize the important role of cognitive operations in promoting and sustaining such growth (Anderson, 1974; Wexler, 1974; Zimring, 1974). Greenwald (1973, p. 27), writing from a humanistic point of view, similarly points out that "There is need for both the experiential approach . . . and for the cognitive approach, if therapy is to be anything but kicks."

which it stimulates the patient to generate new ideas about himself or to begin exploring aspects of his life not previously touched on in therapy. Once accepted and understood, an interpretation should lead to new avenues of self-understanding, and the patient should enter these avenues with some mixture of curiosity, perplexity, anxiety, and enthusiasm. Accordingly, the therapist should listen for the following types of comments from a patient who has agreed with and recapitulated an interpretation: "You know, that reminds me of something I haven't thought of before"; "I really feel good about that, because I think its going to help explain a number of things"; "Now that I understand a little better how I've been handling that type of situation, I'd really like to know more about how I got to be this way"; "Knowing that makes me a little uneasy about the kind of person I'm finding myself to be."

If the patient does not respond in some such manner, indicating that the interpretation is leading him in some new direction, the interpretive effort will have been less than fully effective. Whereas a therapist can help his patient understand an interpretation, he can no more force an interpretation to lead somewhere than he can compel agreement with it. The acceptance and utilization of interpretations have to come from the patient; if they are not forthcoming, the interpretation has been inaccurate, poorly timed, or ill-conceived, and therapist's only recourse will be to drop the matter and do a better job the next time he undertakes an interpretive sequence.

For the reader who is interested in research as well as practice in psychotherapy, a concluding comment is necessary in this section to clarify what otherwise might appear to be a circular approach to judging the effectiveness of interpretations. If the preceding paragraphs are read as stating that an effective interpretation is one the patient accepts, understands, and makes use of, and that the effectiveness of interpretations is judged from the extent to which they are accepted, understood, and productive, then we are left with a tautological definition of effectiveness that precludes an adequate research strategy. An interpretation accompanied by the criteria of effectiveness is defined as effective, and one that is not is defined as ineffective, and there is no way to disprove hypotheses about the impact of effective interpretations.

However, it is not intended to tie the concept of effective interpretation to the same criteria for defining it as for assessing its impact, which would hopelessly contaminate the independent and dependent variables in relevant research studies. Rather, the point is simply that accurate, well-timed, and carefully conceived interpretations are likely to be effective, as measured by patient agreement, understanding, and subsequent productivity. Utilizing this distinction, research studies of the effectiveness of the interpretive process can employ separate measures of the characteristics of an interpretation and of the patient's response to it.

WORKING THROUGH

Just as learning in general rarely occurs on the basis of a single trial, learning about oneself in psychotherapy seldom becomes established with the initial offering of an interpretation. Even an interpretation that is accepted and understood attains little more than the status of a likely possibility the first time the patient hears it. After a number of years of holding certain views of himself and his experiences, a person cannot be expected to embrace alternative views as soon as they are suggested to him. Instead, the alternative views need to be repeated on several occasions, each time helping the patient to understand better some aspect of himself or his behavior. In this way an alternative view develops a cumulative plausibility that gradually allows it to supplant an old view completely. This process is called *working through.*

Working through, then consists of the regular repetition of interpretations in order (a) to establish their validity in accounting for the events that first suggested them and (b) to extend their applicability to new events that come under consideration. Such repetition allows the patient both to reassess the interpretation in its original context and to test it out in new contexts where it should be relevant. In common with other aspects of the interpretive process, working through is the shared responsibility of patient and therapist. On some occasions the patient will spontaneously generate his own working through, on other occasions the therapist will have to institute it, and on all occasions, no matter which party initiates the working through, the patient must end by understanding it in his own words.

To illustrate the process of working through, consider a patient who has been discussing his awareness of never having aspired to anything that might stretch or even approach the limits of his potential, and who with the therapist's help has come to realize that he is so afraid of failing that he avoids any situation where he cannot be absolutely certain of success. Several sessions after first arriving at this new perspective of himself, he states that he was offered a promotion at work but turned it down because it involved changing to a different department where he thought he would enjoy the work less. He then says, "I've been doing some hard thinking about it since it happened; do you suppose it could be that my not liking the different kind of work was just a lame excuse, and that what really was involved was my being afraid of being a failure, like we talked about a while ago?"

With this statement the patient has initiated the process of working through the interpretation of his fear of failure, which he is now observing in a new situation beyond the experiences that introduced it into the therapy. Appreciation of the full extent to which this underlying concern about failure is influencing his behavior and preventing him from utilizing his potential will strengthen both his understanding and his ongoing awareness of it. It is the ongoing awareness of what a person learns about himself from an interpretation, achieved by working through, that allows him to modify his behavior in light of the interpretation. Without such ongoing awareness to mediate between interpretation and behavior change, interpretations are usually doomed to run a barren course.

Before expanding on this important relationship between interpretation and behavior change, there is something more to say about the above example. First, suppose the patient had not initiated his own working through, that is, suppose he had reported turning down the promotion at work because of not liking some of the changes involved but had not said anything more to relate his behavior to previous work in the therapy. The therapist must guard against being disappointed or irritated with a patient who describes maladaptive behavior clearly related to a recent interpretation but does so with no apparent recognition of either the maladaptive nature of the behavior or its relationship to the interpretation. Although such behavior may reflect some resistance on the patient's part, it does not mean that he is dense or insensitive, or that the therapist has not been conducting the treatment properly, or that interpretive psychotherapy is an ineffective procedure.

What it does mean when a patient acts as if a previously accepted and understood interpretation never existed is that he has not yet worked it through. Since virtually all interpretations have to be worked through (excepting those rare instances in which a particularly powerful interpretation results in one-trial learning), the therapist must be prepared for his patient to display minimal behavior change and even minimal recollection following the initial offering and acceptance of an interpretation. Hence, as in the above example, the patient may do just what he would have done before (decline the promotion) but subsequently begin to think about how his behavior may have been influenced by underlying concerns previously interpreted to him. If he does not begin to generate such connections, it then falls to the therapist to use a blend of elliptical statements and partial interpretations to lead the patient to a reexperiencing of the interpretation:

Pt. I was offered a better paying job with more responsibility, but I would have had to switch from the accounting to the advertising department, and I didn't think I would like it there as well so I turned it down.

Th. I think there may be more to it than that.

Pt. Like what?

Th. Like this isn't the first time you've backed off from a chance to take on something more demanding.

Pt. Uh . . . you mean this could be like what we were talking about a while back . . . a situation where I don't do something I really could do and that would get me ahead, because I'm afraid of not succeeding at it. As I think about it now, I'm sure that's what it was again, which means I screwed myself for no good reason.

Second, in addition to helping the patient reexperience an interpretation in contexts similar to the one in which it originally emerged, the therapist should also help him extend the interpretation to other contexts in which it is applicable. Continuing with the example, this patient's fear of failure in work situations could also be contributing to neurotic handling of social situations, leading to the following exchange:

Pt. I would like to become involved with a woman I could really admire and look up to. But somehow the only ones I end up trying to date are ones who don't have much on the ball and who look up to *me*, and I don't enjoy their company very much.

Th. There's a familiar theme to that.

Pt. I'm not sure what you mean.

Th. You're not taking any chances.

Pt. In a way, I suppose. I'm not taking any chances of being unimpressive because the woman's as sharp as I am or sharper, so there's not much risk of—oh, I see what you mean by the same theme. I'm hedging my bets, not risking failure, just as I've been doing in my work.

When the patient has an opportunity to work through the context of an interpretation in this way, seeing it repetitively relevant to understanding his behavior in a variety of situations, he becomes increasingly able to integrate his new knowledge of himself. Concurrently with the process of working through an interpretation, the patient gradually becomes capable of using it to alter his behavior. Initially he may continue to display some maladaptive or self-defeating behavior pattern that has been the subject of an apparently effective interpretation, recognizing how his behavior relates to the interpretation only with the aid of reminders from the therapist. Later, after some working through has taken place, he may persist in the neurotic behavior but he is able to recognize on his own that he could and should have acted in a more constructive and rewarding manner. Over time the lag between his behaving in a neurotic fashion and his recognizing the neurotic determinants of his behavior will continue to shrink, and finally, when the new understanding of himself provided by an interpretation has been fully worked through, he will realize its implication for situations in which he has been behaving neurotically as he encounters them, and *before* he responds, and he then will have achieved fully capacity to control his behavior in those situations.[17]

The necessary role of working through in translating interpretations into potential for behavior change is an important note on which to conclude this chapter, since it has bearing on common misconceptions of psychodynamic psychotherapy. It is frequently presumed, for example, that in the psychodynamic framework interpretations produce insight, which consists of a person's increased understanding of why he has been behaving in certain maladaptive ways, and that this insight produces behavior change. Such a model is subject to and has often received criticism on both conceptual and empirical grounds: conceptually, it appears to represent an authoritarian, judgemental focus on rooting out and correcting the bad in people, to the neglect of positive personality growth and the right of each individual to determine his own destiny; empirically, there is little research evidence to support the notion that insight alone produces behavior change.

However, as the discussion of interpretation in this chapter has hopefully made clear, such criticisms are based on an inaccurate construction of the psychodynamic model of psychotherapy, not only as it has evolved over the years but as it was originally conceived. Freud's notion of the interpretive process was that it serves to make the patient

[17]A detailed analysis of the relationships between insight, learning, and behavior change in psychotherapy is provided by Brady (1967). For further discussions of the general topic of working through, the reader is referred to Freud (1914), Greenson (1965), and Wolberg (1967, pp. 777–791).

conscious of influences on his behavior of which he had not previously been aware: "Where id was, there shall ego be" (Freud, 1933, p. 80). Yet in no way was the making of the unconscious conscious intended or expected to result directly in behavior change. Rather, the explicit purpose of the interpretive process is to bring thoughts and feelings of which a person is not aware, and over which he consequently has no control, into his awareness, where he can examine them, consider their relationship to other thoughts and feelings, and exert some conscious control over the extent to which they will influence his behavior. Once more in Freud's words, the intention of psychoanalysis is "to strengthen the ego, to make it more independent of the super-ego, to widen its field of perception and enlarge its organization, so that it can appropriate fresh portions of the id" (Freud, 1933, p. 80).

Thus the interpretive process is above all an effort to liberate the individual from psychologcal influences over which he has had little control and thereby free him to think, feel, and act in ways he finds gratifying and self-fulfilling. Viewed from this perspective psychodynamic psychotherapy can be seen as stressing rather than ignoring positive personality growth, and as encouraging rather than stifling each individual's determination of his own destiny:

> When the developmental inhibitions are resolved, it happens of itself that the doctor finds himself in a position to indicate new aims for the trends that have been liberated . . . But here again the doctor should hold himself in check, and take the patient's capacities rather than his own desires as guide (Freud, 1912a, pp. 118–119).

Thus it is not a person's after-the-fact understanding of why he behaved in a certain way that allows him to change his behavior, even though such understanding is a necessary step in the interpretive process and may be considered a form of "insight." Only after a person has worked through something new he has learned about himself, to the point where he can recognize its potential influence on his behavior *before* he acts, does he become free to exercise choice, free to behave in some way other than he might have without his increased self-understanding.

Hence in practice as well as theory, psychodynamic psychotherapy emphasizes self-control and self-determination through self-understanding. Yet this approach also stresses that neither self-control nor self-determination is likely to be enhanced until increments in self-understanding have been fully integrated. To expect behavior change to follow on the heels of initial insights will bring disappointment to the psychotherapist and negative results to the psychotherapy researcher.

CHAPTER 9

Interference with Communication: Resistance

Resistance in psychotherapy constitutes a paradoxical reluctance of the patient to participate in the treatment process. The patient who is resisting becomes temporarily unwilling or unable to fulfill the terms of the treatment contract, even though he continues to want help and to believe in the potential helpfulness of the therapist's efforts. Resistance must be differentiated from situations in which a patient truly feels that he has had all the help he wants or needs, or in which he has adequate basis for concluding that psychotherapy has little to offer him. In such situations reluctance to continue treatment represents a rational decision, rather than a paradox, and does not suggest resistance. Once an appropriate treatment contract has been entered into and interpretive work has begun, however, reluctance to participate tends much more to reflect resistance than any genuine conviction that treatment is no longer necessary or potentially helpful.

Resistance interferes with both the sending and receiving aspects of patient communication. A patient in a state of resistance will talk too much about inconsequential matters, too little about important matters, or perhaps not at all. Either way, he ceases to communicate freely the thoughts and feelings that bear most directly on the concerns that have brought him for help. At the same time, the resistive patient stops receiving communications, so that he no longer listens to the therapist, or if listening does not hear, or if hearing does not lend credence to what is being said.

Because resistance always disrupts communication in psychotherapy, it was originally viewed solely as an obstacle to progress. Freud in his early work depicted resistance as a force so antihetical to the aims of psychotherapy that it must be overcome by drawing on almost any available means "by which one man can ordinarily exert psychical influence on another" (Breuer & Freud, 1893–1895, p. 282). Included among these means were hypnosis, insistence, exhortation, and even a procedure in which the therapist presses on the patient's forehead and instructs him that this pressure will elicit previously unrecollected images and associations which he should then communicate.[1] Within a few years, however, Freud began to regard resistance as being itself an important subject for interpretation, to be explored and understood rather than merely removed (Freud, 1904b). The interpretation of resistance has ever since constituted a central aspect of dynamically oriented psychotherapy.

There are several reasons why resistance has come to play a highly important role in psychotherapy. First, resistance inevitably accompanies a patient's efforts to come to grips with interpretations and their implications for behavior change. As noted previously, uncovering psychotherapy confronts a person with unpleasant aspects of himself and his life, and it further leads him to consider adopting some new and unfamiliar ways of doing and looking at things. Few people can sustain participation in such a process without some waxing and waning of their enthusiasm and tolerance for it. Indeed, a patient who coasts merrily along in psychotherapy without intercurrent periods of reluctance to participate usually lacks meaningful engagement in the treatment process.

Second, the therapist's help in reducing or eliminating resistance allows the patient to work more comfortably in the treatment and hastens his progress toward fuller understanding of himself and his behavior. Whatever else may be said about resistance, it does in fact interfere with a person's ability to talk about himself in psychotherapy, and the easing of resistance usually allows thoughts and feelings to emerge that would not otherwise have been expressed.

Third, in addition to what a patient may learn from interview content that emerges following the reduction of some resistance, careful consideration of resistance behavior in its own right, as an aspect of interview process, can augment the person's understanding of himself. Why has the resistance occurred at a particular point? What is the patient resisting and why is he resisting it? How has the patient elected to manifest his resistance? What relationships exist between the resistance behavior seen in the treatment and the patient's behavior outside of psychotherapy? All are questions that can direct the patient toward an

[1]This procedure is described in Freud's chapter on the psychotherapy of hysteria in *Studies in Hysteria* (Breuer & Freud, 1893–1895, pp. 270–278). This book is usually regarded as marking the inception of the psychoanalytic method.

expanded appreciation of his coping style and sources of anxiety.

Fourth, as a subject for interpretation in its own right, resistance often proves more fruitful than the patient's recollected experiences. Because resistance behavior is occuring right at the moment, its manifestations can be directly observed and its impact vividly experienced. Recollected events in the patient's life are seldom a match for events transpiring during the treatment session in providing reliable samples of the patient's personality style and telling opportunities for him to observe himself in action.

To help the therapist recognize resistance behavior and respond to it effectively, it is useful to distinguish four major types of sources of resistance to the treatment process: *resistance to change, character resistance, resistance to content,* and *transference resistance.*[2] These four types of resistance are elaborated below in the sequence in which they are likely to make their first appearance during the course of psychotherapy. Following this discussion of the origins of resistance, the remainder of the chapter is concerned with common manifestations of resistance behavior and alternative ways of responding to it.

RESISTANCE TO CHANGE

It has long been recognized that emotional and behavioral disturbances tend to be accompanied by a reluctance to give them up. In some instances such resistance to change stems from an anticipation that recovery will put an end to certain advantages of being disturbed, in which case the patient is said to display *secondary gain resistance.* At other times change is expected to create specific new disadvantages, the most frequent types of which lead to *neurotic equilibrium resistance, resistance to patienthood,* and *superego resistance.* Whatever form it takes, resistance to change involves feelings and attitudes that pre-date the patient's entering psychotherapy and exist independently of it. Hence, although resistance to change may become exacerbated at various points during psychotherapy, especially when visable progress occurs, it can interfere with a patient's communication from the first moment of his initial interview.

[2]This typology of resistance differs in some respects from the traditional classification proposed by Freud (1926, p. 160) and reviewed by such psychoanalytic writers as Glover (1955, pp. 50–78), Greenson (1967, pp. 85–88), and Menninger and Holzman (1973, pp. 108–112). The modest revisions involved in formulating the types of resistance discussed in this chapter incorporate the traditional types but place them in the context of a somewhat broader frame of reference.

Secondary Gain Resistance

Secondary gain consists of a variety of rewards, benefits, or gratifications that an individual accrues as a consequence of his being psychologically incapacitated and that influence him to resist any significant change in his condition.[3] This is not to say that emotionally disturbed people become disturbed because they enjoy it. To see secondary gain as a source of psychological problems is to conceive of behavior as arising because of its consequences, as in suggesting that people develop emotional problems in order to enjoy having others sympathize with them. Such teleological hypotheses contribute little to comprehending the origins of psychological disturbance and erroneously imply that a disturbed individual can voluntarily give up his psychopathology anytime he decides to forego the advantages stemming from it.

Correctly speaking, secondary gain serves to reinforce already established patterns of disturbed behavior, not to elicit them, and to hinder change, not prevent it. Secondary gain emerges from the fact that a person who is perceived by others as suffering an unfortunate ailment or affliction is likely to receive large doses of sympathy, to be exempted from various kinds of responsibilities, and to have allowances made for outlandish, inconsiderate, and self-indulging behavior that would not otherwise be tolerated. It is difficult to resist becoming attached to having one's needs catered to, his feelings spared, and his energies freed to serve only purposes that please him, and these potential advantages of being incapacitated in turn resist being relinquished. Additionally, it is not uncommon for resistance to change, associated with such secondary gains, to be bolstered by some tangible benefits contingent on the incapacitation, such as a disability pension, extended paid sick leave from a job, or the assistance of a full-time housekeeper.

Yet not everyone who experiences psychological difficulties basks in a supportive response from others, accompanied by special privileges and a reprieve from responsibility. Impatience and irritation, rather than sympathy, may greet a person who becomes disturbed, which means he will realize little secondary gain from persistence of his problems unless he happens to delight in irritating others and trying their patience. Similarly, having psychological difficulties may not lead to a person's being excused from his responsibilities at home, in school, or on the job, but rather to his having to carry on despite the burden of his problems. In

[3]Good descriptions of the nature of secondary gain and of its role in perpetuating emotional disturbance appear in several papers by Freud (1909, pp. 231–232; 1913, p. 133; 1916–1917, pp. 382–385), who first noted the manner in which secondary gain functions as a resistance in psychotherapy (1926, pp. 98–101, 160).

such a case the burden often becomes a stronger motive to overcome the problem than any source of secondary gain is to persist in them.

Furthermore, even when sympathy and freedom from responsibility do accompany psychological incapacitation, there is a limit to how long most people enjoy being dependent and cared for. Not having to work, make decisions, confront delicate interpersonal situations, or be held accountable for one's behavior has a certain temporary appeal, like going on a vacation. But it is in the nature of people to feel best about themselves when they have a sense of doing something meaningful with their lives and of being treated by others as a worthwhile and responsible person capable of making his own decisions. Hence secondary gain emanating from emotional problems tends to be short-lived, except in those relatively few instances in which it becomes entrenched as part of chronic, intransigent disorder that produces psychological invalidism.

Thus secondary gains associated with emotional disturbance may on occasion become sufficiently important to inhibit participation in psychotherapy, but they are usually overshadowed by a patient's motivation to ease his emotional distress and by intrinsic pressures toward positive personality growth. On the other hand, the therapist does need to be prepared to recognize and deal with secondary gain resistance in every patient he sees. No matter how limited the benefits a patient appears to be reaping as a result of having psychological problems, some resistance to change due to secondary gain is bound to develop during the treatment. At the very least, the therapist's interest and respect provide the patient a rewarding experience that will last only so long as he requires treatment. For this reason, a patient who seems fully capable of implementing desirable behavior change may resist changing in order to prolong his relationship with the therapist. This particular pattern of resistance to change has obvious implications for termination in psychotherapy and is elaborated in Chapter 12.

Neurotic Equilibrium Resistance

Whereas resistance to change associated with secondary gain involves a person's reluctance to give up aspects of his condition that are providing him some advantages, other important sources of resistance to change are based on the anticipation of new and distinct disadvantages. Most common in this regard are concerns that change will disrupt current patterns of interpersonal relationships that constitute what is known as a *neurotic equilibrium*.

In a neurotic equilibrium, the people with whom a patient interacts at home, in school, on the job, or in leisure activities have adapted to his behavioral problems and idiosyncracies, so that he feels accepted or at least tolerated in their company and can anticipate how they will respond to him from one day to the next. He may even be valued by significant people in his life because his shortcomings gratify their needs in some complementary way. For example, a man who is psychologically handicapped by a reluctance to assert himself may be married to a maternal woman who thrives on having him depend on her. Or a person whose failures and misadventures seem to be the bane of his family's existence may also be providing them a scapegoat on whom they can blame their other individual and collective difficulties and toward whom they can direct negative feelings they would otherwise direct toward each other. [4]

Either because he and his environment have become accustomed to how he is, even if neurotic, or because his difficulties are meeting the needs of others, a person with psychological problems may be reluctant to change at the risk of disrupting the equilibrium in his life. Early in treatment such reluctance often appears in the form of vague apprehensions about the unkonwn, as if the patient were musing to himself: "I don't like the way I am, but at least I know what to expect of myself and what other people expect of me; if I were to change, what would I be like, how would other people react to me, and what new kinds of experiences would I have to face?" The charting of unexplored waters always provokes anxiety, even for the venturesome person determined to extend his life horizons. Accordingly, psychotherapy may from its beginning include moments when the patient's wish to change is temporarily opposed by a wish to avoid uncertainty, and the therapist must be prepared to help the patient recognize this source of resistance when it arises.

As treatment proceeds and behavior change begins to occur, resistance related specifically to sustaining previous patterns of interpersonal relationships may come to the fore. In particular, progress toward the goals of the treatment may have the adverse effect of alienating key figures in the patient's live, whose needs he is no longer gratifying. If the dependent man mentioned above becomes more assertive and self-reli-

[4]The work of Harry Stack Sullivan (1953, 1956) should be acknowledged as first stressing the interpersonal context in which the onset, nature, and course of psychological disturbance is almost invariably influenced. Subsequent clinical and research findings on the role of complementary neurotic needs and of scapegoating in sustaining individual psychopathology are presented by Ackerman (1958), Eisenstein (1956), Lidz (1963), and Vogel and Bell (1960).

ant, for example, he may frustrate his maternal wife to the point where she becomes depressed, irritable, and perhaps even undecided about continuing in the marriage. If a chronically unsuccessful or deliquent patient deprives his family of a scapegoat by becoming prosperous or law-abiding, he may expose himself to increased family disharmony and decreased family interest in him and his activities.

In such circumstances a patient may feel tempted to persist in his behavior problems and retain the interpersonal equilibrium associated with them, rather than change his behavior and risk disrupting the equilibrium. If so, the therapist will have to ponder whether or not to encourage continued treatment. Would the patient do better to become more self-actualizing and let the interpersonal chips fall where they may? Or is he so locked into his current interpersonal context that equilibrium-disrupting behavior change, no matter how apparently desirable, would be psychologically deleterious?

Whether to change and bear the consequences or remain the same and avoid taking chances is in the end the patient's decision; barring emergency situations, the therapist should not presume to make it for him. Yet a therapist can and should influence his patient's choice between remaining in a neurotic equilibrium or working to change himself, according to his estimate of where the patient's best prospects lie for finding satisfaction in life. Hopefully this estimate will have been accurately made during the assessment phase of the treatment, so that a patient engaged in psychotherapy will have been correctly identified as having more to gain than to lose by modifying his behavior. On the basis of his prior assessment that psychotherapy is appropriate, then, the therapist should ordinarily work to keep his patient in it when a dissolving neurotic equilibrium produces resistance to change.

Assessments are not perfect, however, nor are therapists infallible in their judgments. Information emerging in the course of psychotherapy, including untoward disruption in a patient's life subsequent to behavior change, may indicate that it was a path not wisely taken. The therapist must be prepared to recognize instances of apparent resistance to change that are not paradoxical at all, but instead reflect a patient's well-founded conclusion that he would be better off not to continue in the treatment. Needless to say, such well-founded decisions should be distinguished from resistance and respected for the reality they represent.

Resistance to Patienthood

In some cases resistance to continuing in or benefiting from treatment stems from negative attitudes toward being in the patient's role. Even before beginning treatment, a prospective patient may be repelled by what it means to him to receive professional psychological help. If he perceives entering psychotherapy as evidence that he is a weak, worthless, inadequate, or dependent person, for example, his threatened self-esteem may generate a *resistance to patienthood,* in which the negative connotations of being in psychotherapy outweigh any gains expected from it.

After treatment has begun, resistance to patienthood sometimes originates in or is intensified by the very kinds of behavior change toward which the patient has aspired. In these instances the fact that desired change is being achieved with professional help makes the person feel even more worthless, inadequate, and dependent than he did about entering psychotherapy, and change is resisted because it will be more damaging to self-esteem than just talking with the therapist but not being helped by him.

Unlike neurotic equilibrium resistance, which protects a comforting interpersonal context against the inroads of behavior change, resistance to patienthood provides little benefit beyond some illusory bolstering of self-esteem. Failing to take advantage of available opportunities to receive needed help, simply because of negative attitudes toward receiving such help, is analogous to letting one's teeth decay rather than face up to the dentist's drill. Hence the therapist must be alert to resistance associated with the patient's reservations about being in treatment and take pains to resolve it before the viability of the treatment becomes endangered. Because resistance to patienthood most often arises prior to and during the formulation of the treatment contract, a fuller discussion is found in Chapters 2 and 5.

Superego Resistance

As a patient begins to experience gratifying behavior change in psychotherapy, he may fall prone to another source of resistance to change derived from self-attitudes, namely, *superego resistance.* Superego resistance is spawned by a demanding conscience and nourished by a propensity to feel guilty. A person ruled by conscience attributes his misfortunes to his own culpability, regards hardship and disappointment as his just desserts, and renounces any claims to a more pleasurable existence. People burdened with a harsh superego consequently tend to view any improvement in their lot with suspicion or even alarm. Success and happiness come bittersweet for them, marred by nagging inner whisperings: "It's too good to be true"; "Don't let yourself enjoy it because it won't last and you'll only be let down"; "You don't deserve to have such a good thing happen, and if you go along with it, there will be some price to pay later on."[5]

For people struggling with such attitudes toward themselves, apparent progress in psychotherapy generates skepticism and anxiety. The patient doubts that the beneficial changes are real or permanent, and should events begin to suggest that they may indeed be so, he frets about some future time when he will have to make a Faustian accounting for his gains. Such anxiety emerging from self-punitive attitudes inevitably produces resistance to change in psychotherapy and needs to be recognized when it arises.

CHARACTER RESISTANCE

An individual's character consists of his customary and perferred ways of dealing with his experience. The attitudes and habits that define a person's characterological style often serve positively to foster his productivity and enhance his satisfaction in life. On the other hand, as indicated in the preceeding chapter, some aspects of character constitute defensive operations aimed more at reducing anxiety than at seeking self-fulfillment. Considerable emphasis was placed on the importance of helping a patient in psychotherapy understand and modify such characterological defensive operations, both as an end in iteslf and as a prelude to increased understanding of the underlying concerns that have evoked them. Relevant to the present chapter is the fact that behaviors a person characterologically uses to ward off anxiety will also be used to ward off psychotherapy as a potential source of anxiety, which means that characterological defensive operations may inhibit participation in psychotherapy and constitute a source of resistance.

Several of the ways in which characterological style can interfere with communication in psychotherapy were illustrated in the earlier discussion of interpreting characterological defensive operations (see pp. 123–126). To expand on this subject, it is helpful to classify potential sources of character resistance into three levels of specificity. First, there may be instances in which a patient's reliance on some specific defense mechanism, such as isolation, repression, or reaction formation, prevents direct access to the concerns that would be most useful for the patient to talk about. Second, there may be times when broader aspects of a

[5]The role of the superego in personality functioning is treated at length in Bergler's (1952) *The Superego; Unconscious Conscience* and Lewis' (1971) *Shame and Guilt in Neurosis.*

person's coping style, such as a markedly active or passive approach to life or a predominantly concrete or abstract style of thinking, restrict the range of his conversation in the treatment. And third, there may be patients in whom generalized characterological problems, such as a masochistic personality disorder or a success neurosis, pose particular obstacles to establishing and sustaining the basic treatment contract.

Specific Defense Mechanisms

Defense mechanisms are strategies employed by an individual to avoid conscious recognition of thoughts or feelings that would make him anxious. Since a central aim of psychotherapy is to increase a person's conscious awareness of matters that cause him anxiety in order that he can deal with them more effectively, defense mechanisms always interfere with the patient's working toward the aims of the treatment. For example, people who frequently utilize isolation as a mechanism of defense tend to skirt spontaneous expression of emotion by careful cognitive filtering of their affective experience. When angered they do not explode with "You sonofabitch, I'll get you for this!" but are more like to intone, "I want you to know I'm getting very irritated with you"; when in love they are less likely to say "I love you" than "You mean a great deal to me."

In psychotherapy the characteristic schism between affect and ideation that marks isolation produces excessive attention by the patient to what he thinks rather than what he feels. Emotions are stripped of their immediacy, events are described with pallid objectivity as if from a scenario involving strangers, and efforts by the therapist to elicit feelings produce only grudging , impersonal allusions to affect: "I'm sure I must have been very angry"; "It seems to me right now that I'm feeling pretty good"; "I didn't think I needed to mention feeling sad, since it's obvious anyone would be unhappy in a situation like that." Since such difficulty in experiencing affect directly and expressing it spontaneously inhibits the communication of feelings in psychotherapy, it constitutes a resistance to the treatment. Accordingly, effective interpretation of isolation serves not only to expand a patient's self-awareness, but also to facilitate the emergence of affect-laden material that might otherwise have remained submerged and unavailable for discussion.

Some examples of repression and reaction formation will further illustrate the manner in which specific defense mechanisms produce resistance in psychotherapy. Repression, which is traditionally defined as "unconsciously purposeful forgetting or not becoming aware of internal impulses or external events'' (Fenichel, 1945a, p. 148), can be aimed at either thoughts or feelings, just as isolation can be used to disconnect two thoughts that belong together as well as thoughts from the feelings that correspond to them. However, whereas isolation promotes a predominantly ideational focus on experiences, repression as a generalized defensive mode fosters an immersion in affect and immediacy at the expense of thought and reflection. Hence a person who relies heavily on repressive defense has little difficulty experiencing feelings directly and expressing them spontaneously, but is seldom inclined to reflect on the meaning of his experience and actions.

The repressing individual as a psychotherapy patient freely indicates *how* he feels but gives little attention to *why* he feels that way. If asked why he feels as he does, he is more likely to brush the question off (''I don't know''; ''Just because''; ''The important thing is that I *do* feel this way'') than he is to undertake any analysis of his reactions. Similarly, the repressing individual frequently recounts his affective reactions to events without including enough objective details for the therapist to know what took place. Subsequent requests for such details will try his patience, since he attaches much less significance to facts than to feelings, and they may also exceed his capability to respond, since a repressor tends not to note or remember the kinds of factual details necessary for clear reconstruction of an event. Hence, though in quite an opposite manner from isolation, prominent repressive defenses can also contribute to resistance in psychotherapy and their modification can expand the amount of information that becomes available to work with in the treatment.

Reaction formation involves an overemphasis on certain manifest attitudes or behavior patterns directly contrary to underlying feelings and impulses that would be anxiety-provoking to recognize or express. When reaction formation holds sway, unacceptable enmity becomes transformed into self-sacrificing adoration (''How can I resent my mother when she has been so good to me?''), and frightening aggressive tendencies turn into meek passivity (''If I were to lash out at people the way I'd like to, I'd suffer terrible reprisals''). Whenever psychotherapy begins to unearth any such underlying feelings or impulses that provoke fear, guilt, shame, or embarrassment, the patient who uses reaction formations seeks to disguise them by concentrating on self-reports that suggest just the opposite kind of feelings and impulses—he protests too much. In the face of reaction formation, then, as in instances of isolation and repression, interpretive easing of the patient's defenses allows information to come into the therapy that would otherwise remain outside of awareness.[6]

Coping Styles

Coping styles comprise abiding dispositions or traits that influence the manner in which a person organizes and responds to his experience. Although defense mechanisms similarly influence how a person organizes and responds to experience, coping syles refer to a broader set of behaviors that differs from defensive operations in two respects. First, individual preferences for mechanisms of defense are determined primarily by experiences in anxiety-provoking situations, whereas individual coping styles are influenced not only by experiential factors but also largely by aspects of temperament that are constitutionally determined.

Second, defense mechanisms are protective measures activated to ward off or bind anxiety that would otherwise be experienced in situations a person cannot handle effectively; while thus minimizing anxiety, they also inhibit personality functioning and direct an individual away from coming constructively to grips with the source of his anxiety. Coping styles, on the other hand, constitute modes of dealing with experiences of all kinds, whether anxiety-provoking or whatever; while they may at times be defensive or maladaptive, they also include constructive and self-fufilling ways of behaving and meeting challenge.

Because coping styles consist of certain ways of organizing and responding to experience to the exclusion of other ways, they can narrow a person's behavioral repertoire sufficiently to produce resistance in psychotherapy. For example, some people are by nature relatively active in their approach to life, while others are temperamentally passive. An active person is likely to expect constant interchange, cascading insights, and rapid change in psychotherapy, and for him a process of sober reflection and gradually expanding self-awareness may be difficult to tolerate. A passive person frequently looks to psychotherapy as a treatment that will do something to him, if only he brings his body regularly into the shop, and for him the responsibility for introducing

[6]Extended discussions of the nature of specific defense mechanisms and their implications for characterological style are provided by Fenichel (1945a, pp. 141–167) and in excellent, more recent books by Shapiro (1965), *Neurotic Styles*, and Salzman (1968), *The Obsessive Personality*.

subjects for discussion and helping to explore and learn from them may be difficult to shoulder.

If they are expressed, the manifestations of resistance associated with this activity-passivity dimension of temperament take characteristic forms. The active patient bridles at the slow pace of the treatment, complains that little or nothing is being accomplished, and talks about other treatment methods he has heard or read about that really get things moving quickly. The passive patient grumbles about the lack of direction he is receiving from the therapist, argues that if he could do what is apparently expected of him in the treatment he would not have needed it in the first place, and asks about the possibility of drugs, hypnosis, or other treatment adjuncts that similarly minimize the patient's responsibility.

A somewhat different pattern of resistance related to coping styles derives from certain personality dispositions known as "cognitive styles." As one example of cognitive style, some people are oriented toward thinking about themselves and their experience primarily in concrete terms, while others tend by nature to think more in the abstract. When the work of psychotherapy calls for a focus on concrete details, an abstract cognitive style may interfere with communication, thus causing resistance; when it seems important to generalize beyond details, a concrete cognitive style may be a source of resistance. Other dimensions of cognitive style that have been identified and explored in researech studies include field dependence-independence, constricted versus flexible control, leveling-sharpening, reflection-implusivity, and cognitive complexity-simplicity. As a potential source of resistance, prominent characterological orientation toward either extreme of these dimensions can direct a person away from certain topics or styles of discussion that would facilitate progress in the treatment.[7]

Generalized Characterological Problems

In some instances character resistance in psychotherapy results not from specific defense preferences or from broader aspects of coping style, but from generalized characterological problems that pose

[7]The concept of temperament, its constitutional basis, and its implications for abiding coping styles is elaborated in work by Chess and Thomas (1973), Kagan and Moss (1962), and Thomas et al. (1968). The literature on cognitive style is somewhat diffuse, but seminal research in this area is reported by Gardner et al. (1959), Witkin (1965), and Witkin et al. (1962), and more general reviews are provided by Broverman (1960), Gardner (1964), and Kagan and Kogan (1970).

particular obstacles to effective treatment. Two such problems that merit special attention are *masochistic character disorder* and *success neurosis*.

A person with a masochistic character disorder thrives on psychological pain, no matter how much he complains about it and shrinks from opportunities to improve his lot in life. In psychotherapy such a person presents an exaggerated and pervasive picture of the superego resistance pattern described earlier. Convinced that he does not deserve to be any happier or self-satisfied than he is, he mistrusts and is discomfited by indications of progress—an undeserving person is after all bound to be stripped of his unrightful gains and suffer retribution for having presumed to accept them. As is obvious, then, a masochistic orientation to life can generate unusually refractory resistance to pursuing potentially helpful discussions in the treatment.

The individual with a success neurosis similarly resists progress toward becoming a more effective person, not because he prefers pain to pleasure but because he feels threatened lest he accomplish too much. A success neurosis does not usually preclude a person's enjoying a rich and rewarding social life, but it does inhibit his utilizing his capacities to achieve in academic, occupational, and creative pursuits. Harboring irrational fears of the consequences of surpassing others, the success neurotic holds back in competitive endeavors and avoids accomplishment in such challenging situations as attempting to improve himself in psychotherapy. Like masochism then, fear of success creates specific obstacles to the work of the treatment that must be identified and surmounted for significant progress to occur.[8]

RESISTANCE TO CONTENT

In contrast to resistance to change and character resistance, both of which involve personality characteristics the patient brings with him into psychotherapy, *resistance to content* refers to obstacles to progress that are elicited by and exist uniquely within the treatment situation. Of all the forms of resistance, resistance to content is the least complex in its origin and the least difficult to comprehend. When psychotherapy focuses as it

[8]Although written over 40 years ago, the best available discussion of masochistic character disorder and the obstacles it erects to progress in psychotherapy is provided by Wilhelm Reich (1933, pp. 208–247). Also valuable as an extensive description of masochistic behavior is Theodore Reik's (1941) well-known book, *Masochism in Modern Man*. Success neurosis was first described by Freud (1916) and has been more recently reviewed by Ovesey (1962) and Schuster (1955).

should on the aspects of a person's life that are causing him difficulty, attention will regularly be drawn to subjects that are embarrassing, frightening, aggravating, depressing, or in some other way unpleasant for the patient to think or talk about. Hence the treatment process inevitably evokes content that makes the patient averse to participating fully in it.

Because resistance to content often motivates a patient to avoid certain subjects by keeping them out of his conscious awareness, Freud originally referred to it as "repression resistance," defined as "the persistent, automatic, normative tendency of the ego to try to control dangerous tendencies by blocking them off" (Menninger & Holzman, 1973, p. 108). In view of the advances that have been made in conceptualizing ego psychology and neurotic personality styles, however, it currently seems useful to distinguish between repression as a normative tendency to resist content in psychotherapy, which is present in all patients, and repression as a preferred defensive style that produces specific kinds of resistance in some patients but not others. Accordingly, resistance stemming from a generalized preference for repressive defenses was discussed in the previous section on *character resistance*, and the resistance that all patients display from time to time by avoiding awareness of content is being considered here under the generic label of *resistance to content*.

The relative ease of recognizing resistance to content derives from its close ties to the ongoing interchange in treatment interviews. Resistance to change and character resistance, although exacerbated by psychotherapy, have their origins in life events outside of the treatment. Transference resistance, to be considered next, originates in the treatment situation but is a complex function of the patient's relationships with the therapist and with other current and past figures in his life. Content resistance, on the other hand, is both a unique product of psychotherapy and a fairly simple, transparent reaction to here-and-now events occurring in the treatment.

More specifically, resistance to content emerges either concurrently with the discussion of some topic that is difficult for the the patient to pursue or when such a topic appears about to come up for discussion. Suppose, for example, that a patient who has been discussing some marital problems has become visibly upset while describing a perceived inability to function adequately as a sex partner. He might then attempt to drop the subject, either without comment or perhaps with some statement that he has nothing more to say about it or is finding it too painful or humiliating to pursue further. Such an emergence of resistance would be obvious in its source and meaning. The patient's motivation to escape the psychological distress associated with talking about his sexual problems has temporarily overridden his motivation to work toward resolving the problem, and has thereby produced a reluctance to continue with content pertaining to it.

As for resistance to anticipated content, suppose the patient in this example has been elaborating nonsexual aspects of his marital relationship and has finally volunteered that "I better get into what goes on in regard to sex." Instead of doing so, however, he falls silent, or talks about something other than sex, or begins discussing sex in a general way unrelated to his personal concerns. His behavior then reflects anticipatory resistance to content, and the onset of his resistance just at the time when the topic of his sexuality is about to surface leaves little doubt as to the origin and significance of his having become resistive.

TRANSFERENCE RESISTANCE

In the course of psychotherapy all patients experience various kinds of positive and negative feelings toward their therapist as a result of displacing onto him attitudes they have held toward other important people in their lives. Transference phenomena are of sufficient importance in psychotherapy to justify a separate chapter, and thus Chapter 10 is broadly concerned with their origins, manifestations, and therapeutic utility. The present discussion serves merely to identify transference as one possible source of resistance in psychotherapy and to stress that transference reactions inevitably give rise to resistance behavior.

To understand how transference produces resistance, it is helpful to review briefly the manner in which psychotherapy generally fosters positive and negative feeling toward the therapist. A patient who is extended appropriate amounts of genuineness, warmth, and empathy comes to appreciate his therapist's nonjudgemental interest and admire his sensitivity and dedication to a helping profession. Such attitudes initially cultivate the patient's eagerness to participate in the treatment process, but sooner or later they mount to a point where he begins to idealize the therapist and to crave various kinds of relationships with him that transcend the boundaries of the treatment contract. The patient muses, how wonderful it would be to have or have had this person as a mother or father, a son or daughter, a spouse, a lover, or a close friend. Accompanying these positively toned musings are wishes to be dependent on the therapist or to take care of him, to become an important person in his life, to see him socially, to exchange expressions of love and admiration with him, or to become his sex partner.

As time passes and such positive feelings are not reciprocated in kind, disappointment and frustration set in. Now the therapist ceases to be admirable and lovable; instead, as the callous agent of the patient's disappointment and frustration, he becomes a cold, insensitive, unresponsive, inconsiderate, uncaring individual unworthy of adulation or respect. In this way, positive feelings toward the therapist give way to negative ones, and since the therapist is in reality neither quite so remarkable nor quite so deplorable as the patient perceives him to be, both sets of feelings involve transference elements.

The specific form transference reactions take and the circumstances that elicit them are determined by the individual patient's prior interpersonal experiences, as are the readiness with which transference feelings develop and the manner in which they are expressed (see Chap. 10). For all patients, however, both positive and negative transference reactions interfere with communication in psychotherapy and hence constitute resistance.

Positive transference interferes with communication by fomenting undue concern with the therapist's opinions. A person can talk most freely about himself when he attaches no significance to what his listener thinks of him; the more he ponders the listener's impression of what he has to say, the less spontaneous he can be in saying it. Accordingly, because positive feelings toward a therapist motivate efforts to court his favor, they usually distort a patient's communication in two respects: they incline him to censor his remarks, excluding anything he fears might detract from the impression he hopes to create, and they encourage him to embellish his comments with thoughts, feelings, and self-descriptions he feels will draw the therapist's interest and approval. Either way, the positive transference impedes candid communication and hence leads to resistance.

Negative transference feelings lead to resistance by producing reactions similar to those that accompany unrequited love. Some patients, in their frustration and disappointment at not having their wishes for a closer, more intimate relationship with their therapist gratified, respond in a primarily depressive fashion, either passively or actively. Passive depressive reactions associated with negative transference result in the patient's talking in a subdued and desultory manner, becoming listless and discouraged about his progress, and perhaps expressing reservations about continuing in the treatment. In the latter case, seeing the therapist in the knowledge that the desired relationship with him will never come to pass resembles the experience of a rejected suitor, who may prefer never to see his loved one again rather than endure the agony of being in her presence but denied her love.

The more active depressed patient reacting to ungratified positive wishes toward the therapist is less likely to fall silent or contemplate leaving therapy than he is to hang in there, sullen, pouty, and complaining, in an effort to wheedle the therapist into gratifying him. Without visible anger, he pleads, reprimands, and admonishes: "If only you could tell me more about yourself or we could get together outside of this office, so that I could get to know you better, I would be able to talk to you more easily and you could be of more help to me"; "If you really cared about me, you wouldn't be so remote and distant"; "I would't be surprised if I just slid back into all the problems I was having before if I can't get any more feeling that I'm a person and not just a patient to you." Obviously such statements from the patient require a carefully conceived response from the therapist if he is to avoid either retreating behind a caricatured shell of therapist "objectivity" or stumbling into an interpersonal morass that gratifies the patient for the moment but limits his eventual prospects of benefiting from the treatment.

Continuing with the patterns of transference resistance, some patients react angrily rather than with depression to the therapist's frustration of their positive wishes toward him. The angered patient typically seeks not to prod the therapist into some desired relationship, but to punish him for not reciprocating his positive attitudes. Commonly, then, negative transference is expressed through a variety of maneuvers that complicate the therapist's task, such as failing to appear for sessions, coming late, or refusing to talk. Also frequent are more direct expressions of negative transference couched in criticisms of the therapist's perceived nonresponsiveness ("You're such a cold person, you must have ice water in your veins"; "I've said all I can, its time for you to do some work for a change"); of his conduct of the treatment ("You never seem to have anything useful to say"; "I don't think you're experienced enough to help me with the problem I have"); or of therapy itself ("I don't think this treatment is doing me much good"; "From what I've heard, the evidence for psychotherapy's being worthwhile isn't all that good").

Faced with such remarks, the therapist needs to consider two questions. First, how much of what the patient is saying has a basis in reality and how much is a distortion of reality determined by aspects of the transference? Second, whatever the mixture of reality and transference in the patient's behavior, which elements of each would be most useful to pursue at the particular moment? Deferring to Chapter 10 the discussion of how to answer these questions, the key point to emphasize in the present context is that all of these manifestations of negative transference draw the patient's attention away from the problems that brought him for help and interfere with his talking about himself, and hence they inevitably function as resistance.

Finally, it should be noted that transference feelings can lead to resistance not only by making a patient more intent on impressing or punishing the therapist than he is on pursuing the original goals of the treatment, but also by making him anxious or uncomfortable. When transference feelings are embarrassing or frightening to admit, as feelings of love or hate toward the therapist may often be, they evoke resistance to their content. Thus patients who are generally loath to express affection directly tend to deny or suppress positive feelings toward their therapist, even if doing so means not talking freely and openly with him, and patients who shrink from feeling or venting anger tend to ward off negative transference, even at the price of narrowing their range of self-awareness and self-report. In this way transference feelings that are themselves not expressed, either directly or indirectly, can participate in resistance behavior as content that is difficult for the patient to think about or report.

INDICATIONS OF RESISTANCE

Many of the ways in which resistance is manifest have been illustrated in the preceding discussion of its origins. However, not all indications that a patient is experiencing some reluctance to participate in the treatment are as obvious as the prior examples used, nor are cumulative examples as helpful in learning to identify resistance as a categorization of the kinds of behavior that are likely to reflect it. The following five categories of patient behavior in psychotherapy encompass most of the ways in which resistance is manifest: (a) reducing the amount of time spent in the treatment; (b) restricting the amount or range of conversation; (c) isolating the therapy from real life; (d) acting out; and (e) flight into health.

Reducing the Amount of Time Spent in the Treatment

The simplest way for a patient to resist the impact of psychotherapy without overtly renouncing the treatment contract is for him to find "reasons" for reducing the amount of time he spends in it. In particular, patients who arrive late for sessions, ask to leave early, cancel or miss appointments, or prematurely propose termination are likely to be resisting full participation in the treatment through the simple medium of limiting their exposure to it.

However, despite the straightfoward way in which reducing the time spent in psychotherapy can serve the purpose of resistance, it is not always easy to distinguish resistance from reality when patients cancel or come late for session. "I got caught in traffic," apologizes a woman dashing in 10 minutes late for her session, or "He's home sick in bed," says a wife calling to cancel her husband's appointment. How is the therapist to interpret these events? Everyone gets caught in traffic on occasion and arrives late for an appointment, even when highly motivated to be on time. But could this woman have anticipated heavy traffic and allowed extra driving time? Or could her lateness be due not to any usual traffic congestion but to her having left home later than usual? Or could she have arrived on time despite heavy traffic had she not stopped to chat with an acquaintance she met in the parking lot?

As for a cancellation because of illness, this could certainly constitute reality and not resistance. But is the patient's illness really serious enough to prevent him from keeping his appointment? Or could the "illness" be an anxiety or phobic reaction, perhaps manifest in headache, abdominal pain, or some other physical complaint, symptomatic of some aversion to the treatment? Or could the whole illness story have been contrived to spare the patient from having to tell the therapist directly of prefering not to keep the appointment?

How much resistance and how much reality underlies such events depends then on the specific context in which they occur. As the therapist attempts to make this judgment in the individual case, neither trusting naivety nor relentless skepticism will serve him in good stead. He should be sufficiently suspicious of whatever reasons a patient gives for limiting the time of his participation in the treatment to consider whether they involve elements of resistance; at the same time he should be sufficiently cognizant of reality and of the distinction between near and remote derivatives to accept some explanations at face value and defer exploring others, even when they appear somewhat lame.

In this regard, explanations of missed or abbreviated sessions will usually strike the therapist in one of three ways. Some will appear so realistic and far removed from resistance as to suggest little reason for pursuing them further. A patient who cancels a session because of illness and arrives for his next interview still obviously suffering the effects of a bad cold, for example, or who arrives late but gives a credible account of having been unavoidably detained should not be pressed for possible resistance elements in his behavior.

A second group of explanations seem ambiguous and call for open-ended exploration. Suppose a patient cancels a session because he will be out of town on a business trip. Being out of town on business is seemingly a justifiable reason for missing a session, but is there more to the situation than meets the eye? Was it necessary for the patient to be out of town on the particular day of his session, or did he in fact have some latitude in scheduling his trip that he chose not to exercise? Or, if the day of his trip was inflexible, would it still have been possible for him to leave at noon and keep his morning therapy appointment? In such ambiguous circumstances, where the truth of the matter could lie either in resistance or in reality, the details of the patient's explanation need to be explored until they point clearly in one direction or the other.

A third group of explanations leaves little doubt from the beginning that the patient's behavior reflects resistance and should be responded to accordingly. Either his actions have been too transparently resistive to permit a reasonable explanation, or his initial explanation of otherwise ambiguous behavior rings so false as to relieve it of any ambiguity. With respect to transparency, failing to appear for an uncanceled appointment and asking to end a session early are almost always manifestations of resistance, since nothing short of a major crisis in the patient's life can justify such behavior in reality. Thus a woman who misses a session without calling because her son fell out of a tree and required emergency medical treatment can hardly be perceived as resisting the treatment, whereas a woman who begins a session by saying she has to leave early to take her son to the dentist (for an appointment that presumably could have been scheduled at some other time) is very probably resisting. As for the quality of the explanation offered, a patient who arrives late and says, "I just couldn't get myself moving today," or who cancels an appointment because "I'm not in the mood to talk with you," is almost certainly resisting, even though his behavior might have been more ambiguous if he had attempted to justify it in terms of some mitigating circumstances.

Special attention should be paid to prematurely proposed termination, since it may foreshadow an irreversible reduction in the amount of time spent in the treatment. Patients who raise the question of termination usually do so by indicating either thay they can no longer continue in the treatment, due to circumstances like a move out of town, or that they are disinteresed in continuing, because they no longer feel a need for psychotherapy. As a third alternative, a patient may simply stop appearing for appointments, without having mentioned an inability or unwillingness to continue; however, such drastic action is rarely taken unannounced once a patient and therapist have passed a period of constructive working together.

Each of these three approaches to termination can embrace elements of resistance and reality. A patient who states he is unable to continue may in fact be moving several hundred miles away, to attend school or to take a new job. But perhaps he is just moving across town and facing a longer trip to the therapist's office, or perhaps he is taking on new commitments that will make his regular appointments less convenient. Whereas the first circumstance seems quite realistic, the latter two smack of an excuse to limit the therapy, and they would call for an exploration of probable resistance elements. In the same way. a patient who says he feels he no longer needs or wants therapy may be manifesting resistance or may be presenting an accurate appraisal of his progress in the treatment, in which case his proposal for termination would be appropriate rather than premature. Even a patient who drops out of treatment, and who is therefore very likely to be resisting the impact of further psychotherapy, may instead be reluctant only to tell the therapist that he has achieved his treatment objectives and no longer needs to continue (with the implication that if the therapist had been more alert and perhaps less possessive, he would have recognized the patient's progress and suggested termination himself, without having to be told).

Hints of premature termination are perhaps the most critical resistance behavior for the therapist to confront promptly and effectively, primarily because they may not allow him a second chance. Should overlooked or unresolved resistances rupture the treatment contract, there will not be any subsequent opportunities to recoginize them more quickly or respond to them more usefully: the patient will have dropped out of therapy and canceled the therapist as a helping agent. The important distinction between appropriate termination, which is based on realistic considerations, and premature termination, which indicates resistance, is discussed further in Chapter 12.

Restricting the Amount or Range of Conversation

Whereas reducing the amount of time spent in psychotherapy is the simplest way for a patient to minimuze its impact, the most common manner in which patient's resist the treatment is by restricting the amount or range of their conversation. Reducing the time spent involves the interface between the patient's life inside the therapist's office and his life outside of it, and whether it constitutes resistance depends on whether there are mitigating factors in reality. Restriction of conversation, on the other hand, exists totally within the context of the psychotherapy situation, and any effort by the patient to limit what or how much he says can automatically be taken as a manifestation of resistance (except possibly in the case of laryngitis). To recognize when such limits are being imposed, the therapist should listen for what may be called three kinds of language: the language of *silence*, the language of *fixation*, and the language of *avoidance.*

Silence. Whenever a patient talks noticeably less freely than usual or stops talking altogether, it can be inferred that a wish to avoid discomfort has temporarily unsurped his commitment to the treatment process. Since not talking is an effective way to skirt uncomfortable subjects or circumscribe change in psychotherapy, relative or absolute silence is frequently employed as a means of resisting and points to resistance when it occurs.

When a patient who is talking sparingly comments on his behavior, either spontaneously or in response to being confronted with silence, he may seek to account for it with such statements as "I just don't feel much like talking today" or "Not much has happened so I haven't much to say." Whatever form such statements take, the therapist must not be misled into accepting them as realistic explanations of relative silence. The treatment contract to which the therapist has explicitly agreed (assuming the treatment has been properly initiated as described in Chap. 6) calls for him to talk regardless of how he feels about talking and to say what comes to his mind independently of what may or may not be happening in his life. This does not imply that the therapist's task is to rap his patient on the knuckles whenever he expresses a disinclination to talk. Rather, he needs to recognize that something beyond the obvious is interfering with the patient's ability or willingness to communicate, and he then needs to help the patient identify and resolve the particular source of this resistance.

On occasion a silent patient may report that he simply has nothing to say or that "My mind is a blank." It is doubtful, however, whether in normal circumstances the waking mind ever becomes "blank," without conscious awareness. The patient who says his mind is empty is either dissembling to avoid airing his thoughts or feelings, or he is struggling to keep his mind free to provide justification for his silence. Either way, a patient's claim to have nothing to say is as much an indication of resistance as a frank admission of reluctance to say what is on his mind.

Fixation. In Chapter 8 it is noted that a patient in psychotherapy can vary the content of his remarks along four dimensions. He can talk about past or about present events, in concrete or in abstract terms, about thoughts or feelings, and in specific regard to the treatment process or independently of it. It is further noted that an overemphasis on either pole of these content dimensions provides grist for confrontations addressed to the omitted pole. Having developed the concept of resistance in the present chapter, it is now possible to identify such an overemphasis as a *fixation* that serves the purpose of resistance by restricting the range of the patient's conversation.

To amplify this point, a patient who is talking freely will in various cycles of emphasis touch on both past and present events, employ both abstract and concrete frames of reference, report both thoughts and feelings, and discuss experiences both internal and external to the treatment situation. Whenever the therapist hears the patient focus his conversation in ways that reduce or eliminate such cycling, he is hearing the language of fixation. Thus a patient who talks endlessly about his childhood but rarely volunteers information about his current life is resisting; no matter how poignant his childhood recollections, his reluctance to alternate them with reports of contemporary events suggests that the latter are probably more difficult for him to talk about and more closely related to the problems for which he has sought help.

Likewise, a patient who never refers to the treatment relationship is resisting, as is one who can hardly talk about anything else, and the same significance attaches to fixations involving the abstract-concrete and thought-feeling dimensions of content. A word of caution, however: the language of fixation as a clue to resistance should not be taken to mean that whatever the patient chooses to talk about signifies resistance because he is choosing not to talk about something else. What it does mean is that prolonged or exclusive engagement in certain ways of talking to the exclusion of other ways very probably reflects elements of resistance.

Avoidance. Whereas content fixations constitute a form of avoidance behavior, there is a more specific language of avoidance in psychotherapy that pertains primarily to *what* the patient is not talking about rather than to *how* he is not talking about it. A woman who is afraid of men may be describing her fear only with respect to past events, for example, or only in abstract terms, or without any expression of feelings, or without any reference to her relationship with her male therapist—in each case she is fixating on some ways of talking and probably resisting other ways. However, if she does not mention her fear of men at all, not in any context, then she is demonstrating resistance through the language of avoidance.

In some instances the language of avoidance is easy to hear because the patient constantly talks around rather than about some topic that is obviously on his mind or central to his concerns. Consider again the example of a patient with a marital problem who discusses many aspects of his relationship with his spouse but who stops talking, changes the subject, or drifts off into some digression whenever he seems on the verge of getting into their sex life. Any such avoidance or skirting of a potentially important subject signals resistance at work.

At other times the language of avoidance may be less obvious, in that without appearing to be omitting anything the patient cheerfully fills the interviews with fluent accounts of his thoughts, feelings, and experiences. Yet psychotherapy is intended to direct at least part of a patient's attention to problematic matters that are unpleasant to think or talk about, and patients who are participating freely in the treatment process accordingly talk easily at some points but haltingly at others, and are in good spirits during some sessions but anxious, depressed, or irritable during others. When no such variation occurs, it is very likely that the patient is resisting despite his apparent openness. Even without the slightest inkling of what matters the patient is avoiding talking about, the therapist can infer from persistent breeziness that some potentially important thoughts or feelings are being censored.

Again, however, caution is in order with respect to interpreting smooth sailing in psychotherapy as a manifestation of resistance. Just as psychotherapy cannot accomplish much if it deals only with matters the patient enjoys talking about, it cannot be maximally effective if it dwells without respite on the patient's anxieties, embarrassments, regrets, and failures. Like all learning, learning about oneself in psychotherapy proceeds best if there is some spacing in the introduction of new material and some opportunity for consolidation of the old. A patient needs time to ponder alternative ways of looking at himself and his experiences, and he also needs time to recover from the distress of being confronted with such alternatives.

Patients in psychotherapy typically see to these needs by following work on an interpretive sequence with a period of pulling back or regrouping in which they limit their conversation to relatively mundane matters. Although such behavior constitutes resistance, strictly speaking, it should be recognized as "taking a breather" and distinguished from avoidance behavior that emerges independently of interpretive work or persists longer than seems necessary to regroup following an interpretive sequence. Interventions should be reserved for the latter pattern of avoidance, whereas "taking a breather" constitutes a necessary, expected episode of coasting that should be permitted without comment.

Isolating the Therapy from Real Life

One of the most effective means by which a patient can resist the impact of psychotherapy is by minimizing the extent to which anything that transpires in the treatment generalizes to his life outside of the therapist's office. Although in retrospect this pattern of resistance is easy to identify (it sooner or later becomes obvious when apparent progress by the patient in understanding himself better has not been translated into more effective or rewarding ways of living), the ongoing evidence for it consists only of rather subtle efforts by the patient to divorce his experience as a psychotherapy patient in the interview room from his experience in other roles in other places.

Patients seeking such a divorce usually strive to maintain two separate relationships with the therapist, a "psychotherapy relationship" and a "real relationship." In the "psychotherapy relationship" the patient fills his role as prescribed in the treatment contract, whereas in the "real relationship" he attempts to carve out blocks of time in which he can interact with the therapist in ways that transcend or are irrelevant to the treatment contract. The more he succeeds in maintaining such a separation, the more he erects artificial boundaries between his life as a psychotherapy patient and his life outside the treatment, and the more he can resist allowing progress in the former to influence behavior change in the latter.

Some illustrations of how patients often seek these two different kinds of relationship with their therapist help to clarify this concept of isolating therapy from real life. Consider a patient who enters the office and, while he and the therapist are still standing, says with good humor, "How's life treatin' ya, doc?" Then, as he and the therapist are seated, he becomes somber and subdued and says, "Today I want to talk with you about a really bad thing that happened to me." Who is the real patient? Is it the exuberant, high-spirited person who began so informally, or is it the concerned and troubled person who opened with a formal preview of his subject for the day? Obviously it cannot be both, and what we have is a patient who is presenting one face to the therapist in the form of a greeting and another face as he gets down to business. Certainly the greeting can be understood simply as a forced effort at gaiety intended to cushion the impact of the disturbing incident to be reported—but herein lie the seeds of resistance. If the patient feels that his real life troubles and depressed affect should not intrude on his relationship to the therapist, so that even while being upset he must face him with a smile, then he will just as easily shield his behavior outside the treatment relationship from the impact of what he learns in it.

Once the concept is grasped of how a patient can isolate psychotherapy from life by maintaining two separate relationships with his therapist, numerous illustrations of such behavior can be drawn from common clinical occurrences: a patient stops the therapist on their way into his office and says, "Before we go *in there* (with some ominous emphasis on the "in there"), there's something I have to ask you about"; a patient in the middle of a session says "I'd like you to stop being a therapist for a minute and tell me how you really feel"; a patient on his way to the door after an uneventful session says with more concern in his voice than he has shown in the preceding 50 minutes, "Now that our time is up, there's something important I want to mention to you"; a patient calls on the telephone and says, "I know we don't do this kind of things in our sessions, but I need your advice right now on whether I should take a new job I've been offered." In each of these examples the patient is attempting to divorce some matter from the psychotherapy relationship by casting it beyond the boundaries of time, place, or role behavior defined by the treatment contract.

To identify isolation of psychotherapy from real life, then, the therapist must be alert to any tendency of the patient to compartmentalize the treatment relationship, so that certain topics, styles of talking, or role behaviors arise only at the beginning or the end of sessions, or only outside the confines of the therapist's office, or only on the telephone, or in some other arbitrary disjunction of time or place. On the other hand, the treatment relationship as elaborated in the next two chapters is in fact a complex distillate of reality factors, transference elements, and the "working alliance" between patient and therapist. A patient can alternately emphasize one or another of these three facets of the treatment relationship, with marked shifts in what he chooses to say and how he chooses to say it, without necessarily compartmentalizing them. These shifts in emphasis follow naturally from the course of the treatment and do not involve any arbitrary sectioning off in time, place, or role behavior.

In contrast, when psychotherapy is being isolated from real life, differing role relationships to the therapist will be maintained on an arbitrary basis, so that some subjects are broached only at certain times or in certain ways. It is the patient whose style of relating to the therapist shifts with minimal relevance to the content of the treatment and in ways that strain the treatment contract who is likely to be resisting through isolation of his psychotherapy from real life.

Acting Out

Acting out refers to the resolution of psychological conflict by translating anxiety-provoking impulses directly into behavior. Because acting-out behavior replaces intrapsychic grappling with conflictual impulses, it is temporarily anxiety reducing. However, because acting-out behavior is also typically impulsive and poorly planned, it tends to generate new sources of anxiety. A person who acts out usually does things that make him feel guilty or ashamed, that incur the wrath or derision of others, or that in some other way prove self-defeating.[9]

With these features of acting-out behavior in mind, it is easy to see how it can serve as a resistance in psychotherapy. In general terms, first of all, acting out means that an individual is rejecting both reflection on his thoughts and openness to his feelings in favor of action. Opportunities to experience and observe himself are foreclosed by precipitous behavior, and the behavior itself involves a minimum of self-awareness. Hence acting out is by nature antithetical to the process of psychotherapy, since it involves substituting immediate behavior for any effort to plan more effective behavior on the basis of enhanced self-understanding. Acting out a problem obviates talking about it, and acting-out behavior in a psychotherapy patient suggests that important concerns are not coming up for discussion because they are being translated directly into action.

Turning secondly to the ongoing process of psychotherapy, it is not unusual for acting out to appear specifically in response to anxiety stimulated by discussions in the treatment. Thus a patient reviewing a thorny problem in his life or working through some anxiety-provoking interpretations of his previous ways of handling it may be tempted to take some action that will "end" the problem and thereby abort discussion of it. Returning again to the example of a man with marital problems who is on the verge of discussing some distressing sexual aspect

[9]These unqualified comments on the nature of "acting out" should not obscure the considerable variation and uncertainty that exist among clinicians regarding the definition and use of this term. Fenichel (1945b) elaborates the traditional notion of acting out employed here, and the reader is referred to Abt and Weissman (1965) and Milman and Goldman (1973) for more recent discussions of varying points of view about it.

of the problem, suppose he were suddenly to report that he and his wife had decided on a trial separation and that he had already rented an apartment for himself. "I've solved my marital situation for the time being," his actions would imply, "so we don't need to talk about it anymore."

When a patient responds in this way to distressing aspects of the treatment, it can usually be demonstrated that the actions taken were hastily conceived and have as many drawbacks as advantages. Acting out—an attempt to resolve a problem by precipitous action—will have occurred, and the resistance purposes served by the acting out will be evident. To generalize from the above example, whenever acting out occurs in the context of a treatment focus on a sensitive or upsetting topic, the patient is very probably attempting to resist further attention to the topic by rendering it passé.

One fairly common variant of acting out in psychotherapy merits special comment, since at times it may provide the only clear indication that a patient is resisting participation in the treatment. This pattern of resistance consists of talking to people other than the therapist about problems and concerns germane to the therapy. A person who enters treatment is of course not expected to break off his normal social and interpersonal relationships; indeed, psychotherapy frequently aims to help a person extend the circle of acquaintances with whom he can discuss mutual interests and concerns. What should not occur, however, are regular rehearsals or reviews of the content of psychotherapy sessions with a spouse, relative or friend, especially when these conversations include information that is not shared with the therapist.

Such use of "ancillary" therapists as sounding boards interferes with communication in psychotherapy by diluting both what comes into and what emerges from treatment interviews. The more a patient is airing his problems in conversations outside of psychotherapy, the less spontaneous he will be in the treatment and the less opportunity the therapist will have to work with fresh ideas and vivid affects: the treatment, in Freud's words, will have "a leak which lets through precisely what is most valuable"(1913, p. 136). Likewise, the more a patient is soliciting responses from other people to his thoughts and feelings, the less impact the therapist's comments and observations are likely to have.

Any intimation that a patient is regularly discussing his treatment with someone other than the therapist, or that he has sought outside opinions on matters being considered in the treatment, or that he is reporting pertinent information to other people but not to the therapist should be pursued as a likely manifestation of resistance. In some instances it may even emerge that the patient is contemplating or has entered into another professional relationship concurrently with his psychotherapy. Without having mentioned it, for example, the patient may have begun seeing a marriage counselor, or received personal guidance from his clergyman, or asked his family doctor for tranquilizers, or participated in a weekend group marathon.

A person with psychological problems can certainly be helped by a variety of different approaches, and some patients may profit most from a treatment program that combines individual psychotherapy with group sessions, medication, activities therapy, vocational counseling, or social welfare assistance, to name a few possibilities. When individual uncovering psychotherapy is the primary treatment mode, however, such other relationships dilute rather than sustain the impact of the treatment and should be kept to a minimum agreed on by patient and therapist as a necessary adjunct to their work together. A patient who *unilaterally* seeks medication, counseling, hyponotherapy, encounter group experiences, or any other more or less professional form of help with his problems is resisting psychotherapy by acting to buffer it.

Flight into Health

Patients in psychotherapy commonly begin feeling better or behaving more effectively in the very initial stages of their treatment. Such early benefits derive not so much from the work of the treatment itself, which is just underway, as from positive attitudes the patient has toward being in psychotherapy. In response to the therapist's commitment to work with them and indications of his capacity to be helpful, most people gain some optimism about being able to resolve their psychological difficulties. At the same time, patients are often pleased with themselves for having taken the steps necessary to receive professional help, and their self-esteem may be bolstered further by the therapist's interest in them. Flushed with high expectations and spurred by enhanced self-regard, a new patient may experience sudden symptom relief and increased control over problematic behavior.

In some cases such rapid improvement takes place during the evaluation period, before a treatment contract has been made, and it may even occur between the time a patient schedules a first appointment and is actually seen for evaluation. For some people, in other words, just the opportunity to discuss their concerns and have them evaluated professionally, or just having made an appointment for this purpose, proves to be supportive and reassuring. The initial contacts, even if limited to a telephone call setting up an appointment, signify to the patient that he has taken some definitive action to do something about his problems and that help is on the way. The hopeful expectations and sense of accomplishment associated with these pre-therapy contacts may alone be sufficient to ease a person's concerns and help him function more effectively, at least on a temporary basis.[10]

At times, however, rapid improvement early in psychotherapy indicates resistance to treatment rather than any real benefit derived from being engaged in it. A patient who feels reluctant to continue in psychotherapy may suddenly find himself feeling much better or behaving much more effectually. When such improvement is reported to the therapist, the implied message is clear: "See, I'm doing much better already, and I don't really need to continue with this treatment." Used in this way, a patient's prompt symptom relief constitutes what is known as *flight into health*, and it serves the purpose of resistance (see Oremland, 1973; Train, 1953).

Needless to say, careful distinction must be drawn between actual, enduring improvements produced by the initiation of treatment and illusory, short-lived improvements based on a flight into health. The therapist should not overlook the possibility of meaningful early gains in psychotherapy and should not risk undermining such gains by interpreting them as resistance. Yet he should also be alert to possible resistance elements involved in apparent early improvement, so that he can bring them to his patient's attention before they jeopardize the continuity of the treatment.

Resistance elements in early improvements can be identified by observing the kind of improvement reported, the timing of its occurrence, and the implications attached to it. With respect first to the kind of improvement reported, the more modest, credible, and durable it appears to be, the more likely it is to represent a real gain and not a flight into health. On the other hand, a dramatic report ("Suddenly I'm a new person") of an implausible change ("I've completely lost the self-consciousness that has plagued me for 20 years") that quickly evaporates ("For a while last week I thought I was all straightened out, but now I'm

[10]Early improvement associated only with participating in an evaluation or scheduling an initial interview are aptly referred to by Goldstein (1960, 1962) as "(un)-spontaneous remission." Because of the role that expectations play in influencing behavior change, Goldstein points out, patients who have been evaluated and placed on a waiting list for psychotherapy constitute an inappropriate control group for studying whether psychotherapy facilitates behavior change more effectively than no treatment at all (spontaneous remission). Subotnik (1972) has more recently come to the same conclusion on the basis of a review of the literature.

feeling as self-conscious as ever") points to illusory improvement and probably reflects resistance to continuing in the treatment.

Concerning the timing of early improvements, the more they seem to have occurred in the normal course of the patient's life, independently of the content of his psychotherapy sessions, the more likely they are to constitute reality. If instead the reported improvement seems to follow on the heels of a session in which some anxiety-provoking subjects have come up for discussion and the therapist has offerred some telling confrontations or interpretations, resistance elements in the behavior change should be strongly suspected. Wheelis (1949) aptly refers to this particular form of resistance as "flight from insight."

As for the implications attached to early improvement, patients who report their improvement to the accompaniment of increased enthusiasm for the treatment are likely to have experienced some real gain. The changes they have noted in themselves have heightened their long-range expectations of benefiting from psychotherapy, and the interviews immediately following the reported improvement are likely to be remarkably free of indications of resistance. When on the other hand a patient seems to be concluding from his improvement that he no longer needs treatment or that, since it occurred so quickly, treatment was unnecessary to begin with, the improvement probably represents resistance through a flight into health.

In concluding this section, it should be noted that the rejection of interpretations has not been included as an indication of resistance. Therapists are often tempted to regard refusal to accept an interpretation as resistance behavior. To be so tempted, however, is to regard the therapist as omniscient and the patient as ever culpable. Interpretations exist only as alternative hypotheses, not as absolute truths; as stressed in Chapter 8, it is not the therapist's saying something that makes it so, but the patient's finding it congruent with his experience. When a patient rejects an interpretation, it is because the interpretation has either been inaccurate or poorly timed, and the therapist should direct his attention not to possible resistance elements in the patient's behavior but rather to improving his own sensitivity or his technique in preparing the patient to receive the interpretation.

RESPONDING TO RESISTANCE BEHAVIOR

The manner in which resistance behavior is responded to in psychotherapy has a significant bearing on the course and outcome of the treatment. However, responding to resistance is not synonymous with interpreting resistance however and whenever it occurs. Rather, selective decisions about when and how to interpret resistance should be made according to the general principles of interpretation discussed in Chapter 8. Within the framework of these principles of interpretation, four alternative modes of responding to resistance behavior are available: (a) allowing the resistance to build; (b) circumventing the resistance; (c) exploring the resistance; and (d) breaking through the resistance.

Allowing Resistance to Build

Just as the therapist should refrain from making interpretations unless there is sufficient information to document them, he should not respond actively to resistance behavior until he feels confident he can demonstrate its presence. No matter how certain he is of how and why a patient is resisting, he will make little progress in communicating this understanding unless he can first help the patient appreciate that he is in fact resisting.

Solid evidence is usally necessary to help a patient recognize that some aspect of his behavior is serving the purpose of resistance. Turning again to the common example of a patient's being late, suppose a usually prompt patient arrives five munites late for a session "because of traffic." Such an isolated instance of mild tardiness provides flimsy support for an interpretation of resistance, which even if accurate could be construed by the patient as picayune and unreasonable. The same could be said for a patient who hesitates slightly in bringing up a new subject or on one occasion asks "How are you?" as he enters the office. On the other hand, a patient who arrives 15 minutes late for three successive interviews "because of traffic," or who refuses to say anything further about a subject, or who asks numerous detailed questions about the state of the therapist's health—in short, a patient whose manifestations of resistance are gross or repetitive—can be shown relatively easily that his behavior is probably motivated by a wish to avoid participating fully in the treatment process.

Hence the first step in responding to resistances is to allow them to build to a point where the patient can readily be made aware of them and they can then be profitably explored. If some suggestive behavior like arriving slightly late dissipates quickly without escalating into marked or repetitive tardiness, the patient's possible reluctance to participate in the treatment has been inconsequential and would have been difficult to document. Substantial resistance tends not to dissipate quickly, but rather to generate increasingly repetitive and pronounced resistance behavior that can be readily demonstrated and explored.

By allowing resistance to build, then, the therapist sacrifices little and improves the prospects for being able to interpret resistance behavior effectively. To this end he needs to refrain from jumping on every hint of resistance behavior he detects, just as he generally guards against offering interpretations prematurely or too often. Careful attention to timing and dosage help in the exercise of such restraint, as does keeping in mind that the therapist's task calls more for being helpful than for being clever.

Circumventing Resistance

When resistance reaches a point where its manifestations are obvious and demonstrable, therapist passivity becomes an error of omission. The therapist who ignores marked resistance, waiting and hoping for it to evaporate while he carries on with available interview content, is abdicating his responsibility. Marked resistance left alone tends to fester and may soon infect a patient's commitment to remaining in the treatment or his expectations of benefiting from it. Should the resistance happen to pass of its own accord without inducing the patient to drop out or lose confidence, an opportunity will still have been lost to explore a meaningful process aspect of the psychotherapy. Whether because further progress in the treatment would otherwise have been scuttled or because an opportunity to facilitate progress would have been lost, resistance behavior requires the therapist's active attention whenever it becomes pronounced.

Responding actively to resistance does not preclude attempting to circumvent it, however. On some occasions the therapist may feel that efforts to help a patient understand and learn from his resistance will be less fruitful than helping him pursue a particular subject of concern to him. Usually these occasions involve content resistances that are too pronounced to be ignored but can most usefully be responded to either by providing support, in order to decrease the patient's anxiety about the subject on his mind, or by calling attention to the resistance, as a means of encouraging the patient to proceed in the face of his anxiety.

Providing Support. When intercurrent resistances arise because a patient is too embarrassed, ashamed, or hesitant to report what is on his mind, some reassurance from the therapist may be all that is necessary to relieve his hesitancy and avert any escalation of resistance. Reassurring comments intended to circumvent content resistance can be addressed sometimes to the nature of psychotherapy, as in the first of the two examples below, and at other times to the nature of human behavior, as in the second example:

Pt. I just thought of a sexual thing I did once, but it's awfully hard to talk about.

Th. It's the hard things to talk about that we need to focus on; the things that are easy to talk about are not the ones that are likely to be causing you any problems.

Pt. I just can't tell you about the horrible thoughts I've had about harming my children. You'll think I'm a terrible person.

Th. It's what people *do* that makes them good or bad, not what they think.

As both of these examples indicate, resistances that can be responded to supportively are also usually open to a variety of other approaches. Thus, instead of attempting to encourage elaboration of content, the therapist might have focused attention on the patient's difficulty in talking about sexual matters in the first example above, and on the patient's concern about being regarded as a terrible person in the second example. So long as care is taken not to ignore the resistance in such instances, the decision whether to circumvent or explore it should depend on the therapist's best estimate of which approach will contribute most to the patient's learning about himself at that particular point in the treatment.

Calling Attention to Resistance. It is often possible to circumvent content resistance simply by calling attention to it, without providing support or attempting to explore the origin and meaning of the resistance. The therapist needs only to make a statement on the order of "I get the feeling there's something on your mind that you're reluctant to talk about." If accurate, such observations may provide the patient with all the eoncouragement he needs to plunge into a difficult subject: "Well . . . yes, you're right . . . there is something . . . well, okay, let me tell you." Or instead of going directly into content when his resistance is noted, the patient may reflect on how or why he is resisting: "I usually talk a lot when I'm trying to hide something"; "I'm afraid if I tell you what I'm thinking you won't have much respect for me." One advantage of merely calling attention to a resistance is that it leaves the patient this choice of pursuing either the content with which he is struggling or the nature and origins of his struggle.

Yet, because just calling attention to possible resistance may go beyond a patient's current level of awareness and hence constitute an interpretation, the therapist must be prepared to document his observation. Should a patient ask, "What makes you think there's something on my mind I'm reluctant to talk about?", the therapist should be able to point to firm evidence of such reluctance: "This is the second session in a row you've sat silently for several minutes at a time, whereas you usually have no difficulty finding something to say." Unless such documentation is at hand, even a noncommittal effort to call attention to possible resistance behavior will risk all the disadvantages of a premature interpretation.

Exploring Resistance

When there is no compelling reason for focusing on the content of what a patient is saying or could be saying, resistance that has reached demonstrable proportions should be explored rather than circumvented. To explore resistance effectively, the therapist should follow closely the guidelines presented in Chapter 8 for constructing an interpretive sequence. In particular, interpretations of resistance should be the culmination of a series of clarifications and confrontations that have gradually prepared the patient to recognize that some aspects of his behavior reflect reservations about participating in the treatment process.

The interpretive exploration of resistance accordingly begins with helping the patient perceive discrepancies between how he is behaving and how he agreed to behave in endorsing the treatment contract. Unless a resistive patient can acknowledge that his behavior diverges in certain ways from what might be expected of him and is thereby opposing progress in the treatment, no exploration of the origins and implications of his resistance will be possible. Thus the first step in initiating an interpretive sequence aimed at resistance consists of encouraging the patient to observe his own unusual behavior, as in the following confrontations:

You're talking much less today than usual.

It seems that whenever we have a session in which you get upset, you have a long talk with your wife just afterward.

I've noticed that you begin each session with several minutes of small talk, about the weather and such things.

You've cancelled a number of appointments in the last month or so, and before that you hardly ever missed a session.

The patient may respond to such observations by acknowledging resistance elements in his behavior, or he may instead attempt some rational explanation of it ("I've just had a lot of extra work to do and couldn't make it, even though I really wanted to"). In the latter case the therapist will then have to draw on supplementary data (which should be available if he has allowed the resistance to reach demonstrable proportions) to refute whatever rationalizations are offered ("But from what you've told me, there have been other times when you've been equally busy at work, yet you never missed any sessions then").

A detailed and laborious review of a patient's "explanations" of resistance behavior may be necessary to expose them as masking an underlying reluctance to participate fully in the treatment. Painstaking dissection of the events involved in such behavior as coming late, canceling an appointment, disucssing the therapy with someone else, or experiencing a sudden improvement is well worth the effort if it results in the patient's clearly recognizing that his behavior derives from resistance. On the other hand, when such efforts fail to elicit acknowledgment of apparent resistance elements in the patient's behavior, the therapist should be prepared to recognize that the resistance was either in his imagination or was not yet sufficiently developed to support an effective interpretive sequence.

One fairly common way in which patients seek to justify resistance behavior is by involing a distorted conception of their role in the treatment. For example, a patient confronted with being silent may say, "I think I've been doing my share of the talking and it's your turn now"; or a patient asking to leave a session early may indicate that he has said everything he wanted to say that day; or a patient who has been canceling appointments may assert, "As I see it, I really should come in to talk with you only when something is really bothering me." All such statments distort the usual treatment contract in uncovering psychotherapy, which specifies that it is the patient's primary task to talk and the therapist's to listen, that sessions last for a prescribed length of time regardless of what is or is not being discussed, an that appointments are regularly scheduled independently of how the patient is feeling. To help a patient who responds in this way recognize that his behavior is not so immediately explicable, the therapist should directly contrast the explanation offered with the terms of the treatment contract ("But we discussed initially in planning the treatment that we would meet each time for 50 minutes, so there must be some reason for your wanting to leave early other than just thinking that the sessions end when you're through talking about a particular subject").

This latter example illustrates two important features of interpretive sequences aimed at resistance behavior. First, as noted in Chapter 6, an explicitly stated and mutually endorsed treatment contract often provides the basis for demonstrating to a patient that he is resisting. Without previously specified role behaviors and treatment arrangements to refer to, the therapist may be hard put to convince his patient that there is anything unusual about ways in which he is limiting his participation in the treatment. To continue with the above example, if the therapist has not previously clarified that sessions will be of a fixed length, he is on shaky ground trying to attach significance to his asking to leave early. "Oh," the patient may say, "you never told me that we would always meet for 50 minutes, and if I had known I wouldn't have suggested stopping right now." Thus an adequate treatment contract becomes a valuable ally when resistance interpretations depend on blatant discrepancies between the patient's current behavior and the role he agreed to play in the therapy.

Second, an interpretive sequence aimed at indications of resistance should usually be initiated by arousing the patient's curiosity about his behavior. Although such curiosity may emerge spontaneously, it often must be fostered in gradual stages. In the first stage the apparent resistance behavior is called to the patient's attention for him to acknowledge as existing ("You're right, I'm not talking as much as usual today"). In stage two the behavior now acknowledged as fact is recognized by the patient as being unusual, either because he cannot account for it on a rational basis or because it runs counter to the treatment contract he had previously endorsed. In the third stage the behavior acknowledged as unusual is labeled as a subject worth pursuing (Pt: "So there must be other reasons why I'm acting as I am"; Th: "We have to wonder about what you're feeling this way might mean")

Once interpretation of resistance has reached this point, with the resistance behavior recognized as worthy of exploration, the patient is prepared to begin working on understanding its origins and meanings. He may already have sensed his resistance and been on the verge of talking about it, in which case the therapist's initial observation ("You seem very quiet today") proves sufficient to start him exploring it ("I've been aware of some things we're getting into that I just don't feel like talking about"; "I'm not saying much because I've been having some feelings about you that I'd be embarrassed to have come out"). More commonly, however, progress in unraveling identified resistance behavior requires much more assistance from the therapist than merely arousing his patient's curiosity.

Should the therapist have no impressions or hunches about the origins of acknowledged resistance behavior, the interpretive sequence may go no further than simply marking for future reference the fact that some unaccountable behavior opposing the progress of the treatment has occurred. If on the other hand the therapist has some basis for considering the resistance behavior related to aspects of the patient's characterological style or to his attitudes toward behavior change, the content of the interviews, or the therapist as a person, he can then employ a sequence of clarifications, confrontations, and partial interpretations leading the patient toward sharing in this understanding of his behavior. The following two examples, the first involving resistance to content and the second transference resistance, illustrate such interpretive sequences:

Pt. I can see that there must be something more to my coming so late today, but I don't know what it could be.

Th. It's as if you don't want to talk much.

Pt. How do you mean?

Th. The less time you're here, the less time there is for you to talk.

Pt. Okay, but that would seem to mean there's something I don't want to talk about. Could that be it?

Th. You seemed to have some strong feelings during our last session.

Pt. Did I? Oh yes, I remember, I had just started to tell you about what I did with my husband before we were married—you know, sexually—and how guilty I feel about it, and . . . well, that must be it. I remember when I left I had the thought that I never wanted to come back if it meant I would have to talk more about that subject.

Pt. I know it's different from usual, but I just don't feel like talking today. I suppose there are things I could say, but I'd prefer to keep quiet.

Th. What does keeping quiet mean to you, what comes to your mind about it?

Pt. Oh, I suppose keeping quiet means minding your own business, not getting involved, keeping your feelings to yourself.

Th. So maybe right here and now you have some feelings you want to keep to yourself, to avoid getting involved.

Pt. Uh . . . no . . .uh, I don't think so. Nothing much at all seems to be on my mind. (Patient squirms, appears uncomfortable)

Th. I wonder if you're not having some feelings about me that are difficult to talk about.

Pt. Well, if you must know, I had a dream about you, an intimate kind of dream, and coming in here today I had a feeling of anticipation like I was going on a date or meeting a lover, and I don't know what to make of it.

These examples illustrate two useful techniques for helping a patient explore resistance behavior, in the first case by reconstructing the events leading up to the onset of the resistance and in the second case by encouraging associations to its possible meanings. If a patient can recall when and in what circumstances he experienced some reservations about participating in the treatment, and particularly if he can pinpoint events that were likely to have precipitated these reservations, he will be off to a good start in identifying the origins and meaning of his resistance behavior. Such a reconstruction in the first of the above examples, focused by the therapist's reference to the events of the previous interview, paved the way for the patient to recognize the source of her resistance. When a patient can associate to the meaning of his resistance behavior, his comments will often contain clues to its underlying significance, which is what occurred in the second example: the therapist's request for associations yielded some behavioral descriptions ("not getting involved, keeping your feelings to yourself") that provided him access in the patient's own words to the transference feelings causing the resistance.

When a resistive patient has been helped to understand the origins of his resistive behavior, his resistance will usually abate sufficiently for him to resume communicating freely in the treatment. Additionally, as in the second example above, the nature of the resistance may itself capture the patient's attention ("I don't know what to make of it"). Why, for example, is he uncomfortable or embarrassed to talk about a particular subject? Why, when a situation makes him uncomfortable, does he seek to avoid it in some ways rather than in others? How does his resistance behavior in the treatment relate to other situations in his life in which he has felt uncomfortable and has become maladaptively defensive? Each of these questions and others like them can lead to fruitful areas of exploration, thus illustrating the utility of resistance interpretations not only in helping a patient continue with the current content of the treatment but also in providing new topics for discussion.

Breaking Through Resistance

Exploring resistance, while it occasionally provides dramatic breakthroughs, tends like the interpretive process in general to be a deliberate, low-key reconstruction of a patient's thoughts, feelings and actions during which he gradually arrives at an enhanced understanding of his behavior. At times, however, circumstances call for the therapist to break directly through resistance behavior with a single, unequivocal interpretive statement; for example, to a paitent who has slouched sullenly in his chair for the first five minutes of a session, he may say, "You're angry at me today."

The criteria for attempting to break through resistance in so abrupt a manner, without prior inquiry or exploration, are very stringent. The therapist must be quite certain that the patient is in fact resisting and is cognizant of his reluctance to participate in the treatment; he should be confident that his proffered explanation of the resistance behavior ("You're angry at me today") is accurate and can be readily documented; he should have good reason to expect the patient to accept, understand, and utilize his direct interpretation; and finally, he should be convinced that breaking through the resistance of the moment will be more advantageous than gradually exploring it. Unless the therapist has all of these strong feelings about the appropriateness of an interpretation that breaks directly through resistance behavior, any such interpretation he makes is likely to inject in the treatment the several disadvantages of premature interpretation outlined in Chapter 8.

With few exceptions, the criteria for attempting to break directly through resistance are likely to be met only in instances of repetitive resistance behaviors that have previously been explored and traced to their origins. Consider, for example, a patient who from time to time has been opening his interviews with how-are-you's and subsequent efforts to make small talk about the therapist's life. Suppose further that careful exploration of his behavior on several occasions has clarified (a) that the patient tends to begin this way when he has some delicate or difficult subject on his mind, and (b) that by beginning in this way he attempts to delay getting into the subject, to shift attention from his life to the therapist's, and to cast the patient-therapist relationship more as a mutual friendship than as a working arrangement focused on his problems. In this context, should the patient then begin a session with "How are you today?", the therapist might usefully respond. "There's something on your mind you're hesitant to talk about."

Although such a direct breaking through of resistance is justified only infrequently, it is an oversight for the therapist not to do so when the criteria noted above are met. As in the general process of working through, repetitions of a resistance interpretation should not begin each time from scratch, with detailed exploration as if the behavior in question had never been previously discussed. Rather, each repetition should build on what has gone on before, so that a decreasing amount of therapist effort is necessary to help the patient recapture the probable meaning and implications of the behavior that is being interpreted. In the above example, for the therapist continually to treat "How are you?" as a new and unaccountable process aspect of the treatment, as if no previous understanding of it had been achieved, would both prolong the treatment unnecessarily and sooner or later give the patient cause to wonder whether the therapist was really paying attention and understanding him.

Furthermore, like interpretations in general, interpretations of resistance can become worked through to a point where only minimal therapist activity is necessary to revive them. As a patient progresses from his initial insight into some aspect of his behavior toward being able to use this insight to effect behavior change, breaking through its resistance elements may cease to require statements like "You're angry at me today" or "There's something you're reluctant to talk about." Thus the therapist's response to "There's nothing on my mind" may be "We've heard that before" or perhaps just a raised eyebrow, following which the patient is able to say, "Oh yes, I know, whenever I say that it usually means I've got something to talk about that's hard to say, and I suppose there is something I need to tell you about today." Eventually a point should be reached where the patient interprets his own behavior as quickly as he reports it, even when it involves resistance: "I found myself puttering around today, which would have made me late, and I know that means I'm having some mixed feelings about the treatment; so I got myself to get moving and make it here on time, but I still think it would be important to find out what was bothering me."

Hence, although exploration will remain the most frequently indicated way of responding to demonstrable resistance behavior, resistance interpretations that have been accepted and understood by the patient become part of the working through process. As such, they may be offered with increasingly direct comments that break through rather than explore the resistance behavior. Over time, then, as the working through of resistance interpretations is accomplished, the patient not only learns about himself from his resistances but also achieves sufficient control of his resistance behavior to eliminate its interference with his communication in the treatment.

CHAPTER 10

The Psychotherapy Relationship: Transference

Transference consists of the displacement of feelings, attitudes, or impulses experienced toward previous figures in a person's life onto current figures to whom they do not realistically apply. As such, transference participates to some extent in all interpersonal relationships, since the reactions of one person to another are always subject to the influence of prior interpersonal experience. Like resistance, however, transference behavior is exacerbated by the treatment situation and has considerably bearing on its course.

The role of transference in psychotherapy was first elucidated by Freud (1905, 1912b, 1915), who saw transference reactions as both a useful source of information and a potential impediment to progress in the treatment. As a process aspect of psychotherapy, transference provides vivid clues to the nature of the patient's past and current interpersonal relationships; as a source of resistance, they can cut deeply into the patient's commitment to the treatment contract.

To appreciate the special significance of transference reactions, it is necessary to understand them in the broader context of the treatment relationship. Transference accounts only in part for a patient's feelings and attitudes toward his therapist, since the treatment relationship is also shaped by his realistic responses to the therapist's behavior (the *real relationship*) and by his adherence to the terms of the treatment contract (the *working alliance*). This chapter first elaborates these three components of the patient-therapist relationship and then describes (a) the origins and fostering of transference in psychotherapy, (b) variations in the intensity, feeling tone, and expression of transference reactions, and (c) technical considerations in the exploration and interpretation of transference phenomena.

TRANSFERENCE, REALITY, AND THE WORKING ALLIANCE

The relationship of a psychotherapy patient to his therapist proceeds simultaneously on the three different levels of transference, reality, and the working alliance. As elaborated below, these three components of the patient-therapist relationship differ widely in how they emerge and how they influence the course of treatment, and many aspects of patient behavior in psychotherapy are determined by which component is in ascendance.

Tranference

The distinguishing feature of transference is the *displacement* of feelings, attitudes, or impulses. As displacements, transference reactions are always inappropriate to the actual circumstances of the treatment situation. Some transference reactions are unjustified primarily in kind or quality, and others primarily in their intensity; in either case transference "exceeds . . . anything that could be justified on sensible or rational grounds" (Freud, 1912b, p. 100).

To illustrate first a reaction of inappropriate quality, suppose a patient in the midst of recounting an event suddenly flushes with anger and exclaims, "It really burns me up, the way you sit there scowling at whatever I say, like you wish I wasn't even taking up your time." Why is the patient angry? The therapist has done nothing to incur his wrath except sit and listen, as the treatment contract prescribes and as he presumably has been doing in previous interviews without making the patient angry. Furthermore, assuming that the therapist has not been conducting himself in any typical fashion, why does the patient perceive him as scowling and as begrudging his time commitment? Since the answer to these questions does not lie the reality of the situation, the patient's behavior constitutes a transference reaction unjustified in quality by the circumstances in which it has occurred.

To illustrate a reaction of inappropriate intensity, consider a situation in which the therapist is five minutes late in beginning an interview. The patient in this situation might justifiably feel somewhat irritated or disheartened, since the therapist's tardiness cuts into the time for which he is paying and also indicates that other matters have been allowed to override the therapist's commitment to the treatment contract. In view of such realistic considerations a therapist who begins late owes his patient an apology and should usually extend the session to its contracted length.

But suppose that instead of an appropriately mild reaction the patient flies into a rage and accuses the therapist of unethical practice, or becomes so depressed he can talk only of the therapist's "obvious" disinterest in him. Then the patient's reaction will be appropriate in kind to the actual circumstances but unjustified in intensity, and hence a manifestation of transference.

Implicit in both of these examples is another useful way of conceptualizing transference reactions, namely, that transference represents a *distorted perception* of the therapist's attitudes and behavior. To see the therapist as scowling when he is not, as being disinterested or disapproving when he feels no such way, or as failing to work conscientiously in the patient's behalf when he is are all instances of inaccurate perception. Sullivan (1954, pp. 25–27) coined the term *parataxic distortion* to label the process by which a person's present interpersonal relationships become distorted by inappropriate generalizations from previous interpersonal experience. Although parataxic distortion has not become a widely used term, it nicely captures the role that misperception of the therapist plays in generating and shaping transference reactions.

Reality

A patient's real relationship to the therapist comprises his appropriate and reasonable responses to what the therapist is, says, or does. A patient may respect the therapist for his educational and professional attainments; he may become annoyed if the therapist interrupts an interview to accept a telephone call or appears to have forgotten some important information from a previous session; or, depending on his tastes, he may like or dislike the way the therapist arranges his furniture, combs his hair, selects his ties, displays his books, or whatever. Should such reactions become unrealistically intense—that is, should respect for the therapist generate diffidence, or a brief interruption provoke fury, or opinions of the therapist's personal qualities influence what the patient chooses to talk about—then they will constitute transference. However, so long as they remain within the bounds of how one person might appropriately respond to another, they will be part of the real treatment relationship.

The distinction between transference reactions and the real treatment relationship provides an important guideline for the selection of patient-therapist transactions to interpret. Since transference reactions often contain otherwise unavailable clues to a patient's interpersonal difficulties and may also contribute to resistance, their exploration promises to enhance self-understanding and at the same time relieve obstacles to progress in the treatment. The real relationship, on the other hand, seldom interferes with communication in psychotherapy and provides little information about the patient beyond the superficial and obvious. Attempts to interpret the realistic behavior of a patient toward his therapist therefore contribute minimally to the work of the treatment.

Their differences notwithstanding, transference and reality are rarely exclusive in a patient's behavior toward his therapist. Transference reactions are usually triggered by some event in reality, and realistic reactions are often embellished with transference attitudes. A patient who becomes furious at his therapist for taking a telephone call has after all had his session interrupted, and a patient who denounces a youthful therapist as too young to be competent is correctly perceiving the therapist's age and relative inexperience. A patient who realistically likes the way his therapist looks or arranges his furniture can leave it at that, but if he makes a point of saying "You're a handsome man" or "You have great taste in decorating," some transference elements, involving a wish to court the therapist's favor, are probably participating in his behavior.

The therapist's task is to determine where the balance lies between transference and reality in a patient's reactions to him and to concentrate his attention on those reactions that appear determined primarily by transference. Not only is there more to be gained from pursuing the transference, but there are some distinct disadvantages to probing the real relationship. Consider, for example, a patient who concludes his last session of a calender year with "Happy New Year," or who says to a therapist obviously suffering with laryngitis and a bad cold, "I hope you're feeling better soon." Although such comments may involve transference elements, they also constitute ordinary social amenities that pass between people who have no personal relationship.

Such social amenities are best responded to in psychotherapy by taking them at face value. Aside from yielding minimal information, attempts to explore conventional behavior (e.g., "I wonder what thoughts you have about saying that to me") risk making the patient feel more an object of study than a person worthy of respect. A patient denied the opportunity for a real relationship with his therapist, so that he cannot wish him good health without having his motives impugned, will feel demeaned in the treatment situation and consequently have less likelihood of benefiting from it (see Chap. 3). Unless they blossom into resistance and impede the patient's communication about himself and his problems, conventional social comments call for a response in kind: "Happy New Year" calls for "Same to you," and "I hope you're feeling better soon" calls for "Thank you."[1]

The Working Alliance

The working alliance consists of those aspects of the patient-therapist relationship that are determined by the treatment contract, that is, by the agreement to work in certain prescribed ways toward alleviating the patient's problems. The working alliance is in evidence whenever a patient is reporting his thoughts and feelings openly and participating with the therapist in observing them. Although colored by both transference and reality, the working alliance stands separate from each of these other two components of the treatment relationship.

The working alliance differs from transference because it comprises accurate perception of the treatment situation and strict allegiance to the terms of the treatment contract. When the working alliance holds sway, a patient does not "forget" the essence of his or the therapist's task as initially agreed on, nor does he seek an inappropriately extensive or intimate relationship with the therapist, nor does he distort the nature or meaning of the therapist's behavior. Rather, he goes about the business of describing and looking at himself without displacements and without attempts to cast the therapist in any role other than his contracted one as listener and facilitator of self-understanding.

Although the working alliance is thus reality-oriented and free from distortion, it has a contrived and nonreciprocal quality that also distinuishes it from a real relationship. Interpersonal relationships in the real world are sustained by mutuality, so that people interact on a personal basis only so long as they are gratifying each other's needs. In the relationship formed by a working alliance in psychotherapy, however, one person (the patient) agrees to forego gratification of his needs to allow the other person (the therapist) to help him increase his understanding of these needs. In a real relationship when a person says to a friend, "I really need someone to do it for me," he is told, "Don't worry, you can count on me"; in psychotherapy he is encouraged to explore why he

[1]It should be noted that some theories of psychotherapy do not distinguish between the transference relationship and the real relationship. Within the Kleinian framework, for example, all patient behavior is considered to reflect the transference and is interpreted as such (Klein, 1952; Klein et al., 1952; Heimann, 1956). However, most dynamically oriented therapists endorse the utility of making this distinction, as reviewed in excellent historical surveys by Greenson and Wexler (1969) and by Macalpine (1950).

cannot do it himself. In a real relationship when one person asks another whether he is married, he expects to be told "Yes," or "No," or even "It's none of your business"; in psychotherapy he is asked "What thoughts do you have about it?" or "How would you like it to be?" or "I wonder how it is that you've raised this question at this point."

These examples should be sufficient to demonstrate that the working alliance, even though it proceeds realistically according to the terms of the treatment contract, bears only a passing resemblance to interpersonal relationships as they exist in the real world outside of psychotherapy. The focus on one person as talker and the other as listener, the emphasis on understanding the patient rather than gratifying his needs, and the technique of exploring rather than responding to comments and questions all identify the working alliance as an aritifical situation created to serve the purposes of the treatment, or as what Jackson and Haley (1963) have called a "paradoxical unsymmetric interpretive arrangement."[2]

GENERALIZED AND SPECIFIC TRANSFERENCE REACTIONS

The transference component of the treatment relationship is influenced by typical responses of patients to the therapist's role and by the feelings of each individual patient toward the important people in his life and toward people in general. Typical responses to the therapist's role result in *generalized transference reactions*, whereas the particular interpersonal attitudes of the individual patient contribute to *specific transference reactions*. As elaborated below, this distinction proves helpful in recognizing the origins and significance of transference behavior.

Generalized Transference Reactions

Generalized transference reactions comprise the characteristic ways in which almost all patients respond to the therapist's performance of his task. In the generalized transference a patient first develops unrealistic positive feelings and later unrealistic negative feelings toward his

[2]As noted in Chapter 1, it is not impossible for a psychotherapeutic working alliance to exist in interpersonal relationships other than those between a professional therapist and a patient seeking help. However, such an artificial relationship is unlikely to evolve or be sustained outside of a formal treatment situation and in the absence of a formal treatment contract. Further elaboration of the distinguishing features of the working alliance is provided by Greenson (1965b; 1967, pp. 190–216), who contributed significantly to clarifying the concept of the working alliance as an integral part of the patient-therapist relationship.

therapist, and it was this general pattern to which the brief discussions of transference in Chapters 4 (pp. 46–47) and 9 (pp. 175–176) refer.

To recapitulate these earlier discussions, a psychotherapy patient tends initially to be impressed with his therapist's professional position, his tolerance and self-control, his psychological sensitivity, and his dedication to being helpful. These impressions culminate in an idealized image of the therapist accompanied by longings to be loved or admired by him and to enjoy a more intensive or extensive personal relationship with him than is consistent with the treatment contract. Over time, as the therapist refrains from expressing love and admiration and keeps the real relationship within the boundaries of the treatment contract, the patient begins to feel hurt and rejected. Frustrated and disappointed by the therapist's failure to reciprocate his positive feelings, he starts to view him in a different light: instead of seeing him as sensitive, interested, and helpful, he regards him as callous, uncaring, and inconsiderate—how else could he be so impersonal and unresponsive and be the agent of so much unhappiness?

This prior description of positive and negative feelings in the generalized transference can now be elaborated in terms of the distinction drawn in the present chapter between the real and the transference relationship. The main point to keep in mind is that a patient's generalized positive and negative attitudes toward his therapist may involve reality as well as transference. Thus generalized attitudes toward the therapist constitute transference reactions *only* when they are inappropriate, as when they idealize him as a perfect person or deplore him as a wretched one solely on the basis of his commitment to the working alliance. When they are appropriate to the circumstances, generalized attitudes toward the therapist represent reality, rather than transference, and may appear either independently of transference reactions or concurrently with them.

For example, a patient who respects the therapist's professional reputation or appreciates his being a good listener and sensitive observer, but does not exaggerate his worth as a person on either count, has a positive feeling toward the therapist on the basis of a realistic impression of the therapist as carrying out his prescribed role in the treatment. Such realistic positive responses to therapist competence and dedication can exist without being embellished into positive transference reactions, and they can also persist even in the face of negative reactions based on transference. Thus it is not uncommon for a patient exploring a negative transference reaction to make the following kind of observation of his behavior:

I don't know why I'm angry at you for not saying more. I know in my mind that you're doing your job the way it's supposed to be done [reference to working alliance], and I appreciate your trying to be helpful [reference to realistic positive feelings]. But I still feel mad at you and I think I'm going to stay mad until I get more feedback from you about what you think of me [negative transference].

Generalized negative feelings toward the therapist can also exist either as real or transference reactions, but they are less likely to be justified in reality than positive feelings and hence more consistently likely to indicate transference. Although realistic events can trigger negative transference reactions (see p. 203), a therapist competently doing his job should provide little basis in reality for a patient's becoming upset with him. Should he frequently cancel or arrive late for sessions, or be psychologically insensitive to what is said to him, or bludgeon his patients with poorly conceived, ill-timed, and hypercritical interpretations, the therapist may give just cause for antagonism toward him. However, a conscientious and adequately trained therapist should not be guilty of such irresponsibility, obtuseness, or technical blundering.

Having identified the role of reality elements in a patient's generalized attitudes toward his therapist, it is possible to formulate more fully than before the typical course of feeling tone in the treatment relationship. Since most patients agree to enter into a treatment contract only when they have already formed some respect for the therapist's competence and some belief in his ability to help, psychotherapy usually begins in the context of *positive realistic* attitudes toward the therapist. As the patient subsequently begins to idealize his therapist, he develops *generalized positive transference* feelings that coexist with the positive feelings he has previously developed on a reality basis. When *generalized negative transference* feelings arise in response to the nonreciprocal nature of the working alliance, they submerge positive transference feelings but do not necessarily cancel out realistic positive attitudes toward the therapist. It is for this reason that a patient who is angry at his therapist for not reciprocating intimate personal feelings (transference) can still respect the therapist's credentials and appreciate his effort to be helpful (reality). Furthermore, the process of exploring and interpreting negative transference reactions may enhance a patient's realistic positive attitudes toward the therapist, since this process demonstrates further the therapist's empathic capacity and his willingness to use this capacity on the patient's behalf.

Not only do generalized positive and negative transference feelings alternate and coexist with realistic attitudes toward the therapist, but they also alternate and coexist with each other. Concerning alternation, generalized transference seldom progresses through a single positive-to-negative sequence. Patients vary from session to session in how they are disposed to feel, and sessions vary in the extent to which they leave a patient feeling uplifted or put down. Consequently, although generalized positive transference reactions will almost always appear earlier in treatment than generalized negative ones, both tend to recur in alternating cycles throughout the middle phase of psychotherapy.

As for the coexistence of positive and negative transference, ambivalence is a well-known characteristic of human emotions. Just as one person can love and hate another person at the same time, a patient in psychotherapy can simultaneously hold unrealistic positive and negative attitudes toward his therapist. Ordinarily the stronger or more fully conscious set of attitudes will set the manifest tone of a generalized transference reaction, although it is possible for a patient's transference behavior to reflect a more or less balanced mixture of positive and negative attitudes.

Despite the central role of transference in psychotherapy, very few research studies have been addressed to the central role it plays in psychotherapy (see Luborsky & Spence, 1971, pp. 421–422; Meltzoff & Kornreich, 1970, p. 464). However, what empirical data there are concerning the course of patient-therapist affective tone during therapy prove consistent with the preceding formulation of generalized transference reactions. Most important in this regard are findings of Snyder (1961) that the overall positive affect of patients toward their therapist increases throughout psychotherapy, while overall negative affect rises to a peak midway through treatment and declines thereafter.

These findings can be readily understood in terms of the distinction between realistic and transference aspects of a patient's feelings toward his therapist. Positive feelings toward the therapist arise on both a realistic and a transference basis and proceed in two separate ways: positive transference diminishes or disappears in time, as it is resolved through interpretation or supplanted with negative transference. On the other hand, realistic positive feelings, because they are influenced by appreciation of the therapist's competence and helpfulness, tend to grow in strength as treatment progresses toward its objectives. In successful psychotherapy, then, the patient should feel most positively toward his therapist at the point where termination is mutually agreed on, marking achievement of the treatment goals.

Negative feelings toward the therapist become generalized only on the basis of transference, assuming as noted before that the therapist is sufficiently competent to avoid giving any real cause for patient ill will. Negative transference tends to mount during the middle phase of psychotherapy, in response to the therapist's unrelenting commitment to the working alliance, but also to be disspelled by appropriate interpretations. Since negative feelings based on transference should be resolved by the interpretive process, and since the therapist's behavior should not provide any realistic basis for negative feelings toward him, a patient's overall negative affect can be anticipated to peak and then decline during the course of successful psychotherapy.

A final point to be made about generalized transference reactions is that they are less uniquely influenced than specific transference reactions by the displacement of feelings, attitudes, and impulses onto the therapist. Displacements participate in generalized transference as relatively predictable and uniform features of how patients respond to the helping but frustrating role the therapist plays in sustaining the working alliance. In specific transference reactions, on the other hand, displacements occur as unique reflections of the individual patient's prior interpersonal experience and are triggered more by details of the therapist's behavior than by his general performance of his prescribed role.

Specific Transference Reactions

Specific transference reactions consist of the displacement onto the therapist of thoughts, feelings, and impulses the patient has held toward certain important people in his life or holds toward people in general. Displacements onto the therapist from important people in the patient's life constitute the classical form of transference reaction originally described by Freud (1905, p. 116) as a repetition or reenactment in the therapy of previous interpersonal relationships. Most often these reenactments will reflect the patient's relationship to his parents, primarily because one's parents are the people most likely to have figured in his basic psychological conflicts and to have etched indelible images in his mind.[3] When patients who experience such specific transference reactions are able to verbalize and comment on them, the following kinds of informative self-observations tend to occur:

Sometimes I find myself getting very uneasy while we're talking. I think

[3]Empirical data reported by Mueller (1969) confirm that during psychotherapy a patient's behavior toward his therapist comes increasingly to resemble the ways he behaved or is still behaving toward his parents.

it's the way you clear your throat now and then. My mother had a habit of clearing her throat like that, usually just before she was going to give me a lecture about something.

I have the feeling you're laughing up your sleeve at me, just like my father always did. He had the most irritating way of being patronizing, with a sort of quizzical, mocking expression on his face, and you're doing the same damn thing to me.

You may not understand this, but it bothered me just now to see another patient leaving your office as I was getting here for my appointment. I know it can't be, but I feel like I don't want you to have any other patients—I want you all to myself. It's like when I was a kid, and my parents were always wrapped up with my brothers and sisters and never seemed to have enough time for me.

This is embarrassing to say, but I'm just thinking how nice it would be to go over to you and curl up in your lap. I used to curl up in my father's lap when I was a little girl, and those were some of the happiest moments of my life.

In this way, then, lingering hopes, fears, resentments, and longings experienced originally toward parents during the formative years may become transferred onto the therapist during the course of treatment. In some instances parental surrogates, like an aunt or uncle or much older sibling who played a parental role in the patient's youth, may be the key figures in such specific transference reactions. Similarly, a patient can displace onto his therapist feelings and attitudes he is experiencing toward people who are currently important in his life, such as a spouse or employer. However, because feelings and attitudes toward currently important people usually have more access to direct expression than feelings and attitudes from the past, they are less likely than past feelings and attitudes to figure in displacements.

Nevertheless, current interpersonal relationships do often influence displacement onto the therapist of feelings and attitudes held toward people in general. Transference reactions of this type were first described by Sullivan, who saw them as an inevitable consequence of the previously mentioned "parataxic distortions" to which all people are prone. Sullivan observed that all patients come to psychotherapy with certain interpersonal dispositions determined by their prior experience—fear or resentment of authority figures, dependent or counterdependent needs, readiness or reluctance to divulge intimate concerns, trust or mistrust of the motives of others, and so forth. Through parataxic distortion the therapist becomes inaccurately perceived as a specific instance of people in general, and the patient transfers onto him the feelings, attitudes, and impulses toward others that constitute his interpersonal orientation.[4]

When patients can verbalize transference attitudes they hold toward people in general, the following kinds of remarks are likely to emerge:

I can see that I've been irritated with you for no good reason, at least not for anything you've done. It's just that you seem to be successful in your work and to enjoy it, and I resent anyone who seems to be getting more out of life than I am. And now that I think about it, I guess I see most people that way, and maybe that's why I go around resenting everybody.

This must be the third or fourth time you've pointed out to me that I act as if you won't be interested in hearing what I have to say. I think that's just the way it is with me—I always expect that people won't find me interesting or pay much attention to me, and if I don't say anything, at least I don't give them a chance to ignore me or brush me off.

I suppose I know I can trust you, but it's still not that easy for me to open up. I'm always afraid that if I really let people know what my feelings are, they'll have me in the palm of their hand, so to speak, and be able to take advantage of me. So I always play it close to the vest.

As you say, there must be some reason why I ask you so many personal questions and why I've tried to learn as much as I can about your life outside of this office. I just can't know people at a distance. When I know

[4]Singer (1965, pp. 258–264) provides a useful summary of Sullivan's concept of parataxic distortion and of its similarities and differences with respect to Freud's views on transference. It is important to note that much of Sullivan's thinking about the patient-therapist relationship, if not his terminology, has gained considerable currency among dynamically oriented therapists. In particular, both the notions of transference as a pervasive interpersonal phenomenon rather than a phenomenon unique to the treatment situation, and of transference as reflecting attitudes toward people in general as well as attitudes toward specific people, emerged from the writings of Sullivan and are endorsed by prominent clinicians both within the Sullivanian tradition (e.g., Fromm-Reichman, 1950, pp. 97–107) and outside of it (e.g., Dewald, 1971, Chap. 12; Fenichel, 1941, Chap. 5; Greenson, 1967, pp. 151–155).

people I have to know everything about them, so that I can really feel close to them. I suppose that's why I keep accused by people of being a busybody and being too possessive.

These examples illustrate ways in which envy and resentment, inferiority feelings and anticipated rejection, mistrust and fear of exploitation, and exaggerated needs for intimacy—all as specific attitudes held toward people in general—can become displaced onto the therapist. When a patient's transference allows such attitudes to be assayed in the crucible of the treatment relationship, it greatly facilitates the process of helping him recognize the motives that influence his interpersonal behavior.

THE FOSTERING OF TRANSFERENCE REACTIONS

Whereas transferred feelings and impulses can participate in any interpersonal relationship, the psychotherapy situation tends uniquely to foster transference reactions and bring them into bold relief. This fostering of transference in psychotherapy derives from the unsymmetric and nonreciprocal nature of the working alliance. The therapist encourages the patient to talk, listens permissively and without passing judgment, and concentrates on helping him understand the implications of his remarks. He does not talk about himself, nor does he express his own views, nor does he become personally involved with his patient, except in so far as he feels that these behaviors will strengthen the working alliance and serve the patient's best interests.

The therapist is consequently an ambiguous stimulus, a person whose personal history, tastes and preferences, philosophy of life, sources of pleasure and displeasure, and unresolved concerns become only slightly more apparent to the patient after many months of treatment than they are at the beginning of therapy. It is generally recognized that the less external structure provided by a perceptual field, the more it will be structured in terms of the perceiver's internal needs and dispositions. In other words, the therapist in his ambiguity assumes the dimensions of a projective test, leaving the patient considerable latitude to form impressions of him based on his own fears, wishes, and expectations.[5]

[5]This "projective hypothesis" was introduced by Frank (1939) to provide a theoretical basis for the use of ambiguous stimuli (projective tests) in personality assessment. As noted by Abt (1950) and Holzberg (1968), however, the phenomenon to which the projective

In conceptualizing the manner in which a psychotherapist fosters transference reactions, Tarachow (1963, Chaps. 2–3) draws a useful distinction between the therapist's roles as a *real* object and as an *as if* object. A therapist is always a real object to some extent by virtue of his appearance, his manner, his response to social amenities, and his professional identity. As stated earlier, however, sustaining a helpful treatment relationship requires the therapist to emphasize the working alliance between himself and his patient and to keep any real relationship between them at a carefully controlled minimum. It is in his commitment to the working alliance that a therapist acts as an *as if* object rather than as a *real* object in relation to his patients, taking on a role intended to benefit them but differing from how he would ordinarily behave in interperonal situations:

> The therapist imposes a barrier to reality. . . . The *real* situation is transformed into an *as if* situation demanding attention and comprehension. . . . Nothing in the interaction is permitted to be regarded as real, and everything is subjected to the scrutiny of both parties (Tarachow, 1963, p. 9).

In his relative anonymity, his noncommittal stance, and his emphasis on understanding rather than responding in kind to what is said to him, the therapist becomes a screen onto which each patient projects his interpersonal orientation. The utility of being such a screen was first described by Freud (1912b), who recommended that the therapist "be opaque to his patients and, like a mirror, should show them nothing but what is shown to him" (p. 118). Unfortunately, this "opaque mirror" recommendation has often been interpreted to mean that the therapist should keep himself aloof, impersonal, and emotionally unresponsive at all times. Yet there is no way a therapist can effectively demonstrate the warmth, empathy, and genuineness that contribute to favorable outcomes in psychotherapy without becoming deeply engaged in discussing the patient's concerns and responding to his needs for help.

The proper meaning of being a "screen" is that the therapist, while never becoming indifferent or detached, needs to minimize his participation with the patient as a real object in order to concentrate on his role as an as if object and thereby sustain the working alliance. If the

hypothesis refers has been formulated within the context of numerous theoretical approaches to human behavior and exists independently of whether it is regarded as projection (psychoanalytic theory), as "receptor-orienting responses (learning theory), as "perceptual response tendencies" (perception theory), or as "information processing under conditions of uncertainty" (cognitive theory).

patient's needs for help could be met solely by a real relationship, then they could be met by his friends and loved ones and he would not require professional assistance. If, on the other hand, an individual's personal relationships have proved insifficient to help him resolve his difficulties, then something more than or different from another friendship is called for.[6] Psychotherapy, with its emphasis on understanding rather than exchanging information and on meeting the patient's needs for help rather than establishing a mutually gratifying relationship with him, constitutes such an alternative arrangement.

Although transference reactions provide information that can facilitate progress in the treatment, the fostering of transference should not be conceived as a special activity undertaken by the therapist. Conscious efforts to provoke or manipulate transference reactions will be perceived as ungenuine, and the response to them will not have sufficient spontaneity to be informative. If the therapist merely sticks to his role as prescribed in the treatment contract, he will create an interpersonal climate that in the natural course of events will foster the emergence and expression of transference reactions.

Unflagging allegiance to the treatment contract can be seen as a way of "safeguarding" the transference, that is, of sustaining an atmosphere in which transference reactions are likely to occur with sufficient spontaneity, frequency, and clarity to aid the progress of the treatment. Because of the complex nature of the treatment relationship, however, care must also be taken to safeguard the real relationship and the working alliance, which means that the therapist needs to recognize how and when to protect all three components of the relationship.

Safeguarding the Transference. The therapist needs to safeguard the transference by providing as few opportunities as possible for the patient to form feelings, attitudes, and impulses toward him on a reality basis. The less basis there is in fact for a patient's reactions to his therapist, the more these reactions are likely to involve transference and the more information they will provide about his unique or neurotic dispositions. If a patient concludes that his therapist is bored after seeing him stifle several yawns, or if he begins to regard his therapist as a very maternal figure after learning that she has reared four children, he is reacting in a conventional way to objective data and revealing very little about his

[6]The need and responsibility of the professional psychotherapist to provide his patients something other than a friendship relationship is elaborated in the previously mentioned work of Schofield (1964).

individual needs and attitudes. But if he perceives his therapist as bored without their being any telltale yawn, or as maternal without knowing anything about her family life, then his reaction would point to a propensity for seeing himself as a distinteresting person in the first instance and to a quest for maternal figures to be dependent on in the second case.

Unless the transference is adequately safeguarded, reality factors may act to "contaminate" it: that is, real and transference elements may become so intertwined in a patient's reaction to his therapist as to obscure the inappropriate aspects of the reaction and preclude any fruitful exploration of them. It is for this reason that the therapist should ordinarily not yawn or tell a patient how many children he has, nor should he express any other emotions or provide any other information about himself unless he has specific reasons for doing so. Rather, he should uniformly and consistently concentrate on being an *as if* object. In this way he will minimize the basis for a real relationship in the treatment and maximize the possibility of being able to trace the patient's reactions to him to clinically meaningful displacements.

Safeguarding the Real Relationship. In his zeal to safeguard the transference and thereby facilitate the interpretive work of the treatment, the therapist should be careful not to douse all sparks of the real relationship between himself and his patient. Failure to interact with the patient on a real rather than an as if basis at certain times can detract from the therapist's genuineness, undermine the patient's feeling of being respected as a person, and obstruct the eventual resolution of transference reactions.

With regard to genuineness, first of all, the therapist needs to acknowledge obvious facts about himself and to allow some of his emotional reactions to be expressed. If a patient says "I gather from the diploma on your wall that you went to the University of Michigan, isn't that right?", the appropriate response is "Yes, that's right." To attempt to explore the significance of the patient's questions before or instead of answering it directly, as by responding with "How would you like it to be" or "I wonder what it would mean to you either way" when the facts are hanging squarely on the wall, is to engage in a strained, ungenuine, and probably unproductive subjugation of reality to the as if relationship. Likewise, there will be times when a therapist should smile at a humorous remark or show sympathy with an unfortunate event in the patient's life. Although he may go on to inquire about why the patient has said something funny or whether he played a part in the unfortunate event, he will have responded first as a real person in a situation that called for real rather than as if behavior. Unless the therapist acknowledges facts and expresses emotions in circumstances when it would be natural to do so, the patient will have cause to doubt his genuineness and his three-dimensionality as a feeling, caring, and responsive person.

With regard to respect, neglect of the real relationship inevitably deprives a patient of his due as a person. As illustrated earlier, a patient who says "Merry Christmas" in a conventional fashion deserves a similarly conventional "Same to you." Like the patient who finds his therapist ungenuine, a patient who doubts that his therapist regards him as worthy of personal consideration has fewer prospects for benefiting from psychotherapy than a patient who perceives his therapist as both genuine and respectful (see Chap. 3).

As for the resolution of transference reactions, it has already been noted that the treatment relationship proceeds on multiple levels during the course of psychotherapy, and that successful termination involves the gradual dissolution of transference and the ascendance of reality in the interaction between patient and therapist. If the real patient-therapist relationship is to be available to replace the transference near the end of treatment, it has to be nurtured and kept alive during the middle phase of psychotherapy when the therapist is focusing primarily on transference elements in the relationship. For these reasons, then—to maintain the therapist's genuineness as a three-dimensional person, to sustain the patient's feeling of being respected rather than merely studied or treated in the psychotherapy situation, and to nourish realistic aspects of the treatment relationship that can eventually supplant transference reactions—the real relationship must be safe-guarded even while the therapist is taking steps to safeguard and learn from the transference relationship.

Safeguarding the Working Alliance. The working alliance is implicitly safeguarded by the therapist's efforts to prevent either the transference or the real relationship from intruding on it. Thus whenever the therapist points out the inappropriateness of transference reactions or avoids participating in a mutually intimate relationship, he directs his patient toward the role behaviors prescribed by the treatment contract. At times, however, it becomes necessary to bolster such implicit support for the working alliance with some explicit reaffirmation of it.

Consider, for example, a patient who says, "It's not fair, the way I talk and you listen, and I have to tell you all about myself and you never have to open yourself up at all." Safeguarding the transference in response to this complaint would involve regarding it as inappropriate and setting out to explore its covert significance. Yet because this complaint accurately describes the treatment situation, it would ring most hollow to refuse to take it at face value or to impute some important latent meaning to it.

Furthermore, to regard realistic comments about the working alliance as interpretable transference behavior is to deny the patient his rights as an informed and voluntary participant in the treatment contract. Just as a patient has the right to accept or reject the contract initially, he has the right to suggest reviewing or modifying it during the course of therapy. Perhaps he has good reasons for wanting to change the time of his appointment, or alter his goals in the treatment, or criticize some of the procedures being followed. The patient needs to be accorded an objective discussion of these and similar matters pertaining to the treatment contract, whether or not they contain transference elements, or else his commitment to the working alliance may become seriously frayed.

On the other hand, safeguarding the working alliance does not mean that issues of the treatment contract should be treated solely at the level of the real relationship. Responding realistically to the above complaint about the nonmutuality of the treatment relationship would require saying, "Yes, it is unfair, so we won't operate that way any more." Obviously such capitulation to reality would sacrifice the interpretive approach that characterizes the working alliance and distinguishes psychotherapy from other interpersonal relationships.

To protect the working alliance against reality, the therapist needs to respond to questions and comments about the treatment contract in ways that acknowledge the patient's right to raise them but sustain the nonreciprocal relationship that has been established to accomplish the aims of the treatment. Thus to the complaint about nonmutuality he might respond as follows: "Yes it is unfair, in a way, just as you say; but it is a way of working together in psychotherapy that gives us the most to go on in trying to help you understand yourself and your problems."

VARIATIONS IN THE INTENSITY, FEELING TONE, AND EXPRESSION OF TRANSFERENCE REACTIONS

Whereas transference reactions develop in all psychotherapy patients, they differ widely in their intensity, in the balance of positive and negative feelings that accompany them, and in the extent to which they are directly or indirectly expressed. Variations in these three dimensions of transference account for a wide range of individual differences in how particular patients respond at particular times to the impact of the treatment relationship.

The Intensity of Transference Reactions

Since the psychotherapy situation fosters transference reactions, it follows as a general principle that the longer and more frequently a patient is seen, the more intense his transference reactions are likely to become.[7] If treatment sessions are frequent enough and the treatment continues long enough, transference reactions may build into what is known as a *transference neurosis.* A transference neurosis is said to exist when a patient is reenacting in the treatment relationship a panorama of neurotic conflicts, including many that are rooted in his childhood experience, and when his cumulative transference reactions have become so pervasive as to make therapy and the therapist the central concerns in his life.[8]

General principles notwithstanding, the relationship between frequency and duration of psychotherapy on the one hand and intensity of transference reactions on the other is a highly individual matter. People who give free rein to their feelings, who make friends quickly and become intimate on short notice, and who lean more toward experiencing than observing themselves are relatively prone to forming transference reactions in psychotherapy. Conversely, people who characteristically keep their emotions in check, who relate to others at a distance and become intimate only after prolonged acquaintance, and who incline more toward observing than experiencing themselves tend to be relatively insulated against transference reactions.

Such personality differences in transference proneness influence both the rapidity with which patients develop transference reactions and the intensity of these reactions in response to a particular frequency and

[7]The previously cited findings of Mueller (1969), that patient behavior toward the therapist tends increasingly over time to resemble behavior toward the parents, provides some empiritcal support for this hypothesis.

[8]The usefulness of this term is limited by the lack of any precise criteria for identifying the point at which transference reactions become a transference neurosis. It nevertheless merits attention, since it is commonly used as a synonym for intense transference reactions, and since the formation of a transference neurosis is often proposed as an essential characteristic differentiating psychoanalysis from other forms of dynamically oriented psychotherapy. Extended discussions of psychoanalytic views of how transference neurosis develops and of the role it plays in the therapeutic process are provided by Kepecs (1966) and Weinshel (1971).

duration of psychotherapy. For a relatively transference-prone individual, for example, one with a hysterical personality style, once-weekly psychotherapy may be sufficient to generate pronounced transference reactions in the first few months of treatment. For a person relatively insulated against transference reactions, for example, one with an obsessive-compulsive personality style, once-weekly sessions may elicit only faint whisperings of transference, insufficiently pronounced to support effective interpretation, and two or more sessions per week for several months or longer may be required to foster the emergence of therapeutically useful transference reactions.

It is also relevant that interpersonal affect tends to peak sooner and to dissolve more readily in people who become affectively engaged with others quickly than in those whose engagements are slower to develop. Hence the rapidly emerging transference reactions of the hysterical patient, although sometimes dramatic, tend to be superficial rather than intense and to give way easily to appropriate interpretation. In contrast, the slowly developing transference reactions of the obsessive-compulsive patient, although often expressed in muted fashion, tend to be very intensely felt and to yield only to a lengthy process of interpretation and working through.[9]

These individual differences explain why uncovering psychotherapy with patients who are transference prone may require not only fewer sessions per week but also less total time than similar treatment for patients who are insulated against transference. Such considerations should of course enter into the original treatment planning, since a patient's apparent transference propensities will provide some basis for determining how frequent his sessions should be and for estimating how long his treatment will last. Because initial assessments are imperfect, furthermore, it may become evident after treatment is underway that sessions have not been scheduled frequently enough to elicit transference reactions in a particular patient, in which case plans may have to be made to see the patient more often.

On the other hand, it may develop in some cases that therapy is mobilizing transference reactions of such intensity as to interfere with the patient's capacity to function effectively either in the treatment or outside of it. In his sessions the patient may become so overwhelmed by his transference feelings that he can no longer distinguish them from reality or sustain the working alliance, despite the therapist's best efforts to help

[9]The previously cited books by Salzman (1968) and Shapiro (1965) elaborate on these contrasting personality styles and their implications for individual differences in the handling of interpersonal affect.

him do so. Outside the treament he may become so preoccupied with fantasies and ruminations about the therapist that he cannot attend to his customary responsibilities or carry on in his usual social roles.

When transference reactions become so prepotent that the patient insists they are real, cannot observe or discuss them in ways that further the goals of the treatment, and is prevented by them from continuing in his usual roles and responsibilities, he is said to be suffering a *transference psychosis*. With few exceptions, transference psychotic reactions make themselves painfully evident to the therapist who has evoked them. The patient expresses intense feelings of love and hate toward him and refuses to consider that these feelings may not be justified in reality; he makes egregious demands ("You've got to see me every day and not see any other patients") and becomes furious or deflated when these demands are not met; he reports frequent periods of anxiety, inability to think clearly, or loss of self-control associated with fantasies and daydreams about the treatment relationship.

These and other manifestations of psychotic transference signify a deterioration in the patient's personality organization, since they involve decreased capacity to modulate affective experience and to separate fantasy from reality, and they bring progress in the treatment to a halt, since they represent a complete suffusion of the patient's observing self by his experiencing self. Because psychotic transference reactions are an inevitably deleterious turn of events in psychotherapy, they must be averted wherever possible and reversed whenever they occur.

Susceptibility to psychotic transference reactions usually relates to personality impairments that can be identified during the initial assessment phase of treatment and should steer the therapist away from an uncovering approach. At times, however, particularly in the case of borderline patients whose underlying problems in modulating affective experience are masked by superficial displays of adequate personality integration, a propensity for intense transference reactions may be unsuspected until such reactions actually begin to emerge. It will then be necessary to shift the treatment strategy as soon as possible toward a more supportive and less uncovering approach, which would have been selected in the first place with benefit of a more accurate initial evaluation. Adjustments may also be indicated for patients who can tolerate and benefit from a relatively uncovering approach, but in whom the initially selected frequency of sessions appears to be eliciting a greater intensity of transference reactions than can be accommodated within the working alliance. Then a particularly transference prone patient who is being seen twice weekly, for example, might be continued in uncovering psychotherapy but changed to once-weekly sessions to keep the transference from reaching a disruptive level of intensity.[10]

Positive and Negative Attitudes in the Transference

Every transference reaction is accompanied by some degree of positive or negative feelings toward the therapist. While it has therefore become customary to speak in shorthand terms of "the positive transference" and "the negative transference" in psychotherapy, the positive-negative distinction refers in fact only to the kinds of attitudes the patient holds toward his therapist and not to any global feature of his transference. All transference reactions are essentially negative phenomena, since they always represent distortions of reality and since they invariably produce resistance. Hence the phrases "positive transference" and "negative transference" should be used and interpreted only to mean positive or negative *attitudes* in the transference (see Singer, 1965, pp. 270–278).

Patients vary in the average or typical feeling tone of their transference reactions as a function of their previous experiences and the dispositions they bring to the treatment situation. A surly and suspicious patient who harbors considerable ill will toward the important people in his life is likely to manifest predominantly negative attitudes in the transference, whereas a patient whose interpersonal style revolves around idealizing or ingratiating himself with others will tend to display primarily positively toned transference reactions.

Accurate monitoring of such differences in the emotional tone of a patient's reactions to his therapist provides useful clues to the positive-negative balance of his feelings toward other people in his past and current life. Furthermore, to the extent that unrealistically positive or negative interpersonal attitudes constitute part of the patient's psychological problem, shifts in the prevailing tone of his transference reactions over time can serve as an index of progress toward more balanced emotional relationships with others.

The therapist's appraisal of whether a patient's transference reactions involve primarily positive or primarily negative attitudes can also guide him in deciding how best to intervene, if at all. As will be elaborated shortly, positive and negative transference reactions call for different treatment strategies, particularly since it is generally advantageous to concentrate interventions on negative transference reactions and to be

[10]For additional reading and case illustrations concerning the emergence and resolution of psychotic transference reactions, papers by Hammet (1961), Reider (1957), and Wallerstein (1967) are recommended. The nature of borderline personality organization, including the intense transference propensities of people with this condition, is elaborated by Frank (1970), Kernberg (1967), Knight (1953), and Schmideberg (1959).

somewhat circumspect in the exploration and interpretation of positive attitudes in the transference.

Direct and Indirect Expression of Transference

Transference reactions vary considerably in the directness with which they are expressed, and the behaviors by which a patient reveals that he is experiencing positive or negative feelings toward his therapist on a transference basis range from the very subtle to the patently obvious. First and most indirectly, a patient experiencing transference attitudes may without comment display some suggestive alterations in his behavior or appearance. Under the influence of positive transference attitudes, for example, he may begin coming early for sessions or lingering around after them, perhaps striking up an acquaintance with the therapist's receptionist or secretary, as if by this means to gain a more intimate relationship with him. He may start appearing for sessions particularly well dressed and groomed, in an effort to elicit the therapist's commendation or sexual interest. Or he may in his posture, gestures, and facial expressions convey a wish to become closer, more attractive, or more responsive to him, for example, by leaning forward in his chair or pulling it closer to where the therapist is sitting, by making seductive body movements, or by frequently smiling or nodding his head agreeably.

Under the influence of negative attitudes, a patient may manifest opposite versions of these subtle behavioral indices of transference. He may come late, ask to leave early, and be pointedly uncommunicative with anyone in the reception area, as if to increase his distance from the therapist; he may ignore his dress and grooming, even arriving sloppy and disheveled for his sessions, as if to communicate disdain for the therapist's impression of him or communicate that neither therapy nor therapist is worth the effort of looking presentable; or he may move his chair away from the therapist and sit back in its farthest recesses, or hold his body rigid and unyielding, or scowl, turn down the corners of his mouth, shake his head from side to side, and otherwise present himself as dour and disinterested.

As a second and somewhat less indirect mode of expressing transference, a patient may begin to comment about the therapist's trappings (but not his person) and about his profession. With regard to trappings, the patient may mention that he likes a certain picture in the therapist's office, or that he wishes he had as comfortable a chair at home as the one he sits in during his sessions, or that he likes the selection of magazines in the waiting room, or that he appreciates the convenience of a bus stop right in front of the clinic or office building. Or, if his feeling tone in the transference is primarily negative, he may produce a litany of veiled jibes or complaints: "I wish you didn't keep it so warm in here"; "There sure are a lot of stairs to climb to get to your office"; "You know your receptionist isn't very friendly"; "It's too bad you're not located in a more convenient place to get to." Positive or negative, such comments about extensions of the therapist usually mask similarly toned feelings toward the therapist himself that are not being directly experienced or expressed.

Likewise, implied approval or disapproval of the therapist's profession can be used as an indirect channel for expressing transference. For example, a patient may talk about a friend who profited from psychotherapy, or about society's need for more mental health professionals, or about how interesting and gratifying it must be to listen to people and help them with their problems. Or he may instead give some first-hand accounts of acquaintances who have fared poorly in psychotherapy, or refer to a newspaper article questioning the effectiveness of psychotherapy, or state how dull and unrewarding he would find the therapist's job.

Unlike the transference feelings they express, which involve distortions of reality, such indirect comments may stick closely to fact. The therapist's office may indeed be uncomfortably warm or inconveniently located, and certainly there are both successful and unsuccessful outcomes in psychotherapy and an extensive literature debating its effectiveness. There will accordingly be times when such comments call for a direct answer that addresses the real relationship or the working alliance: "I'm sorry about the stairs, but the elevator should be fixed by next week"; "There is no guaranteed outcome of the work we're doing together, and our agreement involves continuing the treatment only so long as it seems to be beneficial."

For the most part, however, even realistic comments about the therapist's trappings or profession will constitute manifestations of transference and need to be explored as such. Following Dewald (1971, p. 201), it is helpful in identifying the probable transference basis of such comments for the therapist to ask himself, "Why is the patient bringing this up at this time?" So long as this question cannot be answered in ways that call for bolstering the real relationship or the working alliance, the patient's comment can be understood as an indirect expression of positive or negative transference attitudes.

In contrast to the ambiguities of indirect expressions, relatively direct expressions of transference leave little doubt as to their origin in unrealistic feelings and attitudes toward the therapist, even if these feelings and attitudes are not explicitly stated. Most commonly in this regard the patient will make evaluative comments about the therapist as a person or about the course of the treatment. If his feelings are positive, he may express interest in the therapist or approval of him ("I wonder if you're married"; "You have a nice smile"; "I like the way you handle yourself"); he may report pleasant dreams or fantasies in which the therapist played a part; or he may laud the treatment as a means of pleasing the therapist ("I'm really getting a lot out of this"; "You always seem to know just the right thing to say"). If on the other hand he is feeling negatively, he may find fault with the therapist ("I don't think you're interested in me") or with the treatment ("For all my time and money, I don't see where this is doing me much good"), or he may report dreams and fantasies about the therapist that involve themes of hostility or rejection.

Finally, as a fourth stage of directness, a patient may express transference attitudes openly and explicitly. When positive transference attitudes are expressed openly and explicitly, the patient does not merely imply his feelings by pulling his chair closer to the therapist, admiring his office decor, or praising his skill, but comes right out with words to the effect of "I like you" or "I love you" or "I wish I could know you better," or "I wish I could have you for a (parent) (spouse) (lover)." When negative transference attitudes are directly expressed, the patient does not bother with coming late, describing failure cases he has known, or questioning the therapist's competence, but instead lets the therapist know in so many words that "I'm feeling angry at you," or "Everything you do irritates me," or "I don't like talking to you anymore."

Directness of Expression and Awareness of Transference. Appreciating variations in the directness with which transference is expressed helps the therapist not only to recognize its manifestations but also to gauge the patient's awareness of his own feelings. When transference is stated explicitly, the patient's feelings are as apparent to him as they are to the therapist, but as transference manifestations become less direct, the feelings that have given rise to them are increasingly likely to lie outside the patient's awareness.

Thus a patient who complains about not making progress in the treatment when the facts would suggest otherwise may recognize that he is angry with the therapist and attempting to punish him with this complaint, but it is also possible for him to be unaware that his negative attitudes toward the treatment really reflect negative attitudes toward the therapist. If this same patient were to comment only about the purported inefficacy of treatment in general, and not about his own treatment, or if he were just to assume a distant, nonreceptive posture, his behavior would be even farther removed from the transference feelings underlying it and probably even less consciously connected with such feelings.

This is not to say that a patient who expresses transference feelings indirectly will never be aware of them. A woman patient who wears a particularly short skirt or low-cut blouse to a session may know full well that she has dressed to catch the eye of her male therapist, to whom she feels attracted. As a rule, however, the more indirect the expression of transference, the less likely the patient will be to appreicate the meaning and implications of his transference behavior. The distinction between direct and indirect expression of transference thus parallels the distinction between near and remote derivatives drawn in Chapter 8, and suggests similar guidelines for interpretation. Just as near derivatives are more readily interpretable than remote derivatives, relatively direct expressions of transference prove more useful to interpret than relatively indirect transference reactions.

Acting Out of the Transference. One final dimension in the expression of transference that should be recognized when it occurs constitutes a reversal of the usual sequence of events in which transference becomes manifest. Transference reactions, as defined earlier, comprise displacements onto the therapist of thoughts, feelings, and impulses originally experienced toward other people in the patient's life. When powerful affects and attitudes are formed toward the therapist in this way, they may be more or less directly expressed in his presence, *or* they may in turn be displaced onto people with whom the patient interacts in his daily life. Thus a man who is angry at his therapist may come home after a session and pick a fight with his wife, or a woman experiencing sexual feelings toward a male therapist may become attracted to or begin an affair with a man similar to the therapist in age, appearance, or some other characteristic.

This displacement of attitudes toward the therapist onto people external to the treatment is knows as *acting out of the transference* (see Greenson, 1967, pp. 258–263). Although transference feelings can be acted out simultaneously with their being directly or indirectly expressed in the treatment, more often than not the acting out replaces any overt manifestations of transference in the therapist's presence. Hence the acting out of transference inevitably constitutes resistance to the treatment, since it is used by the patient to prevent his transference attitudes from coming to the therapist's attention.

To circumvent this resistance, the therapist needs to listen closely for features of the patient's behavior that suggest the acting out of transference. In patients who are resisting the emergence of transference during their sessions, some otherwise unaccountable behavior outside of the treatment, especially when it is comparable in tone to transference reactions the therapist might have expected to observe in the sessions, may provide the only available clue to the existence of transference reactions that should be identified and explored. Similarly, when a patient who is becoming increasingly direct in expressing transference feelings suddenly ceases to talk about the treatment relationship and begins engaging in some behavior that is atypical for him and seems to express the kinds of feelings he was about to express toward the therapist, acting out of the transference is a likely possibility to be considered.

THE EXPLORATION AND INTERPRETATION OF TRANSFERENCE REACTIONS

Progress in psychotherapy is greatly facilitated by effective exploration and interpretation of transference reactions, for reasons noted at the beginning of this chapter. To mount an effective interpretive sequence in response to manifestations of transference, the therapist should follow closely the general guidelines for interpretation presented in Chapter 8. These guidelines can be elaborated with particular reference to the interpretation of transference phenomena by turning again to the major questions of *what* aspects of the patient's behavior should be selected for interpretation, *when* these interpretations should be made, and *how* an interpretive sequence should be constructed.

Selecting Aspects of Transference to be Interpreted

While there are no aspects of transference reactions that should always or never be interpreted, there are certain priorities in the interpretation of transference just as there are in the general selection of subjects for interpretation. As mentioned earlier, these priorities involve (a) favoring interpretations of negative attitudes in the transference over interpretations of positive attitudes and (b) favoring interpretations of relatively direct expression of transference over interpretations of relatively indirect expressions.

The favoring of negative over positive transference attitudes as subjects for interpretation is based on some potential disadvantages of interpreting positive feelings toward the therapist. First, because all interpretations are implicitly critical and challenging, interpretations of positive transference can be experienced as demeaning and rejecting. Consider the patient who says, "I'm enjoying coming to see you every week," and then proceeds to talk about himself in a productive and resistance-free manner. For the therapist to interrupt in an attempt to capitalize on this off-hand remark—say by exposing its hypocrisy (the patient is after all supposed to be working on personal problems, not enjoying himself) or by laying bare its hidden meanings (the patient is probably displacing positive feelings onto the therapist that are really felt toward someone else)—is like delivering a slap in the face. The patient is made to feel foolish, that his pleasantries are frivolous and of no personal interest to the therapist, and that if such comments have any value it is only in terms of ulterior motives lurking behind them ("Why did you feel a need to say that to me?").

There is seldom much to be learned from exploring fleeting manifestations of transference, and doing so when they are positively toned can abrade a patient's self-respect and diminish his enthusiasm for participating in the treatment. Mild positive transference is too useful an ally in the treatment to be sacrificed by interpretation, especially when the interpretive yield from this effort is insufficient to justify the distress the patient is caused.

Second, because interpretations convey special interest in what the patient is thinking or feeling, exploration of positive transference reactions may have a seductive impact. If in response to a patient who says "I enjoy coming to see you," for example, the therapist smiles pleasantly, leans forward in his chair, and says "Tell me more about that," he cannot help but communicate delight in hearing the patient say nice things about him. Because such delight can imply that the therapist is becoming more than just professionally involved in the relationship, expressions of interest in positive interest may seduce the patient into continuing to feel and report positive attitudes in the expectation that the therapist will soon be reciprocating them. Seductiveness of this kind has the marked disadvantage of stimulating positive transference to peaks of intensity that generate nonproductive resistance and let the patient in for a harder fall when he finally realizes that the therapist is not going to reciprocate.

On the other hand, the possible disadvantages of calling attention to positive transference feelings do not justify ignoring them at the risk of compromising the working alliance. Suppose a patient who is progressing well in treatment to the accompaniment of numerous manifestations of positive transference asks the therapist how old he is and says he will be very upset if he cannot get an answer to his question, or suppose he is obviously skirting some important subject that would probably be painful or embarrassing for him to talk about. To sustain this patient's positive feelings in the treatment situation, the therapist would have to state his age in the first instance and allow continued avoidance of the important subject in the second. To take either course, however, would be to make concessions that violate the treatment contract: the therapist's actions would be serving primarily to help his patient feel good for the moment, rather than to help him understand himself better. The therapist is no longer discharging his responsibility if he becomes so enamored of a patient's positive transference feelings that he bends over backward through acts of omission or commission to sustain them.

The potential disadvantages of rejecting or seducing a patient by calling attention to his positive transference attitudes have no counterparts in the interpretation of negative transference. Since a patient experiencing negative transference is already feeling out of sorts in the treatment relationship, there is little to be lost in the way of enthusiastic participation by setting out to explore these negative feelings. Furthermore, because accurate interpretations demonstrate therapist interest and empathy, they are unlikely to reinforce negative patient attitudes in the way they reinforce positive patient attitudes. To the contrary, when negative transference is producing sticky, unpleasant exchanges in the treatment or threatening to disrupt it completely, timely interpretation of the transference behavior may lead not only to increased understanding by the patient but also to a period of convivial affect and renewed dedication to the work of therapy.

As for favoring direct over indirect expressions of transference as subjects for interpretation, it follows from the discussion on page 227 that interpretive sequences should be preferentially aimed at transference behavior that is relatively clearly and closely tied to the feelings and attitudes underlying it. In reference to the stages of directness delineated earlier, this means that suggestive behaviors and comments about the therapist's trappings and profession will not ordinarily be prime subjects for transference interpretation. Coming late or talking about negative outcomes in psychotherapy may become sufficiently prounced to call for *resistance* interpretations, but any transference sources of such resistance behavior will be relatively remote and provide a less compelling focus for interpretation than possible sources in characterological resistance, content resistance, or resistance to change.

On the other hand, personal comments about the therapist and open expressions of feeling and attitudes toward him point directly to the existence of transference reactions and usually say a good deal about their precise nature and intensity. Transference interpretations of such behavior will therefore have relatively good prospects for being accurate, easy to document, and within the patient's ken. Accordingly, transference interpretations should be reserved for relatively direct expressions of transference attitudes and applied sparingly if at all to its relatively indirect manifestations.

Deciding When To Interpret Transference

Like interpretations in general, a transference interpretation should be made when the patient is bordering on awareness of the interpretation and is in a receptive frame of mind to consider it, and when the therapist is reasonably certain of his interpretation and prepared to document it. The interpretation should neither follow too closely on the heels of prior interpretations or be followed by an inadequate opportunity for discussion (see pp. 132–140). In addition to observing these general requirements of good timing and proper dosage of interpretations, specific decisions to interpret transference should be reserved for times (a) when it is producing marked resistance, (b) when it is of moderate intensity, sufficient to be demonstrable but not so intense as to be intolerable, and (c) when there is something significant to be learned from the interpretive sequence.

When Transference Is Producing Marked Resistance. All transference reactions produce some resistance, since they distract the patient's attention from the problems for which he has sought help. However, just as resistance needs to be allowed to build to a certain point before it can be interpreted effectively, transference is best interpreted when it is markedly interfering with the patient's talking about himself and his difficulties. To illustrate this consideration in timing, suppose that during a session for which the therapist was late the patient talks about expecting too much from people and cites as an example an excessive tendency to feel irritated when someone keeps him waiting. Yet suppose further that, after citing this example, he continues to talk freely and meaningfully about his problems in interpersonal relationships.

In this situation the therapist could with reasonable certainty begin a transference interpretation as follows: "I wonder if you were irritated with me for being late today and keeping you waiting." However, since the patient's irritation had not been sufficiently pressing for him to express it directly or otherwise let it interfere with his continuing to work in the treatment, such an interpretation would have little or no impact. Only if the patient had become so irritated with the delay that he had refused to talk at all or otherwise displayed marked resistance would there be adequate basis for helping him see his transference behavior as unusual and worth exploring.

Timing transference interpretations to coincide with marked resistance is advisable not only because the potential impact of the interpretations are thereby enhanced, but also because there is a potential disadvantage to interpreting transference in the context of fleeting resistance. Specifically, the more the therapist interrupts productive, task-oriented behavior to interpret elements of transference that are producing only minimal resistance, the more the patient is likely to perceive him as picky and depreciatory, as more interested in being clever than in being helpful, and as insensitive to the importance of the real life experience and events he has been attempting to report.

When Transference Is of Moderate Intensity. As already implied, attitudes, feelings, and impulses in the transference should not be interpreted until they have reached an intensity where the patient can readily be made aware of them and can be helped to distinguish them from real reactions to the therapist. In the above example of the patient who "incidentally" mentioned being irritated by people who keep him waiting, considerable effort might have been necessary to convince him that he was really feeling irritated with the therapist for being late. Even if he were to become convinced, furthermore, it would be difficult to argue that his mild irritation in response to the therapist's factual tardiness was in any way inappropriate to the circumstances.

Some degree of intensity, then, usually enough to produce relatively direct behavioral manifestations and to result in clear-cut resistance, is necessary before transference reactions can be effectively interpreted. Yet allowing the transference to build to an interpretable intensity does not mean sitting idly by while transference reactions reach an intensity that overruns the working alliance. Even within a treatment plan formulated to allow the formation of a transference neurosis, no single reaction or set of reactions should be permitted to become so intense that the patient can no longer participate in trying to understand them. A patient who only wants to make love with the therapist or is so angry at him he refuses to continue the treatment has developed a transference intensity that should have been averted by interpretations of these positive and negative feelings while they were still in a more formative stage.

Correct appraisal of the intensity of transference is particularly important whenever intense transference feelings are expressed only indirectly and without the patient's awareness. For example, a patient who scrupulously avoids saying anything personal to or about the therapist during sessions but who brings him gifts, "forgets" things in his office, drives by his house every day, and begins to affect some of his mannerisms may be on the verge of uncomfortably intense positive transference feelings. Because of the intensity of feeling they reflect, such behaviors call for interpretation, even though as indirect expressions of positive transference they would ordinarily have low priority as subjects for interpretation. Indirect manifestations of strong negative attitudes similarly need to be recognized and responded to before the transference builds to a disruptive intensity.

To summarize the considerations in interpreting transference presented thus far, indirect expressions of mild positive transference attitudes should receive the least interpretive attention and direct expressions of intense negative transference the most. The appropriateness and potential utility of interpreting transference increases as positive transference elements shade into negative ones, as mild transference reactions become moderately intense, and as indirect expressions of transference grow increasingly direct.

When There Is Something Significant to Be Learned from the Interpretive Sequence. Generally speaking, there is always something to be learned from an accurately conceived, properly timed, and aptly phrased interpretation. In a situation calling for interpretation, however, interpretations addressed to transference elements in the patient's behavior may be more or less informative in comparison to other aspects of his behavior that might be interpreted. Independently of its feeling tone, directness, and intensity, a transference reaction should therefore be weighed for its information value before it is selected for interpretation.

To clarify what is meant by the "information value" of a transference reaction, it needs first to be emphasized that the interpretation of transference is not itself an end in the psychotherapy process, to be implemented whenever possible. Rather, transference interpretations are a vehicle for facilitating progress in the treatment, to be employed when they will help to alleviate resistances or to identify aspects of the patient's interpersonal life that might otherwise escape notice. Because there are resistances in which transference elements play only a peripheral role, and manifestations of transference that reveal nothing about the patient beyond what he is already aware of, there will be circumstances in which little stands to be learned from selecting transference as the focus of an interpretive sequence, even when it is possible to do so.

The example of the tardy therapist and the patient irritated with being kept waiting can be used to illustrate both kinds of circumstances in which transference interpretations will have negligible information value. The patient in this instance followed his passing reference to being irritated when people make him wait by talking freely and meaningfully about his interpersonal problems, and his working productively in this way obviated any therapist intervention. Suppose, however, that he had continued as follows: "I remember one time just last week. . . . I don't even like to think about it. . . . I guess it really wasn't the same kind of thing anyway." Then his comments would have suggested resistance and called for an interpretation, but still not an interpretation of transference. The type of resistance most probably involved in "I don't even like to think about it" is resistance to content, not transference resistance. Hence a transference interpretation, even if appropriate to some aspects of the patient's behavior, would contribute little to understanding or resolving his resistance of the moment.

As for what the patient is already aware of in this example, the major inference to be drawn from his feeling irritated at the therapist for keeping him waiting is that he is generally prone to irritability in interpersonal situations because he expects too much of people—yet this is exactly what he goes on to say without benefit of therapist intervention. When transference reactions thus mirror interpersonal attitudes and dispositions the patient already appreciates full well and can discuss freely, chiming in with interpretations will offer no more than a blinding glimpse of the obvious.

On the other hand, behavior suggesting transference resistance or some previously unmentioned interpersonal attitudes offers considerable potential for something to be learned from a transference interpretation. Suppose the patient in the example, invited into the therapist's office five minutes later than his session was scheduled to begin, had sat silently for a while and then said, "There were some things I wanted to tell you about today, but now I don't feel like it—I'm feeling irritated with you instead." This response would constitute resistance, since it pushes aside the work of the treatment, and it would identify transference as the source of the resistance, since it is the patient's preoccupation with his feelings toward the therapist that is preventing him from taking up his task.

Furthermore, the patient's poutiness in response to only a delay of five minutes—as if to say "You were mean so now I'm not going to talk to you"—would suggest that he may overreact to similar situations outside of the treatment. Hence an interpretive focus on his exaggerated, maladaptive response to the therapist could serve both to relieve his resistance and to help him recognize a personality disposition that has been limiting his pleasure and effectiveness in interpersonal relationships.

Constructing Interpretive Sequences Aimed at Transference

Effective interpretation of transference reactions requires a sequence of interventions intended to help the patient clarify, explore, and understand aspects of his behavior that are influenced by unrealistic feelings, attitudes, and impulses toward the therapist. In considering specific procedures for the interpreation of transference, it should be kept in mind that the question of how to interpret transference becomes relevant only when the previously discussed criteria for what and when to interpret are satisfied.

Clarifying Transference Reactions. The therapist's first response to relatively direct expressions of transference otherwise suitable for interpretation should be to clarify that they represent a distortion of reality and accordingly merit the patient's curiosity and attention. As noted earlier, the distortions that underlie transference behavior may involve inaccurate perception of either the therapist or of the treatment contract, and one or both possibilities may have to be addressed as the patient is helped to recognize that his transference reactions constitute unusual behavior that needs to be observed as well as experienced.

When a transference reaction involves misperception of the therapist, the therapist's task is to point out how the patient's perceptions diverge from reality. The following two examples, similar in kind and both taken from the beginning of sessions, illustrate such initial clarification of relatively directly expressed transference feelings:

Pt. You seem in a sour mood today, like you're ready to bite my head off.

Th. What suggests that to you?

Pt. I don't know. I'm just not getting the right vibes, like you're not in a good mood or you're feeling down on me.

Th. I'm not aware of being in a bad mood or feeling down on you. I wonder if there might be some reason why you're perceiving me in that way.

Pt. (Pauses, appears thoughtful) Well, I suppose maybe there is. I've got something I think I should tell you, and I don't know how you'll take it. (Pause) I've decided to move in with my boyfriend, and I have the feeling you may disapprove.

. . .

Pt. (Long pause) I don't know what to talk about today. (Pause) It seems hard to get started. (Pause) You look tense and anxious.

Th. I hear you saying that *you* are finding it hard to talk, but that *I* look anxious.

Pt. (Quickly and loudly) Oh I can talk, that's for sure, I wouldn't have

> any trouble talking—(breaks off, then proceeds more softly) I guess you're right. I am feeling anxious because I should tell you about something that's happened and I don't know how you'll take it.

Both of these examples are richly revealing in terms of the psychotherapy process. Both illustrate resistance manifest in reluctance to talk; in both the resistance seems clearly derived from transference concerns, namely, apprehension about what the therapist will think or how he will respond; and the transference reaction in each case appears primarily positive, centering around a wish to retain the therapist's approval. Additionally in the first example, the patient's reference to moving in with her boyfriend could be subtly seductive (an attempt to arouse the therapist's jealousy or sexual fantasies) or could signify some acting out of the transference.

When transference distorts the treatment contract, the therapist needs first to contrast the patient's feelings with the relevant terms of the original agreement. Suppose as commonly happens a patient expresses irritation with the therapist for not talking more, or not giving him advice, or not answering all of his questions. The therapist might then make the following kind of response:

> You say you're angry at me because I'm not telling you what to do, as if I'm not interested in helping you. Yet the basis on which we agreed to proceed in psychotherapy is that I would try to help you understand yourself better, so that you could make your own decisions about what to do, not that I would advise you. So there must be some other reason aside from what I'm actually doing that is causing you to feel angry at me.

As is true of resistance behavior, such transference phenomena accentuate throughout the middle phase of therapy the importance of having an explicit and mutually endorsed treatment contract. Without such prior agreement to refer back to, little progress may be possible in helping a patient recognize that his transference reactions embody feelings and attitudes inappropriate to the reality of the treatment situation. Only if it can be clarified to the patient's satisfaction that his transference behavior is unusual and stems from other than apparent motives can the transference be used effectively to enhance self-understanding.

Exploring Transference Reactions. Once the presence of a transference reaction has been clarified, so that the patient perceives it as behavior not rooted in current reality and hence worthy of being understood further, the transference behavior should be explored to pursue as far as possible its origins and implications. Consider, for example, a patient who has angrily and without justification accused his therapist of not being interested in him. What is it like for this patient to feel angry and what fantasies are associated with the experience? In what other situations, past and present, has he experienced anger related to the perceived disinterest of others? Toward what other people has he felt such anger and how has he typically expressed it? The answers to these and similar questions help to elucidate the original instances of interpersonal conflict that are being reenacted in the transference and to identify the underlying feelings and attitudes toward significant people in the patient's life that are being displaced onto the therapist.

Exploring the dimensions, history, and more widespread expressions of a transference reaction can of course proceed only as far at a particular point in the treatment as the patient is prepared to go in his recollection and reporting of events. Partial interpretations and requests for associations may help press the inquiry beyond where it initially seems destined to end, but when the patient has exhausted his available ideas bearing on a transference reaction, the exploration will have to be dropped until some further expressions of the particular reaction occur.

Understanding Transference Reactions. When exploration of a transference reaction has yielded sufficient information to support appropriate interpretations, the patient should then be helped to understand his transference experience in ways that teach him about his interpersonal experience in general. The key element in this process is assisting the patient to generalize from his transference reactions to the previously unrecognized attitudes, feelings, and impulses toward others that have shaped his transference behavior.

Interpretations aimed at helping a patient use the treatment relationship to draw inferences about his interpersonal experiences in general may focus on either past or current events in the patient's life. To illustrate the use of the transference in recapturing interpersonal experiences from the past, consider the following exchange between a female patient with chronic feelings of inferiority, especially in relation to men, and a male therapist toward whom some negative reactions on her part have just been clarified as transference:

Pt. Now that you've pointed it out, I can see that you haven't been acting any different than usual, and you probably had no expression on your face at all. Yet when I started talking today, I did have the impression you had some kind of superior look about you, like you were mocking me, and it really made me feel bad. Where did I get that impression from?

Th. I wonder what other people in your life may have given you the same impression.

Pt. Other people? Let me think a minute. (Pause) Hey, you know I haven't thought about this in a long time, and I don't like to think about it now, but my father always used to do that to me. Anytime I wanted to tell him something, or about something I was proud of doing, he'd sit back there with that smug smile on his face, mocking and patronizing as hell, and make me feel like I was an insignificant worm. Boy, did that get to me—I never knew whether to feel more angry or more crushed, and I think I felt a mixture of both.

Th. So you were reacting to me just now as if I were your father and you were still a little girl.

Pt. It seems silly, but that's right.

Th. So here you are, a grown woman, feeling inferior to men because you still see yourself as an insignificant little girl and men as being superior to you, like your father was.

In this example, then, the transference phenomena were used as a clue to real experiences in the patient's past life that had probably contributed to her psychological problems as an adult, and the therapist was able to help her recall and begin reexperiencing some relevant and unresolved conflicts from her childhood. A possible alternative in the example would have been to encourage the patient to explore further her memories about her father and to vent more of her pent-up affect toward him, rather than move so directly to the transference interpretation that was offered. As with interpretation of transference, however, the reworking of past experience is not an end in psychotherapy, but only a vehicle for increased self-understanding and positive behavior change in the present. Hence the emphasis in the example was placed first on helping the patient answer her very relevant question ("Where did I get that impression from?") by accounting for her distorted perception of the therapist, and secondly on helping her appreciate that similar distortions in her present experience, based on childhood feelings and attitudes lingering beyond the time when they were justified in reality, probably participate in her current difficulties in relationships with men.

Transference reactions can be used in much the same fashion to generalize directly to current interpersonal relationships outside of the treatment, without necessarily proceeding through a recollection of past events. Suppose in the above example the therapist instead of saying, "I wonder what other people in your life may have given you the same impression," had said, "If you've had this kind of impression here, there must be other situations in which you have a similar reaction without there being any real basis for it." The patient might then have begun talking about some of her current relationships with men, recognizing in the process that she was indeed prone to feeling patronized and inferior without sufficient cause, just as she had in relation to the therapist.

In this latter version of the example, the patient is helped to recognize *how* she is distorting her current interpersonal experience, whereas in the original version, which involves tracing back the origins of transference feelings before attempting to generalize from them, the patient is helped to understand *why* as well as how she tends to misperceive the attitudes of others. The choice between a past or current focus in the interpretation of transference will depend on the salient content of the interviews and on the intensity of the treatment. With regard to interview content, a focus on either past or present concerns may be closer to the patient's awareness and hence more timely to pursue. If the woman in the above example had been talking about childhood experiences, perhaps describing members of her family but pointedly omitting to mention her father, there would have been good reason to direct the interpretation of her transference reaction toward her earlier experiences with people, with particular expectation that previously repressed thoughts about her father might emerge. If on the other hand she had not been talking about childhood at all but had been complaining at length about current interpersonal difficulties, then an effort to generalize directly from the transference to those ongoing situations would have been indicated.

Regarding the intensity of the treatment, it needs to be kept in mind that the origins of transference reactions will usually be more remote from a patient's awareness than their implications for his current behavior. Hence a relatively uncovering treatment approach will be necessary to trace the origins of transference as well as elucidate its current impact, and a relatively supportive approach may have to limit the interpretation of transference to a focus on current rather than past events.

Yet in planning his strategy the therapist should not overlook that a patient's needs may be adequately met by generalizations from transference reactions to current interpersonal behavior, whether or not the patient has the interest and capacity to unravel the origins of his interpersonal attitudes. The recognition based on his experiences in the transference that he is currently misperceiving other people in his life may be sufficient to help a person gradually bring his perceptions into better tune with reality and thereby resolve the problems that have brought him into treatment. The therapist must be prepared to recognize such improvement as meaningful and not to insist that the causes of the patient's problems must all be traced to their earliest origins. When the goals of the treatment, as expressed in desired changes in behavior or self-attitudes, are met within the context of a contemporary focus on transference reactions, there is little reason to push for a historical accounting of their origins. This point of view concerning the interpretation of transference has obvious implications for deciding on when to terminate psychotherapy, which is the topic considered in Chapter 12 following discussion in Chapter 11of the therapist's side of the treatment relationship.

CHAPTER 11

The Psychotherapy Relationship: Countertransference

Countertransference in psychotherapy consists of inappropriate or irrational reactions by a therapist to his patient's behavior. Countertransference reactions parallel transference in reverse, in that they comprise displacements by the therapist onto the patient of thoughts, feelings, and impulses that are not justified in reality by anything the patient has said or done.

Like transference, countertransference was originally viewed solely as a hinderance to psychotherapy that must be avoided in order for progress to occur. Freud (1910b) admonished each therapist to "recognize this counter-transference in himself and overcome it," because "no psycho-analyst goes further than his own complexes and internal resistances permit" (p. 145). Yet subsequent work has indicated that countertransference reactions can at times be turned to advantage, since they have the potential for teaching the therapist something about himself and about unverbalized feelings and attitudes of his patient.

In further parallel with transference, countertransference interacts with real aspects of the treatment relationship and with the working alliance between patient and therapist. Additionally, as with transference, the ways in which countertransference develops and becomes manifest can be described by distinguishing between generalized and specific reactions and by elaborating individual differences in the intensity, feeling tone, and directness with which these reactions are expressed.

THE NATURE, COURSE, AND CONTROL OF COUNTERTRANSFERENCE REACTIONS

Because countertransference reactions mirror transference reactions, virtually everything said in Chapter 10 about inappropriate or irrational reactions of patient to therapist (transference) applies equally to inappropriate or irrational reactions of therapist to patient (countertransference). Without reiterating each parallel between these two phenomena, the following discussion translates the nature, course, and control of transference reactions into the language of countertransference.

Countertransference, Reality, and the Working Alliance

Defining countertransference as *inappropriate* or *irrational* reactions by a therapist to his patient's behavior implies that the treatment relationship is complex and multifaceted from the therapist's as well as from the patient's point of view. Although some clinicians have suggested that all of a therapist's feelings toward his patient constitute countertransference, it is generally considered more accurate and useful to distinguish countertransference both from realistic reactions to a patient's behavior and from attitudes based on the working alliance.[1]

The Real Relationship. As a person in his own right, every therapist carries a set of values with him into the treatment room. He may feel personal dislike for a patient who is racially bigoted or anger toward one who is cruel to his children. He may feel more sympathy for a patient who has suffered financial reversals than for one who has been disappointed in love, or vice-versa. He may find some patients physically attractive, consider some particularly admirable for their talents or achievements, and regard some as people he would enjoy knowing socially had he met them in that context.

Such reactions, stemming as they do from congruities between a therapist's values and his patient's actual characteristics or behavioral style, constitute reality. Unlike countertransference, they do not involve distorted perceptions of the patient or displacements onto him of approval or opprobrium that has not been merited. While there is accordingly little to be learned from exploring these real reactions, the therapist needs to be sufficiently aware of them to prevent them from

[1]The issues relevant to a precise definition of countertransference are elaborated in two important papers by A. Reich (1951, 1960). Other good survey articles on countertransference are provided by Baum (1970, 1973), Kernberg (1965), Orr (1954), and Tower (1956).

diluting his commitment to the working alliance. Whenever real reactions threaten to impair therapist effectiveness, as for example when the therapist finds it difficult to like or respect his patient as a person, serious consideration should be given to transfering the patient to another therapist.

Similarly inevitable are realistic reactions to specific bits of patient behavior in the interview, especially expressions of transference. A therapist may feel irritated with a patient who drops cigarette ashes on his floor; he may take pleasure in being complimented for his perspicacity and take umbrage at being assailed for his lack of understanding; he may feel gratified when a patient is progressing well in the treatment and disappointed when progress comes to a standstill. Whereas these kinds of reactions may escalate into countertransference, they can also remain at the level of the real relationship between therapist and patient, so long as the therapist's feelings remain appropriate in kind and intensity to the patient's behavior.

To elaborate, a therapist may realistically be annoyed at having ashes dropped on his floor; if he becomes furious, he is probably experiencing a countertransference reaction. He may realistically take some pleasure in compliments and offense at criticisms; if he is thrilled by the patient's praise or devastated by his censure, he is experiencing countertransference. He may realistically feel better about the treatment when it is progressing well than when it is not; if his dedication to the treatment ebbs and flows with the tides of its progress, he is experiencing countertransference.

In addition to experiencing realistic emotional reactions to his patients, the therapist as described in Chapter 10 also initiates or responds to certain aspects of the patient's real relationship to him. He says "Hello" and "Goodbye," he responds to "Merry Christmas" with "Same to you," he smiles at humorous events, and he expresses condolences should tragedy cross his patient's life. When appropriately modulated, these expressions of humanity sustain a patient's belief in his therapist's wish and capacity to be of help, and they participate in distinguishing the real relationship between therapist and patient from either countertransference or the working alliance.

The Working Alliance. From the therapist's point of view the working alliance comprises the ways he feels and behaves toward his patient as a function of his commitment to the treatment contract. He is dedicated to helping the patient understand himself better, resolve his psychological difficulties, and more fully realize his human potential. He is obliged to respect his patient's integrity and his right to be himself, even while he is attempting to help him find more effective and rewarding ways of being himself. He is required to listen in a relatively nonjudgmental manner, to respond primarily for the purpose of deepening the patient's self-understanding, and to refrain from using the treatment relationship to gratify his own personal needs.

The therapist's behavior in these respects, being rational and appropriate, does not constitute countertransference. Yet the working alliance is not a real relationship any more so for the therapist than it is for the patient. Unlike real interpersonal relationships, which involve a measure of spontaneity and mutual need gratification, the working alliance invokes an asymmetrical, nonmutual relationship and specifies how and when the parties to it shall interact. In keeping most of his personal feelings to himself, in passing no judgments, in seeking satisfaction only for his professional needs, in responding interpretively to what is said to him, in setting a schedule of appointments, and in continuing the relationship for as long as the patient requires, the therapist is behaving in a manner contrived to serve the aims and goals of psychotherapy and not as he would ordinarily behave in conducting his interpersonal affairs.

Countertransference. When a therapist feels or acts toward a patient in ways that are neither part of the real relationship, rationally justified by the circumstances, nor part of the working alliance, appropriate to the terms of the treatment contract, he is manifesting countertransference. More than from the real relationship or the working alliance, it is from these countertransference aspects of his relationship with a patient that a therapist has an opportunity to increase his understanding of himself and of the person he is trying to help. Whereas he must be sufficiently attentive to his parts in the real relationship and the working alliance to modulate the former and sustain the latter, neither will provide him much information beyond what is already explicit in content of the treatment. Countertransference reactions, on the other hand, consisting as they do of inappropriate or irrational reactions of the therapist to his patient's behavior, often furnish otherwise unavailable clues to both his and the patient's underlying motives and concerns.

The ways in which the *therapist's* distortions can provide information about his *patient's* personality may initially be difficult to conceive. Yet countertransference, like transference, always has some foundation in reality on which the edifice of unjustified feelings or attitudes is built. A patient who observes his therapist stifling a yawn and accuses him of not caring about the treatment is overreacting to the situation (transference), but he has after all seen his therapist behave in a manner usually indicative of boredom or disinterest (reality). Likewise, searching out the real features of the patient's behavior that have served to trigger a countertransference reaction can often turn up previously undetected aspects of his personality.

It is by alerting the therapist to otherwise obscured patient characteristics that countertransference provides a bridge from his own reactions to the patient's underlying motives and concerns. Suppose, for example, that a therapist finds himself feeling drowsy during a session, even though he has had ample sleep the night before and his patient is talking volubly. Since there is no realistic basis for his being drowsy and since the working alliance calls for him to be attentive at all times, his apparent disinterest in what the patient is saying is irrational and inappropriate and constitutes a countertransference reaction. But why should the therapist be inattentive, and what could the patient be doing to precipitate his inattentiveness at this particular time? The answer may be that the patient, despite talking freely about seemingly important matters, is really talking around rather than about issues central to the work of the treatment. If so, then the therapist's difficulty in paying attention will furnish a clue to the existence of such resistance behavior.

In a similar vein, suppose a therapist is finding himself regularly irritated with a patient, out of proportion to any real circumstances and contrary to his prescribed nonjudgmental role. Why is he becoming inappropriately irritated and what is the patient doing to irritate him? Could the patient have some underlying motives for wanting to irritate him? Is he as a manifestation of resistance hoping to terminate the treatment by provoking the therapist into discharging him, or does he perhaps have masochistic needs that he is seeking to gratify by goading the therapist into being punitive towards him? It is by raising such questions and possibilities in the therapist's mind that countertransference reactions can help to identify needs and impulses that the patient is not verbalizing.

The Course of Countertransference Reactions

Countertransference, like transference, follows a fairly uniform and predictable course with respect to its onset and feeling tone. Before describing these features of countertransference reactions, mention should be made of empirical findings that document the existence of countertransference phenomena in most if not all psychotherapy relationships. Research indicates, for example, that patient expressions of hostility are likely to produce anxiety and hostility in the therapist (Heller, Myers, & Kline, 1963; Russell & Snyder, 1963); that therapists tend to respond with decreased effectiveness when patients present material bearing on their own conflicts (Cutler, 1958; Yulis & Kiesler, 1968); and that the likelihood of premature termination increases when therapists encounter patients with problems similar to unresolved problems in themselves (Fielding, 1972). In fact, countertransference reactions are so inevitably a part of a meaningful psychotherapy interaction that their absence may indicate insufficient involvement of the therapist in his work. Snyder (1961) in his previously mentioned investigation of the psychotherapy relationship found considerable evidence "for the existence and desirability of some expression of countertransference in good psychotherapy" (p. 242), and his data tend to support the earlier conclusion of Reich (1951) that if countertransference does not exist, "the necessary talent and interest is lacking" (p. 31).

Although inevitable in effective psychotherapy, countertransference does not emerge full-blown in the initial stages of treatment. Rather, it tends to take shape gradually as a patient's behavior and verbalizations exert a cumulative impact on his therapist. Research findings confirm that the manner in which a therapist behaves toward a patient becomes increasingly similar over time to the ways in which other people behave toward that patient (Mueller, 1969). In light of this convergence over time of the therapist's behavior toward a patient onto the behavior of others toward him, countertransference can be conceived as the therapist's reaction to a patient's "pull" on him: the patient as a stimulus elicits certain kinds of reactions to himself from people in general, and the therapist is increasingly influenced to share in these reactions as he becomes increasingly familiar with him.

Although similar in onset to transference, countertransference reactions display a different pattern of variation in feeling tone over the course of psychotherapy. As described in Chapter 10, positive feelings of patient toward therapist tend to increase gradually throughout psychotherapy and in successful cases to reach their peak at termination. Negative patient feelings, it was noted, tend to increase markedly during the middle phase of psychotherapy and subsequently to decline as treatment nears termination. In contrast, the feelings of therapists toward their patients tend to fluctuate fairly evenly over the course of psychotherapy, without showing any consistent positive or negative trends. Only at the very end of psychotherapy are some directional shifts in feeling tone likely to occur, and then primarily in relation to the outcome of the treatment.

Toward patients who have made substantial progress, therapists tend to experience increasingly positive feelings as therapy nears termination, whereas toward patients who have derived minimal benefit, there is a marked increase in negative feelings at the end of treatment (see Snyder, 1961).

Rabiner et al. (1971) have more recently confirmed that therapists' attitudes toward their patients vary substantially over time, primarily in relation to the patient's clinical state. Specifically, therapists were found to feel relatively positive toward their patients when they were doing well and relatively negative toward them when they appeared increasingly upset, disturbed, or unable to function effectively. The conclusion Rabiner et al. draw about variation in countertransference feelings bears repeating:

> Apparently, therefore, at times when patients' attitudes and behavior in the dyadic situation are most consistent with the therapists' personal and professional interests, providing affirmation of the effectiveness of their "science," their competence in its use, and even of the institution with which they are affiliated, therapists find patients more likeable and savor more their work together (p. 568).

Controlling the Countertransference

Attention was called in Chapter 10 to the importance of "safeguarding" the transference component of the treatment relationship, which dictates that the therapist be circumspect in how much he reveals about himself in order to maximize what can be learned from how the patient perceives him. With respect to countertransference, however, such safeguarding is neither possible nor desirable. The therapist needs to discover as much as he can about his patient, not to remain in shadowy ignorance to avoid contaminating his impressions with fact. The more effectively he functions in this task, identifying the true nature of his patient's feelings and attitudes, the less opportunity there will be for him to misperceive these feelings and attitudes on a countertransference basis.

While the therapist should therefore do nothing to safeguard the countertransference, he does need to prevent countertransference reactions from interfering with his commitment to the working alliance, just as he strives to prevent the patient's commitments from being eroded by transference reactions. To exert such control over his countertransference reactions, a therapist must be able to recognize them when they occur and abort any untoward influence they might have on his conduct of the treatment.

Suppose, for example, a therapist finds himself feeling unusually sympathetic or solicitous toward a patient and allowing sessions to run several minutes overtime. Suppose further that the additional time is not being offered in response to some crisis or emergency in the patient's life, but only because the patient asked for it or because the sessions seemed "too interesting" to cut off. Then the therapist is probably experiencing some positive countertransference that he should immediately bring under control by returning to the prescribed session length. Otherwise, if he continues out of insensitivity to his countertransference to give more of himself than is called for by the treatment contract or by some urgent circumstances, he risks seducing his patient into unrealistic positive expectations about their relationship and thereby complicating resolution of the transference.

For another example of controlling countertransference, suppose a patient mentioning a concern that has already been the subject of several detailed interpretive sequences says, "I just don't have any idea what that could relate to," and the therapist finds springing acerbicly to his lips, "We've been over that a dozen times, but you just don't seem to be making any use of our work together." Although the patient's behavior may indeed reflect resistance or even an inability to profit from uncovering psychotherapy, neither possibility would justify the therapist expressing so much pique. Disappointment and frustration he may realistically feel in such situations, but anger toward the patient would need to be recognized as countertransference and kept from entering into either his words or the tone of his voice. Otherwise he risks responding to gratify his own needs rather than to meet his commitment to helping the patient understand himself.

Thus countertransference is important in psychotherapy not only because of what the alert therapist may learn from it, but also because recognizing and controlling it is a necessary duty of the therapist to maintain his commitment to the working alliance and provide his patient with a therapeutic climate. In his zeal to restrain expressions of countertransference, however, the therapist should be careful not to suppress appropriate responses in the context of the real relationship. The therapist who holds all of his personal comments and reactions firmly in check fails to demonstrate the human qualities essential to sustain the real relationship, and total suppression of freedom in the therapist's reactions to his patient isolates the treatment from real life in a manner that is as disadvantageous for the therapist as for the patient to do (see Fenichel, 1941, p. 74). Rather, the therapist needs to assess carefully whether his feelings and reactions are congruent with reality and might therefore be directly aired, or constitute countertransference and need instead to be understood and controlled.

Interestingly in this latter regard, there is empirical evidence for an inverse relationship between the amount of negative countertransference experienced by a therapist and the competence and effectiveness with which he is able to conduct psychotherapy. Fiedler (1951) demonstrated a greater incidence of negative attitudes toward patients in less competent than in more competent therapists, and Gurman (1972) has more recently reported a direct relationship between the therapist being in a good mood and his being able to display empathy, warmth, and genuineness in a treatment session. Although no cause-effect conclusions can be drawn from these correlational data, they affirm the association between negative therapist affect in the treatment situation and impaired therapist effectiveness. This association is sufficient to underline the importance for each therapist to learn to recognize and control his countertransference reactions.

ORIGINS AND MANIFESTATIONS OF COUNTERTRANSFERENCE

Countertransference originates when a patient's personality characteristics and behavior impinge in an affect-arousing manner on the underlying needs and concerns of his therapist. Depending on the nature of this interplay, countertransference reactions may be generalized or specific, positive or negative in feeling tone, and directly or indirectly felt and expressed.

Generalized and Specific Countertransference Reactions

All therapists are prone to countertransference reactions based on the needs and attitudes that generally characterize their interpersonal relationships. A therapist with strong needs to be nurturant, for example, may be particularly attracted to patients who become dependent on him and put off by patients who resist a dependent relationship. A therapist with voyeuristic needs may feel more enthused about his work with a patient who furnishes him extensive details of his sex life than one who does not. A therapist with unresolved problems with authority figures may be more prone to feeling irritated and defensive while conducting psychotherapy with a pompous and overbearing patient than while treating someone who is humble and deferential.

Interactions of this kind between a therapist's personality and his patient's attributes constitute generalized countertransference and pose potential obstacles to progess in the treatment. A highly nurturant therapist who fails to control countertransference may become inordinately supportive of a dependent patient, while offering fewer interpretations than the patient could have benefited from. A voyeuristic therapist may become preoccupied with ferreting out details that satisfy his own curiosity but contribute little to enhancing his patient's self-understanding. And a therapist with unresolved concerns about authority may devote more time to reacting in a defensive or retaliatory manner to a patient's pomposity than to helping the patient appreciate the nature and implications of his overbearing behavior.

By recognizing and controlling any such potential influences of his personality on the performance of his task, the therapist can prevent generalized countertransference from impairing his capacity to be helpful. Additionally, by identifying early in the relationship any patients toward whom his generalized countertransference tendencies are likely to exceed his ability to control them, the therapist can improve his judgment of whom he should attempt to treat and whom he should refer to another therapist. Virtually any abiding personality characteristic of the therapist can spawn generalized countertransference in relation to a patient's personality style, or to such attributes of the patient as his age, sex, social class, physical appearance, and mannerisms, or to how the patient responds and progresses in the treatment. The better a therapist understands himself and the more experience he has had with different kinds of patients, the more adept he becomes in anticipating his generalized countertransference and controlling it when it occurs.

Specific countertransference reactions comprise inappropriate or unjustified thoughts, feelings, or actions toward the patient in response to something particular he says or does that touches on problems the therapist himself has faced or is still facing. For example, a therapist with unresolved homosexual concerns may become anxious listening to a patient describe a homosexual encounter, and a therapist struggling with a marital problems may have difficulty attending with equanimity to a patient recounting difficulties in his marriage.

Unless such countertransference reactions are recognized and controlled, the therapist may inadvertently project his own limitations onto his patient and think poorly of him for not being able to handle the particular problem more effectively; he he may become angry at the patient for having brought up a subject that has made him feel anxious; or, without realizing the source of his anxiety, he may intervene so as to discourage the patient from continuing with the anxiety-arousing topic, as by directly changing the subject or suggesting that the patient is resisting talking about something else. In other circumstances countertransference may induce the therapist to think well rather than poorly of his patient, to become kindly disposed toward him for making him feel good, or to encourage him to pursue some enjoyable topic further than the needs of the treatment would indicate. Under the influence of specific countertransference, then, the therapist may think, feel, and act toward his patient in ways that have more to do with defending or gratifying himself than with understanding or being helpful to the patient.

Specific countertransference reactions tend to be short-lived, arising and dissipating as a patient introduces and finishes with the subject matter that provokes them. Hence they have fewer long-term implications for the course of psychotherapy than do generalized countertransference reactions, and fewer implications for which kinds of patients a particular therapist can or cannot effectively treat. Yet it should be obvious that moment-to-moment recognition and control of specific as well as generalized countertransference reactions is necessary for a therapist to maintain effective commitment to the working alliance in the face of material that impinges on his personal concerns.

Positive and Negative Countertransference

Countertransference reactions always involve a prevailing feeling tone that casts the patient in either a favorable or unfavorable light. As in the case of positive and negative transference, however, positive and negative countertransference refer only to the primary attitudes in the therapist's reaction to his patient, not to two separate forms of reaction. Like transference reactions, all countertransference reactions are essentially negative, in that they distort reality and suspend the therapist's attention to helping his patient toward increased self-understanding. Singer (1965, pl. 295) expresses this communality of positive and negative transference-countertransference as follows: ". . . a distortion, whether perpetrated by patient or by therapist and regardless of its overt form—irrational admiration or irrational dislike—is inevitably negative and pathological in the sense that it bespeaks a reduction of personal awareness and simultaneously does violence to the other person."

Yet differentiating the prevailing feeling tone of countertransference reactions can facilitate controlling them, especially since inappropriate positive and negative feelings toward a patient contribute to different kinds of therapist error. In reference to previous examples in the chapter, a therapist influenced by positive countertransference may tend to be oversolicitous, to back off from making interpretations, to allow sessions to run overtime or the treatment to last too long, and to be seductive with patients of the opposite sex or ingratiating with patients of the same sex. A therapist influenced by negative countertransference may tend to be patronizing or unresponsive, to bludgeon his patient with interpretations, especially interpretations of resistance and transference, to be overly casual about tardiness or missed sessions, and to seize prematurely on possibilities for termination.

The more alert the therapist is to these and other common manifestations of positive and negative countertransference, the better prepared he is to anticipate and reverse their influence. Thus a therapist, aware that his own needs are causing him to feel positively toward a patient, should warn himself in advance against being so solicitous or seductive as to preclude his being helpful; conversely, a therapist aware of feeling negatively toward a patient should be prepared to guard against being too cold and distant or using interpretations as a tool to vent his anger rather than as a means of communicating understanding.

Direct and Indirect Expressions of Countertransference

Countertransference reactions vary in the directness with which they are expressed and correspondingly in the degree to which their meaning is obvious. Most direct among countertransference reactions are consciously experienced feelings toward the patient of love, hate, anger, jealousy, repugnance, sexual arousal, pride, parental fondness, and the like. The countertransference basis for such strong affects is usually apparent, provided the therapist does not err in considering them a justifiable part of the real relationship. The psychotherapy interaction—asymmetrical as it is, confined at most to only a few hours of contact per week, and constrained within a set of prescribed role behaviors—provides neither patient nor therapist with the kinds of mutually shared experiences from which one person can develop genuinely strong feelings toward another. Consequently, any strong feelings of like or dislike must be regarded as transference if the patient has them and as countertransference if they emerge in the therapist.

This point is emphasized because even experienced therapists may fall prey on occasion to believing that strong positive or negative feelings they develop toward a patient are realistically based on his being a marvelous or despicable person. In fact, however, no matter how marvelous or despicable a patient may be in his impact on others, he cannot be either in his relationship with the therapist: the relatively limited amount of time he spends with the therapist and the extent to which this time is devoted to the work of the treatment allow the patient little opportunity to intrude either marvelously or despicably on the therapist's personal life. Because the reality of the treatment relationship provides insufficient basis for a therapist to develop strong positive or negative feelings toward his patient, the origin of such feelings should always be sought in countertransference, no matter how tempted the therapist might be to regard them otherwise (see Marmor, 1970, 1972).

Somewhat less direct but also fairly obvious expressions of countertransference comprise feelings or fantasies concerning the patient that clearly imply but do not explicate positive and negative therapist attitudes. Common in this regard is dreaming about a patient, which constitutes clear evidence that the patient is affecting the therapist more than could be expected from either the real relationship or the working alliance. If correctly interpreted, the content of dreams about a patient can tell the therapist a good deal about the nature of his countertransference reactions, as can the theme and emotional tone of any waking fantasies he has about a patient, whether during or outside of treatment sessions.

Countertransference feelings may also appear in thinly disguised form as positive or negative attitudes toward the treatment. For example, a therapist may experience mounting or waning interest in his work with a particular patient, or he may find himself looking forward to sessions with eager or unpleasurable anticipation, or he may feel uneasy, depressed, elated, or relieved following sessions. Similarly indirect but obvious manifestations of countertransference are present when the therapist takes great satisfaction in a patient's praising his sensitivity and helpfulness or becomes markedly upset at having his competence or dedication impugned. With allowance for the satisfactions and disappointments to which a therapist is entitled as a professional person observing the success or failure of his efforts, strong positive or negative emotional reactions to a patient's comments on these efforts indicate that he is attaching special importance to the patient's opinion of him.

A third and less obvious type of countertransference expression consists of therapist behaviors that are not accompanied by feelings or attitudes toward the patient or the treatment but that on closer inspection seem very likely to derive from such feelings or attitudes. In the case of negative countertransference, for example, a therapist may become careless about his obligations to a patient, "forgetting" an appointment, giving discourteously short notice of an impending vacation, losing track of details from one session to the next, or letting his mind wander during an interview.

Similarly reflecting countertransference is a therapist's inclination to discuss with colleagues his treatment of a particular patient. Although informal sharing of experiences among psychotherapists can contribute to their continuing professional growth, it may also be used as a vehicle for the indirect expression of attitudes toward a patient of which the therapist is not otherwise aware. In speaking with relish and enthusiasm about his work with a patient, for example, a therapist experiencing positive countertransference may in effect be telling the world "Look at what a wonderful patient I have, and how much progress he is making, and how well I am conducting the therapy." If countertransference is primarily negative in tone, communication to colleagues may instead focus on the difficulty of the treatment, on the strength of the patient's resistances, or on "humorous" aspects of the patient's problems. Any such complaining about a patient or laughing at his foibles in discussion with a colleague bears close scrutiny for its possible origins in negative countertransference. As a general principle, all discussions among therapists of their ongoing treatment should be examined with respect to whether they represent solely an academic sharing of clinical experience or are additionally expressing countertransference feelings to which one or more of the participating therapists should be alerted.

Fourth and least directly indicative of countertransference are variations in the therapist's conduct of the treatment that can easily be rationalized and hence escape notice as countertransference manifestations unless the therapist is vigilant to them. As described earlier, for example, the therapist may at various points in the treatment be providing unnecessary reassurance or insufficient emotional support; he may be offering too few interpretations, couched in exceedingly tentative terms, or an excessive number of interpretations phrased with undue certainty; he may be prematurely encouraging consideration of termination or inappropriately deferring such considerations; and he may be alternating between feeling confident in his plan of action and uncertain about how best to conduct the treatment.

The therapist's judgment in these and similar respects should be guided by his understanding of how best to conduct effective psychotherapy. However, if countertransference is distorting his perception of the treatment situation, he may have difficulty identifying the indications for one or another technical procedure. Is the patient really ready to begin thinking about termination, or is the therapist in his negative reactions to a difficult patient seizing too eagerly on some slight references to the possibility of discontinuing treatment? Is the patient really presenting bland information that does not call for interpretation, or is the therapist in his wish to have his patient like him overlooking appropriate interpretations that might make the patient anxious or angry?

These kinds of questions should be constantly on the therapist's mind, to help him address his behavior in the therapy to the needs of the patient rather than to countertransference distortions of what these needs may be. Whenever the therapist cannot satisfy himself that his actions are fully justified by the reality of the treatment situation, he should suspect some countertransference basis for his behavior and take steps to mitigate its influence.

RECOGNIZING AND LEARNING FROM COUNTERTRANSFERENCE REACTIONS

The first and most important thing a therapist must do with his countertransference reactions is to recognize them when they occur. Without such recognition there are few prospects for controlling countertransference, as discussed in this chapter, or learning from it, as will be considered in the final section. To hone his sensitivity to countertransference, the therapist should anticipate that he will develop some countertransference reactions toward every patient with whom he works in a conscientious and dedicated fashion. Furthermore, drawing on his understanding of himself and on his cumulative clinical experience, he should come to anticipate the kinds of countertransference reactions he is likely to form toward patients in general and toward some types of patients in particular.

It is this latter regard that self-awareness becomes particularly important to a therapist's effectiveness. As noted in Chapter 3 and emphasized again here, a trained professional does not have to be a paragon of psychological adjustment, free from all neurotic concerns, in order to function effectively as a psychotherapist. However, he does have to be sufficiently aware of his own concerns to prevent them from interfering with his clinical work and to guide him in determining which patients he is most likely to benefit and which he should refer to a colleague. Thus each therapist must be aware of qualities within himself that tend to impair his effectiveness with patients of a particular age, sex, social class, or personality style, and he needs to know in advance whether he is likely to feel intimidated by an overbearing patient or exasperated with a timid one, gratified by a highly dependent patient or impressed with a highly independent one, aroused or alienated by a sexually seductive patient, envious of or captivated by an intellectually brilliant one, and so on.

Awareness of his own dispositions to generalized and specific countertransference reactions and of the various ways in which countertransference is expressed prepare a therapist to recognize the emergence of feelings and attitudes in himself that are not justified in reality or by the nature of the working alliance. The more promptly countertransference is recognized, the more adequately the therapist can prevent it from impairing his sensitivity to his patient's communications, from blurring his perspectives on the implications of the patient's behavior, or from inducing him to act in ways that impede progress in the treatment. He can become more careful about scheduling appointments, for example, or concentrate harder on paying attention, or offer fewer interpretations, or give additional attention to possibilities for terminating, or do whatever else is necessary to reverse features of his behavior that, as products of countertransference, have been serving his needs and not the needs of his patient.

When countertransference reactions are clearly recognized, the therapist may be able to learn a good deal about himself and his patients from them. With respect to generalized countertransference, a therapist cannot help but acquire from his clinical experience knowledge of his own interpersonal attitudes and how they dispose him to react to various kinds of patients and patient problems. Hopefully a clinician who assumes responsibility for providing psychotherapeutic services will already have attained a large measure of self-understanding, so that he will not need to look upon psychotherapy as a major growth experience for himself. Psychotherapy is after all intended for the benefit of the patient not the therapist.

On the other hand, genuine involvement as a participant observer with his patients always has the potential for adding to a therapist's self-understanding. It is partly for this reason that experience contributes to competence in doing psychotherapy. The more patients with whom a therapist has worked, the more opportunity he has had to identify interpersonal dispositions that are likely to affect his conduct of psychotherapy and to learn which types of patients are most likely to profit from being in therapy with him. Cumulative clinical experience thereby allows each therapist to improve his selection of patients to treat or refer and to work more effectively with those he decides to treat.

In terms of specific countertransference reactions, a therapist can use any intercurrent anxiety or other discomfort he experiences during the treatment to identify unresolved areas of conflict in himself. If, for example, he feels unsettled or finds himself changing the subject when a patient describes failure to perform sexually or problems in asserting himself, he probably has some unresolved concerns in these areas. As just noted, a therapist should bring to his clinical work a fairly thorough understanding of any such areas of conflict in his own personality that might untowardly influence his conduct of the treatment. Yet it is to be expected that the diverse pathways of psychotherapy will from time to time cross areas of conflict that the therapist has not previously recognized in himself, and what he learns from observing the countertransference reactions he experiences in these instances will enhance his self-understanding and make him a better therapist, better prepared to anticipate and control such reactions in the future.

Sensitivity to countertransference of course brings with it increased potential for the therapist to understand his patient as well as himself. Although most clinicians consider the recognition and control of countertransference as more important to effective psychotherapy than any clues it offers to the nature of the patient's personality (see Reich, 1960), prevailing opinion nevertheless agrees with the view presented here that countertransference can alert the therapist to important unverbalized attitudes and impulses in the patient (see Menninger & Holzman, 1973, pp. 87–94; Racker, 1953, 1957).

To use countertransference reactions in this way, the therapist needs first to understand his inappropriate feelings or attitudes toward the patient and then to seek in the patient's behavior themes that might have triggered the particular countertransference reaction. Suppose, for example, that a therapist becomes anxious during a session in which the patient talks about how much progress he has made, and suppose further the therapist is aware of having become attached to or gratified by the patient in ways that will make termination a personally unhappy experience for him. Although it may seem fairly obvious that a patient talking about how much progress he has made has termination on his mind, sensitivity to his countertransference can help the therapist recognize this implication of the patient's remarks more quickly or clearly than he might otherwise, especially if it is something he would prefer not to hear because of his attachment to the treatment relationship.

As a patient's comments or actions become less directly related to unverbalized themes or impulses than in the above example, countertransference becomes potentially more instrumental in bringing these themes or impulses to the therapist's attention. Suppose a patient is not doing or saying anything apparently related to thoughts about termination, but the therapist is nevertheless experiencing some anxiety he associates with an imminent rupture of the treatment relationship. He might then have adequate basis for at least raising the topic for exploration: "I wonder if you've been having some thoughts about how much longer we should continue to work together."

Whenever a therapist's countertransference reactions sensitize him in this way to unverbalized attitudes or impulses in the patient, he is likely to begin recognizing other subtle clues to these attitudes and impulses tht he had previously overlooked. Continuing with the above example, a patient satisfied with his progress may find few things to talk about in his sessions, require minimal help to explore and understand what he does say, and display little concern about circumstances that force cancellation of sessions. Although any of these behaviors should signal the therapist that his patient may be nearing termination, a countertransference investment in continuing to work with the patient could cloud his vision of them. Then only his anxiety, compensating for his insensitivity to the other available clues, could alert him that the patient may be considering termination.

Countertransference thus provides a barometer of patient feelings and attitudes that can help a therapist keep abreast of the climate of the treatment relationship when other indices are unavailable or escape his notice. In this sense Tauber and Green (1959, Chap. 10) have appropriately described countertransference as a form of "subthreshold communication." On the other hand, countertransference should not be equated with all forms of subthreshold communicaton that reach the therapist in the treatment relationship, because such an equation would make countertransference synonymous with empathy and strip it of its unique significance.

To illustrate this distinction of countertransference from empathy, suppose a therapist talking with a seriously disturbed patient in a hospital setting suddenly feels apprehensive and steps back from him—just in time to evade a punch aimed at his jaw. Or suppose a therapist listening to a male patient describing repetitive clumsiness in spilling his drinks at cocktail parties, especially while he is talking to a woman, has an association to premature ejaculation, which is a form of spilling, and it turns out on exploration that premature ejaculation is an important concern of the patient he has not yet been able to verbalize.

In these instances empathy and not countertransference has determined the therapist's subthreshold communications. Anticipating that the first patient was about to strike at him could have been based on sensitivity to a number of visible clues, such as a slight clenching of the patient's teeth or fist or a change in the intensity of his facial expression. Whatever the stimuli that triggered the therapist's apprehension, he was accurately perceiving his patient's impulse, and both his fear and his drawing back were appropriate responses to the situation. As a reaction based on reality, then, independently of any perceptual distortion influenced by his prior dispositions or his own unresolved conflicts, his behavior would have constituted empathic understanding, not countertransference.

Similarly in the second example, the therapist's association from the spilling of a drink to the spilling of semen, which allowed him to identify the patient's unverbalized concerns about premature ejaculation, would have involved accurate rather than distorted perception and conflict-free utilization of the therapist's fantasy to serve the purpose of the treatment. This latter type of sensitivity, in which the therapist uses his own associations to the patient's productions to enrich his understanding of them, is discussed at length in Reik's (1948) *Listening with the Third Ear*, the third ear being the one the therapist tunes in to his own inner voices. However, so long as the therapist's emotional reactions are appropriate to the reality of the treatment situation and his associations are not disturbed by his own unresolved conflicts, attention to minimal clues and listening with the third ear constitute empathy and not countertransference.

PART FOUR

The Final Phase of Psychotherapy

CHAPTER 12

Termination

The final phase of psychotherapy is exceeded perhaps only by the initial phase in its importance for determining the amount of help a patient receives. The middle phase of treatment, involving as it does the communication of understanding through interpretation and the utilization of resistance, transference, and countertransference phenomena for this purpose, constitutes the main work of therapy. Yet this work becomes possible only if the therapist is first able to assess accurately a patient's likelihood of benefiting from psychotherapy and then to implement an adequate treatment contract for engaging in it. Similarly, the manner in which psychotherapy is brought to a close determines in large measure whether self-learning during the middle phase of treatment persists as a life-enriching resource or pales into a transiently interesting but no longer meaningful experience.

To bring psychotherapy to an effective close, the therapist must be able to judge when an appropriate point of termination has been reached and what procedures will serve best to consolidate the gains that have been made. To complicate this task, there are no fixed criteria for when psychotherapy should end, and there are often circumstances external to the treatment that mandate termination. However, several considerations relating to the necessary duration of psychotherapy can guide the therapist in evaluating the appropriateness of termination, and a number of procedures can be specified for conducting the final phase of treatment under conditions of both voluntary and forced termination.

THE NECESSARY DURATION OF PSYCHOTHERAPY

It is deceptively simply to say that psychotherapy should last until the goals of the treatment have been achieved. In actual practice, however, the goals of psychotherapy are seldom sufficiently delineated for either patient or therapist to identify precisely when they have been achieved. If the initial treatment contract was aimed toward the resolution of psychological problems through increased self-understanding, then how completely should the patient resolve his problems and how thoroughly should he understand himself before psychotherapy is considered to have achieved its goals? If treatment began with more specific objectives in mind, such as relief from symptoms of anxiety or depression, improved functioning in social work situations, or better control of certain impulses or emotions, how much symptom relief, improved functioning, or better self-control must be achieved to meet the objectives of the treatment? Even if treatment is started with clearly delineated goals that should leave little doubt as to when it has served its purpose, such as resolving a marital problem or graduating from college, patients who enter psychotherapy to achieve such narrow goals more often than not become interested during the course of the treatment in pursuing broader concerns they have about themselves. Hence they too will face ambiguities in deciding when the treatment has gone far enough.

It may seem possible to eliminate these ambiguities by positing complete self-understanding, total symptom relief, full self-actualization, and perfect self-control as indications that psychotherapy has achieved its goals. But such perfection rarely if ever characterizes the human condition; it exists only as an abstraction when measured against each person's quest for realization of his potential and satisfaction in his interpersonal relationships. Freud (1937) in one of his last and most significant papers, "Analysis Terminable and Interminable," cautioned that if therapists continue treatment until the patient is "cured" or has reached a state of complete freedom from neurotic inhibitions or concerns, the treatment will never end. More realistically, therapy will have reached its necessary duration when the patient's freedom from symptoms, anxieties, and inhibitions has been "approximately fulfilled" (p. 219):

> Our aim will not be to rub off every peculiarity of human character for the sake of a schematic "normality," nor yet to demand that the person who has been "thoroughly analysed" shall feel no passions and develop no internal conflicts. The business of the analysis is to secure the best possible psychological conditions for the function of the ego; with that it has discharged its task (p. 250).

Successful psychotherapy, in other words, should be conceived as making progress toward goals, not necessarily as reaching these goals in all of their ramifications. Extending treatment until all of its objectives have been realized may bind the patient to life-long psychotherapy, which only in the most unusual circumstances could be in his best interest. Psychotherapy is after all an unreal relationship, in which certain contrived and nonmutual roles are prescribed for the participants (see Chaps. 10–11), and, no matter how much responsibility a patient assumes for the conduct of the treatment, being in psychotherapy still places him in a dependent relationship rather than on his own two feet. Psychotherapy is a means by which a person can help himself live more fully, but it should never be allowed to become itself a way of living life to the full.

The fact that the work of psychotherapy is never fully completed, and that termination accordingly occurs at a point of progress toward its goals rather than upon full attainment of these goals, does not mean that therapists should denigrate the fruits of their efforts or regard psychotherapy as a seriously limited procedure. One of the most important accomplishments of psychotherapy is that it teaches the patient a method of looking at himself. In addition to whatever degree of self-knowledge, self-control, or symptom relief he attains during treatment, a patient brings away from therapy some training in how to observe past and current experiences so as to learn from them more effective ways of dealing with future experience.

A patient's experience in learning self-observation allows him to make continued progress toward the goals of psychotherapy even after treatment has been terminated. Interpretations that have been fairly well worked through prior to termination continue to be worked through as the patient encounters new situations in which they help him understand and modulate his behavior. Self-esteem that has been enhanced during psychotherapy continues to increase following termination as the patient realizes personal ambitions made possible by his gains in the treatment. Thus psychotherapy constitutes a process that, once set in motion, can help a patient sustain progress toward a richer and more rewarding life even after the formal treatment relationship has been terminated.[1]

In this same vein, termination does not need to be deferred until the therapist feel certain his patient will never again encounter the difficulties that brought him for help. While substantial progress toward a more

[1]Research evidence in this regard, although meager, confirms that beneficial effects of uncovering psychotherapy continue to accrue following termination of the treatment (see Reisman, 1971, p. 36). Kubie (1973) concludes on the basis of clinical experience that "for some patients therapy as a process of continuing psychological change and maturation may start only after formal therapy has been terminated" (p. 882).

effective and rewarding life style should have occurred before termination is seriously considered, the possibility of new or recurrent psychological problems does not contraindicate a decision to terminate. Just as perfection is an ideal, so psychological problems can never be avoided completely, and termination of psychotherapy should not presume that the patient has received all the help he will ever need. Future and unforeseen circumstances may cause him difficulties for which some return visits with the therapist would be helpful. Like booster shots, such follow-up periods of treatment help sustain improved functioning and should neither be discouraged nor interpreted to mean that the original psychotherapy was unsuccessful.

Consistently with the fact that there are no fixed criteria for when psychotherapy should end, no linear relationship has been demonstrated between either the duration of treatment (as measured in weeks, months, or years) or the amount of treatment (as measured by total number of sessions) and successful or unsuccessful outcome (see Meltzoff & Kornreich, 1970, pp. 340–357; Reisman, 1971, pp. 37–43). About one-half of the relevant research studies report a positive relationship between amount of treatment and successful outcome, whereas the remainder report either a curvilinear relationship between them or no relationship at all. The value of these studies is unfortunately limited by widespread failure to control for degree of disturbance among the patient samples and by reliance on outcome ratings obtained from the patients' own therapists, whose judgments may have been biased by the amount of treatment they had provided.

Nevertheless, the therapist can be guided in the individual case by certain factors that affect how long the treatment needs to last. Additionally, even though successful outcome must usually be measured in terms of progress toward various goals rather than attaining them, there are some definite minimum criteria for beginning to consider the appropriateness of termination.

Factors Affecting the Duration of Psychotherapy

The duration of psychotherapy in the individual case will be influenced by three factors: (a) the depth and intensity of the treatment, (b) the orientation and skill of the therapist, and (c) the needs and capacities of the patient.

Depth and Intensity of the Treatment. Uncovering psychotherapy proceeds by evoking thoughts and feelings of which the patient has not been fully aware and that bear on the problems for which he has sought help. The more intensively the treatment is pursued, as measured by the frequency of the sessions, the more numerous these uncovered thoughts and feelings become and the more time is necessary to discuss them adequately. Furthermore, the more intensive the treatment is, the more deeply involved the treatment relationship is likely to become and the longer the time will be to explore and resolve its transference elements. Because any increase in session frequency thus broadens and deepens the scope of treatment, with a corresponding increase in its intensity, it is generally the case that the more intensive psychotherapy is, the longer it will need to last.[2]

Two exceptions to this general relationship between frequency of sessions and duration of psychotherapy, both of which involve primarily supportive treatment, should be noted. In instances of crisis intervention, first of all, the treatment plan may involve very frequent sessions but over just a short period of time, until the crisis has passed. For example, an acutely suicidal patient may be seen daily for only a week or two and then, if the immediate suicide risk has abated, be terminated or placed on a different treatment schedule. Second, in some circumstances supportive treatment may be arranged on a relatively infrequent basis but with the expectation of an extended duration. Especially for patients with mild but chronic psychological problems, psychotherapy on a bi-weekly or monthly basis over a period of years may be the most appropriate way of promoting gradual movement toward a more effective life style or of providing sustenance through a transitional phase in the life cycle. Allowing for these two exceptions, however, the direct relationship will generally hold between the frequency of psychotherapy sessions and the necessary duration of the treatment.

Orientation and Skill of the Therapist. Some psychotherapists approach their work in the belief that people are innately resilient and remarkably capable of redirecting their lives on the basis of even minimal flashes of insight or a "corrective emotional experience" (see Alexander & French, 1964, Chap. 4). Other therapists, though equally dedicated to helping their

[2]As noted in the discussion of transference proneness in Chapter 10, patients vary in how intensively they become involved in psychotherapy of a given frequency, so that, for example, a relatively expressive person may be engaged in more intensive psychotherapy on a once-weekly basis than a relatively reflective person is with two sessions per week. By and large, however, it is reasonable to expect that the more frequently a patient is being seen the more intensive his psychotherapy will become and the longer its duration will have to be.

patients live a fuller life, share Freud's (1937) more pessimistic view that neurotic inhibitions and conflicts are stubbornly persistent phenomena that yield, if at all, only to extensive and hard-won increments in self-understanding. Therapists of the first persuasion tend to proceed with the expectation that psychotherapy can be brought to a satisfactory point of termination in relatively short order, whereas those holding the latter view anticipate a much longer period of psychotherapy prior to reaching an appropriate termination point.

Such differences in orientation produce corresponding differences among therapists in their setting of criteria for termination. Those who are optimistic about their patients' capacities for self-growth are inclined to accept initial symptom relief and beginning progress toward more effective coping as sufficient basis for termination, and they regard prolonging therapy beyond this point as fostering the patient's dependency and discouraging him from seeking his own best destiny. Therapists who are more conservative in their expectations about personality change tend to view such initial progress as only a first step toward improvement and to consider termination based on it as premature and risking reversal of the prior treatment gains.

One noteworthy outgrowth of optimism concerning the possible brevity of psychotherapy has been an effort to specify in the initial contract how many sessions there will be or over how long a period of time the treatment will continue. Such use of time-limited therapy is believed to create some urgency about the treatment, to encourage both patient and therapist to use their time together more efficiently than they would in the absence of such limitations, and to reduce patient dependence on the therapist (see Mann, 1973; Meltzoff & Kornreich, 1970, pp. 337–339). Although the available research evidence in this regard is neither abundant nor conclusive, it is not unusual for short-staffed clinics serving large numbers of people to place administrative limits on the length of time any patient can be seen for psychotherapy. Hence the practice of time-limited psychotherapy is probably more common than convictions about its effectiveness would otherwise dictate.[3]

[3]It should be acknowledged that the labels "optimistic" and "pessimistic" used to describe different attitudes toward the necessary duration of psychotherapy would probably be unacceptable to therapists firmly convinced either that therapy should usually be an extended investigation process, or that it should regularly be a brief, time-limited encounter. From the former point of view the "pessimistic" attitude would be considered appropriate and the "optimistic" attitude unrealistic, whereas from the latter point of view just the opposite opinions would prevail. Nevertheless, given the evidence that there is no optimal duration of psychotherapy applicable to all patients, and in the absence of strong empirical

In the absence of time restrictions, the pace at which treatment progresses toward a satisfactory termination point is influenced by the therapist's skill as well as his orientation. The more readily he can understand his patient's communications and the more incisively he can communicate this understanding to the patient, the more rapidly the treatment will yield benefits and the shorter its necessary duration will be. Yet it should be remembered from Chapter 3 that therapist skill is a dyadic variable and not a fixed personality trait of the therapist. Whatever his general level of competence, a therapist will prove more skillful in working with certain kinds of patients and patient problems than with others. With regard to the necessary duration of psychotherapy, each therapist will accordingly require more time to complete a satisfactory course of treatment with some patients than with others.

Needs and Capacities of the Patient. With respect to the patient's needs, people who enter treatment with relatively serious, complicated, long-standing problems tend to require more prolonged therapy than those seeking help for relatively mild and straightforward problems of recent onset. Likewise, people who wish to achieve sweeping personality changes in psychotherapy usually require a more extended course of treatment than those who seek less ambitious goals. Generally speaking, then, the greater the gap between the seriousness and the chronicity of the patient's difficulties on the one hand, and the state of improved personality functioning he would like to achieve on the other, the longer the psychotherapy can be expected to last.

This general principle notwithstanding, patients as well as therapists differ in the amount and kind of treatment progress they consider sufficient basis for terminating. Some patients doubt their capacity to change permanently or for the better; in treatment such patients mistrust initial signs of progress, anticipate recurrence of their difficulties, and hesitate to think about termination until there has been extensive working through in the therapy and prolonged improvement outside of it. Other patients are optimistic about being able to improve rapidly in therapy and maintain their improvement if the therapist can get them moving in the right direction; these patients thrive on initial signs of progress, which they see as signifying the beginning of the end of the treatment, and they

support for either extended or brief therapy as *the* best form of treatment, "optimistic" and "pessimistic" serve adequately to describe these two differing expectations concerning the necessary duration of psychotherapy. The history and treatment implications of these differing points of view on the capacity of people to change are discussed further by Chrzanowski (1960).

are reluctant to delay termination once they have begun to cope more effectively with their experience.

The capacities of the individual patient influence the necessary duration of psychotherapy in much the same way as the skill of the therapist. The more freely a person can talk about himself in the treatment situation, the more sensitively he can address his own needs and attitudes, the more perceptively he can draw on the therapist's interventions to expand his self-understanding, and the more readily he can allow the psychotherapy experience to influence his behavior in other situations, the more rapidly he will progress in treatment and the sooner he will complete it.

The extent to which the needs and capacities of the patient affect the necessary duration of psychotherapy challenge the widespread practice of distinguishing between "long-term" and "short-term" therapy on the basis of some arbitrary number of sessions or months of treatment, whether for clinical or research purposes. Efforts to abbreviate the time necessary to meet the psychological needs of people seeking psychotherapy have led to a number of books in the last decade specifically addressed to "brief" psychotherapy (e.g. Barten, 1971; Bellak & Small, 1965; Phillips & Wiener, 1966; Sifneos, 1972; Wolberg, 1965). However, so long as the nature of the treatment and the skill and orientation of the therapist are appropriate to the patient's needs and capacities, there is no such thing as psychotherapy that is "brief" or "prolonged," except in terms of an arbitrary numerical criterion, but only psychotherapy that lasts a particular length of time (see Appelbaum, 1972).

Minimum Criteria for Considering Termination

The discussion to this point has hopefully clarified that many factors influence the necessary duration of psychotherapy and that there are no fixed criteria for identifying the point at which treatment is complete. However, despite the complexities of deciding whether psychotherapy has lasted long enough and the uncertainties in choosing an ideal time for termination, there are three minimum criteria that should be satisfied before termination is even considered as a possibility.

First, some substantial progress should have been made toward achieving the goals of the treatment. Although "substantial progress" is open to different interpretations, each patient and therapist should be able to agree on what constitutes progress toward the goals they have set and on whether such progress has taken place. Except in those instances when patient and therapist agree to discontinue treatment because *no* progress is being made, then, the principle will generally hold that termination should not be considered until both parties to the treatment contract concur in perceiving substantial progress toward their goals.

Second, the patient should appear capable of continuing to work independently on understanding and alleviating his problems. As noted earlier, successful psychotherapy teaches a person method as well as substance: he learns not only about himself as a person but also about how to observe his own behavior, how to relate his thoughts and feelings to each other and to the actions he takes, and how to apply his self-knowledge in pursuing a more effective and rewarding life style. Before termination of psychotherapy is considered, a patient should have demonstrated capacity to initiate without the therapist's help such observation, understanding, and realigning of his behavior in situations of conflict and opportunity. Only then will there be sufficient likelihood of his sustaining and building on his treatment gains to justify a decision to terminate.

Third, the patient's transference relationship to the therapist should have been resolved sufficiently for the real relationship between them to gain ascendance. This does not mean that patient and therapist now become personally intimate in ways that transcend their original treatment contract. Rather, it means that fewer transference reactions will occur and that a correspondingly larger part of the treatment interaction will consist of reality-oriented conversations, in which the patient recounts his experiences with minimal evidence of distortion and the therapist listens and comments with minimal utilization of an as if, interpretive stance. If therapy is terminated before such a resolution of the transference is achieved, the patient's unexpressed feelings toward his therapist may trouble him in the future, in the same manner as other unresolved feelings toward important people would trouble him. It is also likely that patients who leave therapy with unresolved transference feelings probly leave with other unresolved problems as well, for which additional treatment would have been helpful.

These three minimum criteria for considering termination in psychotherapy—substantial progress toward the goals of the treatment, the patient's apparent capacity to continue independently to observe and learn about himself, and resolution of the transference—is elaborated throughout the rest of this chapter with respect to the specific planning and implementation of termination. In ideal circumstances termination occurs when a patient and therapist who are working together with few external constraints become fully satisfied that an appropriate stopping point has been reached. Not uncommonly, however, some external circumstances mandate termination of the therapy regardless of what stage of progress it has reached. Since considerations in planning and implementing termination vary with whether it is occurring on a voluntary or forced basis, these two patterns of termination will be discussed separately.

CONSIDERATIONS IN VOLUNTARY TERMINATION

Voluntary termination of psychotherapy occurs when the parties to a treatment contract come mutually to the conclusion that it should end. Unless an inappropriately conceived treatment contract prompts a decision to terminate shortly after therapy has begun, mutual agreement that psychotherapy should end usually begins to emerge after the patient has gone through a period of learning more about himself and working through the implications of his enhanced self-knowledge. Then the initial suggestion to consider termination may come from either the patient or the therapist, depending on the particular nature of their treatment relationship and the demands of the situation.

Termination Proposed by the Patient

The most desirable way for termination to evolve is for a patient spontaneously to report that he believes he has accomplished his objectives in psychotherapy, that he feels capable of handling on his own any further difficulties he might encounter, and that he would like to discuss how much longer the treatment needs to continue. Such a proposal from a patient eminently satisfies the minimum criteria for beginning to consider termination: the patient will have stated in as many words that he has made substantial progress in the treatment, that he has good prospects for sustaining this progress, and that he is prepared to review at the level of the real relationship when and how termination should be implemented.

The therapist's first task in responding to such direct expressions of interest in termination is to consider whether they reflect an accurate estimate of progress or instead mask resistance to further treatment. As noted in Chapter 9, resistance to change, resistance to interview content, and resistance associated with transference attitudes may all contribute to premature suggestions to terminate. When termination is proposed in the context of obvious resistance, the proposal should be interpreted as a manifestation of the resistance; when it is proposed in the absence of obvious resistance but also in the absence of evidence for the improvement the patient claims to feel, the proposal should be explored for its possible origins in resistance that is not otherwise being manifest.

On the other hand, when a patient who asks about termination seems not to be resisting and has in fact made substantial progress toward the goals of the treatment, his questions should be taken at their face value—that is, a thorough and reality-oriented review should be initiated of the changes that have occurred during treatment and the extent to which these changes fill the treatment goals. The more satisfying the conclusions that emerge from such a review are to both patient and therapist, the more clearly the time has come for them to begin planning the termination of their treatment relationship.

If a progress review instituted at the patient's request paints a less positive picture of improvement than the patient has surmised, the opportunity can be utilized to help him identify what kinds of changes or developments remain to be accomplished before an advantageous termination point will be reached. However, identifying unfinished business does not mean impressing on the patient dire consequences of his terminating at the moment. Persuading a patient to remain in psychotherapy has no more place in an effective treatment contract than seducing him into beginning it. Rather, the therapist needs to present as realistically as he can the gaps that still exist between what the treatment set out to accomplish and what has thus far been achieved, after which it is in the patient's hands to decide whether he wants to continue working toward these remaining goals.

In contrast to situations in which the therapist must help his patient recognize that progress has not yet been as substantial as he thought, a treatment review initiated at the patient's request may sometimes reveal more progress than the therapist had heretofore recognized. A patient who surprises his therapist with a request to terminate may be resisting and he may be overestimating the progress he has made, especially if he has strong needs to bolster his self-image as a competent person (see Crowne & Strickland, 1963); yet it is also possible for him to have made gains considerably beyond what the therapist has appreciated, especially if the therapist's personal needs have clouded his observations. In this latter circumstance the therapist should not hesitate to revise his estimate of the patient's progress and accelerate plans for arranging termination.

Indirect Expression of a Wish to Terminate. A patient who is eager to consider termination may be reluctant to say so directly and instead express his eagerness in some indirect fashion. He may talk at length about how well he is doing, for example, or he may stop bringing pressing problems to the therapist's attention. Assuming he is not trying to please the therapist in the first instance or resist the treatment in the second, such behavior may be his way of attempting to communicate that he regards the work of the treatment as finished. It will then fall to the therapist to recognize and respond to this communication, as by saying, "It sounds as if you feel that therapy has accomplished what you wanted it to."

Occasionally a patient may indirectly communicate a feeling that the therapy is finished by suddenly dropping out of treatment. Patients who drop out of psychotherapy without discussing their decision to terminate usually do so early in the treatment, prior to the establishment of a firm working alliance.[4] In the event that a patient drops out after getting well into the middle of treatment and engaging in some useful interpretive work, his unilateral termination still does not necessarily signify an unsuccessful treatment outcome. A patient who genuinely feels he has derived full measure of benefit from psychotherapy may decide that, instead of trying to convince the therapist of his progress or going through a drawn-out separation process, he will simply stop appearing for sessions.

Obviously it is preferable for a patient to talk out termination plans before acting on them, and reluctance to do so may indicate some lingering neurotic problems. Why, for example, should a patient shrink from reviewing his progress with the therapist, and why should he find it inordinately difficult to say goodbye rather than just drop out of sight? Yet a unilateral terminator may be correct in his estimate that he has achieved his treatment goals, and he may leave therapy considerably improved and with substantial capacity to sustain his improvement.

This possibility that a patient who drops out of treatment may have made significant gains merits careful attention, not because the therapist should encourage or be fully satisfied with unilateral termination, but because he should avoid automatically regarding it as a negative outcome. There has been an unfortunate tendency in some research studies to label all such patients as "defectors" and to designate them as "failure cases," that is, persons not helped by psychotherapy. Yet aside from the fact that the unilateral terminator may have improved before he drops out, the

[4]As reviewed by Meltzoff and Kornreich (1970, pp. 358–373) the relevant research evidence indicates that it is very difficult to predict which patients will terminate therapy during the first few sessions following the arrangement of a treatment contract and which will continue on beyond this point. Among the few apparently reliable findings in this regard is that relatively experienced therapists are more likely to hold on to their patients than relatively inexperienced therapists.

previously cited evidence of posttermination gains demonstrates the unreliability of any such designation: only careful follow-up investigation can identify which unilateral terminators derived no benefit from psychotherapy and which achieved considerable and lasting improvement.

The Wish to Terminate As a Ceiling Effect. The circumstances discussed thus far in which a patient proposes termination have been predicated on his feeling satisfied with his progress and no longer in need of help. There are also times when patients ask about discontinuing treatment not because they have made as much progress as they would like, but because they feel they have made as much progress as they can. Although it is preferable to have therapy end because the patient believes he has achieved his goals rather than because he anticipates no further progress toward them, the latter circumstance—a ceiling effect—may nevertheless signify an appropriate stopping point.

The appropriateness of a patient's feeling that he has reached his ceiling in benefiting from psychotherapy depends on the extent to which the treatment goals have in fact been achieved and whether what remains to be accomplished appears within reasonable expectations from continued psychotherapy. A patient who has been making steady gains in the treatment and whose remaining objectives are similar to those which have already been achieved is being unrealistic if he feels he has made as much progress as he can. On the other hand, a patient whose gains have become increasingly fewer and farther between may quite accurately perceive that psychotherapy has little more to offer him, even though some of his difficulties persist.

In addition to helping his patient appraise whether psychotherapy has reached a ceiling in benefiting him, the therapist also needs to recognize points at which some other form of help should be instituted to build on what has been accomplished. Thus a patient who has learned in psychotherapy to understand himself better and deal with his experience more effectively may still require marital counseling to resolve some issues with his spouse or vocational counseling to make a career choice consistent with his interests and talents. Or a patient who has enhanced his self-image and his capacity to utilize his ability may still be troubled with some focal symptoms, like a specific phobia, for which a course of systematic desensitization might be helpful.

In evaluating a patient's wish to terminate because maximum progress has been made, the therapist should have in mind that all psychotherapy sooner or later reaches a point of diminishing returns. Even the most modest of treatment goals can contribute to a ceiling effect, in the sense that substantial progress toward these goals tends to make the remaining increments of gain progressively more difficult to achieve.[5] As current progress and future prospects are evaluated in the individual case, then, it is necessary to weigh the progress yet to be made against the time, effort, and expense that will be necessary to make it. If the therapist agrees with his patient that little stands to be gained from further psychotherapy, he should simply proceed with plans for termination. If progress has slowed as its apparent ceiling has been approached, but has not yet ground to a halt, the patient should have an opportunity to review whether the gains still possible are worth the cost to him of continuing the treatment contract.

The realistic weighing of psychotherapy's cost in time, effort, and money against the possible benefits to be derived from it should be viewed neither as fatalistic surrender nor as any subjugation of the spiritual value of increased self-understanding to crass practical concerns. Rather, a cost-benefit analysis with a patient who asks about terminating serves to emphasize the gains he has made to date and to help preserve them. Because therapy that seeks ultimate aims will be interminable, prolonging treatment beyond a point of diminishing returns risks the erosion of its prior benefits. A patient who is continued in psychotherapy to a point where few additional gains are realizable, and these only with enormous effort, can easily grow disenchanted with the treatment process and with the therapist. Working hard at a task that is no longer as rewarding as it once was can lead one to wonder whether it was ever as rewarding as he thought; being encouraged to continue in this now unrewarding task can lead one to wonder whether the preson doing the encouraging really knows his job and has one's best interests at heart.

Hence, as part of allowing the patient to participate on an informed basis in deciding whether therapy should continue in light of cost-benefit considerations, the therapist should be wary of permitting it to extend into a stage of disenchantment. If a patient is to leave therapy not fully satisfied with the progress he has made, it is much better for him to leave with a sense that the treatment worked well as far as it was possible for it to go rather than with a sense that it petered out in a dilatory and unprofitable fashion. It is primarily in the former circumstance that it is reasonable to expect sustained benefits from the treatment and continued engagement by the patient in the kinds of self-observation he has learned from it.

[5]Although no universal point of diminishing returns can be specified, there is ample supportive evidence that psychotherapy beyond a certain point cannot be expected to return commensurate additional benefits (see Meltzoff & Kornreich, 1970, pp . 340–354).

Termination Proposed by the Therapist

Whereas most patients monitor their progress closely and sooner or later inquire about how much longer the therapy needs to continue, some either ignore evidence of their own progress or refrain from calling attention to it. Such behavior inevitably has its origins in some form of resistance. With respect to *characterological resistance*, for example, a patient who has made substantial progress in therapy may have lingering masochistic or self-deprecatory tendencies that interfere with his accepting his progress as real and taking pleasure in it. Only if his self-abnegation is confronted directly in this regard will he be able to begin appreciating his improvement and considering the work of the therapy accomplished.

In terms of *resistance to change*, some secondary gain elements derived from being in psychotherapy can create as much resistance to terminating the treatment as to entering it in the first place. Patients not uncommonly become very attached to their relationship with the therapist and loath to give it up. Such resistance to change emerges not so much from any particular feelings the patient has toward his therapist as from the comforting knowledge that, no matter what else happens in his life, continued treatment will provide him regularly scheduled opportunities to meet with a competent and sensitive person who respects, listens to, and stands ever ready to help him.

Secondary gains can also produce resistance to termination in relation to the patient's identified role as being in psychotherapy. Just as patients may hesitate to begin treatment out of reluctance to sacrifice some accrued benefits of being considered psychologically disturbed, they may delay terminating it because doing so will cost them some benefits they have derived from being in treatment. A person known to his family, friends, and employers as "being in psychotherapy" or "seeing someone" or "getting some help" may receive special consideration at home, time off from work, and sympathetic encouragement in his social circle, and he may give pause to endangering any of these benefits by becoming a person who has finished treatment and is presumably no longer in need of having allowances made for him.

Finally, *transference resistance* can make a patient reluctant for very specific reasons to give up his relationship with his therapist. Particular feelings of liking and respect formed toward the therapist can motivate a patient to avoid seeing or saying things about his progress that might hasten the end of the relationship. It is also possible for a patient who has not yet resolved his positive transference to be concerned about somehow hurting or offending the therapist by being first to raise a question about terminating the relationship.

Whatever the reasons why a patient who has made sufficient progress to consider termination does not spontaneously begin to do so, the therapist can explore them only by assuming responsibility himself for proposing termination and instituting a status review of the therapy. Suppose, for example, that a patient who has achieved significant gains in the treatment has for some time been rehashing old material in his sessions while concurrently demonstrating self-sufficiency in thinking through and resolving any new difficulties he encounters. The therapist should then consider the following kind of remarks:

For some time now things have been going along fairly smoothly for you, and any problems you've had you've been working out on your own. There really hasn't been much for us to talk about or that we needed to work on together. So I wonder if we've reached a point where we might consider how much longer we should continue to meet.

As this sample remark illustrates, the therapist who decides to broach termination should do so gently, alluding to positive aspects of the patient's progress and avoiding any criticism of his failure to perceive and comment on these improvements himself. The therapist furthermore needs to speak of these improvements as being just his impression, rather than an established fact, and of termination as only a matter for consideration, not an already confirmed implication of the patient's recent conduct. Broaching termination in such a gentle, positively toned, and open-ended fashion encourages the patient to participate actively in a progress review, much as if he had been the one to propose terminating. Failure to involve the patient in reviewing his progress can complicate termination by giving him cause to think that the therapist is making his decision for him or is perhaps overeager to discontinue working with him.

Although termination proposed by the therapist should therefore consist of no more than raising the topic for discussion, his raising the issue is obviously likely to influence a decision that a good stopping point has been reached. Hence the therapist must attend carefully to the timing of any suggestion he makes to discuss termination. In particular, he needs to be alert to countertransference feelings that might induce him to be either premature or dilatory in proposing termination to a patient who is disinclined to ask about it himself.

If a patient has made frustratingly slow progress, if he has proved sticky to work with and unattractive as a person, if he is occupying an appointment time the therapist would like to have free for other purposes, or if in some other way he has generated marked negative feelings in the treatment relationship, the therapist may rush to judgment in concluding that satisfactory or maximum progress has been made. If a patient has been a delight to work with, on the other hand, moving rapidly toward the treatment goals, demonstrating admirable life achievements, or otherwise providing the therapist an enjoyable relationship he eagerly renews with each session, then the therapist may be tempted to overlook progress and to prolong the treatment beyond a point of diminishing returns. Such countertransference feelings obviously need to be recognized with sufficient clarity to prevent them from influencing the therapist to act in either way contrary to the patient's best interests.

While ensuring that his decisions to proceed with or defer proposing termination are based on realistic considerations and not countertransference, the therapist can often take natural interruptions in the treatment as occasions for suggesting a progress review. Illnesses, vacations, or business commitments inevitably require patient or therapist to cancel sessions from time to time. If a patient who seems to have reached a point where termination might begin to be considered sustains his progress during a break in the continuity of the treatment, the moment may be propitious to comment as follows:

> We haven't met for two weeks now, while I've been on vacation, but from what you've been telling me it was a good two weeks for you and you were able to work things out very well on your own. Perhaps this means we should give some thought to what has been accomplished in the treatment and how much longer it needs to continue.

As in the previous illustration, the tone here is gentle and open-ended, complimenting the patient on his progress but not jumping to any conclusions about its implications. Although the therapist should avoid using every interruption in the treatment for such review purposes, interruptions at a point where termination might otherwise be considered can provide his most natural opportunity for proposing to do so.

IMPLEMENTING TERMINATION

When patient and therapist agree that satisfactory or maximum progress has been made, the therapist needs to implement the actual termination of treatment by (a) consolidating the decision to terminate, (b) arranging for either a time-limited or spaced method of proceeding to the final sessions,

(c) reinforcing the patient's self-observational abilities, and (d) fostering the resolution of the transference.

Consolidating the Decision to Terminate

No matter how firmly and unequivocally a review of progress in psychotherapy indicates that a termination point has been reached, time should always be allowed for this conclusion in turn to be reviewed and become consolidated. Although the conduct of psychotherapy is governed largely by relative rather than absolute principles, an absolute prescription can be written with respect to termination: never terminate psychotherapy with the session in which termination first comes up for discussion, regardless of how appropriate it is agreed to be. There are four compelling reasons for adhering strictly to this principle.

First, the patient or the therapist may be mistaken in their initial impression of the patient's readiness to terminate. All of the relevant facts may simply not come to mind on the first occasion of a progress review, and further reflection may yield a different perspective on the appropriateness of terminating. Additionally, transference and countertransference attitudes are both capable of influencing a premature conclusion that treatment should end. A patient may claim no further need for therapy either as a means of rewarding the therapist should he feel positively toward him, or of escaping the treatment should he be experiencing strong negative transference. A therapist may erroneously decide that the work of the treatment is accomplished because he wants the satisfaction of believing he has "cured" the patient or because he wants to be able to justify discontinuing a difficult or distasteful treatment relationship. Only if there is an opportunity in further sessions for both parties to reconsider their wish to terminate will it be possible to identify and adjust for any such transference or countertransference elements.

Second, even if patient and therapist are correct at the time in concluding that the treatment seems no longer necessary or beneficial, they may be failing to anticipate subsequent events that would suggest otherwise. Psychological functioning is inevitably cyclical, so that it is in the nature of people to feel better about themselves on some days and worse on others, and to deal more effectively with their experience on some occasions than on others. Accordingly, any conviction that psychotherapy has reached its termination point should be tempered by attention to the patient's likely future prospects. Unless the patient has already passed an extended period of sustained improvement, special care must be taken to assure that his apparent improvement of the moment will not succumb to the next life problem he faces, nor cycle of its own accord into a state of markedly decreased self-feeling or reduced personal effectiveness. Only by continuing the treatment beyond the session in which termination is first considered reasonable can the therapist adequately determine how enduring the patient's gains have become.

Third, even if a patient's improvement is real and enduring, the therapist who suggests terminating treatment the first time such a possibility comes up for discussion risks injecting a note of rejection into the treatment relationship. No matter how gratified the patient may be at having completed the work of the treatment, he is unlikely to savor breaking it off at a moment's notice. Indeed, the terminal phase of psychotherapy is a period of separation for the patient, often mourned in the same way as other separations from familiar people, places, and activities are mourned. The pain of such separations tends to be eased by opportunities to prepare for them, especially if feelings about the separation can be aired and worked through before it becomes final.

If treatment is terminated as soon as the possibility is considered, the patient has no such opportunity to prepare for separation from the treatment relationship, and he also has good reason to wonder about the motives of the therapist's preemptory behavior. It is as if the patient has said, "I don't think I need to see you any more" and the therapist has promptly replied, "Okay, goodbye." Even in the absence of such crudity, a therapist's willingness to end the treatment as soon as it seems reasonable to do so can leave his patient musing, "It's as if he couldn't wait to get rid of me." Hence, both to allow the patient a gradual separation process and to avoid appearances of rejecting him, it is obligatory to extend psychotherapy beyond the point at which termination is first considered.

Fourth, if all of the preceding potential disadvantages of hasty termination could be avoided in a particular case, valuable opportunities for a closing burst of activity in the therapy will be lost if it is ended abruptly. Very often a mutual decision that psychotherapy has reached a good stopping point motivates effective use by the patient of the time between when the decision is made and when it is carried out. Knowing that the treatment is soon to terminate encourages the patient to raise issues that have not yet been covered in the treatment and to tie up loose ends of previous discussion. What takes place, then, is the kind of useful integrative summary that occurs in many kinds of work situations when a period of time is specified as constituting its final phase. If termination is enacted when it is first considered appropriate, no space of time is provided for such a concluding period of useful work.

For these four reasons, then, some number of sessions should always be allotted to consolidating the decision to terminate psychotherapy. Because a first impression of progress can be erroneous, because current progress does not necessarily assure sustained progress, because termination is a separation process, and because an extended summary period can be very useful, the therapist should refrain from implementing termination abruptly and should resist any pressure from the patient to do so. In this latter regard, suppose a patient follows an initial agreement that the necessary work of the treatment appears completed by saying, "I guess this will be our last session, then, because I don't see any need for me to come again." The therapist should always attempt to defer such decisions with a comment on the order of the following: "Even though everything right now appears to point to your having completed treatment, it is usually helpful to allow a little time to make sure our impressions are correct; so I suggest that we begin now to plan on stopping but arrange for some further sessions between now and when we stop completely." A response of this kind, framed in terms of realistic considerations and inviting the patient to begin the work of consolidating his decision to terminate, helps to avert abrupt termination and encourages the patient to work through a termination process.

Arranging for Time-Limited or Spaced Termination

The final phase of psychotherapy, between the point at which termination is agreed to be reasonable and the time of the final session, can be arranged in two ways. In *time-limited termination* a fixed duration of time is set during which sessions continue at their usual frequency and then stop completely. For example, a patient being seen in once-weekly psychotherapy might be scheduled for one additional month of weekly sessions between the time when termination is agreed on and when it is to be implemented. In *spaced termination* the time between sessions is gradually extended, so that the date of the final session is not set in advance but is approached in measured steps. With spaced termination a patient being seen weekly might be changed first to bi-weekly sessions and then to some monthly visits before the treatment is finally ended.

From the patient's point of view, the most obvious difference between time-limited and spaced termination is that the former method designates when the final session will occur and the latter does not. Thus time-limited termination implies that the patient seems fully prepared to go his own way but will find some final period for tying up loose ends helpful. Spaced termination, on the other hand, implies that a wait-and-see period is in order, during which the patient will be gradually weaned from the treatment as he is able to sustain his improvements over increasingly longer periods of time. Even with spaced termination, however, there eventually comes a time when the next regularly scheduled session is intended in advance to be the last ("Let's plan to meet but one more time, two months from now, and if things still appear to be going as well for you, we can make that session our last one").

Despite their different implication, neither time-limited nor spaced termination should be considered an irrevocable arrangement. In effective time-limited termination the patient will usually pass through a period of tying up loose ends and preparing for separation, following which he will find less and less to talk about and the sessions will gradually tail off into pleasant but mundane conversation. Should the patient instead continue right into the last scheduled session to bring up new or unresolved issues, then it may be advisable for the therapist to propose amending the time-limit agreement: "In view of all that has been coming up in the last few weeks, it may be that we set our stopping point too early; perhaps we should allow some additional time to make sure you have an opportunity to finish thinking through the kinds of issues you have been raising recently."

Needless to say, any decision to extend time-limited termination in response to a last-minute flurry of activity must take into account the possibility that the patient's activity level represents resistance to termination. A patient who has completed the work of the treatment but nevertheless wants to retain his patient role or his relationship with the therapist may suffer an apparent "relapse" or begin to dredge up "new" or "urgent" matters for discussion as termination approaches. The message in such behavior is "See I've really got a lot of problems yet and a lot to talk with you about, so we better not terminate after all." If upon inquiry the reports of relapse prove exaggerated and the problems being presented neither new nor urgent, the therapist should then proceed with the time-limited termination as planned, allowing extra sessions only as they seem necessary to help the patient work through his specific concerns about ending the treatment.

Spaced termination must similarly be guided by flexibility in deciding which is to be the final session. If a patient decreases in a regular progression his use of his treatment sessions for working on continuing issues and concerns, spaced termination may proceed in a corresponding progression toward less frequent sessions and the scheduling of a final follow-up visit. Should new or pressing problems emerge during this spacing-out period, however, it may be necessary to revise the termination plan. Then a therapist who has reduced once-weekly visits to bi-weekly visits may find it necessary to suggest, "Since a number of new things have come up recently that seem useful to talk about, perhaps we should go back to having sessions every week for a while." Similarly, a presumably final follow-up visit may reveal that the patient has had unanticipated difficulty sustaining his improvement and that some further follow-up sessions seem in order.

As in the case of time-limited termination, the therapist evaluating some apparent continuation or recrudescence of difficulties during spaced termination should consider the possible role of resistance to termination in causing the patient to experience or report continuing problems. Yet he must also prevent his wariness from closing his ears to actual continuing problems, and his determination to complete the treatment should not bind him fast to the original termination agreement. At the very least, if he has some reservations about the patient's capacity to sustain and build on his improvements but still feels that termination should be implemented, he should make it clear that his door is open to the patient in the event he subsequently experiences a need to contact him.

Choosing Between Time-limited and Spaced Termination. The choice between a time-limited or spaced approach to termination depends on the nature and goals of the treatment contract. Generally speaking, time-limited termination works most effectively in uncovering psychotherapy, whereas spaced termination becomes increasingly appropriate the more supportive the treatment has been. Because time-limited termination gives the patient a fixed period of time to finish his business, it presumes considerable capacity on his part to utilize this time effectively and then promptly discontinue the treatment. For a patient who has been fufilling the obligations of participating in uncovering psychotherapy, these demands of time-limited termination are consistent with what has previously been expected of him, and they are furthermore rewarding in the confidence they express in him. The more supportively a patient has been seen, however, the more the requirements of time-limited termination will diverge from his previous role responsibilities in the treatment and burden him with anxiety about being able to meet them.

Spaced termination, on the other hand, meets the needs of the patient in supportive psychotherapy by granting him an intitially unspecified length of time in which to extricate himself gradually from the treatment and to test out in measured steps his capacity to function adequately without it. To offer such an opportunity for gradual weaning from treatment to a patient in uncovering psychotherapy would have the disadvantage of appearing to baby him, as if the therapist lacked confidence in his ability to end the treatment as responsibly as he had thus far participated in it. To maintain consistency with the previous tenor of the treatment, then, and thereby promote smooth transit from it, time-limited or spaced termination should be selected according to the relative prior emphasis on uncovering or supportive goals in the treatment.

With either the time-limited or spaced method of termination, the length of the terminal period will usually be commensurate with the frequency and duration of the treatment that has proceeded it. In both primarily uncovering and primarily supportive psychotherapy, the more frequent sessions have been, and the longer the therapy has lasted, the more the patient will have become engrossed in and accustomed to it, and the longer he will require to tie up loose content ends of the treatment and work through his separation from it. Thus for example the interval set for time-limited termination of uncovering psychotherapy will be longer for a patient who has been seen twice-weekly than for one seen once-weekly, and longer for a patient whose treatment has lasted for two years than for one whose treatment has lasted one year. Similarly in supportive psychotherapy, a patient who has been seen weekly for 18 months should have his termination spaced out in more gradual increments and over a longer total period of time than a patient who has been seen bi-weekly for six months.

Reinforcing Self-Observational Abilities

The decision to terminate psychotherapy should be made with the confidence that the patient will not only be able to sustain his improvements but will also be capable of building on them through continued self-observation. As a patient in the final phase of treatment becomes increasingly capable of self-initiated and adaptive reflection on his experience, he will bring progressively fewer issues to the treatment sessions that require interpretive comments from the therapist. This means that the less work the therapist finds to do on the patient's behalf, the more likely it is that the patient has become sufficiently capable of sustaining and building on his improvements to justify termination.

On the other hand, in the absence of resistance to termination, the emergence of major new difficulties following an agreement to work toward termination may signify either that the extent of the patient's unresolved problems has not been fully appreciated or that his capacity to confront problems solely with his own resources is not yet firmly enough established for the treatment to end. In the first case some new interpretive work may be necessary that will delay termination and continue the treatment in a middle phase, while in the second case the therapist's task will be not so much to engage in new interpretive work as to help the patient make better use of his previously developed capacity to understand and modify his behavior.

The techniques for helping a patient make better use of his self-observational capacities consist of reinforcing him when he acts as his own therapist and confronting him when he does not. To reinforce effective self-observation, the therapist in the final phase of treatment should make liberal use of the following kind of comment:

I think it's important for you to pay special attention to what happened this week. You ran into a problem on Monday that was similar to many of the problems you were having when we began working together. Yet you were able to think it through, without letting it make you anxious, and you were able to find some way of dealing with it that worked out very well. So now on Wednesday, when you come in for your session, you've taken care of the whole thing by yourself, and there's really nothing that we need to discuss about it.

To confront a patient with his reluctance or failure to initiate self-observation of which he appears capable, comments of the following kind may be called for:

It strikes me that the problem you're raising for discussion today is really one that we've talked about a number of times and that you understand pretty well. In fact, I can think of some occasions in the last few months you've handled some similar problems very well on your own, without even finding it necessary to discuss them with me first. So I wonder whether right now you're not using all the ability you have to work through this particular situation on your own.

The first of these illustrative comments is obviously reinforcing and aimed toward consolidating the decision to terminate. The second comment confronts the patient with his apparent failure to utilize his self-observational capacities, but note that it also refers to evidence of the patient's prior progress. The emphasis, in other words, is less on criticizing the patient for what he is not currently doing than on reminding him of how much he has been able to do in the past and engaging his curiosity about what may be preventing him from sustaining his prior accomplishments. If correctly timed and aptly phrased, such confrontation can lead the patient into a productive exploration of whatever influences may be suppressing his capacity for independent self-observation.

Fostering Resolution of the Transference

In successful psychotherapy transference becomes resolved in concert with the working through of transference interpretations. As a patient recognizes his dispositions to misperceive the therapist or the treatment situation, he becomes capable of modifying or at least anticipating and controlling them. As he nears completion of the treatment, he will accordingly display progressively fewer instances of transference behavior, and these instances will increasingly be accompanied by accurate and self-initiated observations on the nature of the displacements they involve.

Although resolution of the transference is a process that must emanate from the patient, the therapist can play an important role in fostering and reinforcing it. Attention is given in Chapter 10 to means by which the therapist should act to safeguard each of the three components of the treatment relationship, the transference, the real relationship, and the working alliance (see pp. 216–219). In the final phase of therapy, when the time has come for transference to be resolved and the real relationship to gain ascendence, the therapist can facilitate this change by discontinuing his efforts to safeguard the transference and concentrating on safeguarding the real relationship.

The most effective way for the therapist to promote the real relationship at the expense of transference is for him to act increasingly as a real rather than as an as if object. Now he will take certain questions at their face value and answer them directly, rather than construe them as behavior to be understood. To a patient who says, "I wonder why I didn't realize sooner that I could never make a living as a salesman," the response is no longer "What thoughts do you have about it?" but instead, "As we've learned, for a long time you felt you had to be the kind of brash, back-slapping person you associated with being a salesman."

Now the therapist will expand in certain ways the information he provides about himself, rather than act to preserve his relative anonymity. To a patient who says, "I'm really curious to know whether you're married," the response is no longer "How would you like it to be?" or "What makes you curious about that right now?" but instead, "Yes, I am" or "No, I'm not." Now the therapist expresses certain personal feelings instead of trying to prevent them from influencing the treatment relationship. To a patient who reports, "I got a promotion at work" or "I got engaged over the weekend," the response is no longer limited to "Tell me about it" but also includes "I'm pleased to hear that" or "Best wishes."

In making such responses the therapist should be striving not to rush headlong into an intimate personal relationship with the patient, but to change subtly his emphasis within the role prescribed for him by the treatment contract. Instead of continuing to attempt to foster transference by maintaining his stimulus ambiguity, he should respond in ways that diminish opportunities for the patient to form impressions of him on any but a realistic basis. Instead of maintaining the asymmetric interpretive arrangement in which the patient is identified primarily as the talker and the therapist as the listener, he should gradually establish a more mutual, egalitarian relationship in which he talks more while interpreting less.

By becoming more of a real object in his patient's life, the therapist can help him complete and sustain the resolution of transference that should already have begun by the time a termination plan is agreed on. Some caution is necessary, however, lest the therapist by changing overnight from a relatively restrained listener to an unbridled mutual participant in the relationship suppress unsuspected transference reactions that the patient still needs to resolve. As with other aspects of consolidating the decision to terminate, there must be some opportunity to assess whether transference is sufficiently resolved for the treatment to end successfully. Should the initial decision to enter a final phase of treatment be followed by an upsurge of transference feelings, further interpretive work may be required, even to the extent of deferring the termination plan. Only by proceeding slowly to exchange his interpretive stance for a more mutual approach to the treatment relationship can the therapist be sure to allow remaining transference issues to emerge for further discussion.

CONSIDERATIONS IN FORCED TERMINATION

As desirable as it may be for psychotherapy to wind down of its own accord and lead naturally into a final phase, the therapist must be prepared for external circumstances that force termination of treatment prior to any substantial realization of its goals. Patients may move out of town to take a new job, get married, go away to school, or enter the military, or they may become realistically unable to sustain the cost in time or money of further sessions. Therapists may also move for personal or professional reasons, and, if they are in training, they may complete an assignment and leave an agency or be rotated to a different service.

Although forced termination does not automatically cancel out the prior benefits of treatment, special care is required to prevent its having a disruptive impact. The closing phase of psychotherapy that must be ended should as in voluntary termination emphasize the trying up of loose ends, the subjugation of the transference relationship to the real relationship, and the encouragement and reinforcement of the patient's independent capacity to sustain and build on his improvements. Additionally, forced termination of psychotherapy needs to include a careful review of which goals of the treatment have been fairly well realized and which have not, and also a realistic discussion of the patient's future plans, particularly with regard to how he will utilize what he has learned in the treatment and whether or not he will seek further psychotherapy. The specific techniques for implementing forced termination in this way vary somewhat with whether the termination is being forced by the patient or by the therapist, and these two possibilities are accordingly discussed separately.

Termination Forced by the Patient

When a patient states that he will not be able to continue in psychotherapy beyond a certain date, the therapist needs first to determine whether this statement reflects real contraints or is instead a manifestation of resistance. Whenever resistance appears responsible for a unilateral decision to terminate, every effort should be made to help the patient recognize the origin of his descision and to dissuade him from acting on it until he has given it further thought. However, if circumstances external to the psychotherapy process will make it very difficult or impossible for the patient to continue treatment beyond a certain date, then it is necessary to institute terminal work even if the progress to date would not otherwise call for doing so.

To move psychotherapy into a final phase prior to its evolving naturally, the therapist can begin with a remark such as the following: "Since with your leaving town it appears we will have only another two months to work together, we should start to review what has gone on in the therapy, especially matters we've considered but haven't finished with." Such an overture sets a review process in motion and also encourages the patient to focus on problems and concerns that he feels need further work.

While thus inviting the patient to pursue unfinished business, the therapist needs to be cautious about getting into new problems that cannot be adequately worked through in the time remaining. It is a disservice to the patient to allow him to unravel psychological concerns only to send him forth from therapy with their loose ends still flapping. Once the therapist has proposed a period of review and consolidation, with forced termination pending, he should concentrate on conducting such a review and discourage the patient from opening up major new avenues for exploration.

To this end, the therapist in the final phase of forced termination therapy must exchange the relatively noncommital, unstructured approach by which he has previously encouraged the patient's spontaneous associations for a more focused approach to summarizing and concluding the work of the treatment. Without probing for new areas of concern, he should review at the level of the real relationship the amount and kind of progress that has been made and identify the treatment goals that have not yet been achieved. He should also discuss the patient's future plans with him and not hesitate to advise the patient about ways in which the finished and unfinished work of the treatment are likely to affect him in the future, as in the following example:

In the time we've worked together you've been able to overcome much of the work inhibition that was holding you back, and one result of your progress is the promotion you've received that is taking you to a different city. But we've also learned that you have a tendency to doubt yourself at first when you take on a new or challenging task, and we haven't had time to work out that particular problem. So you should keep in mind that you may experience some initial self-doubts in the new job and take care not to let them discourage you or interfere with your keeping at your work.

Such counsel may seem too superficial or gratuitous to provide a patient much protection against continuing neurotic concerns, and indeed it might be in the absence of any prior treatment gains. However, if a patient who must terminate has previously been engaged in acquiring and consolidating new learning about himself, it is reasonable to expect him to draw on parting advice from the therapist to help sustain and enhance his improvements after the treatment ends. Just as a patient who terminates voluntarily should continue to build on his gains from therapy, one who must end prematurely should be able to progress on his own following the therapy if the therapist provides him some guidance for doing so.

Considering Further Treatment. A very important consideration in reviewing future plans with a patient who must terminate psychotherapy is abvisability of further treatment in the new locale or at some future time. Judgments about further psychotherapy will depend on the same considerations that enter into an initial evaluation and assessment, including the extent of the patient's need for help and the likelihood that psychotherapy will provide such help (see Chap. 5). If patient and therapist agree that treatment should be resumed, either with a different therapist in another location or with the same therapist after an unavoidable interruption, then the therapist needs to curtail somewhat the thoroughness of his progress review and the extent of his emphasis on the real relationship.

With regard to previous progress, otherwise admirable closure in reviewing and summarizing the treatment may seal over areas of concern that should be left exposed if therapy is to resume. The above example, in which the therapist explicates for the patient his continuing propensity for self-doubt, represents a helpful procedure primarily when treatment will not be resumed. Yet it is generally the case that patients derive more benefit from participating actively in coming to such understandings of themselves than from having the therapist do the work for them. Hence with a patient who will be resuming treatment in the near future, specific advice concerning the handling of likely future problems should be soft-pedaled to allow these matters to emerge spontaneously in the continuing treatment and be worked on independently of prior formulations or judgments about them.

As for the treatment relationship, an emphasis on reality in terminal work with a patient who will be resuming treatment seriously compromises the position of the next therapist. Because of its mutuality, the real relationship is inherently more gratifying and comfortable than the asymmetric working alliance, which patients agree to put up with as the price of learning more about themselves in psychotherapy. Once a patient has progressed through a middle phase of psychotherapy, with its stress on the working alliance and on safeguarding the transference, to a terminal phase, with its stress on the real relationship and on resolving the transference, it is very difficult for him to acccept a return to nonmutuality. A therapist who attempts to reinstitute interpretive psychotherapy with a patient who has recently completed a final phase of treatment that stressed a real patient-therapist relationship is likely to be seen as harsh, ungiving, and disinterested and to be compared unfavorably with the previous therapist, who is remembered for his warm, active, and direct engagement during termination.

For this reason, a therapist doing terminal work with a patient who will soon be resuming treatment should refrain from becoming too much of a real object in the treatment relationship, lest he pose an unsurmountable challenge for his successor. At the same time he should work to resolve the patient's pressing transference attitudes toward him as much as possible, to prevent them from carrying over into the subsequent treatment as a potent source of initial resistance. Ideally, then, a patient who must terminate psychotherapy but will soon continue with another therapist should have worked through his transference reactions to his first therapist without having come to interact with him primarily as a real object. The more fully the final phase of the first treatment relationship satisfies both of these aims, the better the patient's prospects will be for participating effectively in and benefiting from continued treatment with a second therapist.

Termination Forced by the Therapist

Whereas in private office practice forced termination of psychotherapy tends to be instigated primarily by the patient when it occurs, there are numerous settings in which termination forced by the therapist is a common or even regular occurrence. Most notable in this regard are clinical training centers in which psychotherapy is provided under staff supervision by trainees in the various mental health disciplines who leave the center upon completion of their assignment to it. Even among practicing clinicians, especially those who hold academic appointments or agency positions, there is sufficient mobility to generate a substantial frequency of therapist-forced termination.

In arranging for a termination he must impose, the therapist as in other treatment situations, must attend to helping the patient complete unfinished business, resolve transference issues, and plan for the future. Of these, resolution of the transference is most likely to prove problematic, since termination forced by the therapist inevitably foments negative patient reactions. There is no way a therapist can avoid having his cancellation of the treatment contract perceived as a hostile and rejecting act. No matter how rational or understandable the patient finds the therapist's action to be from the *therapist*'s point of view, from the *patient*'s point of view it still represents a voluntary decision by the therapist to terminate the treatment relationship. Whatever his intellectual grasp of the therapist's reasons for terminating, emotionally the patient will be saying to himself, "If you cared enough for me, you wouldn't be leaving."[6]

[6]Numerous additional examples of negative patient reactions to termination forced by the therapist are provided by Dewald (1965) and Glenn (1971).

There is of course some reality to a patient's feeling this way. If the therapist did care enough about continuing to work with him, he would turn down his new job opportunity, or refuse to allow his superiors to rotate him to a different service, or make whatever other changes in his plans that would be necessary to allow continuation of the treatment. Yet it would be both unrealistic and beyond the obligations of the treatment contract for a therapist to reverse the normal course of his personal and professional life in order to avoid terminating a treatment relationship. Without allowing either guilt or positive countertransference to draw him into extending psychotherapy at the expense of seriously disrupting his own life, the therapist needs to take account of these inevitable negative reactions to his leaving in three important respects.

First, he should make certain that the patient's reactions to his leaving are aired and discussed as fully as possible. Other efforts at achieving some resolution of the transference prior to termination will go for naught if the patient is left with unexpressed anger at the therapist for deserting him. Often the patient will manifest such anger with sufficient directness for the therapist to recognize it promptly and deal with it as he would other transference behavior. Should the patient give no hint of emotional reactions to the therapist's leaving, he should be asked specifically about them: "I wonder if you've been having any feelings about my leaving in just a few more weeks." If even this invitation fails to elicit clear-cut expressions of affect, the therapist should go one step further: "It's likely that you've been having some feelings about my leaving, and it would be helpful if we could talk about them."

Such a direct approach is justified by the inevitability of a patient's having some feelings about his therapist's forcing termination on him and by the importance of having these feelings expressed, even if the therapist must probe for them. Once such feelings are aired, the patient can be helped to recognize their transference elements and to reduce their intensity to the level of realistic disappointment at the imminent separation. If they are not aired, their continued rankling may prevent the patient from sustaining and building on his gains in the treatment and from resuming treatment effectively with another therapist.

Second, the therapist must give the patient as much advance notice as possible concerning his having to terminate the treatment, to allow him sufficient time to work through his reactions to termination. Sometimes a therapist will know in advance that his time for treating a particular patient will be limited, in which case the time limitation should be discussed as part of the treatment contract. For example, a therapist who expects to be working for only a year in a particular clinic should tell each patient with whom he considers possible psychotherapy exactly how many months he has remaining in his tour of duty, and a judgment should be made concerning whether this length of time will be adequate to meet the patient's needs. Should either or both parties anticipate that the work of the treatment cannot be accomplished in the time available, referral should be made to a therapist whose availability is less limited.

In other instances the circumstances that cause the therapist to terminate arise during the treatment, without having been anticipated, and it then behooves the therapist to share his plans with his patients as soon as they become definite. Exceptions to this principle should be entertained only if the treatment appears certain to reach a voluntary conclusion prior to the time when the therapist will have to leave. For example, a therapist who learns he will have to terminate his patients in eight months' time may elect not to mention this constraint to a patient already in the final phase of treatment with a fixed termination date just one month away. Similarly, a therapist beginning a one-year assignment in a clinic may elect not to mention this time limitation to a patient he sees early in the year who appears to require only brief supportive psychotherapy.

Third, out of respect for the patient as a person and in order to safeguard the real relationship, the therapist needs to state candidly his reasons for terminating treatment. "Candor" does not mean a sharing of all the issues involved in the therapist taking a different job or being shifted to a new assignment, but it does mean presenting an accurate and reasonable explanation of the change that will take place:

> I need to tell you of a change in my life that will affect our working together. I've accepted a position in [*name of city*] beginning next July 1, which means I will be seeing patients here only until next June. That means we will have about another six months to continue your therapy, and then we'll have to stop.

Although patients vary in their initial response to such an announcement of forced termination, sooner or later their reaction will touch on all three components of the treatment relationship, transference, the real relationship, and the working alliance. On a transference basis, the patient may begin to feel angry or dejected as soon as the therapist tells him he will be leaving. Directly or indirectly he will then communicate beliefs that the therapist is a calculating hypocrite ruthlessly dropping him to seek greener pastures elsewhere, or that he himself is unworthy of any else's sustained interest and has only rejection and disappointment to anticipate in his interpersonal relationships. The therapist's corresponding task will be to disabuse the patient of such distorted perceptions of what his leaving signifies and thereby attenuate the patient's transference reactions to the termination.

At the level of the real relationship, the patient is likely to be curious about the therapist's plans and ask about many specific details of them: what kind of job is he taking, where is he moving to, how did he decide on this change, will he continue to do psychotherapy, and so forth. The number of such questions the therapist answers and the amount of detail he provides will depend on his judgment concerning an advantageous balancing of the transference and the real relationship. The closer the therapy is to termination and the stronger the emphasis on fostering ascendance of the real relationship, the more directly and fully the therapist will respond to inquiries about his future plans, within what he sees as the appropriate limits of the treatment contract. If the nature of his work with a particular patient suggests he had best be circumspect in talking about his plans, he should still be certain to inform the patient clearly of his reason for terminating and of the origin of this reason in his life rather than in the patient's behavior.

In terms of the working alliance, the therapist's announcement that he must terminate the treatment will evoke numerous questions from the patient about the future course of his therapy: will there be enough time to finish treatment, how should he make best use of the time remaining, what should he do if he needs more help, and so forth. Most questions of this kind can be answered in terms of the general guidelines for terminating therapy discussed earlier in the chapter. However, special attention may have to be given to helping the patient plan for further treatment if his needs for help are likely to extend beyond the time when the therapist must terminate.

Specifically, the therapist should provide a patient who wishes to continue treatment with a list of recommended therapists. Usually this list should include more than one name, so as to spare the second therapist the burden of being the first therapist's designated heir apparent. If the second therapist is a hand-picked successor, the patient may come to him with underlying resentments at having had the new therapist chosen for him, without having participated in the choice; he may come with an exaggerated expectation that, because the second therapist was the one person from among the entire local professional community selected to continue the treatment, he will be capable of working wonders in bringing it to a prompt and gratifying conclusion; and if for some reason he is unable to work out a feasible time schedule with this one therapist, or finds him difficult to relate to, he will be stranded without anyone else to turn to.

For these reasons a patient being terminated should be given at least two or three names of other therapists who might continue the treatment. Some thought should also be given to the personality style and usual clientele of the therapists being recommended to minimize the likelihood of a poor patient-therapist match. The terminating therapist should also ascertain whether the therapists he would like to recommend have time available to take on the patient should he call them. The patient will then have the names of at least a few recommended therapists, each of whom is accustomed to working with patients having his type of problems and has space on his calendar to devote to him, and he can exercise some choice in deciding which one to contact first.

A patient being offered such a list may of course ask his current therapist whom he would recommend *most*, in which case the therapist should simply emphasize that all of the people he has recommended are competent and available. The patient is then free to select among them by any means he wishes, including going alphabetically or flipping a coin. In this way the patient makes the selection rather than having it made for him; he does not view any of the people on the list as *the* best person for him to see; and he has some equally recommended alternatives if there is some failure to connect with the first therapist he chooses from the list.

When psychotherapy is primarily supportive in nature, a therapist who must terminate the relationship may be somewhat more directive in arranging a successor than has been described above. To the extent that dependent gratification has participated in the supportive measures of the treatment, for example, or the patient lacks sufficient personality resources himself to decide on and arrange for a new therapist, the current therapist may specifically designate his successor and even go so far as to arrange the initial appointment with him. In clinic and hospital settings in which staff in training are being rotated, it is often helpful in supportive work with seriously disturbed or chronic, marginally adjusted patients for the departing therapist to invite a designated successor to attend one of his final sessions so that he can personally introduce the patient to him.[7]

What remains to be mentioned are those situations in which terminated patients initiate subsequent contact with the therapist through letters or telephone calls. Although such efforts to sustain some relationship with

[7]Problems and techniques of transferring patients in clinics with rotating staff are discussed further by Keith (1966), Pumpian-Mindlin (1958), and Schiff (1962).

the therapist can occur following any form of termination, they understandably appear to occur primarily in situations where the therapist has forced the termination, before the patient would otherwise have been ready for it. The therapist who receives letters or calls from patients he has terminated must be careful to sustain the same level of real relationship with which he hopefully concluded their sessions together. He cannot let himself be dragged into explorations of current problems, lest he interfere with the patient's work with a subsequent therapist or open up issues that he is in no position to help the patient resolve. At the same time he cannot adopt a personally involved style of relating to the patient, as if he is now letting out real feelings previously held in check by the working alliance, lest he be seductive or cause the patient to have second thoughts about the true nature of their previous relationship. Rather, in keeping with his manner of ending the treatment, he should concentrate on being a real rather than a transference object in the patient's life while avoiding any personal engagements that might reflect his lingering countertransference feelings.

References

Abroms, G.M. The new eclecticism. *Archives of General Psychiatry*, 1969, **20,** 514–523.

Abroms, G. M., & Greenfield, N. S. A new mental health profession. *Psychiatry*, 1973, **36,** 10–22.

Abt, L. E. A theory of projective psychology. In L. E. Abt & L. Bellak (Eds.), *Projective Psychology*. New York: Knopf, 1950. Pp. 33–66.

Abt, L. E., & Weissman, S. L. (Eds.) *Acting out: Theoretical and clinical aspects.* New York: Grune & Stratton, 1965.

Ackerman, N. W. *The psychodynamics of family life.* New York: Basic Books, 1958.

Alexander, F., & French, T. M. *Psychoanalytic therapy.* New York: Ronald Press, 1946.

Allison, J., Blatt, S. J., & Zimet, C. N. *The interpretation of psychological tests.* New York: Harper & Row, 1968.

Allport, G. W. The functional autonomy of motives. *American Journal of Psychology*, 1937, **50,** 141–156.

Anderson, W. Personal growth and client-centered therapy: An information processing view. In D. A. Wexler & L. N. Rice (Eds.), *Innovations in client-centered therapy*. New York: Wiley, 1974.

APA Committee on Training in Clinical Psychology. Recommended graduate training program in clinical psychology. *American Psychologist*, 1942, **2,** 539–558.

Appelbaum, S. A. How long is long-term psychotherapy? *Bulletin of the Menninger Clinic*, 1972, **36,** 651–655.

Arieti, S. (Ed.) *American handbook of psychiatry*. New York: Basic Books, 1959.

Aronson, H., & Overall, B. Treatment expectations of patients in two social classes. *Social Work*, 1966, **11,** 35–41.

Auld, F., & White, A. M. Sequential dependencies in psychotherapy. *Journal of Abnormal and Social Psychology*, 1959, **58,** 100–104.

Baltes, P. B. (Ed.) Strategies for psychological intervention in old age: A symposium. *Gerontologist,* 1973, **13,** 4–38.

Bandura, A. *Principles of behavior modification.* New York: Holt, Rinehart & Winston, 1969.

Banks, W. M. The differential effects of race and social class in helping. *Journal of Clinical Psychology*, 1972 , **28,** 90–92.

Barten, H. H. (Ed.) *Brief therapies.* New York: Behavioral Publications, 1971.

Baum, O. E., Countertransference. *Psychoanalytic Review*, 1972, **56,** 621–636.

Baum, O. E. Further thoughts on countertransference. *Psychoanalytic Review*, 1973, **60,** 127–140.

Beck, A. T. Reliability of psychiatric diagnosis. **I.** A critique of systematic studies. *American Journal of Psychiatry*, 1962, **119,** 210–216.

Beery, J. W. Therapists' responses as a function of level of therapist experience and attitude of the patient. *Journal of Consulting and Clinical Psychology*, 1970, **34,** 239–243.

Bellak, L. Free association: Conceptual and clinical aspects. *International Journal of Psycho-Analysis*, 1961, **42,** 9–20.

Bellak, L., & Small, L. *Emergency psychotherapy and brief psychotherapy.* New York: Grune & Stratton, 1965.

Bergin, A. E. Some implications of psychotherapy research for therapeutic practice. *Journal of Abnormal Psychology*, 1966, **73,** 235–246.

Bergin, A. E. Further comments on psychotherapy research and psychotherapeutic practice. *International Journal of Psychiatry*, 1967, **3,** 317–323.

Bergin, A. E. The evaluation of therapeutic outcomes. In A. E. Bergin & S. L. Garfield (Eds.), *Handbook of psychotherapy and behavior change.* New York: Wiley, 1971. Pp. 217–270.

Bergler, E. *The superego: Unconscious conscious.* New York: Grune & Stratton, 1952.

Berzins, J. I., Dove, J. L., & Ross, W. F. Cross-validational studies of the personality correlates of the A-B therapist "type" distinction among professionals and nonprofessionals. *Journal of Consulting and Clinical Psychology*, 1972, **39,** 388–395.

Beutler, L. E., Johnson, D. T., Neville, C. W., & Workman, S. N. "Accurate empathy" and the A-B dichotomy. *Journal of Consulting and Clinical Psychology*, 1972, **38,** 372–375.

Beutler, L. E., Johnson, D. T., Neville, C. W., & Workman, S. N. Some sources of variance in "accurate empathy" ratings. *Journal of Consulting and Clinical Psychology*, 1973, **40,** 167–169.

Blake, R. R., & Ramsey, G. V. (Eds.) *Perception: An approach to personality.* New York: Ronald Press, 1951.

Blank, L. *Psychological evaluation in psychotherapy.* Chicago: Aldine, 1965.

Blum, G. S. *Psychodynamics: The science of unconscious mental forces.* Belmont, Cal.: Brooks/Cole, 1966.

Bonime, W. *The clinical use of dreams.* New York: Basic Books, 1962.

Bordin, E. S. *Psychological counseling.* (2nd ed.) New York: Appleton-Century-Crofts, 1968.

Boss, M. *Psychoanalysis and daseinalaysis.* New York: Basic Books, 1963.

Boucher, M. L. Effect of seating distance on interpersonal attraction in an interview situation. *Journal of Consulting and Clinical Psychology*, 1972, **38,** 15–19.

Bowden, C. L., Endicott, J., & Spitzer, R. L. A-B therapist variable and psychotherapeutic outcome. *Journal of Nervous and Mental Disease*, 1972, **154,** 276–290.

Brady, J. P. Psychotherapy, learning theory, and insight. *Archives of General Psychiatry*, 1977, **16,** 304–311.

Brenner, C. *An elementary textbook of psychoanalysis.* (Rev. ed.) New York: International Universities Press, 1973.

Breuer, J., & Freud, S. (1893–1895) Studies on hysteria. *Standard Edition,* Vol. II. London: Hogarth, 1955. Pp. 1–319.

Brill, H. Psychiatric diagnosis, nomenclature, and classification. In B. Wolman (Ed.), *Handbook of clinical psychology.* New York: McGraw-Hill, 1965. Pp. 639–650.

Brill, N. Q., & Storrow, H. A. Social class and psychiatric treatment. *Archives of General Psychiatry*, 1960, **3,** 340–344.

Broverman, D. M. Dimensions of cognitive style. *Journal of Personality*, 1960, **28,** 167–185.

Bruner, J. S., & Goodman, C. C. Value and need as organizing factors in perception. *Journal of Abnormal and Social Psychology*, 1947, **42,** 33–44.

Bugental, J. F. T. The person who is the psychotherapist. *Journal of Consulting Psychology*, 1964, **28,** 272–277.

Bugental, J. F. T. *The search for authenticity.* New York: Holt, Rinehart & Winston, 1965.

Buhler, C., & Allen, M. *Introduction into humanistic psychology.* Belmont, Cal.: Brooks/Cole, 1971.

Butler, R. N. Intensive psychotherapy for the hospitalized aged. *Geriatrics*, 1960, **1 5,** 644–653.

Cameron, N. *Personality development and psychopathology.* Boston: Houghton Mifflin, 1963.

Carr, J. E. Differentiation similarity of patient and therapist and the outcome of psychotherapy. *Journal of Abnormal Psychology*, 1970, **3,** 361–369.

Carson, R. C. A & B therapist "types": A possible critical variable in psychotherapy. *Journal of Nervous and Mental Disease*, 1967, **144,** 47–54.

Carson, R. C., & Heine, R. W. Similarity and success in therapeutic dyads. *Journal of Consulting Psychology*, 1962, **26,** 38–43.

Chartier, G. M. A-B therapist variable: Real or imagined? *Psychological Bulletin*, 1971, **75,** 22–33.

Chess, S., & Thomas, A. Temperament in the normal infant. In J. C. Westman (Ed.), *Individual differences in children.* New York: Wiley, 1973. Pp. 83–104.

Chessick, R. D. *Why psychotherapists fail.* New York: Science House, 1971.

Chrzanowski, G. Termination in psychoanalysis. *American Journal of Psychotherapy*, 1960, **14,** 48–62.

Corsini, R. J. *Current psychotherapies.* Itasca, Ill.: Peacock, 1973.

Cozby, P. C. Self-disclosure: A literature review. *Psychological Bulletin*, 1973, **79,** 73–91.

Crowne, D. P., & Strickland, B. R. Need for approval and the premature termination of psychotherapy. *Journal of Consulting Psychology*, 1963, **27,** 95–101.

Cutler, R. L. Countertransference effects in psychotherapy. *Journal of Consulting Psychology*, 1958, **22,** 349–356 .

Deutsch, F. Analysis of postural behavior. *Psychoanalytic Quarterly*, 1947, **16,** 195–213.

Deutsch, F. Some principles of correlating verbal and non-verbal communication. In L. A. Gottschalk & A. H. Auerbach (Eds.), *Methods of research in psychotherapy*. New York: Appleton-Century-Crofts, 1966. Pp. 166–184.

Deutsch, F., & Murphy, W. F. *The clinical interview.* 2 vols. New York: International Universities Press, 1955.

Dewald, P. A. Reactions to the forced termination of therapy. *Psychiatric Quarterly*, 1965, **39,** 102–126.

Dewald, P. A. Therapeutic evaluation and potential: The dynamic point of view. *Comprehensive Psychiatry*, 1967, **8,** 284–298.

Dewald, P. A. *Psychotherapy: A dynamic approach.* (2nd ed.) New York: Basic Books, 1971.

Dollard, J., Auld, F., & White, A. *Steps in psychotherapy.* New York: Macmillan, 1953.

Durlak, J. A., Myths concerning the nonprofessional therapist. *Professional Psychology*, 1973, **4,** 300–304.

Eisenstein, V. W. (Ed.) *Neurotic interaction in marriage.* New York: Basic Books, 1956.

Ekman, P., & Friesen, W. V. Nonverbal behavior in psychotherapy research. In J. M. Shlien (Ed.), *Research in psychotherapy*. Vol. III. Washington, D.C.: American Psychological Association, 1968. Pp. 179–216.

Ekman, P., Friesen, W. V., & Ellsworth, P. *Emotion in the human face: Guidelines for research and an integration of findings.* New York: Pergamon, 1972.

Ellis, A. *Reason and emotion in psychotherapy.* New York: Lyle Stuart, 1962.

Eriksen, C. W. Perceptual defense as a function of unacceptable needs. *Journal of Abnormal and Social Psychology*, 1951, **46,** 557–564.

Eron, L. D. (Ed.) *The classification of behavior disorders.* Chicago: Aldine, 1966.

Fagan, J., & Shepherd, I. L. (Eds.) *Gestalt therapy now.* Palo Alto, Cal.: Science and Behavior Books, 1970.

Fancher, R. E., McMillan, R. S., & Buchman, N. A. Interrelationships among accuracy in person perception, role taking, and the A-B variable. *Journal of Consulting and Clinical Psychology*, 1972, **39**, 22–28.

Feather, B. W., & Rhoads J. M. Psychodynamic behavior therapy. *Archives of General Psychiatry*, 1972, **26**, 496–511.

Feldman, S. S. *Mannerisms of speech and gestures in everyday life.* New York: International Universities Press, 1959.

Fenichel, O. *Problems of psychoanalytic technique.* New York: Psychoanalytic Quarterly, 1941.

Fenichel, O. *The psychoanalytic theory of neurosis.* New York: Norton, 1945.(a)

Fenichel, O. Neurotic acting out. *Psychoanalytic Review*, 1945, **32**, 197–206.(b)

Fiedler, F. E. A comparison of therapeutic relationship in psychoanalytic, nondirective, and Adlerian therapy. *Journal of Consulting Psychology*, 1950, **14**, 436–445.

Fiedler, F. E. A method of objective quantification of certain countertransference attitudes. *Journal of Clinical Psychology*, 1951, **7**, 101–107.

Fielding, B. Aspects affecting premature termination at a training clinic. *American Journal of Psychotherapy*, 1972, **26**, 268–276.

Fierman, L. B. Myths in the practice of psychotherapy. *Archives of General Psychiatry*, 1965, **12**, 408–414.

Fisher, E. H., & Cohen, S. L. Demographic correlates of attitude toward seeking professional psychological help. *Journal of Consulting and Clinical Psychology*, 1972, **39**, 70–74.

Fitzgibbons, D. J., Cutler, R., & Cohen, J. Patient's self-perceived treatment needs and their relationship to background variables. *Journal of Consulting and Clinical Psychology*, 1971, **37**, 253–258.

Ford, D. H., & Urban, H. B. *Systems of psychotherapy: A comparative study.* New York Wiley, 1963.

Frank, G. H. The effect of directive and nondirective statements by therapists on the content of patient verbalizations. *Journal of General Psychology*, 1964, **71**, 323–328.

Frank, G. H. Psychiatric diagnosis: A review of research. *Journal of General Psychology*, 2969, **81**, 157–176.

Frank, G. H. On the nature of borderline psychopathology: A review. *Journal of General Psychology*, 1970, **83**, 61–77.

Frank, J. D. Therapeutic factors in psychotherapy, *American Journal of Psychotherapy*, 1971, **25**, 350–361.

Frank, J. D. *Persuasion and healing.* (Rev. ed.) Baltimore, Md.: Johns Hopkins University Press, 1973.

Frank, L. K. Projective methods for the study of personality. *Journal of Psychology*, 1939, **8**, 389–413.

Freedman, A. M., & Kaplan, H. I. (Eds.) *Comprehensive textbook of psychiatry.* Baltimore, Md.: Williams & Wilkins, 1967.

Freud, A. (1936) *The ego and the mechanisms of defense.* New York: International Universities Press, 1946.

Freud, S. (1900) The interpretation of dreams. *Standard Edition*, Vols. IV & V. London: Hogarth, 1953. Pp. 277–508.

Freud, S. (1901) The psychopathology of everyday life. *Standard Edition*, Vol. VI. London: Hogarth, 1960.

Freud, S. (1904a) On psychotherapy. *Standard Edition*, Vol. VII. London: Hogarth, 1953. Pp. 257–268.

Freud, S. (1904b) Freud's psycho-analytic procedure. *Standard Edition*, Vol. VII. London: Hogarth, 1953. Pp. 249–254.

Freud, S. (1905) Fragment of an analysis of a case of hysteria. *Standard Edition*, Vol. VII. London: Hogarth, 1953. Pp. 7–122.

Freud, S. (1909) Some general remarks on hysterical attacks. *Standard Edition*, Vol. IX. London: Hogarth, 1959. Pp. 229–234.

Freud, S. (1910a) 'Wild' psycho-analysis. *Standard Edition*, Vol XI. London: Hogarth, 1957. Pp. 221–227.

Freud, S. (1910b) The future prospects of psycho-analytic therapy. *Standard Edition*, Vol. XI. London: Hogarth, 1957. Pp. 141–151.

Freud, S. (1911) The handling of dream interpretations in psycho-analysis. *Standard Edition*, Vol. XII. London: Hogarth, 1958. Pp. 91–96.

Freud, S. (1912a) Recommendations to physicians practicing psycho-analysis. *Standard Edition*, Vol. XII. London: Hogarth, 1958. Pp. 111–120.

Freud, S. (1912b) The dynamics of transference. *Standard Edition*, Vol. XII. London: Hogarth, 1958. Pp. 99–108.

Freud, S. (1913) On beginning the treatment (further recommendations on the technique of psycho-analysis I). *Standard Edition*, Vol. XII. London: Hogarth, 1958. Pp. 123–144.

Freud, S. (1914) Remembering, repeating, and working through. *Standard Edition*, Vol. XII. London: Hogarth, 1958. Pp. 145–156.

Freud, S. (1915) Observations on transference-love. (Further recommendations on the technique of psycho-analysis III). *Standard Edition*, Vol. XII. London: Hogarth, 1958. Pp. 159–171.

Freud, S. (1916) Some character-types met with in psychoanalytic work. *Standard Edition*, Vol. XIV. London: Hogarth, 1957. Pp. 311–333.

Freud, S. (1916–1917). Introductory lectures on psycho-analysis . *Standard Edition*, Vols. XV–XVI. London: Hogarth, 1963.

Freud, S. (1923) Remarks on the theory and practice of dream interpretation. *Standard Edition*, Vol. XIX. London: Hogarth, 1961. Pp. 109–121.

Freud, S. (1926) Inhibitions, symptoms, and anxiety. *Standard Edition*, Vol. XX. London: Hogarth, 1959. Pp. 87–174.

Freud, S. (1933) New introductory lectures on psycho-analysis. *Standard Edition*, Vol. XXII. London: Hogarth, 1964. Pp. 5–182.

Freud, S. (1937) Analysis terminable and interminable. *Standard Edition*, Vol. XXIII. London: Hogarth, 1964. Pp. 216–253.

Fromm-Reichmann, F. *Principles of intensive psychotherapy*. Chicago: University of Chicago Press, 1950.

Gardner, R. W. The development of cognitive structures. In C. Scheerer (Ed.), *Cognition: Theory, research, promise*. New York: Harper & Row, 1964. Pp. 147–171.

Gardner, R. W., Holzman, P. S., Klein, G. S., Linton, H., & Spence, D. P. Cognitive control: A study of individual consistencies in cognitive behavior. *Psychological Issues*, 1959, **1** (4).

Garduk, E. L., & Haggard, E. A. Immediate effects on patients of psychoanalytic interpretations. *Psychological Issues*, 1972, **7** (4).

Garfield, S. L. Research on client variables in psychotherapy. In A. E. Bergin and S. L. Garfield (Eds.), *Handbook of psychotherapy and behavior change*. New York: Wiley, 1971. Pp. 271–298.

Garfield, S. L., & Bergin, A. E. Personal therapy, outcome, and some therapist variables. *Psychotherapy: Theory, Research and Practice*, 1971, **8**, 251–253.

Garrett, A. *Interviewing: Its principles and methods*. (2nd ed.) New York: Family Service Association of America, 1972.

Gassner, S. M. Relationship between patient-therapist compatibility and treatment effectiveness. *Journal of Consulting and Clinical Psychology*, 1970, **34**, 408–414.

Gendlin, E. T. Initiating psychotherapy with "unmotivated" patients. *Psychiatric Quarterly*, 1961, **35**, 134–139. (a)

Gendlin, E. T. Experiencing: A variable in the process of psychotherapeutic change. *American Journal of Psychotherapy*, 1961, **15**, 233–245. (b)

Gill, M. M. Topography and systems in psychoanalytic theory. *Psychological Issues*, 1963, **3** (2).

Gill, M., Newman, R., & Redlich, F. *The initial interview in psychiatric practice*. New York: International Universities Press, 1954.

Glenn, M. L. Separation anxiety: When the therapist leaves the patient. *American Journal of Psychotherapy*, 1971, **25**, 437–446.

Gliedman, L. H., Stone, A. R. , Frank, J. D., Nash, E. H., & Imber, S. D. Incentives for treatment related to remaining or improving in psychotherapy. *American Journal of Psychotherapy*, 1957, **11**, 589–598.

Glover, E. *The technique of psycho-analysis*. New York International Universities Press, 1955.

Goin, M. K., Yamamoto, J., & Silverman, J. Therapy congruent with class-linked expectations. *Archives of General Psychiatry*, 1965, 13, 133–137.

Goldfried, M. R., & Merbaum, M. A perspective on self-control. In M. R. Goldfried & M. Merbaum (Eds.), *Behavior change through self-control*. New York: Holt, Rinehart & Winston, 1973. Pp. 3–34.

Goldstein, A. P. Patient's expectancies and non-specific therapy as a basis for (un)-spontaneous remission. *Journal of Clinical Psychology*, 1960, **16,** 399–403.

Goldstein, A. P. *Therapist-patient expectancies in psychotherapy*. New York: Pergamon, 1962.

Goldstein, A. P. Maximizing the initial therapeutic relationship. *American Journal of Psychotherapy*, 1969, **23,** 430–451.

Goldstein, A. P. *Psychotherapeutic attraction*. New York: Pergamon, 1971.

Goldstein, A. P. *Structured Learning therapy: Toward a psychotherapy for the poor*. New York: Academic Press, 1973.

Gough, H. Some reflections on the meaning of psychodiagnosis. *American Psychologist*, 1971, **26,** 160–167.

Gould, R. E. Dr. Strangeclass or: How I stopped worrying about the theory and began treating the blue collar worker. *American Journal of Orthopsychiatry*, 1967, **37,** 78–86.

Greenson, R.R. The problem of working through. In M. Schur (Ed.), *Drives, affects, behavior*. New York: International Universities Press, 1965. Pp. 277–314. (a)

Greenson, R.R. The working alliance and the transference neurosis. *Psychoanalytic Quarterly*, 1965, **34,** 155–181. (b)

Greenson, R. R. *The technique and practice of psychoanalysis*. Vol. I. New York: International Universities Press, 1967.

Greenson, R. R., & Wexler, M. The nontransference relationship in the psychoanalytic situation. *International Journal of Psycho-Analysis*, 1969, **50,** 27–39.

Greenspoon, J. The reinforcing effect of two spoken sounds on the frequency of two responses. *American Journal of Psychology*, 1955, **68,** 409–416.

Greenwald, H. From client-centered to therapist-centered. *Contemporary Psychology*, 1973, **18,** 26–27.

Grotjahn, M. Analytic psychotherapy with the elderly. *Psychoanalytic Review*, 1955, **42,** 419–427.

Guerney, B. *Psychotherapeutic agents: New roles for nonprofessionals, parents, and teachers*. New York: Holt, Rinehart & Winston, 1969.

Gurman, A. S. Therapist's mood patterns and therapeutic facilitativeness. *Journal of Counseling Psychology*, 1972, **19,** 169–170.

Gurman, A. S. Instability of therapeutic conditions in psychotherapy. *Journal of Counseling Psychology*, 1973, **20,** 16–24.

Gutheil, E. A. *The handbook of dream analysis*. New York: Liveright, 1951.

Hall, C. S., & Lindzey, G. *Theories of personality*. (2nd ed.) New York: Wiley, 1970.

Hall, R. A., & Closson, W. H. An experimental study of the couch. *Journal of Nervous and Mental Disease*, 1964, **138,** 474–480.

Hammer, M. Psychotherapy with the aged. In M. Hammer (Ed.), *The theory and practice of psychotherapy with specific disorders.* Springfield, Ill.: Thomas, 1972. Pp. 376–399.

Hammet, V. O. Delusional transference. *American Journal of Psychotherapy,* 1961, **15,** 574–581.

Harper, R. A. *Psychoanalysis and psychotherapy: 36 systems.* Englewood Cliffs, N. J.: Prentice-Hall, 1959.

Harrower, M. *Personality change and development as measured by the projective techniques.* New York: Grune & Stratton, 1958.

Hart, J. T., & Tomlinson, T. M. *New directions in client-centered therapy.* Boston: Houghton Mifflin, 1970.

Heilbrun, A. B. Effects of briefing upon client satisfaction with the initial counseling contract. *Journal of Consulting and Clinical Psychology,* 1972, **38,** 50–56.

Heimann, P. Dynamics of transference interpretations. *International Journal of Psycho-Analysis,* 1956, **37,** 303–310.

Heine, R. W. A comparison of patient's reports on psychotherapeutic experience with psychoanalytic, nondirective, and Adlerian therapists. *American Journal of Psychotherapy,* 1953, **7,** 16–23.

Heine, R. W. *Psychotherapy.* Englewood Cliffs, N. J. : Prentice-Hall, 1971.

Heller, K., Myers, R. A., & Kline, L. V. Interviewer behavior as a function of standardized client roles. *Journal of Counseling Psychology,* 1963, **20,** 501–508.

Henry, W. E., Sims, J. H., & Spray, S. L. *The fifth profession: Becoming a psychotherapist.* San Francisco: Jossey-Bass, 1971.

Hersen, M. The complementary use of behavior therapy and psychotherapy: Some comments. *Psychological Record,* 1970, **20,** 395–402. (a)

Hersen, M. The use of behavior modification techniques within a traditional psychotherapeutic context. *American Joural of Psychotherapy,* 1970, **24,** 308–313. (b)

Hiatt, H. Dynamic psychotherapy with the aging patient. *American Journal of Psychotherapy,* 1971, **25,** 591–600.

Hobbs, N. Sources of gain in psychotherapy. *American Psychologist,* 1962, **17,** 741–747.

Hofling, C. K. & Meyers, R. W. Recent discoveries in psychoanalysis. *Archives of General Psychiatry,* 1972, **26,** 518–523.

Hohen-Saric, R., Frank, J. D., Imber, S. D., Nash, E. H., Stone, A. R., & Battle, C. C. Systematic preparation of patients for psychotherapy. **I.** Effects on therapy behavior and outcome. *Journal of Psychiatric Research,* 1964, **2,** 267–281.

Holmes, D. J. *The adolescent in psychotherapy.* Boston: Little, Brown, 1964.

Holt, R R. (Ed.) *New horizons for psychotherapy: Autonomy as a profession.*

New York: International Universities Press, 1970.

Holt, W. E. The concept of motivation for treatment. *American Journal of Psychiatry*, 1967, **123,** 1388–1394.

Holzberg, J. D. Psychological theory and projective techniques. In A. I. Rabin (Ed.), *Projective techniques in personality assessment*. New York : Springer, 1968. Pp. 18–63.

Holzman, P. S. *Psychoanalysis and psychopathology*. New York: McGraw-Hill, 1970.

Jackson, A. M. Psychotherapy: Factors associated with the race of the therapist. *Psychotherapy: Theory, Research & Practice*, 1973, **10,** 273–277.

Jackson, D. D., & Haley, J. Transference revisited. *Journal of Nervous and Mental Disease*, 1963, **137,** 363–371.

Jourard, S. M. *The transparent self: Self-disclosure and well-being*. Princeton, N. J.: Van Nostrand/Reinhold, 1964.

Jourard, S. M. *Self-disclosure: An experimental analysis of the transparent self*. New York: Wiley, 1971.

Jourard, S. M., & Jaffee, P. E. Influence of an interviewer's disclosure on the interviewees. *Journal of Counseling Psychology*, 1970, **17,** 252–257.

Kadushin, C. *Why people go to psychiatrists*. New York: Atherton, 1969.

Kagan, J., & Kogan, N. Individual variations in cognitive processes. In P. H. Mussen (Ed.), *Carmichael's manual of child psychology*. Vol. I. New York: Wiley, 1970. Pp. 1273–1365.

Kagan, J., & Moss, H. A. *Birth to maturity: A study in psychological development*. New York: Wiley, 1962.

Kanfer, F. H. Verbal conditioning: A review of its current status. In T. R. Dixon & D. L. Horton (Eds.). *Verbal behavior and general behavior theory*. Englewood Cliffs, N. J.: Prentice-Hall, 1968. Pp. 254–290.

Kanfer, F. H. Self-regulation: Research, issues, and speculations. In C. Neuringer & J. L. Michael (Eds.), *Behavior modification in clinical psychology*. New York: Appleton-Century-Crofts, 1970. Pp. 178–220.

Kanfer, F. H., & Phillips, J. S. *Learning foundations of behavior therapy*. New York: Wiley, 1970.

Kanzer, M. Verbal and nonverbal aspects of free association. *Psychoanalytic Quarterly*, 1961, **30,** 327–350.

Kaplan, M. L., Colarelli, N. J., Gross, R. B., Leventahl, D., & Siegel, S. M. *The structural approach in psychological testing*. New York: Pergamon, 1970.

Keith, C. Multiple transfers of psychotherapy patients. *Archives of General Psychiatry*, 1966, **14,** 185–189.

Kelly, G. A. *The psychology of personal constructs*. Vol. 2. *Clinical diagnosis and psychotherapy*. New York: Norton, 1955.

Kepecs, J. G. Theories of transference neurosis. *Psychoanalytic Quarterly*, 1966, **35,** 497–521.

Kernberg, O. Notes on countertransference. *Journal of the American Psychoanalytic Association*, 1965, **13**, 38–57.

Kernberg, O. Borderline personality organization. *Journal of the American Psychoanalytic Association*, 1967, **15**, 641–685.

Kernberg, O. F., Burstein, E. D., Coyne, L., Applebaum, A., Horowitz, L., & Voth, H. *Psychotherapy and psychoanalysis: Final report of the Menninger Foundation's psychotherapy research project*. Topeka, Kan.: The Menninger Foundation, 1972.

Khaton, O. M., & Carriera, R. P. An attitude study of minority group adolescents toward mental health. *Journal of Youth and Adolescence*, 1972, **1**, 131–142.

Klein, M. The origins of transference. *International Journal of Psycho-Analysis*, 1952, **33**, 433–438.

Klein, M., Heimann, P., Isaacs, S., & Riviere, J. *Developments in psycho-analysis*. London: Hogarth, 1952.

Knight, R. P. Borderline states. *Bulletin of the Menninger Clinic, 1953*, **17**, 1–12.

Krasner, L. Verbal conditioning and psychotherapy. In L. Krasner & L. P. Ullman (Eds.), *Research in behavior modification*. New York: Holt, Rinehart & Winston, 1965. Pp. 211–228.

Kris, E. Defense mechanisms and psychoanalytic technique. *Journal of the American Psychoanalytic Association*, 1954, **2**, 318–326.

Kubie, L. S. The pros and cons of a new profession: A doctorate in medical psychology. *Texas Reports on Biology and Medicine*, 1954, **12**, 692–737.

Kubie, L. S. A school of psychological medicine in the framework of a medical school. *Journal of Medical Education*, 1964, **39**, 476–480.

Kubie, L. S. The process of evaluation of therapy in psychiatry. *Archives of General Psychiatry*, 1973, **28**, 880–884.

Langs, R. *The technique of psychoanalytic psychotherapy*. Vol. 1. New York: Aronson, 1973.

Langs, R. *The technique of psychoanalytic psychotherapy*. Vol 2. New York: Aronson, 1974.

Lassen, L. J. Effect of proximity on anxiety and communication in the initial psychiatric interview. *Journal of Abnormal Psychology*, 1973, **81**, 226–232.

Leader, A. L. The argument against required personal analysis in training for psychotherapy. In R. R. Holt (Ed.), *New horizons for psychotherapy*. New York: International Universities Press, 1971. Pp. 231–240.

Lee, S. D., & Temerlin, M. K. Social class, diagnosis, and prognosis for psychotherapy. *Psychotherapy: Theory, Research and Practice*, 1970, **7**, 181–185.

Lennard, H. L., & Bernstein, A. *The anatomy of psychotherapy*. New York: Columbia University Press, 1970.

Lerner, B. *Therapy in the ghetto: Political impotence and personal disintegration*. Baltimore, Md.: Johns Hopkins University Press, 1972.

Lerner, B., & Fiske, D. W. Client attributes and the eye of the beholder. *Journal of Consulting and Clinical Psychology*, 1973, **40,** 272–277.

Levy, L. H. *Psychological interpretation.* New York: Holt, Rinehart & Winston, 1962.

Lewis, H. B. *Shame and guilt in neurosis.* New York: International Universities Press, 1971.

Lichtenberg, J. D., & Slap, J. W. On the defense mechanism: A survey and synthesis. *Journal of the American Psychoanalytic Association, 1972,* **29,** 776–792.

Lidz, T. *The family and human adaption.* New York: International Universities Press, 1963.

Lindner, R. M. *The fifty-minute hour.* New York: Holt, Rinehart & Winston, 1955.

Locke, E. A. Is "behavior therapy" behavioristic? *Psychological Bulletin*, 1971, **76,** 318–327.

Loewenstein, R. M. Some remarks on defenses, autonomous ego and psychoanalytic technique. *International Journal of Psychoanalysis*, 1954, **35,** 188–198.

Loewenstein, R. M. Some considerations on free association. *Journal of the American Psychoanalytic Association*, 1963, **11,** 451–473.

Lorand, S. Historical aspects and trends in psychoanalytic therapy. *Psychoanalytic Review*, 1972-1973, **59,** 497–525.

Lorion, R. P. Socioeconomic status and traditional treatment approaches reconsidered. *Psychological Bulletin*, 1973, **79,** 263–270.

Lott, G. Psychotherapy of the mentally retarded: Values and cautions. In F. J. Menolascino (Ed.), *Psychiatric approaches to mental retardation.* New York: Basic Books, 1970. Pp. 227–250.

Luborsky, L., Auerbach, A. H., Chandler, M., & Cohen, J. Factors influencing the outcome of psychotherapy: A review of quantitative research. *Psychological Bulletin*, 1971, **75,** 145–185.

Luborsky, L., & Spence D. P. Quantitative research on psychoanalytic therapy. In A. E. Bergin & S. L. Garfield (Eds.), *Handbook of psychotherapy and behavior change.* New York: Wiley, 1971. Pp. 408–438.

Macalpine, I. The development of the transference. *Psychoanalytic Quarterly*, 1950, **19,** 501–539.

McGinnies, E. Emotionality and perceptual defense. *Psychological Review*, 1949, **56,** 244–251.

MacKinnon, R. A., & Michels, R. *The psychiatric interview in clinical practice.* Philadelphia: Saunders, 1971.

Maggon, T. M., Golann, S. E., & Freeman, R. W. *Mental health counselors at work.* New York: Pergamon, 1969.

Mahl, G. F. Gestures and body movements in interviews. In J. M. Shlien (Ed.),

Research in psychotherapy. Vol. III. Washington, D. C.: American Psychological Association, 1968. Pp. 295–346.

Mahl, G. F. *Psychological conflict and defense*. New York: Harcourt Brace Jovanovich, 1971.

Mann, J. *Time-limited psychotherapy*. Cambridge, Mass.: Harvard University Press, 1973.

Mariner, A. S. A critical look at professional education in the mental health field. *American Psychologist*, 1967, **22**, 271–281.

Mariner, A. S. Psychotherapists' communications with patients' relatives and referring professionals. *American Journal of Psychotherapy*, 1971, **25**, 517–529.

Marmor, J. Psychoanalytic therapy as an educational process: Common denominators in the therapeutic approaches of different psychoanalytic "schools." In J. H. Masserman (Ed.), *Science and psychoanalysis*. Vol. 5. New York: Grune & Stratton, 1962. Pp. 286–299.

Marmor, J. The seductive psychotherapist. *Psychiatry Digest*, 1970, **31**, 10–16.

Marmor, J. Dynamic psychotherapy and behavior therapy. *Archives of General Psychiatry*, 1971, **24**, 22–28.

Marmor, J. Sexual acting-out in psychotherapy. *American Journal of Psychoanalysis*, 1972, **32**, 3–8.

Marston, A. R., & Feldman, S. E. Toward the use of self-control in behavior modification. *Journal of Consulting and Clinical Psychology*, 1972, **39**, 429–433.

Maslow, A. H. *Toward a psychology of being*. Princeton, N. J.: Van Nostrand/Reinhold, 1962.

Masserman, J. H. (Ed.) *Handbook of psychiatric therapies*. New York: Aronson, 1973.

Matarazzo, J. D., & Wiens, A. N. *The interview: Research on its anatomy and structure*. Chicago: Aldine-Atherton, 1972.

Matarazzo, J. D., Wiens, A. N., Matarazzo, R. G., & Saslow, G. Speech and silence behavior in clinical psychotherapy and its laboratory correlates. In J. M. Shlien (Ed.), *Research in psychotherapy*. Vol III. Washington, D. C. : American Psychological Association, 1968. Pp. 347–394.

Matarazzo, J. D., Wiens, A. N., & Saslow, G. Studies in interview speech behavior. In L. Krasner & L. P. Ullman (Eds.), *Research in behavior modification*. New York: Holt, Rinehart & Winston, 1965. Pp. 179–210.

May P. R. Psychotherapy and ataraxic drugs. In A. E. Bergin & S. L. Garfield (Eds.), *Handbook of psychotherapy and behavior change*. New York: Wiley, 1971. Pp. 495–540.

May, R., Angel, E., & Ellenberger, H. F. (Eds.) , *Existence: A new dimension in psychiatry and psychology*. New York: Basic Books, 1958.

Meeks, J. E. *The fragile alliance: An orientation to the outpatient psychotherapy of the adolescent*. Baltimore: Williams & Wilkins, 1971.

Meltzoff, J., & Kornreich, M. *Research in psychotherapy*. New York: Atherton, 1970.

Menninger, K. *The vital balance: The life process in mental health and illness*. New York: Viking Press, 1963.

Menninger, K. A., & Holzman, P. S. *Theory of psychoanalytic technique*. (2nd ed.) New York: Basic Books, 1973.

Milman, D. S., & Goldman, G. D. (Eds.), *Acting out*. Springfield, Ill.: Thomas, 1973.

Minuchin, S., Montalvo, B., Guerney, B. G., Rosman, B. L., & Schumer, F. *Families of the slums: An exploration of their structure and treatment*. New York: Basic Books, 1967.

Moos, R. H., & MacIntosh, S. Multivariate study of the patient-therapist system: A replication and extension. *Journal of Consulting and Clinical Psychology*, 1970, **35**, 298–307.

Mueller, W. J. Patterns of behavior and their reciprocal impact in the family and in psychotherapy. *Journal of Counseling Psychology*, 1969, **16** (2, Part 2).

Munroe, R. L. *Schools of psychoanalytic thought*. New York: Dryden Press, 1955.

Murray, E. J., & Jacobson, L. I. The nature of learning in traditional and behavioral psychotherapy. In E. A. Bergin & S. L. Garfield (Eds.), *Handbook of psychotherapy and behavior change*. New York: Wiley, 1971. Pp. 709–747.

Norton, J. Treatment of a dying patient. *Psychoanalytic Study of the Child*, 1963, **18**, 541–460.

Oremland, J.D. Transference cure and flight into health. *International Journal of Psychoanalytic Psychotherapy*, 1972, **1**, 61–75.

Ornston, P. S., Cicchetti, D. V., Levine, J., & Fierman, L. B. Some parameters of verbal behavior that reliably differentiate novice from experienced psychotherapists. *Journal of Abnormal Psychology*, 1968, **73**, 240–244.

Ornston, P. S., Cicchetti, D. V., & Towbin, A. P. Reliable changes in psychotherapy behavior among first-year residents. *Journal of Abnormal Psychology*, 1970, **75**, 7–11.

Orr, D. W. Transference and countertransference: A survey. *Journal of the American Psychoanalytic Association*, 1954, **2**, 621–670,

Ostow, M. *Drugs in psychoanalysis and psychotherapy*. New York: Basic Books, 1962.

Ovesey, L. Fear of vocational success. *Archives of General Psychiatry*, 1962, **7**, 82–92.

Peck, A. Psychotherapy of the aged. *Journal of the American Geriatrics Society*, 1966, **14**, 748–753.

Perlman, G. Change in "central therapeutic ingredients" of beginning psychotherapists. *Psychotherapy: Theory, Research and Practice,* 1973, **20,** 48–51.

Phillips, E. L., & Wiener, D. N. *Short-term psychotherapy and structured behavior change.* New York: McGraw-Hill, 1966.

Phillips, L., & Draguns, J. G. Classification of the behavior disorders. *Annual Review of Psychology,* 1971, **22,** 447–482.

Polatin, P. *A guide to treatment in psychiatry.* Philadelphia: Lippincott, 1966.

Polster, E., & Polster, M. *Gestalt therapy integrated.* New York: Brunner/Mazel, 1973.

Pope, B., & Scott, W. H. *Psychological diagnosis in clinical practice.* New York: Oxford University Press, 1967.

Pope, B., Siegman, A. W., Blass, T., & Cheek, J. Some effects of discrepant role expectations on interviewee verbal behavior in the initial interview. *Journal of Consulting and Clinical Psychology,* 1972, **39,** 501–507.

Pumpian-Mindlin, E. Comments on techniques of termination and treatment in a clinic setting. *American Journal of Psychotherapy,* 1958, **12,** 455–464.

Rabiner, E. L., Reiser, M. F., Barr, H. L., & Gralnick, A., Therapists' attitudes and patients' clinical status: A study of 100 psychotherapy pairs. *Archives of General Psychiatry,* 1971, **25,** 555–529.

Racker, H. A contribution to the problem of counter-transference. *International Journal of Psycho-Analysis,* 1953, **34,** 313–324.

Racker, H. The meanings and uses of countertransference. *Psychoanalytic Quarterly,* 1957, **26,** 303–357.

Rapaport, D., Gill, M. M., and Schafer, R. (R. Holt, Ed.) *Diagnostic psychological testing.* New York: International Universities Press, 1968.

Raskin, N. J. The psychotherapy research project of the American Academy of Psychotherapists. *Proceedings APA,* 1965, 253–254.

Raush, H. L., & Bordin, E. S. Warmth in personality development and in psychotherapy. *Psychiatry,* 1957, 351–363.

Razin, A. M. A-B variable in psychotherapy: A critical review. *Psychological Bulletin,* 1971, **75,** 1–21.

Reich, A. On counter-transference. *International Journal of Psycho-Analysis,* 1951, **32,** 25–31.

Reich, A. Further remarks on countertransference. *International Journal of Psycho-Analysis,* 1960, **41,** 389–395.

Reich, W. (1933) *Character Analysis.* (3rd ed.) New York: Orgone Institute Press, 1949.

Reider, N. Transference psychosis. *Journal of the Hillside Hospital,* 1957, **6,** 131–149.

Reik, T. *Masochism in modern man.* New York: Grove Press, 1941.

Reik, T. *Listening with the third ear.* New York: Grove Press, 1948.

Reisman, J. M. *Toward the integration of psychotherapy.* New York: Wiley 1971.

Rioch, M. J., Elkes, C., Flint, A. A. , Usdansky, B. S., Newman, R. G., & Silber, E. National Institute of Mental Health pilot study in training of mental health counselors. *American Journal of Orthopsychiatry*, 1963, **33,** 678–689.

Ripley, H. S. Psychiatric interview. In A. M. Freedman & H. I. Kaplan (Eds), *Comprehensive textbook of psychiatry.* Baltimore, Md.: William & Wilkins, 1967. Pp. 491–498.

Roback, H. B. Inexact personality interpretations and behavior change. *Ontario Psychologist*, 1972, **4,** 92–99.

Roback, H. B. Insight: A bridging of the theoretical and research literatures. *Canadian Psychologist*, 1974, **15,** 61–88.

Rogers, C. R. *Client-centered therapy.* Boston: Houghton Mifflin, 1951.

Rogers, C. R. The necessary and sufficient conditions of therapeutic personality change. *Journal of Consulting Psychology*, 1957, **21,** 95–103.

Rogers, C. R. *On becoming a person: A therapist's view of psychotherapy.* Boston: Houghton Mifflin, 1961.

Rosner, S. Free association and memory. *Psychotherapy: Theory, Research and Practice*, 1973, **10,** 278–280.

Russell, P. D. , & Snyder, W. U. Counselor anxiety in relation to amount of clinical experience and quality of affect demonstrated by clients. *Journal of Consulting Psychology*, 1963, **27,** 358–363.

Salzinger, K. Experimental manipulation of verbal behavior: A review. *Journal of Genetic Psychology*, 1959, **61,** 65–94.

Salzman, L. *The obsessive personality.* New York: Science House, 1968.

Sampson, H., Weiss, J., Mlodnosky, L., & Hause, E. Defense analysis and the emergence of warded-off mental contents. *Archives of General Psychiatry*, 1972, **26,** 524–531.

Sands, W. L. Psychiatric history and mental status. In A. M. Freedman & H. I. Kaplan (Eds.), *Comprehensive textbook of psychiatry.* Baltimore, Md.: Williams & Wilkins, 1967. Pp. 499–508.

Schiff, S. Termination of therapy. *Archives of General Psychiatry*, 1962, **6,** 77–82.

Schlesinger, H. J. Diagnosis and prescription for psychotherapy. *Bulletin of the Menninger Clinic*, 1969, **33,** 269–278.

Schmideberg, M. The borderline patient. In S. Arieti (Ed.), *American handbook of psychiatry.* Vol. 1. New York: Basic Books, 1959. Pp. 398–418.

Schofield, W. *Psychotherapy: The purchase of friendship.* Englewood Cliffs, N. J.: Prentice-Hall, 1964.

Schofield, W. The psychotherapist as friend. *Humanitas*, 1970, **6,** 211–223.

Schonbar, R. Interpretation and insight in psychotherapy. *Psychotherapy: Theory, Research & Practice*, 1965, **2,** 78–84.

Schuster, D. B. On the fear of success. *Psychiatric Quarterly*, 1955, **29,** 412–420.

Shakow, D. Recommended graduate training program in clinical psychology. *American Psychologist*, 1947, **2,** 539–558.

Shakow, D. The role of classification in the development of the science of psychopathology with particular reference to research. *Bulletin of the Menninger Clinic*, 1966, **30,** 150–161.

Shapiro, A. K. Placebo effects in medicine, psychotherapy, and psychoanalysis. In A. E. Bergin & S. L. Garfield (Eds.), *Handbook of psychotherapy and behavior change*. New York; Wiley, 1971. Pp. 439–473.

Shapiro, D. *Neurotic styles*. New York: Basic Books, 1965.

Sifneos, P. E. *Short-term psychotherapy and emotional crisis*. Cambridge, Mass.: Harvard University Press, 1972.

Silverman, J. Personality trait and ''perceptual style'' studies of the therapists of schizophrenic patients. *Journal of Nervous and Mental Disease,* 1967, **145,** 5–17.

Singer, E. *Key concepts in psychotherapy*. New York: Random House, 1965.

Sloane, R. B. The converging paths of behavior therapy and psychotherapy. *American Journal of Psychiatry*, 1969, **125,** 877–888.

Sloane, R. B., Cristol, A. H., Pepernik, M. C., & Staples, F. R. Role preparation and expectation of improvement in psychotherapy. *Journal of Nervous and Mental Disease*, 1970, **150,** 18–26.

Snyder, W. U. *The psychotherapy relationship*. New York: Macmillan, 1961.

Solley, C. M., & Murphy, G. *Development of the perceptual world*. New York: Basic Books, 1960.

Speisman, J. C. Depth of interpretation and verbal resistance in psychotherapy. *Journal of Consulting Psychology*, 1959, **23,** 93–99.

Spielberger, C. D. Anxiety as an emotional state. In C. D. Spielberger (Ed.), *Anxiety: Current trends in theory and research*. New York: Academic Press, 1972. Pp. 24–49.

Stein, L. S., Green, B. L., & Stone, W. N. Therapist attitudes as influenced by A-B therapist type, patient diagnosis, and social class. *Journal of Consulting and Clinical Psychology*, 1972, **39,** 301–307.

Stein, M. I. (Ed.) *Contemporary psychotherapies*. Glencoe, Ill. : Free Press, 1961.

Sterba, R. F. The fate of the ego in analytic therapy. *International Journal of Psycho-Analysis*, 1934, **5,** 117–126.

Stevenson, I. The psychiatric interview. In S. Arieti (Ed.), *American handbook of psychiatry*. Vol. 1. New York: Basic Books, 1974. Pp. 1138–1156.

Stevenson, I., & Sheppe, W. M. The psychiatric examiniation. In S. Arieti (Ed.), *American handbook of psychiatry.* Vol 1. New York: Basic Books, 1974. Pp. 1157–1180.

Strupp, H. H. An objective comparison of Rogerian and psychoanalytic techniques. *Journal of Consulting Psychology*, 1955, **19,** 1–7. (a)

Strupp, H. H. Psychotherapeutic techniques, professional affiliation and experience level. *Journal of Consulting Psychology*, 1955, **19**, 97–102. (b)

Strupp, H. H. The performance of psychoanalytic and client-centered psychotherapists in an initial interview. *Journal of Consulting Psychology*, 1958, **24**, 219–226. (a)

Strupp, H. H. The psychotherapist's contribution to the treatment process. *Behavioral Science, 1958*, **3**, 34–67. (b)

Strupp, H. H. *Psychotherapists in action: Explorations of the therapist's contribution to the treatment process*. New York: Grune & Stratton, 1960.

Strupp, H. H. Specific vs. nonspecific factors in psychotherapy and the problem of control. *Archives of General Psychiatry*, 1970, **23**, 393–401.

Strupp, H. H. On the technology of psychotherapy. *Archives of General Psychiatry*, 1972, **26**, 270–278.

Strupp, H. H. On the basic ingredients of psychotherapy. *Journal of Consulting & Clinical Psychology*, 1973, **41**, 1–8.

Strupp, H. H., & Bergin, A. E. Some empirical and conceptual bases for coordinated research in psychotherapy: A critical review of issues, trends, and evidence. *International Journal of Psychiatry*, 1969, **7**, 18–90.

Strupp, H. H., & Williams, J. V. Some determinants of clinical evaluations of different psychiatrists. *Archives of General Psychiatry*, 1960, **2**, 434–440.

Sturm, I. E. A model for the delineation of the psychotherapeutic intervention. *Journal of Nervous and Mental Disease*, 1972, **154**, 332–343.

Subotnik, L. Spontaneous remission: fact or artifact? *Psychological Bulletin*, 1972, **77**, 32–48.

Sullivan, H. S. *The interpersonal theory of psychiatry*. New York: Norton, 1953.

Sullivan, H. S. *The psychiatric interview*. New York: Norton, 1954.

Sullivan, H. S. *Clinical studies in psychiatry*. New York: Norton, 1956.

Swenson, C. H. Commitment and the personality of the successful therapist. *Psychotherapy: Theory, Research and Practice*, 1971, **8**, 31–36.

Szurek, S. A., & Philips, I. Mental retardation and psychotherapy. In I. Philips (Ed.), *Prevention and treatment of mental retardation*. New York: Basic Books, 1966. Pp. 221–246.

Tarachow, S. *An introduction to psychotherapy*. New York: International Universities Press, 1963.

Tauber, E. S., & Green, M. R. *Prelogical experience*. New York: Basic Books, 1959.

Tedesco, P. C. The twenty-minute hour: An approach to the postgraduate teaching of psychiatry. *American Journal of Psychiatry*, 1967, **123**, 786–791.

Tedesco, P. C. The "20-minute hour" revisited: A follow-up. *Comprehensive Psychiatry*, 1970, **11**, 108–122.

Thomas, A., Chess, S., & Birch, H. G. *Temperament and behavior disorders in children.* New York: New York University Press, 1968.

Tower, L. E. Countertransference. *Journal of the American Psychoanalytic Association,* 1956, **4,** 224–255.

Train, G. F. "Flight into health." *American Journal of Psychotherapy,* 1953, **7,** 463–483.

Truax, C. B., & Carkhuff, R. R. *Toward effective counseling and psychotherapy.* Chicago: Aldine, 1967.

Truax, C. B., & Mitchell, K. M. Research on certain therapist interpersonal skills in relation process and outcome. In A. E. Bergin & S. L. Garfield (Eds.), *Handbook of psychotherapy and behavior change.* New York: Wiley, 1971. Pp. 299–344.

Truax, C. B., and Wargo, D. G. Psychotherapeutic encounters that change behavior for better or for worse. *American Journal of Psychotherapy,* 1966, **20,** 499–520.

Vogel, E. F., & Bell, N. F. The emotionally disturbed child as a family scapegoat. *Psychoanalysis and the Psychoanalytic Review,* 1960, **47,** 21–42.

Vriend, J., & Dyer, W. W. Counseling the reluctant client. *Journal of Counseling Psychology,* 1973, **20,** 240–246.

Waite, R. R. The Negro patient and clinical theory. *Journal of Consulting and Clinical Psychology,* 1968, **32,** 47–433.

Wallerstein, R. S. Reconstruction and mastery in the transference psychosis. *Journal of the American Psychoanalytic Association, 1967,* **15,** 551–583.

Wallerstein, R. S. The psychotherapy research project of the Menninger Foundation: A seminfinal view. In J. M. Shlien (Ed.), *Research in psychotherapy.* Vol. III. Washington, D.C.: American Psychological Association, 1968. Pp. 584–605.

Wallerstein, R. S., & Robbins, L. L. The psychotherapy research project of the Menninger Foundation. *Bulletin of the Menninger Clinic,* 1958, **22,** 117–166.

Weiner, I. B. *Psychodiagnosis in schizophrenia.* New York: Wiley, 1966.

Weiner, I. B. *Psychological disturbance in adolescence.* New York: Wiley, 1970.

Weiner, I. B. Does psychodiagnosis have a future? *Journal of Personality Assessment,* 1972, **36,** 534–546.

Weinshel, E. M. The transference neurosis: A survey of the literature. *Journal of the American Psychoanalytic Association,* 1971, **19,** 67–88.

Weiss, J. The integration of defenses. *International Journal of Psychoanalysis,* 1967, **48,** 520–524.

Weitzman, B. Behavior therapy and psychotherapy. *Psychological Review,* 1967, **74,** 300–317.

Wexler, D. A. A cognitive theory of experiencing, self-actualization, and therapeutic process. In D. A. Wexler & L. N. Rice (Eds.), *Innovations in client-centered therapy.* New York: Wiley, 1974.

Wheelis, A. B. Flight from insight. *American Journal of Psychiatry,* 1949, **105,** 915–919.

Whitehorn, J. C. Guide to interviewing and clinical personality study. *Archives of Neurology and Psychiatry*, 1944, **52,** 197–216.

Whitehorn, J. C., and Betz, B. A study of therapeutic relationships between physicians and schizophrenic patients. *American Journal of Psychiatry*, 1954, **111,** 321–331.

Wilkins, W. Expectancy of therapeutic gain: An empirical and conceptual critique. *Journal of Consulting and Clinical Psychology*, 1973, **40,** 69–77.

Williams, J. H. Conditioning of verbalizations. *Psychological Bulletin*, 1964, **62,** 383–393.

Williams, R. I., & Blanton, R. L. Verbal conditioning in a psychotherapeutic situation. *Behavior Research and Therapy*, 1968, **6,** 97–103.

Winston, A., Pardes, H., & Papernik, D. S. Inpatient treatment of blacks and whites. *Archives of General Psychiatry*, 1972, **26,** 405–409.

Witkin, H. A., Dyk, R. B., Faterson, H. F., Goodenough, D. R., & Karp, S. A. *Psychological differentiation.* New York: Wiley, 1962.

Witkin, H. A. Psychological differentiation and forms of pathology. *Journal of Abnormal Psychology*, 1965, **70,** 317–336.

Wolberg, L. R. *Short-term psychotherapy*. New York: Grune & Stratton, 1965.

Wolberg, L. R. *The technique of psychotherapy.* (2nd ed.) New York: Grune & Stratton, 1967.

Wolff, K. Individual psychotherapy with geriatric patients. *Disease of the Nervous System*, 1963, **24,** 688–691.

Wolitzky, D. L., & Wachtel, P. L. Personality and perception. In B. B. Wolman (Ed.), *Handbook of general psychology.* Englewood Cliffs, N. J.: Prentice-Hall, 1972. Pp. 826–857.

Wolkon, G. H., Moriwaki, S., & Williams, K. J. Race and social class as factors in the orientation toward psychotherapy. *Journal of Counseling Psychology*, 1973, **20,** 312–316.

Wolman, B. B. *Handbook of clinical psychology*. New York: McGraw-Hill, 1965.

Wolman, B. B. (Ed.) *Success and failure in psychoanalysis and psychotherapy.* New York: Macmillan, 1972.

Woody, R. H. *Psychobehavioral counseling and therapy: Integrating behavioral and insight techniques*. New York: Appleton-Century-Crofts, 1971.

Wrenn, R. L. Counselor orientation: Theoretical or situational. *Journal of Counseling Psychology,* 1960, **7,** 40–45.

Yalom, I. B. *The theory and practice of group psychotherapy.* New York: Basic Books, 1970.

Yates, A. J. *Behavior therapy*. New York: Wiley, 1970.

Yulis, S., & Kiesler, D. J. Countertransference response as a function of therapist anxiety and content of patient talk. *Journal of Consulting and Clinical Psychology*, 1968, **33,** 413–419.

Zimring, F. Theory and practice of client-centered therapy: A cognitive view. In D. A. Wexler & L. N. Rice (Eds.), *Innovations in client-centered therapy*. New York: Wiley, 1974.

Zubin, J. Classification of the behavior disorders. *Annual Review of Psychology*, 1967, **18,** 373–506.

Author Index

Subject Index